iPod touch Made Simple

Martin Trautschold
and
Gary Mazo

Apress®

iPod touch Made Simple

ISBN-13 (pbk): 978-1-4302-3195-0

ISBN-10 (electronic): 1-4302-3195-5

Printed and bound in the United States of America 9 8 7 6 5 4 3 2 1

President and Publisher: Paul Manning
Lead Editor: Steve Anglin
Development Editor: James Markham
Editorial Board: Steve Anglin, Mark Beckner, Ewan Buckingham, Gary Cornell, Jonathan Gennick, Jonathan Hassell, Michelle Lowman, Matthew Moodie, Duncan Parkes, Jeffrey Pepper, Frank Pohlmann, Douglas Pundick, Ben Renow-Clarke, Dominic Shakeshaft, Matt Wade, Tom Welsh
Coordinating Editor: Laurin Becker
Copy Editor: Mary Behr, Mary Ann Fugate, Patrick Meador, Sharon Terdeman
Compositor: MacPS, LLC
Indexer: BIM Indexing & Proofreading Services
Cover Designer: Anna Ishchenko

Distributed to the book trade worldwide by Springer Science+Business Media, LLC., 233 Spring Street, 6th Floor, New York, NY 10013. Phone 1-800-SPRINGER, fax (201) 348-4505, e-mail orders-ny@springer-sbm.com, or visit www.springeronline.com.

For information on translations, please e-mail rights@apress.com, or visit www.apress.com.

Apress and friends of ED books may be purchased in bulk for academic, corporate, or promotional use. eBook versions and licenses are also available for most titles. For more information, reference our Special Bulk Sales–eBook Licensing web page at www.apress.com/info/bulksales.

This book is dedicated to our families—to our wives, Julie and Gloria, and to our kids, Sophie, Livvie and Cece, and Ari, Dan, Sara, Billy, Elise and Jonah.

Without their love, support, and understanding, we could never take on projects like this one. Now that the book is done, we will gladly share our iPods with them – for a little while!

Contents at a Glance

Contents

About the Authors

Martin Trautschold is the founder and CEO of Made Simple Learning, a leading provider of Apple iPad, iPhone, iPod touch, BlackBerry, Android, and Palm webOS books and video tutorials. He has been a successful entrepreneur in the mobile device training and software business since 2001. With Made Simple Learning, he helped to train thousands of BlackBerry Smartphone users with short, to-the-point video tutorials. Martin has now co-authored nineteen "Made Simple" guide books. He also co-founded, ran for 3 years, and then sold a mobile device software company. Prior to this, Martin spent 15 years in technology and business consulting in the US and Japan. He holds an engineering degree from Princeton University and an MBA from the Kellogg School at Northwestern University. Martin and his wife, Julia, have three daughters. He enjoys rowing with the Halifax Rowing Association in Daytona Beach, Florida and cycling with friends. Martin can be reached at martin@madesimplelearning.com.

Gary Mazo is Vice President of Made Simple Learning and is a writer, a college professor, a gadget nut, and an ordained rabbi. Gary joined Made Simple Learning in 2007 and has co-authored the last seventeen books in the Made Simple series. Along with Martin, and Kevin Michaluk from CrackBerry.com, Gary co-wrote *CrackBerry: True Tales of BlackBerry Use and Abuse*—a book about BlackBerry addiction and how to get a grip on one's BlackBerry use. The second edition of this book will be published by Apress this fall. Gary also teaches writing, philosophy, technical writing, and more at the University of Phoenix. Gary has been a regular contributor to CrackBerry.com—writing product reviews and adding editorial content. He holds a BA in anthropology from Brandeis University. Gary earned his M.A.H.L (Masters in Hebrew Letters) as well as ordination as Rabbi from the Hebrew Union College-Jewish Institute of Religion in Cincinnati, Ohio. He has served congregations in Dayton, Ohio, Cherry Hill, New Jersey and Cape Cod, Massachusetts. Gary is married to Gloria Schwartz Mazo; they have six children. Gary can be reached at: gary@madesimplelearning.com.

About the Technical Reviewer

Rene Ritchie is editor of TiPb.com, the iPhone iPod touch and iPad blog, which covers the full range of news, how-tos and app, game, and accessory reviews. Part of the Smartphone Experts network, TiPb also provides a full range of help and community forums and has a thriving YouTube channel (http://www.youtube.com/theiphoneblog/), Facebook page (http://www.facebook.com/tipbcom/) and Twitter following (http://twitter.com/tipb). A graphic designer, web developer, and author, Rene lives and works in Montreal. He can be reached via rene@tipb.com or @reneritchie on Twitter.

Acknowledgments

A book like this takes many people to successfully complete. We would like to thank Apress for believing in us and our unique style of writing.

We would like to thank our Editors, Jim and Laurin, and the entire editorial team at Apress.

We would like to thank our families for their patience and support in allowing us to pursue projects such as this one.

Part I

Quick Start Guide

In your hands is one of the most exciting devices to hit the market in quite some time: the new iPod touch. This Quick Start Guide will help get you and your new iPod touch up and running in a hurry. You'll learn all about the buttons, switches, and ports, and how to use the innovative and responsive touch screen and multitask with the new App Switcher bar. Our App Reference Tables introduce you to both the built-in apps and some valuable additions from the App Store—and serve as a quick way to find out how to accomplish a task.

Getting Around Quickly

This Quick Start Guide is meant to be just that—a tool that can help you jump right in and find information In this book, as well as learn the basics of how to get around and enjoy your iPod touch right away.

We'll start with the nuts and bolts in the "Learning Your Way Around" section, which covers what all the keys, buttons, switches, and symbols mean and do on your iPod touch. In this section, you'll see some handy features, such as multitasking by double-clicking the **Home** button. You'll also learn how to interact with the menus, submenus, and set switches—tasks that are required in almost every application on your iPod touch.

> **TIP:** Check out Chapter 2: "Typing Tips, Copy/Paste and Search," for great typing tips and more.

In the "Touch Screen Basics" section, we will help you learn how to touch, swipe, flick, zoom, and more.

Later, in the "App Reference Tables" section, we've organized the app icons into general categories, so you can quickly browse through the icons and jump to a section in the book to learn more about the app a particular icon represents. This guide also includes several handy tables designed to help you get up and running with your iPod touch quickly:

- Getting Started (Table 1)
- Staying Connected and Organized (Table 2)
- Being Entertained (Table 3)
- Staying Informed (Table 4)
- Networking Socially (Table 5)
- Being Productive (Table 6)

So let's get started!

Learning Your Way Around

To help you get comfortable with your iPod touch, we start with the basics—what the buttons, keys, and switches do—and then move into how you start apps and navigate the menus. Probably the most important status indicator on your iPod touch, besides the battery, is the one that shows Wi-Fi status in the upper-left corner.

Keys, Buttons, and Switches

Figure 1 shows all the things you can do with the buttons, keys, switches, and ports on your iPod touch. Go ahead and try out a few things to see what happens. Swipe left to search, swipe right to see more icons, try double-clicking the **Home** button to bring up the multitasking **App Switcher** bar, and press and hold the **Power/Sleep** key. Have some fun getting acquainted with your device.

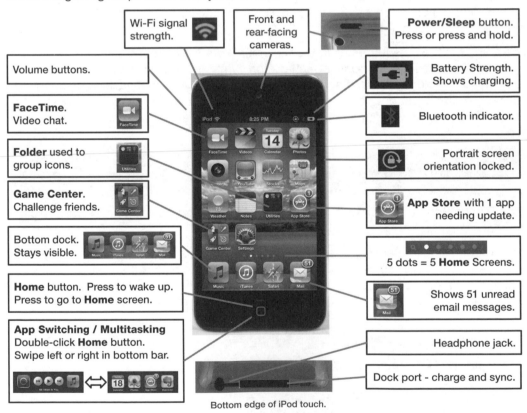

Figure 1. *The iPod touch's buttons, ports, switches, and keys*

Switching Apps (Multitasking)

One of the great new features introduced with the iPod touch is the ability to multitask, or jump between applications (see Figure 2).

Double-click the **Home** button to bring up the **App Switcher** bar at the bottom of the screen. Next, swipe right to see more icons and tap the icon of any app you want to start. If you don't see the icon you want, then click the **Home** button to see the entire **Home** screen. Repeat these steps to jump back to the app you just left. The nice thing is that the app you just left is always shown as the first app on the **App Switcher** bar.

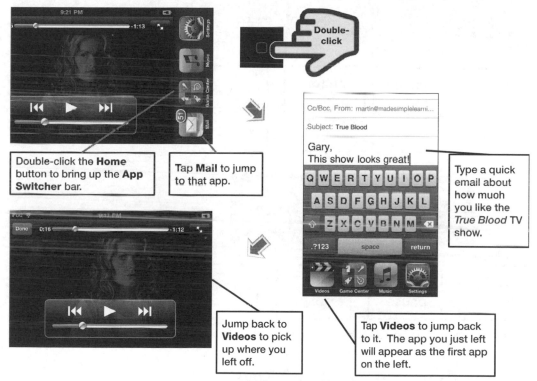

Double-click the **Home** button to bring up the **App Switcher** bar.

Tap **Mail** to jump to that app.

Type a quick email about how much you like the *True Blood* TV show.

Jump back to **Videos** to pick up where you left off.

Tap **Videos** to jump back to it. The app you just left will appear as the first app on the left.

Figure 2. *Multitasking (app switching) by double-clicking the Home button*

Music Controls and Portrait Screen Rotation Lock

You will see a few more icons if you swipe from left to right in the **App Switcher** bar. You can lock the screen rotation by tapping the leftmost icon, and control the currently playing music or video using the middle buttons. The icon on the right will start the app that was most recently playing music or videos on your iPod touch. This might be **Music**, **Videos** or even an app like **Slacker** internet radio. If you were not playing anything, then you will see your **Music** app here as shown in Figure 3.

> **TIP:** The previous track and next track icons will rewind and fast forward within the current track if you press and hold them.

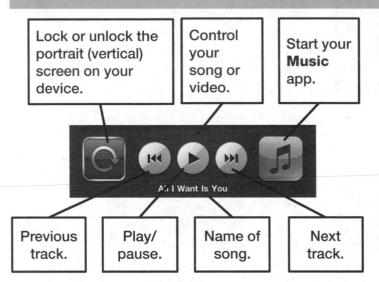

Lock or unlock the portrait (vertical) screen on your device.

Control your song or video.

Start your **Music** app.

Previous track.

Play/ pause.

Name of song.

Next track.

Figure 3. *The Screen Rotation Lock button, media controls, and Music icon in the App Switcher bar*

Starting Apps and Using Soft Keys

Some apps have soft keys at the bottom of the screen, such as the **Music** app shown in Figure 4.

To see and use the soft keys in the **Music** app, you must have some content (e.g., music, videos, podcasts, etc.) on your iPod touch. See Chapter 3: " Sync Your iPhone with iTunes," for help with syncing your music, videos, and more to your iPod touch. Follow these steps to launch the **Music** app and become familiar with using the soft keys to get around:

1. Tap the **Music** icon to start the **Music** app.

2. Tap the **Albums** soft key at the bottom to view your albums.

3. Tap the **Artists** soft key to view a list of your artists.

4. Try all the soft keys in **Music**.

5. In some apps, such as the **Music** app, you will see the **More** soft key in the lower-right corner. Tap this key to see additional soft keys or rearrange your soft keys.

> **TIP:** You know which soft key is selected because it is highlighted—usually with a color. The other soft keys are gray, but can still be touched.

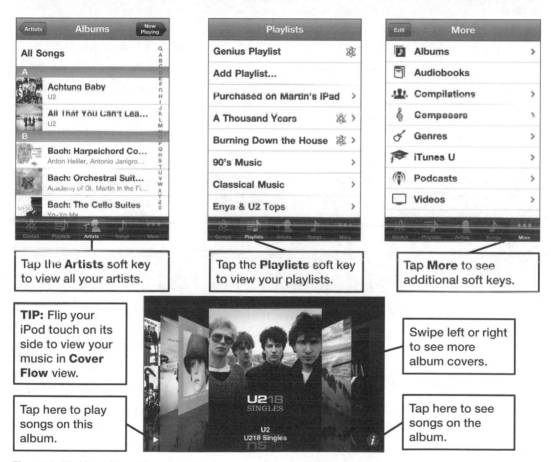

Figure 4. *Working with soft keys in apps*

Menus, Submenus, and Switches

Once you are in an app, you can select any menu item by simply touching it. Using the Settings app as an example, tap **General**, and then tap **Auto-Lock**, as shown in Figure 5.

Submenus are any menus below the main menu.

> **TIP:** You know there is a submenu or another screen if you see the greater-than symbol (>) next to the menu item.

To get back up to the previous screen or menu, simply tap the button at the top of the menu. If you're in the **Auto-Lock** menu, for example, you'd touch the **General** button.

You'll see a number of switches on the iPod touch, such as the one next to **Airplane Mode**, as shown in Figure 5. To set a switch (e.g., to toggle it between **OFF** and **ON**), just touch it.

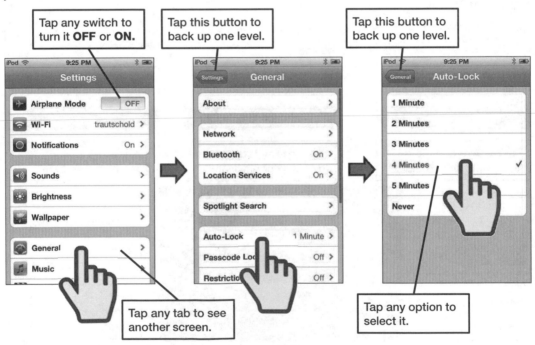

Figure 5. *Selecting menu items, navigating submenus, and setting switches.*

Reading the Wi-Fi Connectivity Status Icons

Most of the functions on your iPod touch work only when you are connected to the Internet (e.g., email, your browser, the **App Store**, **iTunes**, and so on), so you need to know when you're connected. Understanding how to read the status bar can save you time and frustration.

The following are some examples of Wi-Fi network signal strengths:

- *Strong*:

- *Weak*:

- *Off*:

Chapter 5: "Wi-Fi Connectivity," shows you how to connect your iPod touch to a Wi-Fi Network.

Touch Screen Gestures

In this section, we will describe how to interact with the iPod touch's touch screen. The iPod touch has an amazingly sensitive and intuitive touch screen. Apple, renowned for making its iPad, iPod touch, and iPod devices easy to use, has come up with an excellent, even higher-resolution, highly responsive touch screen.

If you are used to a physical keyboard and a trackball or trackpad, or even an iPod's intuitive scroll wheel, then this touch screen will take a little effort to master. With a little practice, though, you'll soon become comfortable interacting with your iPod touch.

You can do almost anything on your iPod touch by using a combination of the following:

- Touch screen gestures

- Touching icons or soft keys on the screen

- Clicking the **Home** button at the bottom

The following sections describe the various gestures you can use on your iPod touch.

Tapping and Flicking

To start an app, confirm a selection, select a menu item, or select an answer, simply tap the screen. To move quickly through contacts, lists, and the music library in **List** mode, flick from side to side or up and down to scroll through items. Figure 6 shows both of these gestures.

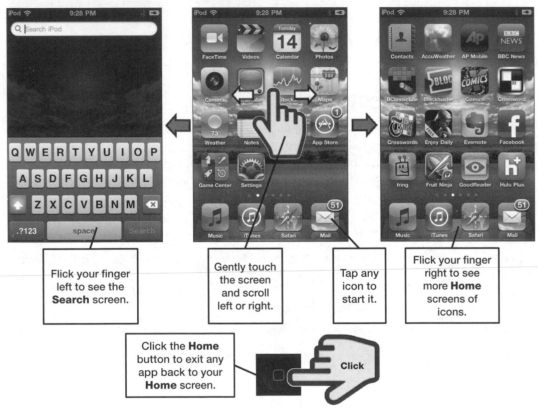

Flick your finger left to see the **Search** screen.

Gently touch the screen and scroll left or right.

Tap any icon to start it.

Flick your finger right to see more **Home** screens of icons.

Click the **Home** button to exit any app back to your **Home** screen.

Click

Figure 6. *Basic touch screen gestures*

Swiping

To swipe, gently touch and move your finger as shown in Figure 7. You can also do this to move between open **Safari** web pages and pictures. Swiping also works in lists, such as the **Contacts** list.

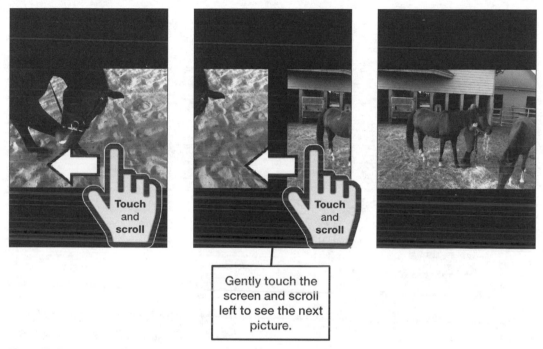

Gently touch the screen and scroll left to see the next picture.

Figure 7. *Touch and swipe to move between pictures and web pages.*

Scrolling

Scrolling is as simple as touching the screen and sliding your finger in the direction you want to scroll (see Figure 8). You can use this technique in messages (email), the **Safari** web browser, menus, and more.

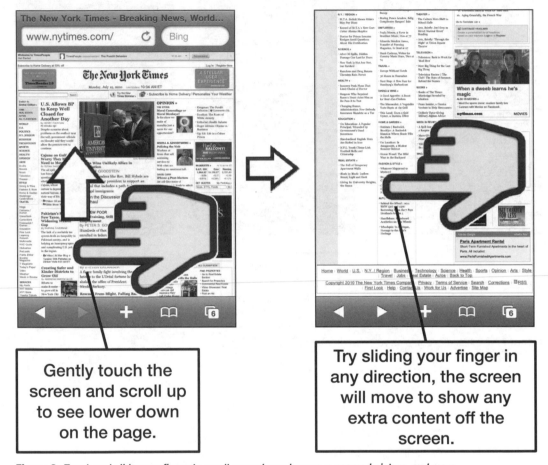

Gently touch the screen and scroll up to see lower down on the page.

Try sliding your finger in any direction, the screen will move to show any extra content off the screen.

Figure 8. *Touch and slide your finger to scroll around a web page, a zoomed picture, and more.*

Double-Tapping

You can double-tap the screen to zoom in and then double-tap again to zoom back out. This works in many places, such as web pages, mail messages, and pictures (see Figure 9).

TIP: Interestingly, double-tapping the title of a TV episode from a show or season in the iTunes is how you access the individual episodes to buy or rent.

Figure 9. *Double-tapping to zoom in or out*

Pinching

You can also pinch open or closed to zoom in or out. This works in many places, including web pages, mail messages, and pictures (see Figure 10). Follow these steps to zoom in using the *pinching* feature:

1. To zoom in, place two fingers that touch each other on the screen.

2. Gradually slide your fingers open, and the screen will zoom in.

Follow these steps to zoom out using the pinching feature:

1. To zoom out, place two fingers with space between them on the screen.

2. Gradually slide your fingers closed so they touch, and the screen will zoom out.

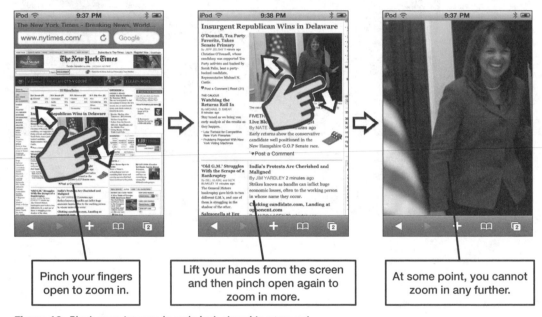

Pinch your fingers open to zoom in.

Lift your hands from the screen and then pinch open again to zoom in more.

At some point, you cannot zoom in any further.

Figure 10. *Pinch open to zoom in and pinch closed to zoom out.*

App Reference Tables

This section gives you a number of handy reference tables that group the various apps that are preinstalled on your iPod touch by their functionality. Also included in the tables are other useful apps you can download from the **App Store**. Each table gives you a brief description of the app and tells you where you can find more information about it in this book.

Getting Started

Table 1 provides some quick links to help you connect your iPod touch to the Web (using Wi-Fi), buy and enjoy songs or videos (using the **iTunes** and **iPod** apps), make your iPod touch sleep or power off, unlock your iPod touch, use the electronic **Picture Frame**, and more.

Table 1. *Getting Started*

To Do This...	Use This...		Where to Learn More
Turn the iPod touch on or off.		The **Power/Sleep** button: Press and hold the button on the top right edge of the iPod touch.	Chapter 1
Adjust settings and connect to the Internet (via Wi-Fi or 3G).		**Settings > Wi-Fi** or **Settings > General > Network**	Chapter 5
Return to the **Home** screen.		The **Home** button	Chapter 1
Unlock the iPod touch.		Slide your finger to unlock your iPod touch.	Chapter 1
Completely power down your iPod touch.		Press and hold the power key, and then slide this button to power the device off.	Chapter 1
Sync music, videos, pictures, addresses, calendar, email, and notes with your computer.	**iTunes** (for Windows and Apple Mac) **MobileMe Sync Service** **Google/Exchange Sync**		Chapter 3 Chapter 4
Set a really amazing new wallpaper.		**WallpapersHD**	Chapter 7

Staying Connected and Organized

Table 2 provides links for everything from organizing and finding your contacts to managing your calendar, working with email, sending messages, getting driving directions, calling people with FaceTime, and more.

Table 2. *Staying Connected and Organized*

To Do This...	Use This...		Where to Learn More
Manage your contact names and numbers.		**Contacts**	Chapter 15
Manage your calendar.		**Calendar**	Chapter 16
Surf the Web.		**Safari**	Chapter 12
Use video conferencing.		**FaceTime**	Chapter 13
Control your iPod touch with your voice (press and hold the **Home** button).		**Voice Control**	Chapter 8
View and send email.		**Mail**	Chapter 14
Find just about anything, get directions, avoid traffic, and more.		**Maps**	Chapter 27

Being Entertained

You can have lots of fun with your iPod touch; Table 3 shows you how. For example, you can use your iPod touch to buy or rent movies, check out free Internet radio with **Pandora**, or buy a book and enjoy it in a whole new way using **iBooks**. If you already use a **Kindle**, you can sync all your **Kindle** books to your iPod touch and enjoy them right away. You can choose from more than 200,000 apps in the **App Store** to make your iPod touch even more amazing, fun, and useful. You can also rent a movie from **Hulu** or **iTunes**, downloading it immediately for later viewing (e.g., on an airplane or train).

Table 3. *Being Entertained*

To Do This...	Use This...		Where to Learn More
Buy music, videos, podcasts, and more.	iTunes	**iTunes on** your iPod touch	Chapter 19
Use your computer to sync, buy music apps, and listen to music and other content.	iTunes	**iTunes** on your computer	Chapter 29
Browse and download apps right to your iPod touch.	App Store	**App Store**	Chapter 20
See playlists, artists,songs, albums, audiobooks, videos, and more.	Music	**Music**	Chapter 9
Watch movies, music videos, TV episodes, video podcasts, and more.	Videos	**Videos**	Chapter 10
Listen to free Internet radio.	Pandora	**Pandora**	Chapter 9
Read a book anytime, anywhere.	iBooks	**iBooks**	Chapter 11

To Do This...	Use This...		Where to Learn More
Read your Kindle books.		**Kindle**	Chapter 11
Take pictures and videos with your iPod touch.		**Camera**	Chapter 17
Look at, zoom in on, and organize your pictures.		**Photos**	Chapter 17
Watch TV shows.		**Hulu Plus**	Chapter 10
Watch a video from YouTube.		**YouTube**	Chapter 10
Play a game.		Games icons	Chapter 21
Play games with friends.		**Game Center**	Chapter 21
Work on a crossword puzzle by tapping your finger.		**Times Crosswords**	Chapter 20
Interact with comics in a whole new way.		**Marvel** comics	Chapter 26

Staying Informed

You can also use your iPod touch to read your favorite magazine or newspaper with vibrant, up-to-the-minute pictures and videos (see Table 4). Or, you can use it to check out the latest weather reports.

Table 4. *Staying Informed*

To Do This...	Use This...		Where to Learn More
Check your favorite radio news program.	NPR News	**NPR News**	Chapter 20
Read the newspaper.	NYTimes	**New York Times**	Chapter 26
Check the weather.	TWC	**The Weather Channel**	Chapter 20
Check out the latest headlines.	AP Mobile	**AP Mobile**	Chapter 26

Networking Socially

You can also use your iPod touch to connect and stay up to date with friends, colleagues, and professional networks using the social networking tools on your iPod touch (see Table 5).

Table 5. *Networking Socially*

To Do This...	Use This...		Where to Learn More
Use Skype to make free phone calls to other Skype users around the world.	Skype	**Skype**	Chapter 13
Network on LinkedIn.	LinkedIn	**LinkedIn**	Chapter 22
Stay connected with friends on Facebook.	Facebook	**Facebook**	Chapter 22
Follow your favorites on Twitter.	Twitter	**Twitter**	Chapter 22

Being Productive

An iPod touch can also help you be more productive. You can use it to access and read just about any PDF file or other document with the **GoodReader** app. You can take notes with the basic **Notes** app, or step up to the advanced **Evernote** app, which has amazing capabilities for integrating audio, pictures, and text notes, and as well as syncing everything to a web site. You can also use your iPod touch to set an alarm, calculate a tip, see what direction you are walking in, and record a voice memo (see Table 6).

Table 6. *Being Productive*

To Do This...	Use This...		Where to Learn More
Access and read almost any document.		**GoodReader**	Chapter 26
Take notes, store your grocery list, and more.		**Notes**	Chapter 23
Take and organize your notes in a whole new way.		**Evernote**	Chapter 23
Use folders to organize your icons.		Folders	Chapter 6
Set an alarm, countdoun timer, and more.		**Clock**	Chapter 25
Calculate a tip or find the cosine of 30 degrees.		**Calculator**	Chapter 25
Take a note without using your hands or typing.		**Voice Memos**	Chapter 25

Part II

Introduction

Welcome to your new iPod touch—and to the book that tells you what you need to know to get the most out of it. In this part we show you how the book is organized and where to go to find what you need. We even show you how to get some great tips and tricks sent right to your iPod touch via short e-mail messages.

Introduction

Congratulations on Your New iPod touch!

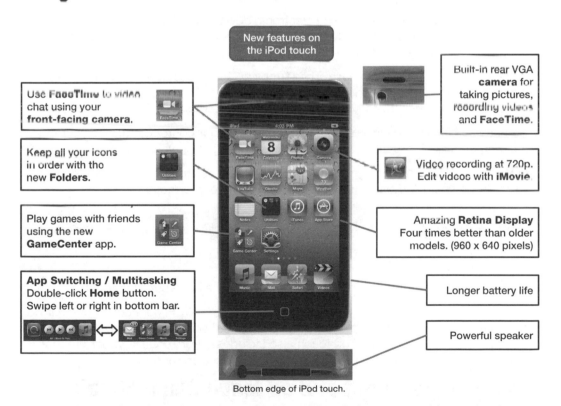

New features on the iPod touch

Use **FaceTime** to video chat using your **front-facing camera**.

Keep all your icons in order with the new **Folders**.

Play games with friends using the new **GameCenter** app.

App Switching / Multitasking
Double-click **Home** button.
Swipe left or right in bottom bar.

Built-in rear VGA **camera** for taking pictures, recording videos and **FaceTime**.

Video recording at 720p. Edit videos with **iMovie**.

Amazing **Retina Display** Four times better than older models. (960 x 640 pixels)

Longer battery life

Powerful speaker

Bottom edge of iPod touch.

You hold in your hands perhaps the most powerful and elegant portable music player available, a phone that is also a media player, e-book reader, gaming machine, life organizer, and just about everything else available today: the iPod touch.

The iPod touch can do more than just about any other music player on the market. In a beautiful and elegantly designed package, the iPod touch will have you listening to music, playing games, surfing the web, checking email, and organizing your busy life in no time.

> **NOTE**: Take a look at Chapter 13: "FaceTime Video Messaging and Skype," where we show you how to use the **Skype** app and the new **FaceTime** video chat feature on your iPod touch!

With your iPod touch, you can view your photos and interact with them using intuitive touch-screen gestures. You can pinch, zoom, rotate, and email your photos—all by using simple gestures.

Interact with your content like never before. News sites and web sites look amazing due to the incredibly clear and crisp Retina display. Flip through stories, videos, and pictures, and interact with your news.

For the first time, reading a book on an electronic device feels like you're reading a paper-page book. Pages turn slowly or quickly, and you can even see the words on the back of the pages when you turn them.

Manage your media library with ease. The **iTunes** app features a beautiful interface, letting you choose music, watch videos, organize playlists, and more—all in an effortless and fun way on the iPod touch's high definition quality screen.

Do you have a Netflix account? You can now manage your content, organize your queue, and stream high-quality movies and TV shows right on your iPod touch.

Hulu Plus is available now, so you can watch complete seasons of your favorite TV shows right on your iPod touch (see Chapter 10 for more information).

> **NOTE**: The Netflix app was recently released in the US and Canada; it requires a subscription to Netflix.

Update your **Facebook** status and receive push alerts—all on your iPod touch.

Stay connected to the web and your email with the built-in Wi-Fi connection of the iPod touch. All the latest high-speed protocols are supported, so you can always be in touch and get the latest content. The iPod touch also includes a horizontal keyboard to type out emails and notes when you use the device in **Landscape** mode.

Getting the Most out of *iPod touch Made Simple*

Read this book cover-to-cover if you choose, but you can also peruse it in a modular fashion, by chapter or topic. Maybe you just want to check out the **App Store** app, try **iBooks**, set up your email or contacts, or just load up your phone with music. You can do all this and much more with our book.

You will soon realize that your iPod touch is a very powerful device. There are, however, many secrets "locked" inside, which we help you "unlock" throughout this book.

Take your time—this book can help you understand how to best use and have fun with your new iPod touch. Think back to when you tried to use your first Windows or Mac computer. It took a little while to get familiar with how to do things. It's the same with the iPod touch. This book will help you get up to speed and learn all the best tips and tricks more quickly.

Also remember that devices this powerful are not always easy to grasp—at first.

You will get the most out of your iPod touch if you can read a section and then try out what you just read. We all know that reading and then doing an activity gives us a much higher retention rate than simply reading alone.

So, in order to learn and remember what you learn, we recommend the following:

Read a little, try a little on your iPod touch, and repeat!

How This Book Is Organized

Knowing how this book is organized will help you quickly locate things that are important to you. Here we show you the main organization of this book. Remember to take advantage of the abridged table of contents, detailed table of contents, and comprehensive index. All of these elements can help you quickly pinpoint items of interest to you.

Day In the Life of an iPod touch User

Located inside the front and back covers, the "Day in the Life of an iPod touch User" reference is an excellent guide to your phone's features, providing ideas on how to use your iPod touch and lots of easy-to-access, cross-referenced chapter numbers. So, if you see something you want to learn, simply thumb to that page and learn it—all in just a few minutes.

Part I: Quick Start Guide

Touch Screen Basics: This book's many practical and informative screen shots will help you quickly learn how to touch, swipe, flick, zoom, and more with your iPod touch's touch screen.

App Reference Tables: Quickly skim the icons or apps grouped by category. Get a thumbnail of what all the apps do on your iPod touch, including a pointer to the relevant chapter numbers so you can jump right to the details of how to get the most out of each app in this book.

Part II: Introduction

You are here now . . .

Part III: You and Your iPod touch

This is the meat of the book, organized in 28 easy-to-understand chapters, all of them packed with loads of pictures to guide you every step of the way.

Part IV: iPod touch's Soulmate, iTunes

As a special bonus for our readers, we have provided an extensive iTunes Guide in Chapter 29. This special bonus chapter walks you through many of the **iTunes** app's best features such as the new Ping social networking feature, iTunes Remote, Home Sharing, iTunes DJ and Genius. We show you how to maximize not just the features of **iTunes**, but the iPod touch itself. The more comfortable you can get with the **iTunes**, the more you can arrange and use content from your computer on your iPod touch—making a great and enjoyable user experience even more so.

Quickly Locating Tips, Cautions, and Notes

If you flip through this book, you can instantly see specially formatted **TIPS**, **CAUTIONS**, and **NOTES** that highlight important facts about using the iPod touch. For example, if you want to find all the special tips relevant to using the iPhone's Calendar, you can flip to the Calendar chapter and search for these highlighted nuggets of information.

> **TIP**: **TIPS**, **CAUTIONS**, and **NOTES** are all formatted like this, with a gray background, to help you see them more quickly.

Free iPod touch Email Tips

Finally, check out the author's web site at www.madesimplelearning.com for a series of very useful "bite-sized" chunks of iPod touch tips and tricks. We have taken a selection of the great tips out of this book and even added a few new ones. Click the "Free Tips" link and register for your tips in order to receive a tip right in your iPod touch inbox about once a week. Learning in small chunks is a great way to master your

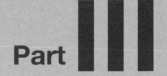

You and Your iPod touch

This is the heart of *iPod touch Made Simple*. In this section, you'll find clearly labeled chapters—each explaining the key features of your iPod touch. You'll see that most chapters focus on an individual app or a specific type of application. Many of the chapters discuss applications that come with your iPod touch, but we also include some fun and useful apps you can download from the App Store. Sure, the iPod touch is for fun, but it's for a whole lot more, too. We finish with some handy troubleshooting tips that can help if your iPod touch isn't working quite right.

Chapter 1

Getting Started

You've got a brand-new iPod touch and you can't wait to get started. Well, that's what we're here for. We'll take you on a step-by-step tour of your new device—and everything you get in the box. And we'll look at how to charge your iPod touch and how to make your battery last longer.To get started, your first step is to connect your IPod touch to iTunes to get it activated and registered.In our "iPod touch Basics" section at the end of this chapter, we'll give you the essentials to get you up and running quickly.

Getting to Know Your iPod touch

In this section we show you how to use everything you get in the box with your iPod touch. We also give you some iPod touch battery and charging tips, help you determine if your iPod touch is already activated, and take a look at the **Slide to Unlock** feature.

What's in the Box

While the clear plastic box may seem skimpy if you're new to the iPod touch, it does contain everything you need to get started and enjoy your iPod touch—except for a good manual, which is why we wrote this book!

iPod touch: On the very top, as soon as you open the box, you see your new iPod touch, attached to the clear plastic holder. Pull the tape on the back of the holder from the direction of the arrow to release your precious iPod touch.

Under the plastic holder for the iPod touch you'll find a paper flap, which covers the following:

- **Finger Tips**: A small fold-out booklet with nine panels of basic information on your iPod touch.

- **iPod touch Product Information Guide**: A small booklet with a font that's way too small to read, containing all the legal terms, conditions, warnings, and disclaimers related to your iPod touch.

- **Apple Logo Stickers**: Two of those nice white Apple logos you sometimes see on car windows. Enjoy!

In the bottom of the box you'll find the rest of your gear, as shown in Figure 1–1.

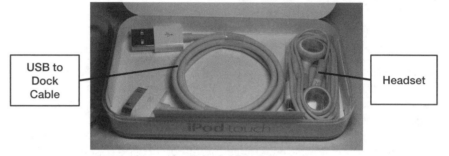

Figure 1–1. *The USB cable and headset in the bottom of the box.*

iPod touch Headset

The headset consists of two white earphones for listening to anything on your IPod touch—music, videos, audiobooks, FaceTime calls, and more. Plug this into the hole on the bottom right edge of your iPod touch. Make sure it's inserted all the way—it can be a little tough to press in.

USB to Dock Cable

This is the cable to connect to your computer, and it also doubles as your power cable.

Wall Plug Adapter Accessory

The iPod touch does not come with this useful piece of hardware, but you may want to purchase one so you can charge your iPod touch directly from a wall outlet without having your computer around. All you do is plug the USB cable into this wall adapter and the other end into your iPod touch. Current pricing for this plug adapter is less than US $10 at discount online stores.

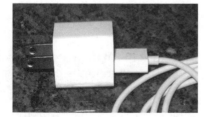

Charging Your iPod touch, and Battery Life Tips

Your iPod touch may already have some battery life, but it's a good idea to charge it completely so you can enjoy uninterrupted hours of use as soon you get it set up. While it's charging, you can take the opportunity read the rest of this chapter, install or update iTunes, or check out all the cool iPod touch apps in Chapter 20: "The Amazing App Store."

Charging from the Power Outlet

As we mentioned, if you buy the wall plug adapter, you can charge your iPod touch the fastest way possible—directly from the wall outlet.

You can tell your iPod touch is charging by looking at the screen. You'll see a lightning bolt or plug icon inside the battery indicator in the upper right corner.

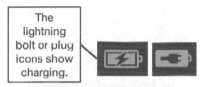

The lightning bolt or plug icons show charging.

The main battery icon will show your charge level. See the image to the right, which shows a charging iPod touch with an almost-full battery.

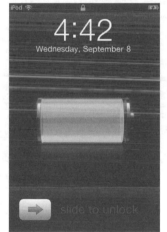

TIP: Some newer cars have built-in power outlets just like in your home, where you can plug in your iPod touch power cord. Some also have a Dock option that allows you to control the **Music** app from your car radio headset. These outlets are sometimes buried in the middle console next to the front seat.

Charging from Your Computer

You can also charge your iPod touch when you plug it into your computer.

TIP: Try different USB ports on your computer. Some USB ports share a bus and have less power, while others have their own bus and more power.

For best charging, your computer should be plugged into the wall power outlet. If it's not, your iPod touch will charge, but at a slower rate.

Keep in mind that if your laptop computer goes to sleep or you close the screen, your iPod touch will stop charging.

Charging from Other Accessories

Some accessories designed to work with an iPod touch will also charge it. The most common of these are iPod touch/iPhone music docks. These are speaker systems you plug into your iPod touch to listen to music. Note that your iPod touch won't charge in some older accessories, or those not designed specifically for the iPod touch. In such cases, you'll see a warning message on your screen saying, "Charging is not supported with this accessory."

> **TIP:** A number of manufacturers supply cases that actually have external batteries built into the case. One provider, Mophie (www.mophie.com), has produced such cases for previous iPod touch models and is currently developing an iPod touch battery with case called a "Juice Pack."

Expected Battery Life and Charging Times

Apple says battery life on the new iPod touch, with its bigger battery and advanced technology, should last longer than the previous version. See Table 1–1.

Table 1–1. *Battery Life Specifications from Apple*

Video Playback	7 hours of video playback
Audio Playback	40 hours of audio playback
Charging Time	2 hour to get 80% in a Fast Charge, 4 hours to get fully charged

These battery life durations are in ideal conditions with a new, fully charged battery. You will notice that over time, your actual battery life will diminish.

Battery and Charging Tips

There's nothing worse that running out of juice just when you need it, so the key question is, how can you maximize your battery life and make sure your iPod touch is ready when you are? Here are a few tips that can help.

Getting More Out of Each Charge

To extend your battery life, try these tips.

1. **Put the iPod touch into Sleep mode.** Tap the **Power/Sleep** button on the upper right edge of the device to put it into sleep mode.

2. **Turn off Wi-Fi when not needed.** The Wi-Fi antenna uses power even if you're not connected to a Wi-Fi network, so turn it off when you don't need it. Tap **Settings**, then **Wi-Fi**, set **Wi-Fi** to **Off**.

3. **Lower your screen brightness**: Tap **Settings** and then **Brightness**. Use the slider bar to lower your brightness to a level less than halfway across that still works for you. Also, make sure **Auto-Brightness** is set to **On**.

4. **Turn off Location Services**: If you don't need your actual location to be transmitted to your apps, you can turn this off. Tap **Settings**, then **General**, and **Location Services**. Set **Location Services** to **Off**. If you start an app that wants your location, you'll be reminded to turn it back on.

5. **Set a Shorter Auto-Lock**: Shortening the time your iPod touch takes to turn off the screen when not being used and go into sleep mode can help save your battery. To do this, tap **Settings, General**, and **Auto-Lock**. Set **Auto-Lock** as short as possible—you can set as short as **1 minute** if you like.

6. **Turn off push email** and push notifications. Tap **Settings**, then **Mail, Contacts, Calendars**, tap **Fetch New Data,** and set **Push** to **Off.**

7. **Learn more** about battery life and get more tips from the Apple web site at http://www.apple.com/batteries/ipods.html

Making the Battery Last Longer

A rechargeable battery loses its ability to maintain a charge over time, and has only a limited number of cycles during its useful life. You can extend the life of your iPod touch battery by making sure you run it down completely at least once a month. The rechargeable battery will last longer if you do this complete draining on a regular basis.

Finding More Places to Charge

No matter what you do, if you use your iPod touch a lot, you'll want to find more places and more ways to charge it. Besides using your power cord or connecting it to your computer, Table 1–2 gives you some other options.

Table 1–2. *Other Places and Ways to Charge Your iPod touch*

Airport Charging Station	Most airports have wall sockets available today where you can top off your iPod touch while waiting for your flight. Some airports have designated "charging stations," while others just have wall sockets that may even be hidden behind chairs or other objects. You may have to do a bit of hunting to beat out all those other power-hungry travelers!
External Battery Pack	This accessory allows you to extend the life of your iPod touch battery by five times or more. You can buy them for about US $40–65. Search for "external iPod touch battery" on the Web to find the latest and greatest options.
Car Charger	If you are using your iPod touch heavily for phone calls during the day, you may want to invest in a car charger or another way to give it a little more juice in the middle of a long day. These chargers plug directly into the cigarette lighter socket in your car and run about US $15–25.
Car Power Inverter	If you are taking a long car trip, you can buy a power inverter to convert your 12V car power outlets into a power outlet where you can plug in your iPod touch charger. Do a Web search for "power inverter for cars" to find many options for under US $50. This is a small price to pay for hours of enjoyment on your iPod touch!
Other Accessories	As we mentioned, you can also charge your iPod touch in many accessories designed to do other things, like play your music over speakers. Just look for the plug or lightning bolt icons to make sure your iPod touch is charging in such accessories.

iTunes and Your iPod touch

Now that you've taken your iPod touch out of the box and learned how to get the most out of your battery, you are ready to start enjoying it. Connecting it to iTunes is the next step. iTunes allows you to activate and register your iPod touch and tie it to your Apple ID (iTunes account). Once you do that, you can buy songs, movies, books, and just about anything else right from your iPod touch or in iTunes on your computer.

You can also use iTunes to load up your music and videos and to back up your iPod touch and later restore it. If you don't have iTunes, you'll need to install the latest version (10 at time of writing).

Do You Need to Activate Your iPod touch?

You need to connect your iPod touch to iTunes to activate it if you see a black screen like the one here, showing a USB cable plugging into iTunes.

If that's the case, skip to the "iTunes and Your iPod touch" section later in this chapter to find out how to get your iPod touch going.

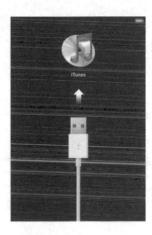

Slide to Unlock and Your Home Screen

After your iPod touch has been activated, you'll see the **Slide to Unlock** screen, as shown in Figure 1–2. Touch your finger to the screen and follow the path of the arrow to slide the unlock button to the right.

When you do that, you'll see the Home screen.

Notice that the four icons locked in the Bottom Dock (Figure 1–2, bottom right) don't move while the rest of the icons can move back and forth in "pages." Check out our "Moving Icons" section in Chapter 7 to learn how to move your favorite icons into the Bottom Dock.

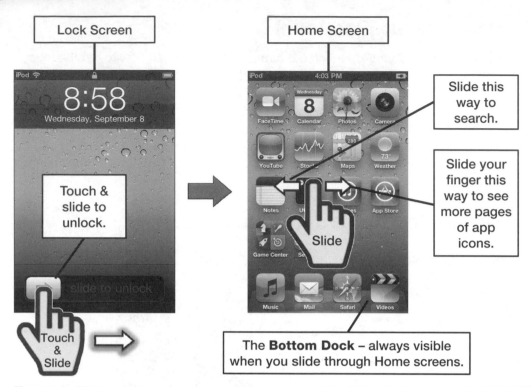

Figure 1–2. *Slide to unlock, moving around your Home screen, and the Bottom Dock*

Install or Upgrade iTunes on Your Computer

If you don't have iTunes loaded on your computer, open a web browser and go to www.itunes.com/download to download the software.

> **TIP:** You'll find detailed instructions on how to install iTunes in the "How to Download and Install iTunes" section, and the "iTunes Upgrade" section in Chapter 29: "Your iTunes User Guide" tells you how to update iTunes if you have an older version.

If you already have iTunes on your computer, check to see if an updated version is available. Version 10 was the latest at publishing time.

1. Start iTunes.

2. If you are a Windows user, select **Help** from the menu, and then **Check for Updates**.

3. If you are a Mac user, select **iTunes** from the menu, and then **Check for Updates**.

4. If an update is available, follow the instructions to update iTunes.

Connecting Your iPod touch to iTunes the First Time

Once you've installed or upgraded to iTunes version 10 or higher, you are ready to connect your iPod touch to iTunes on your computer.

TIP: Using the iTunes Home Sharing feature, you can share your purchased content (music, apps, videos, iBooks, and more) from the same iTunes account across authorized computers on your home network. And all of this content can be synced to any iPod//iPhone/iPod touch under the same iTunes account. Learn more about syncing content using iTunes in Chapter 3: "Sync Your iPod touch with iTunes," and about Home Sharing in Chapter 29: "Your iTunes User Guide."

By connecting your iPod touch to iTunes, you'll register or associate your iPod touch (via the device serial number) to a particular iTunes account (Apple ID).

TIP: The benefit of this approach is that if you've purchased apps or other content for another iPod touch or iPhone, you can run all those apps on your new iPod touch! Note that all content you sync to your iPod touch has to originate from a single computer. So you need to select your "main" computer to sync with your iPod touch.

If you don't yet have an iTunes Account (Apple ID), we'll show you how to create one.

Start iTunes

If iTunes isn't already running, double-click the **iTunes** icon on your desktop.

- Mac users, click the **Finder** icon, select the **Go** menu, and then select **Applications** to look for iTunes. (Shortcut: **Shift+Command+A** for Applications.)

- Windows users, click the **Start** menu or **Windows logo** in the lower left corner, select **All Programs**, and then **iTunes**.

iTunes should open, showing the left and main window nav bars as shown to the right.

Registering or Activating Your iPod touch the First Time

Once you have iTunes installed or updated on your computer, you are ready to connect your iPod touch for the first time and get it registered or activated so you can start using it.

> **NOTE:** If your iPod touch has already been registered (you see the "Slide to Unlock" message or your Home screen of icons when you tap the **Home** button on the bottom of your device), you can skip this section and jump to the "Set Up Your iPod touch" section later in this chapter.

1. Start iTunes on your computer.

2. Connect your iPod touch to your computer. Plug in the wide end of the white USB cable to the bottom port on your iPod touch and the small USB connector end to an available USB port on your computer.

> **NOTE:** You need to use the USB cable, not Bluetooth or Wi-Fi, to connect your iPod touch to iTunes on your computer.

3. When you connect your iPod touch to your computer the first time, your Windows computer should automatically install the necessary drivers. If you are on a Mac computer, you may see messages recommending you upgrade to the latest version of the operating system before using your iPod touch. Follow the steps shown on the screen to complete the process.

4. To see the setup screen, you may need to click **iPod touch** under **DEVICES** in the left nav bar. Then you should see the new iPod Wecome screen, as shown in Figure 1–3.

Click **iPod touch** undor DEVICES

Then, click **Continue**.

Figure 1–3. *The iPod touch Welcome window in iTunes, which you'll see after clicking on "iPod touch" in the left navigation bar.*

5. Click the **Continue** button to see the iPod Software License Agreement.

6. Assuming you agree with the legal terms, check the box that says **i have read and agree to the iPod Software License Agreement** and click the **Continue** button.

7. You will be given the opportunity to sign in using your Apple ID or to create a new Apple ID. Enter your Apple ID and password or click **I do not have an Apple ID** and select your country.

8. Click the **Continue** button.

   ■ If you tried to enter your Apple ID and password and received an error message that "additional security information is required," read the "Troubleshooting: Fixing the Apple ID Security Error" section in Chapter 29: "Your iTunes User Guide."

9. You should now see the **Register your iPod** screen. Type or verify that your information is correct and click **Submit** to complete your registration.

If everything has been entered correctly, you'll see either the **MobileMe** ad or the **Set Up Your iPod** screen.

Apple's MobileMe Sync Service

After registering your iPod touch for the first time, you may see a screen advertising the MobileMe wireless sync service from Apple. To keep setting up your iPod touch, click the **No Thanks** button to continue to the next screen.

What is MobileMe?

MobileMe is a way to keep your email, contacts, calendar, and web bookmarks shared across all your computers and mobile devices. You can even use MobileMe to locate a missing iPod touch! At publishing time, photo-sharing is limited to Mac computers with MobileMe iPhoto folders. MobileMe is free for a limited time (currently 60 days), and then it costs US $99.00 for a single user or US $149.00 for a family plan.

See our MobileMe Tour section in Chapter 5: "Wi-Fi Connectivity."

Set Up Your iPod touch

After your registration is complete, the first time you connect your iPod touch, you'll see the screen shown in Figure 1–4.

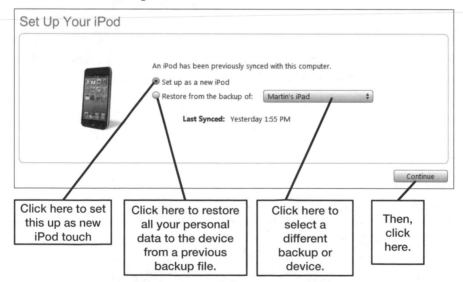

Figure 1–4. *The iPod touch setup screen.*

1. If you'd like to set up a new iPod touch, do the following:

   a. Click the selection next to **Set up as a new iPod**.

   b. Click the **Continue** button and skip to Step 3.

NOTE: If you want to keep your existing iPod touch and/or iPhone and set up your new iPod touch, you should select **Set up a New iPod**, as shown.

2. If you'd like to restore from a backup of another iPod touch (or iPad or iPhone), do the following:

   a. Click the button next to **Restore from the backup of**.

   b. Select the particular backup file from the drop-down menu.

   c. Click the **Continue** button to restore data to your iPod touch from the backup file.

   d. Now you are done with the initial setup of your iPod touch.

CAUTION: We've heard of people experiencing problems (lock-ups, reduced battery life, etc.) when they restored a backup from a non-iPod touch (an iPad or iPhone) to the iPod touch. Also, selecting **Restore** here assumes you've already made a backup of your old device in order to restore the latest information to your new iPod touch.

3. As Figure 1–5 shows, you have the option of naming your iPod touch and setting up basic sync options in iTunes.

4. Give your iPod touch a **Name**. Each time you plug in your iPod touch—to this or any other computer—your iPod touch will show the name you choose here. In this case, we'll call it **Martin's iPod**.

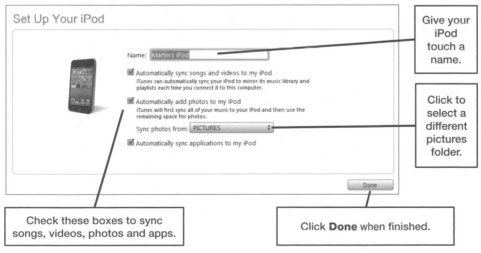

Figure 1–5. *Naming your iPod touch and selecting sync options.*

TIP: Get Moving Quickly without Syncing Anything

The first sync to your iPod touch can take a long time (15 minutes or more). If you want to start playing with your new iPod touch right away, uncheck both boxes shown in Figure 1–5 and click **Done**. Don't worry—you can check or uncheck these boxes in iTunes later. We show you the details in Chapter 3: "Sync Your iPod touch with iTunes."

5. To use iTunes to sync information between your computer and your iPod touch, leave the box checked next to **Automatically sync songs and videos to my iPod.**

CAUTION: Your iPod touch does not have as much memory as your computer, so be careful selecting **automatically sync** when you have thousands of songs, photos, or videos in your computer iTunes library.

6. To have your photos synced between your computer and your iPod touch, check the box next to **Automatically add photos to my iPod** and click the drop down menu to adjust the folder location where you store your photos on your computer.

TIP: You can select only a single folder from this screen to sync photos. If you have several folders you want to sync, please skip this step and check out the "Sync Photos" section of Chapter 3: "Sync Your iPod touch with iTunes" to learn how.

7. Leave the box checked next to **Automatically sync applications**, if you'd like apps you purchase on your iPod touch backed up to your computer and other apps you have purchased from iTunes on your computer automatically synced to your new iPod touch. We recommend leaving this checked. This option also allows you to update apps from iTunes on your computer and be able to manage and arrange your app icons and Home screens using iTunes on your computer.

8. Click **Done** to complete the set up screen.

Setup Complete: The iPod touch Summary Screen

Once you confirm your choices and click **Done**, you'll be taken to the Summary screen (Figure 1–6).

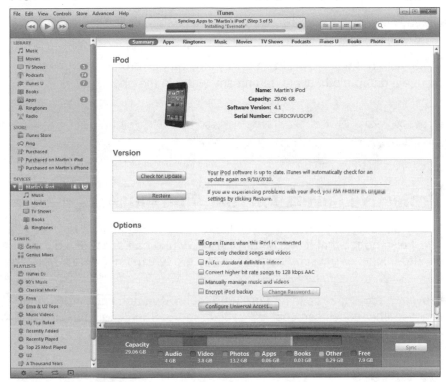

Figure 1–6. *iPod touch Summary screen in iTunes.*

Maintaining Your iPod touch

Now that you've set up your iPod touch with iTunes, you will want to know how to safely clean the screen and keep it protected.

Cleaning Your iPod touch Screen

After using your iPod touch a little while, you'll see that your fingers (or other fingers besides yours) have left smudges and oil on the formerly pristine screen. You will want to know how to safely clean the screen. One way to keep the screen cleaner in general is to place a protective screen cover (discussed in the next section) on the iPod touch, which may have the added benefit of cutting down on glare.

As for cleaning the screen, we recommend the following:

1. Turn off your iPod touch by pressing and holding the **Sleep/Power** key on the top edge, and then use the slider to turn it off.

2. Remove any cables, such as the USB sync cable.

3. Rub the screen with a dry, soft, lint-free cloth (like a cloth supplied to clean eyeglasses or something similar).

4. If the dry cloth does not work, try adding a very little bit of water to dampen the cloth. If you use a damp cloth, avoid getting any water in the openings.

> **CAUTION:** Never use household cleaners, abrasive cleansers such as SoftScrub, ammonia-based cleaners such as Windex, or alcohol, aerosol sprays, or solvents.

Cases and Protective Covers for Your iPod touch

Once you have your iPod touch in your hands, you'll notice how beautifully it is constructed. You will also notice that it can be fairly slippery and can easily slip out of your hands, bump into things, or get scratched when you are typing on it. And it gets smudged.

We recommend buying a protective case for your iPod touch. Average cases run about US $10–40 and fancy leather cases can cost US $100 or more. Spending a little to protect your iPod touch, which costs $200 or more, makes good sense.

Where to Buy Covers

You can purchase your iPod touch protective cover at the following locations:

- Amazon.com (www.amazon.com)
- The Apple Accessory Store: (http://store.apple.com)
- iLounge: (http://ilounge.pricegrabber.com)
- TiPB – The iPod touch + iPad Blog Store (http://store.tipb.com/)

You can also do a Web search for "iPod touch cases" or "iPod touch protective covers."

> **TIP:** You *may* be able to use a case designed for another type of smartphone for your iPod touch. If you go this route to save some money, just make sure your iPod touch fits securely in the case or cover.

What to Buy . . .

The following sections tell you a little about the types of cases and price ranges you can choose from.

Rubber / Silicone Cases ($10–30)

What these do: Provide a cushioned grip, absorb iPod touch bumps and bruises, and isolate the edges of the phone (antennas) from your fingers.

Pros: Inexpensive, colorful, and comfortable to hold.

Cons: Not as professional as a leather case.

Combined Cases with External Battery Packs ($50-80)

What these do: Combine the protective features of a hard shell case with a rechargeable external battery pack.   Manufacturers such as Mophie and Case-Mate are busy working on new iPod touch versions of these cases. Hopefully they'll be available by the time you read this book.

Pros: Protect your iPod touch while getting a tremendous boost to your battery life – some boast 50% or more battery life.

Cons: Adds weight and bulk to the phone.

Waterproof Cases ($10–40)

What these do: Provide waterproof protection for your iPod touch and allow you to safely use your device near water (in the rain, at the pool, at the beach, on the boat).

> **TIP:** If you like to row or paddle, you'll want a waterproof case. Check out the **SpeedCoach Mobile** app. You can buy this app for about $65 from the App Store.

Pros: Provide good water protection.

Cons: May make the touch screen harder to use; usually doesn't protect against drops or bumps.

Hard Plastic / Metal Case ($20–40)

What these do: Provide hard, solid protection against scratches, bumps, and short drops.

Pros: Provide good protection.

Cons: Add some bulk and weight. You may need to remove when charging because the iPod touch could overheat.

Leather or Special Cases ($50–100+)

What these do: Provide good protection and more of a luxury feel.

Pros: Attractive and luxurious; protects the front and back.

Cons: More expensive; add bulk and weight.

Front Screen Glass Protectors ($5–40)

What these do: Protect the screen of the iPod touch from scratches.

Pros: Help prolong life of your iPod touch, protect against scratches, decrease screen glare.

Cons: Some may increase glare or affect touch sensitivity of the screen.

iPod touch Basics

Now that you have your iPod touch charged, clean, registered, and decked out with a new protective case, let's take a look at some of the basics to help you learn how to get around.

Powering On/Off and Sleep/Wake

To power on your iPod touch, press and hold the **Power/Sleep** button on the top edge of the device for a few seconds (Figure 1–7). Tapping this button quickly won't power on the iPod touch if it's completely off—you really need to hold it until you see the iPod touch power on.

When you are no longer using your iPod touch, you have two options: you can either put it into sleep mode or turn it off completely.

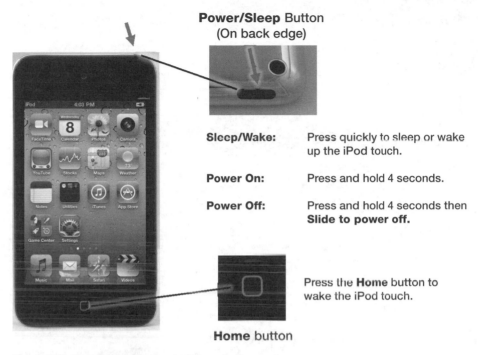

Power/Sleep Button
(On back edge)

Sleep/Wake: Press quickly to sleep or wake
up the iPod touch.

Power On: Press and hold 4 seconds.

Power Off: Press and hold 4 seconds then
Slide to power off.

Press the **Home** button to
wake the iPod touch.

Home button

Figure 1–7. *Power/Sleep button and Home button.*

The advantage of sleep mode is that when you want to use your iPod touch again, just a quick tap of the **Power/Sleep** button or the **Home** button will wake it up. According to Apple, the iPod touch has up to a month of stand-by power.

If you want to maximize your battery or if you know you won't be using your iPod touch for some time—say when you go to sleep—you should turn it off completely. The way to do this is to press and hold the **Power/Sleep** button until you see the **Slide to Power Off** bar. Just slide the bar to the right and the iPod touch will power off.

Moving Around Inside Apps and the Settings Screens

Getting around the screens inside the apps on your iPod touch is as simple as tapping on the screen, as Figure 1–8 shows.

1. Tap any icon to start an app. Tap the **Settings** icon to start the Settings app.

2. Touch **General** to see the General settings.

3. Touch **Network** to see Network settings.

4. You set any switch by tapping it. So, next to **Data Roaming**, touch the **OFF** switch to turn it **On**.

5. To go back a level in the screens, touch the button in the upper left corner. In this case, you'd touch the **General** button to get out of the **Network** screen.

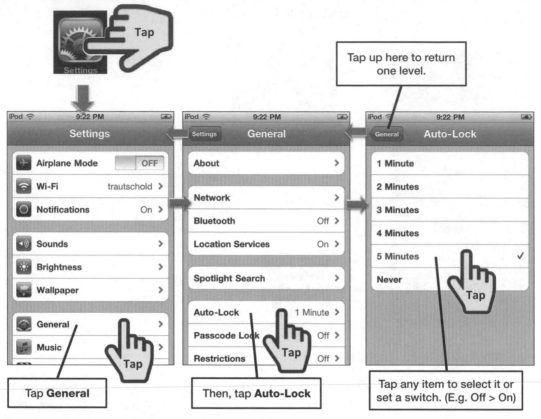

Figure 1–8. *Navigating through icons and settings screens*

The Home Button

The button you'll use most often is your **Home** button (at left). This button starts everything you do with your iPod touch. It also jumps you out of any app and brings you back to your Home screen. If your iPod touch is sleeping, press the **Home** button once to wake It up.

TIP: Double-tapping the **Home** button launches the fast app switcher. If the phone is locked and playing music, a double tap will launch the iPod controls.

Multitask by Double-Clicking the Home Button

One of the features of the new iPod touch is multitasking, which means you can have more than one app open at a time. To multitask, simply double-click the **Home** button.

TIP: You'll find more details on multitasking in Chapter 8:

"Multitasking and Voice Control."

1. While in any app or from the Home screen, double-click the **Home** button. See Figure 1–9.

2. You'll see a small bar of icons appear in the bottom row. These represent the apps you've started since you powered on your iPod touch.

3. Tap any icon to return to that app.

4. Swipe your finger left or right to see more icons.

5. Swipe all the way to the left to see an additional set of controls for the Music and to lock the screen in portrait (vertical) orientation.

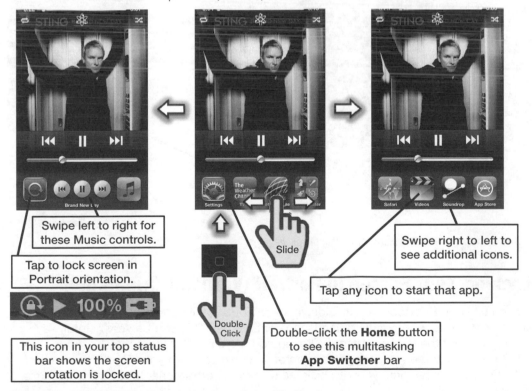

Figure 1–9. *Double-click the Home button to see the multitasking bar*

Volume Keys for Ringer and Audio/Video Playback

Located on the upper left-hand side of the iPod touch (Figure 1–10), these are simple **Volume Up/Volume Down** keys that you'll find very handy.

Ringer Volume

If you're not playing a song, video, or other content, pressing these **Volume** keys will adjust the volume of your phone ringer.

Adjusting Playback or FaceTime Voice Volume

When you are listening to music, video, or other content, or when you are on a FaceTime call, you can use the **Volume** keys to raise or lower the volume. If you are listening to music or videos, you can also use the onscreen slider bar to adjust the volume, as Figure 1–10 shows.

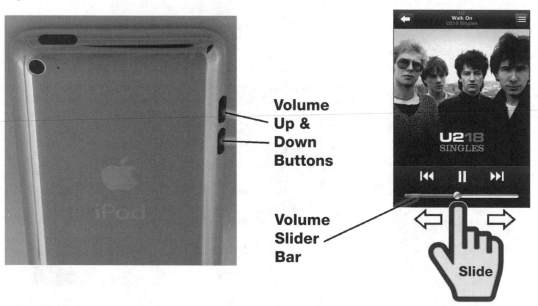

Figure 1–10. *Adjusting the volume or muting the phone ringer*

Locking Your Screen in Portrait (Vertical) Orientation

As you tilt your iPod touch on its side, in some apps you'll notice that the iPod touch screen rotates to a horizontal or landscape orientation. This can be very helpful, say when you want the larger landscape keyboard for typing. But there may be times you don't want the screen to change its orientation when you turn your iPod touch on its side. On such occasions, you can lock the screen in portrait orientation (refer back to Figure 1–9).

1. Double-click the **Home** button.

2. Swipe left to right to see the iPod and screen-lock controls.

3. Touch the **Portrait Orientation Lock** button in the left end of icons.

4. To disable the lock, tap the same button again.

> **TIP:** The iPod touch is great for reading iBooks in bed. If you prefer the larger page view in portrait mode, enable Portrait Orientation Lock. This way, when you set your iPod touch on your lap or hold it almost flat, the screen will not accidentally rotate to landscape mode. Check out Chapter 14: "Email on Your iPod Touch," for more.

Adjust or Disable the Auto-Lock Time-Out Feature

You'll notice that your iPod touch will auto-lock and go into sleep mode with the screen blank after a short amount of time. You can change this time or even disable this feature altogether inside the **Settings** icon.

1. Touch the **Settings** icon from your Home screen.

2. Touch **General**.

3. Touch **Auto-Lock**.

4. You'll see your current Auto-Lock setting next to Auto-Lock on this screen. The default setting is that the iPod touch locks after 3 minutes of sitting idle (to save battery life.) You can change this to **1**, **2**, **3**, **4**, or **5** minutes, or **Never**.

5. Touch the desired setting to select it—you'll know it's selected when you see the checkmark next to it.

6. Then, touch the **General** button in the upper left corner to get back to the General screen. You should see your change now reflected next to **Auto-Lock**.

> **BATTERY LIFE TIP:** Setting a shorter lock time for Auto-Lock (e.g., 1 minute) will help save battery life.

Adjusting the Date, Time, Time Zone, and 24-Hour Format

Usually, the date and time is either set for you or adjusts when you connect your iPod touch to your computer, as we cover in Chapter 3: "Sync Your iPod touch with iTunes." You can, however, easily adjust the date and time manually. You may want to do this when you are traveling with your iPod touch and need to adjust the time zone when you land.

1. Touch the **Settings** icon.

2. Touch **General**.

3. Scroll down and touch **Date & Time** to see the Date & Time settings screen.

4. If you prefer to see **09:30** and **14:30** instead of **9:30 AM** and **2:30 PM**, tap the **24-Hour Time** setting switch to **On**.

5. To set your time zone, tap **Time Zone** and type in the name of a major city in your time zone. Tap the city name when it appears.

6. After selecting the city, you are brought back to the main Date & Time screen with your selected city shown next to **Time Zone**. Tap **Set Date & Time** to adjust your date and time.

7. To adjust the date, tap the date at the top of the screen.

8. To adjust the time, tap the time at the top of the screen.

9. Once you tap the date or time at the top, then you can adjust the date and time, by touching and sliding the wheels up or down as shown in the image here.

10. When you are done, tap the **Date & Time** button in the upper left corner.

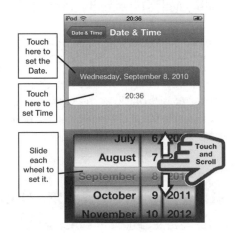

Adjusting the Brightness

Your iPod touch has an **Auto-Brightness** control that's turned on by default. It uses the built-in light sensor to adjust the brightness of the screen. At night or when it is darker outside, the auto-brightness control dims the screen. When it is bright and sunny, the screen will automatically brighten so it's easier to read. Generally, we advise you keep this set to **On**.

If you want to adjust the brightness, use the controls in your **Settings** app.

1. From your Home screen, touch the **Settings** icon.

2. Touch **Brightness**.

3. Move the slider control to adjust the brightness.

4. Set the switch next to Auto-Brightness to **On** or **Off**.

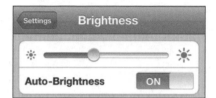

TIP: Setting the brightness lower helps you save battery life. A little less than halfway across seems to work fine.

Chapter 2

Typing Tips, Copy/Paste, and Search

In this chapter, we show you how to save valuable time typing on your iPod touch, whether you use the portrait (vertical, smaller) keyboard or the landscape (horizontal, larger) keyboard. You'll learn how to select different language keyboards, how to type symbols, and more.

Later we'll delve into the Spotlight search and copy-and-paste functions. Copy and paste will save you lots of time as well as increase your accuracy when working with your iPod touch.

Keyboards on Your iPod touch

You'll find two onscreen keyboards on your iPod touch: the smaller one visible when you hold your iPod touch in a vertical orientation, and the larger landscape keyboard when you hold the iPod touch horizontally. You can easily choose the keyboard that works best for you, and switch whenever you want.

Typing on the Screen with Two Thumbs

When you first start out with your iPod touch, you'll probably find you can most easily type with one finger—usually your index finger—while holding the iPod touch with your other hand.

After a little while, try experimenting with thumb typing (like you see so many people doing on their phones). Once you practice a little, typing with two thumbs instead of one finger will really boost your speed. Just be patient, it does take some practice to become proficient with your thumbs.

TIP: Have large hands and fingers? Flip your iPod touch on its side to get the larger landscape keyboard!

You'll actually notice after a while that the keyboard touch sensitivity assumes you are typing with two thumbs. What this means is that the letters on the left side of your keyboard are meant to be pressed on their left side, and the keys on the right are meant to be pressed on their right side (Figure 2–1).

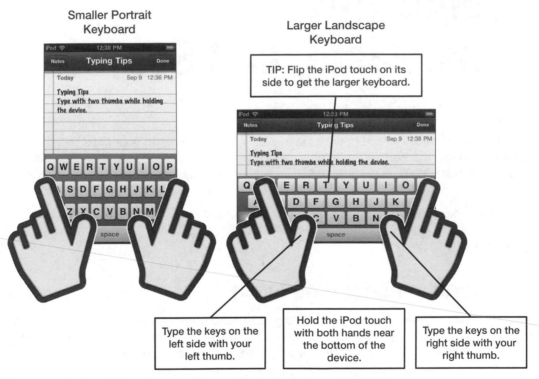

Smaller Portrait Keyboard

Larger Landscape Keyboard

TIP: Flip the iPod touch on its side to get the larger keyboard.

Type the keys on the left side with your left thumb.

Hold the iPod touch with both hands near the bottom of the device.

Type the keys on the right side with your right thumb.

Figure 2–1. *Typing with two thumbs can be much faster than using a single finger.*

Saving Time with Auto-Correction

After typing for a while, you may to notice a little pop-up window directly below some of the words you're typing—this is called Auto-Correction.

NOTE: If you never see the Auto-Correction pop-up window, you will have to enable it by going to **Settings** > **General** > **Keyboard** > Set **Auto-Correction** to **ON.**

You can save typing time when you see the correct word guessed by just pressing the **Space** key at the bottom of the keyboard.

In the example in Figure 2–2 we start typing the word "especially" and when we get to the c, the correct word appears below in a pop-up. To select it, we simply press the **Space** key on the keyboard.

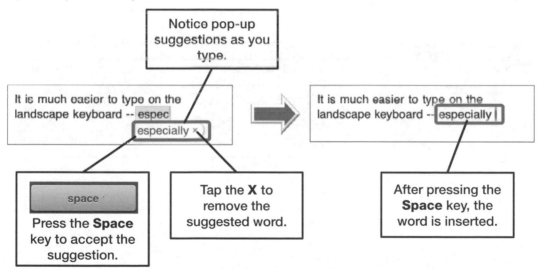

Figure 2–2. *Using Auto-Correction' suggested words*

Your first inclination might be to tap the pop-up word, but that just erases it from the screen. It's ultimately faster to keep typing or press the **Space** key when you see the correct word, as there will be more situations in which the word is either correct or will become correct as you keep typing—less finger travel in the long run.

TIP: Auto-Correction also looks through your **Contacts** list to make suggestions. For example, if Martin Trautschold was in your **Contacts** list, you'd see "Trautschold" come up as a suggestion after typing "Trauts."

Once you become accustomed to using the **Space** key this way, you'll find that this pop-up guessing can be quite a time-saver. After all, you'd have to type a space at the end of the word anyway.

Sometimes the Auto-Correction word is incorrect; in this case, you can simply press the **Backspace** key 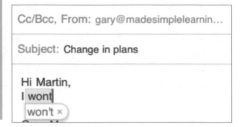 and you'll see a pop-up appear with the original word before Auto-Correction changed it. See Figure 2–3.

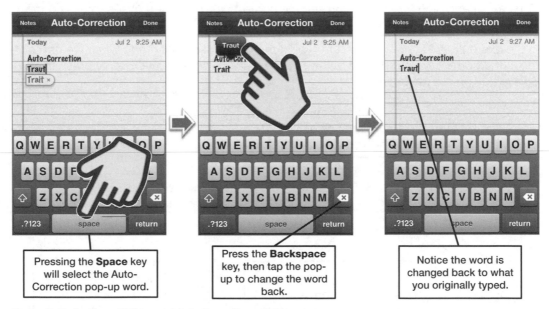

Figure 2–3. *Dealing with incorrect Auto-Correction words*

TIP: With Auto-Correction, you can save time by not having to type the apostrophe in many common contractions, such as "wont" and "cant." Auto-Correction will present its little pop-up window with the contraction spelled correctly and all you need to do is to press the **Space** key.

Hearing Auto-Correction Words Out Loud

You can set your iPod touch to say the Auto-text and Auto-Correction words as they appear. This might be helpful for selecting the correct word. To enable this feature:

1. Tap the **Settings** icon.

2. Tap **General**.

3. Tap **Accessibility** near the bottom of the page (you need to swipe down).

4. Set the switch next to **Speak Auto-text** to **On**.

Now whenever you're typing, you'll hear the Auto-Correction word that pops up. If you agree with the word you hear, press the **Space** key to accept it; otherwise, keep typing. Not having to look up at the keyboard can save you some time.

Spell Checker

Working together with Auto-Correction is the built-in spell-checker. Most of the time, your misspelled words will be caught and corrected automatically by Auto-Correction, but not always. When Auto-Correction thinks a word is misspelled, it underlines the word with a red dotted line, as in Figure 2–4. If you tap the word, you'll see some suggestions for what might be the correct word and you can simply select the correct one.

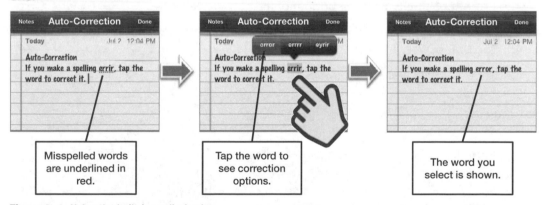

Figure 2–4. *Using the built-in spell-checker*

> **TIP:** If your spell-checker has too many incorrect words, you can give it a fresh start by clearing out all the custom words. To do this: Tap **Settings** > **General** >**Reset** > **Reset Keyboard Dictionary.** Then tap **Reset Dictionary** to confirm. This will clear out all custom words added to your iPod touch dictionary. You can also turn off spell check entirely if you like; tap **Settings** > **General** > **Keyboard** and turn of the spell check feature.

Accessibility Options

There are a number of accessibility features on the iPod touch that can be useful, even if you don't have any special problems. The VoiceOver option, for example, reads to you from the screen, while the **Zoom** feature can help you see what's on screen better.

Getting Your iPod touch to Speak To You (VoiceOver)

One cool feature of the iPod touch is that you can turn on the VoiceOver feature so that the iPod touch will speak anything on the screen—even entire screens of text if you want. It will also tell you what you tap on, what buttons are selected, and any available options. You can even get it to read you an e-mail, text document, or an iBook page.

> **TIP:** If you're using VoiceOver in a public place, use your headphones to better hear what's said and to avoid bothering others.

To enable **VoiceOver**:

1. Tap the **Settings** icon.

2. Tap **General**.

3. Tap **Accessibility** near the bottom of the page.

4. Tap **VoiceOver**.

5. Set the **VoiceOver** switch to **On**.

> **CAUTION:** As shown on the screen to the right, the VoiceOver gestures are different from the normal gestures. Tap the **Practice VoiceOver Gestures** button to get used to them.

Scroll down the **VoiceOver** screen to see more settings.

Adjust whether hints are spoken by changing the setting for **Speak Hints.**

When you type with **VoiceOver**, by default every character you type will be spoken. You can change this by tapping **Typing Feedback** and then, on the next screen, you can set feedback to **Characters, Words, Characters and Words**, or **Nothing**.

On this setting screen, you can also adjust the **Speaking Rate** by sliding the bar.

You can specify whether **Phonetics** and **Pitch Change** are used by setting the switches.

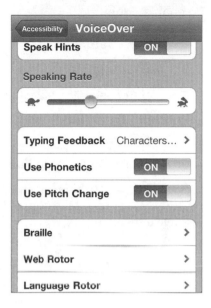

To have **VoiceOver** read you an entire page in the **Notes** or **iBooks** app, tap the bottom and top of the block of text on the screen simultaneously. If you tap in the text with just one finger, only a single line will be read.

Using Zoom to Magnify the Entire Screen

It's a good idea to turn on the **Zoom** feature if you find that the text, icons, buttons, or anything on the screen is too hard to see. With **Zoom** turned on, you can enlarge the entire screen to almost twice its normal size. Everything is much easier to read.

NOTE: You can't use VoiceOver and Zoom at the same time. Also, if you don't want to magnify the entire screen, you can increase just the font sizes for your major apps using the **Large Text** feature, as we describe in the "Use Larger Text Size for Easier Reading" section below.

To enable **Zoom**:

1. Tap the **Settings** icon.

2. Tap **General**.

3. Tap **Accessibility** (near the bottom of the page).

4. Tap **Zoom**.

5. Set the switch next to **Zoom** to **On**.

Like **VoiceOver**, **Zoom** uses the three-fingered gestures. Be sure to take note of them before you leave the screen.

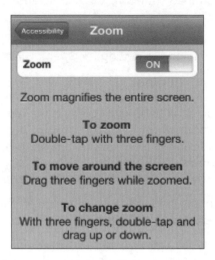

White on Black

If the contrast and colors are difficult to see, you might want to turn on the **White on Black** setting. To change this setting:

1. Get into the **Accessibility** screen in the **Settings** app, as shown previously.

2. Set the **White on Black** switch to **On**.

   With this setting **On**, everything that was light on the screen becomes black, and everything that was dark or black becomes white.

Use Larger Text Size for Easier Reading

You can really expand the size of the font in **Contacts**, **Mail**, **Messages,** and **Notes** using the **Large Text** feature.

1. Tap the **Settings** icon.

2. Tap **General**.

3. Tap **Accessibility** near the bottom of the page (you need to swipe down).

4. Tap **Large Text**. You will then see a screen of font size options: **Off, 20pt text, 24pt, 32pt, 40pt, 48pt** and **56pt** text. Tap the size you want to use. In the image to the right, we select the 48pt font.

5. Tap the **Accessibility** button in the upper left corner to return to the previous screen, then tap the **Home** button to exit **Settings**.

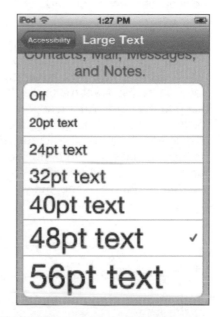

NOTE: The Accessibility section also has a mono audio mode in case you have no hearing in one ear.

Triple-Click Home Button Options

You can set a triple-click of the **Home** button to do various things related to **Accessibility**.

1. Get into the **Accessibility** screen in the **Settings** app, as shown previously.

2. Tap **Triple-click the Home Button** near the bottom of the page.

3. Choose from **Off**, **Toggle VoiceOver**, **Toggle White on Black**, or **Ask**.

Magnifying Glass for Editing Text/Placing the Cursor

How many times have you been typing something and wanted to move the cursor precisely between two words or between two letters?

This can be hard to do until you figure out the magnifying glass trick. What you do is this: Touch and hold your finger on the place where you want the cursor (see image to the right). After a second or two, you'll see a magnifying glass appear. While holding your finger on the screen, slide the magnifying glass around to position the cursor. When you let go, you'll see the copy/paste pop-up menu, but you can just ignore it.

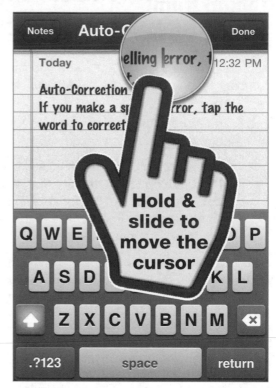

Typing Numbers and Symbols

How do you type a number or a symbol using the iPod touch's onscreen keyboard? When you are typing, tap the **123** key in the lower left corner to see numbers and common symbols such as **$! ~ & = # . _ - +**. If you need more symbols, tap the **#+=** key on the number keyboard, just above the **ABC** key in the lower left corner (see Figure 2–5).

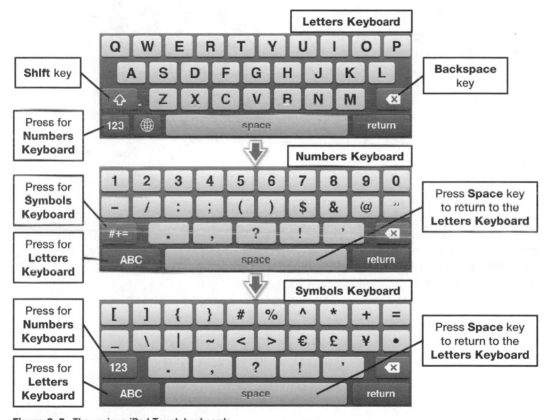

Figure 2–5. *The various iPod Touch keyboards*

TIP: Notice that the number and basic symbols keyboard will stay active until you either hit the **Space** key or press the key for another keyboard, such as **ABC**.

Touch and Slide Trick

These tips are courtesy of Rene Ritchie from the iPhone/iPod touch Blog (www.tipb.com).

Typing Uppercase Letters

Normally, to type uppercase letters, you press the **Shift** key, then the letter.

The faster way to type single uppercase letters and symbols that require the **Shift** key is to press the **Shift** key, keep your finger on the keyboard, slide over to the key you want, and release.

For example, to type an uppercase **D**, press the right **Shift** key, then slide over to the **D** key and release.

Rapidly Typing a Single Number

If you have to type just a single number, press the **123** key and slide your finger up to the number. However, to type several numbers in a row, it's best to press the **123** key, let go, and then press each number.

Press and Hold to Type More Symbols

What about symbols not shown on the keyboard?

All you need to do is press and hold a letter, number, or symbol that is related to the symbol you want.

> **TIP:** You can type more symbols than are shown on the screen.

For example, if you wanted to type the YEN symbol (¥), you would press and hold the $ key until you saw the other options, slide up your finger to highlight, and then let go on the YEN symbol.

This tip also works with the **.com** key in the Safari web browser and when typing e-mail addresses by pressing and holding the **period** (.) key. You can get additional web site suffixes by pressing and holding the **.com** or **period** keys.

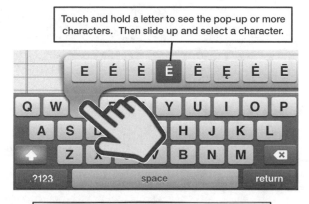

Touch and hold a letter to see the pop-up or more characters. Then slide up and select a character.

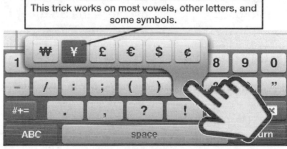

This trick works on most vowels, other letters, and some symbols.

The screen above shows items not on the standard US keyboard: **.co.uk**, **.ie**, **.de**, **.ca**, **.eu**. That's because we've installed additional international keyboards. See how to do this in the "Typing in Other Languages—International Keyboards" section later in this chapter.

> **TIP:** A few more useful symbols.
>
> You'll find a good bullet-point character on the **Advanced Symbols** keyboard, just above the **Backspace** key. You can get a **degree** symbol if you press and hold the **Zero** key (0). And press and hold the **?** and **!** keys to get their Spanish inverted cousins.

Caps Lock

Double-press the **Shift** key to turn on **Caps Lock**. You know it's turned on when the key turns blue.

To turn off Caps Lock, just press the **Shift** key again.

Quickly Deleting or Changing Text

If you need to change or delete some text, the quickest way is to select it first.

1. Begin selecting the text by double-tapping it.

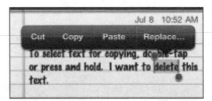

2. Adjust the selection by dragging the blue handles.

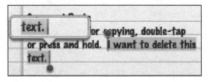

3. To erase the selected text, press the **Backspace** key.

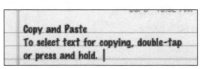

4. To replace the text, simply start typing. The text will be instantly replaced by the letters you type.

Keyboard Options and Settings

There are a few keyboard options to make typing on your iPod touch easier. The keyboard options are located in the **General** tab of your **Settings**.

1. Tap the **Settings** icon.

2. Tap **General**.

3. Tap **Keyboard** near the bottom of the page.

Auto-Capitalization

When you start a new sentence, the first word will be automatically capitalized if **Auto-Capitalization** is **ON**.

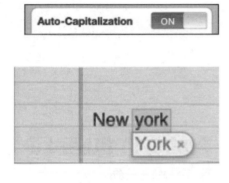

Also, common proper nouns will be correctly capitalized. For example, if you typed "New york," you'd be prompted to change it to "New York"— again, just pressing the **Space** key will select the correction. If you backspace over a capital letter, the iPod touch will assume the new letter you type should be capital as well. This is also set to **ON** by default.

Auto-Correction ON/OFF

Using the built-in dictionary, Auto-Correction will automatically make changes to commonly misspelled words. For example, if you type in "wont," **Auto-Correction** will change it to "won't" on the fly. Make sure this is ON (the default setting) if you want this feature to work.

Check Spelling

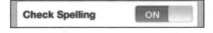

The built-in spell-checker is set to ON by default, and underlines words with red dotted lines to show they appear to be misspelled. Tap the word to view suggestions or add the word to your custom dictionary.

Enable Caps Lock

Sometimes when you type, you may want to lock the caps by double-tapping the Shift key. Enabling Caps Lock will allow you to do this.

This is set to OFF by default.

"." Shortcut

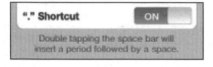

You might be familiar with this time-saving feature that will automatically put in a period at the end of the sentence when you double-press the Space key. This is exactly the same feature that you can enable on the iPod touch. By default, this is also set to ON.

Typing In Other Languages—International Keyboards

At publishing time, the iPod touch lets you type in over a dozen different languages. Some of the Asian languages, such as Japanese and Chinese, offer two or three keyboards for different typing methods.

Adding a New International Keyboard

To enable various language keyboards, follow these steps:

1. Touch the **Settings** icon.

2. Tap **General**.

3. Tap **Keyboard** near the bottom of the page.

4. Tap **International Keyboards**.

5. Tap **Add New Keyboard** (see Figure 2–6).

6. Tap any language listed to add that keyboard.

7. Now you'll see that keyboard among the available keyboards.

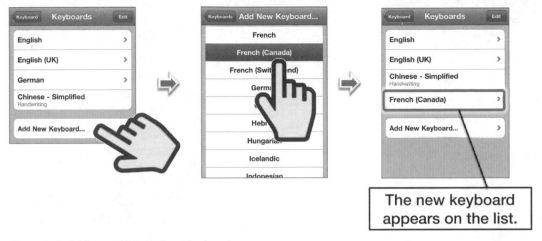

The new keyboard appears on the list.

Figure 2–6. *Adding new international keyboards.*

Editing, Reordering, or Deleting Keyboards

You may want to adjust options for a keyboard, reorder, or simply remove a keyboard that you no longer use.

1. Follow steps 1-4 under **Adding a New International Keyboard** above to view the list of International Keyboards.

2. To adjust options for a specific keyboard, tap it. In our example, we tapped **French (Canada)**.

3. Change the **Software Keyboard Layout** by tapping a choice in that section.

4. Change the **Hardware Keyboard Layout** by tapping a choice in that section.

5. Tap the **Keyboards** button in the upper left corner to save your choices and return to the list of keyboards.

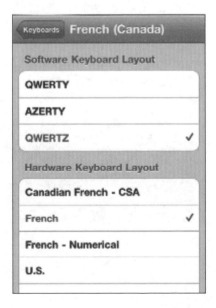

6. To reorder the list of keyboards or delete a keyboard, tap the **Edit** button in the upper right corner.

7. Touch and drag the right edge of the keyboard (the three gray bars) up or down.

Touch and drag to re-order the keyboards.

8. To delete a keyboard, tap the **red minus sign** so it swings to the vertical position, then tap **Delete.**

9. To finish editing your keyboards, tap the **Done** button in the upper right corner.

When you've installed at least one international keyboard, you'll see a little Globe key appear (see Figure 2–7). Press the **Globe** key to cycle between the installed languages.

TIP: Press and hold the **Globe** key to see a list of available keyboards. Then you can quickly select the keyboard you wish to use.

Japanese, Chinese, and some other languages provide several keyboard options to meet various typing preferences.

In some of the languages (such as Japanese), the typed letters change into characters, or you can draw characters. You may also see a row of other character combinations above the keyboard. When you see the combination you want, tap it.

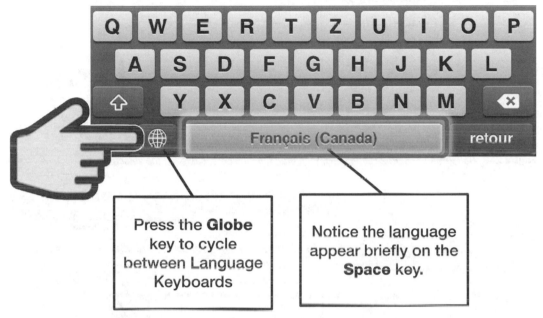

Press the Globe key to cycle between Language Keyboards

Notice the language appear briefly on the Space key.

Figure 2–7. *Press the Globe key to cycle between International Keyboards.*

Copy and Paste

The copy-and-paste function can save time and increase your accuracy. You can use it for taking text from e-mail (such as meeting details) and pasting it into your Calendar, or you may want to copy an e-mail address from one place to another so you don't have to retype it. (We show you this technique in the "Setup Exchange/Google Account" in Chapter 4: "Other Sync Methods.") You can even copy text or images from your Safari web browser and paste them into a Note or a Mail message. You'll find lots of places to use copy and paste; the more comfortable you are with it, the more you'll use it.

Selecting Text with Double-Tap

To copy text, first you have to select it, which you do by double-tapping it. You'll see a box with blue dots (handles) at opposite corners. Just drag the handles to select the text you want to highlight and copy, as shown in Figure 2–8.

This works well in Mail, Messages, and Notes.

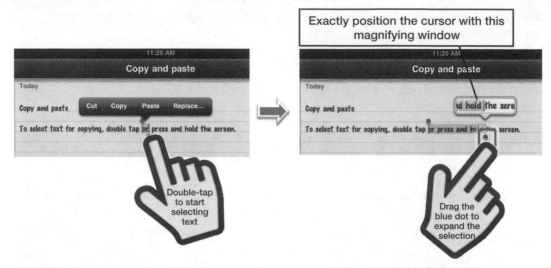

Figure 2–8. *Double-tap to start selecting text, then drag the blue dots to expand the selection.*

TIP: If you want to select all the text, tap and hold the screen on the text or double-tap the screen above or below the text. You'll see a pop-up asking you to Select or Select All. Tap **Select** to select a word. Tap **Select All** to highlight all the text.

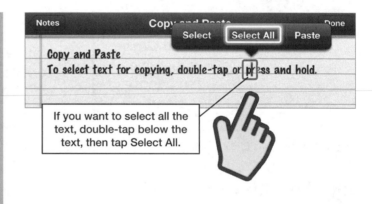

Selecting Text with Two-Finger Touch

The other way to select text requires that you touch the screen simultaneously with two fingers. This seems to work best if you are holding your iPod touch with one hand and use your thumb and forefinger from your other hand. You can also set the iPod touch down on the table and touch with a finger from both hands.

1. Touch the screen simultaneously at the beginning and end of the text you want to select. Don't worry if you can't get the selection exactly on the first touch.

2. After the two-finger touch, use the blue handles to drag the beginning and end of the selection to the correct position, as shown in Figure 2–9.

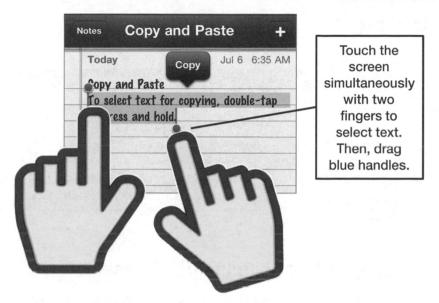

Touch the screen simultaneously with two fingers to select text. Then, drag blue handles.

Figure 2–9. *Select text by touching the screen at the same time with two fingers.*

Selecting Non-Editable Text with Touch and Hold

In the Safari web browser and other places where you can't edit the text, hold your finger on some text and the paragraph will become highlighted with handles at each of the corners.

Drag the handles to select more or less text.

Touch and hold to select web site text.

> **NOTE:** If you drag less than a paragraph, the selector will switch to fine-text mode and give you the blue handles on both ends of the selection to let you pick just the characters or words you want. If you drag your finger beyond a paragraph, you get the gross-text selector that you can drag up or down to select whole pages of text and graphics.

Cut or Copy the Text

Once you've selected the text you want to copy, touch the **Copy** tab at the top of the screen. The tab will turn blue, indicating that the text is on the clipboard.

NOTE: If you've previously cut or copied text, you'll also see the Paste option, as shown here.

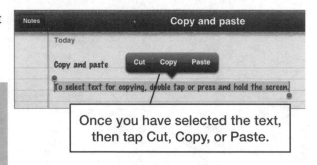

Once you have selected the text, then tap Cut, Copy, or Paste.

Jumping Between Apps/App Switching/Multitasking

After you copy text, you may want to paste it into another app. The easiest way to jump between apps is to use the App Switcher.

1. Copy or cut your text.

2. Double-tap the **Home** button to bring up the App Switcher at the bottom of your screen (see Figure 2–10).

3. If you had an app running in the background, you'll be able to find it on the App Switcher bar.

4. Swipe right or left to find the app you want and tap it.

5. If you don't see the app you want in the App Switcher bar, tap the **Home** button and start the app from the **Home** screen.

6. Now paste the text by pressing and holding the screen and selecting **Paste** from the pop-up.

7. Double-tap the **Home** button again and tap the app you just left to jump back to it.

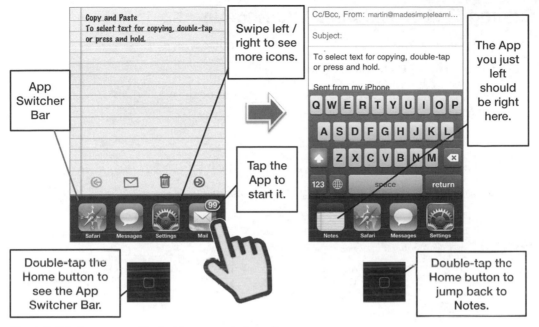

Figure 2–10. You can copy the text from one app to another.

Pasting the Text

If you are pasting the text into the same Note or Mail message:

1. Use your finger to move the cursor to where you want to paste the text. Remember the magnifying glass trick we showed earlier in this chapter to help you position the cursor.

2. Once you let go of the screen, you should see a pop-up asking you to **Select**, **Select All**, or **Paste**.

3. If you don't see this pop-up, double-tap the screen.

4. Select **Paste** to paste your you are pasting the text into the same Note or Mail selection.

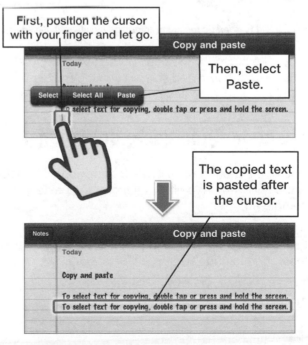

Pasting Text or an Image into Another App

To paste the text or image you have copied into another app:

1. Tap the **Home** button (see Figure 2–11).

2. Tap the icon for the app into which you want to paste the text. In this case, let's tap **Mail**.

3. Tap the **Compose** icon 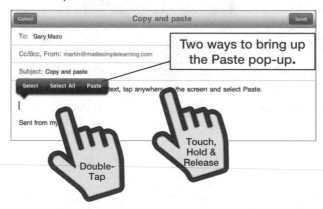 to write a new e-mail.

4. Double-tap anywhere in the body of the message.

5. Tap **Paste**.

Figure 2–11. *Bring up the Paste command by either double-tapping or touching, holding, and releasing.*

Move the cursor to the body of the text and either double-tap or touch, hold, and release your finger and you will see the Paste pop-up. Tap **Paste** and the text in the clipboard will be pasted right into the body of the e-mail.

Shake to Undo Paste or Typing

One of the great new features for copying and pasting is the ability to undo either typing or the paste you just completed.

All you have to do is shake your iPod touch after typing or pasting. A new pop-up appears giving you the option to undo what you've just done.

Tap **Undo Typing** or **Undo Paste** to correct the mistake.

TIP: Quickly Delete Text with the Backspace Key

If you ever want to delete a number of lines of text, a paragraph, or even all the text you just typed with only one or two taps, this tip is for you. Just select the text you want to delete, then

press the **Backspace** key  in the lower right corner of the keyboard to delete all the selected text.

Find What You Need with Spotlight Search

Your iPod touch has a great feature for finding information—**Spotlight Search**, Apple's proprietary search method for globally searching through your iPod touch for a name, event, or subject.

Let's say you're looking for something related to Martin. You can't remember if it was an e-mail, a Note, or a Calendar event, but you do know it was related to Martin.

This is the perfect time to use **Spotlight Search** to find everything related to Martin on your iPod touch.

Using Spotlight Search

First, you need to get into **Spotlight Search**, which resides to the left of the first page of the **Home** screen.

To the left of the first circle (indicating the first page of your **Home** screen) is a very small magnifying glass.

Swipe your finger from left to right on the first page of icons to see the **Spotlight Search** page.

> Type your search words here.
>
> Swipe your finger from left to right on the first page of icons to see the Spotlight Search page.

1. On the **Spotlight Search** page), type in one or a few words for your search.

2.   Tap the **Search** button in the lower right corner to execute your search.

> **TIP:** If you are looking for a person, type their full name to more accurately find items from only that person (for example, "Martin Trautschold"). This will eliminate any other Martins who might be in your iPod touch and make sure you find items only related to Martin Trautschold.

3.   In the search results (see Figure 2–12,) you'll see all e-mails, appointments, meeting invitations, and contact information found. Swipe down to see more results.

4.   Tap one of the results in the list to view its contents.

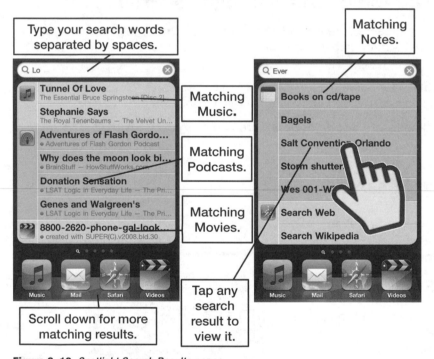

Figure 2–12. *Spotlight Search Results pages.*

Your search results stay in place until you clear them, so you can go back to **Spotlight Search** once again by swiping to the right from your **Home** screen.

To clear the search field, just touch the **X** in the search bar. To exit **Spotlight Search**, press the **Home** key or swipe to the left.

Search Web or Search Wikipedia

After you perform a Spotlight Search, you'll see at the very bottom of the results **Search Web** and **Search Wikipedia**.

Tap either of these to execute your search on the Web or in Wikipedia.

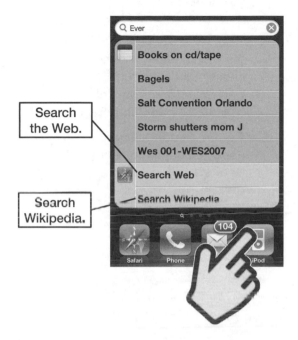

Search the Web.

Search Wikipedia.

Customizing Spotlight Search

You can customize your **Spotlight Search** by removing certain apps or types of data from the search. You can even change the order in which each type of data is searched. This might be useful if you want to search only your **Contacts** and **Mail** messages, but nothing else. Or, if you know that you always want to search **Mail** first, then **Calendar**, then **Music**, you could set those items in the proper order.

1. Tap the **Settings** icon.

2. Tap **General**.

3. Tap **Spotlight Search**.

4. To change the order of the items searched, touch and drag the right edge of the item with the three gray bars up or down.

5. To remove a specific item from the search, tap it to remove the check mark next to it. Unchecked items are not searched by **Spotlight Search**.

6. Tap the **General** button in the upper left corner to return to the **Settings**.

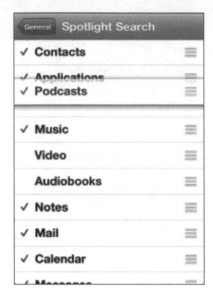

Chapter 3

Sync Your iPod touch with iTunes

In this chapter, we will show you how to set up or adjust the synchronization of information between your iPod touch and your Windows or Mac computer using iTunes.

We'll also take a look at what to consider before you sync and how to set up both automatic and manual sync of your personal information. With iTunes, you can sync or transfer contacts, calendar, notes, apps, music, videos, iBooks, documents, and picture libraries.

Moreover, as you'll see, iTunes will automatically back up your iPod touch whenever you connect it to your computer. And, because nothing ever works right all the time, we'll show you a few simple troubleshooting tips. Finally, you'll see how to check for updates and install updated operating system software for your iPod touch.

> **TIP:** iTunes can do so much more than just syncing—organize your music, create playlists, buy songs and videos—and it includes the Home Sharing and Genius features. To learn about all of the iTunes features and capabilities— and the brand new Ping Social Networking features - especially if you're new to iTunes—please check out Chapter 29: "Your iTunes User Guide."

Before You Set Up Your iTunes Sync

There are a few things you need before you can start using iTunes to sync. We cover the prerequisites and answer a few common questions about the reasons to use iTunes. We also help you understand what happens if you own another Apple device, such as an iPad or iPod, and start syncing with your iPod touch.

Prerequisites

There are just a few things you need to do before you sync your iPod touch with iTunes.

TIP: If you followed all the steps in Chapter 1: "Getting Started," chances are you've already completed the steps listed here and the initial sync of your contacts, calendar, bookmarks, notes, and email accounts to your iPod touch. If so, you may want to skip ahead to the "Apps: Sync and Manage Them" section later in this chapter.

1. Make sure you've installed version 10 or higher of iTunes on your computer. For help with installing or updating iTunes, see Chapter 29: "Your iTunes User Guide."

2. Create an iTunes account (Apple ID); see the "Create iTunes Account" section in Chapter 29.

3. Get the white sync cable that came with your iPod touch. One end plugs into the bottom of your iPod touch near the **Home** button and the other plugs into the USB port on your computer.

Can You Sync iTunes with an iPhone or iPad *and* Your iPod touch?

Yes! As long as you are syncing to the same computer, you can sync several Apple devices (Apple says up to five, but we've heard of people syncing more) to the same iTunes account on a single computer.

CAUTION: You can't sync the same iPod touch, iPad, or iPod to two different computers. If you attempt to do this, you'll see a message like: "Would you like to wipe this device (iPod touch, iPad, iPhone) and resync the new library?" If you answer **Yes**, any music and videos on the device will be erased.

However, you can stream music from the iPod touch (or any iOS device) even if it's not in manually manage music mode. Just plug it in, navigate to its music contents and play.

There Are Other Sync Options (MobileMe and Exchange/Google)—Should You Use iTunes?

There are other ways to synchronize your personal information and email, such as Exchange/Google and MobileMe, which we cover in Chapter 4: "Other Sync Methods." Keep in mind, however, that even if you choose one of these, you'll still need to use iTunes to:

- Backup and restore your iPod touch

- Update the iPod touch operating system software

- Sync and manage your applications (apps)

- Sync your music library and playlists

- Sync movies, TV shows, podcasts, and iTunes U content

- Sync books

- Sync photos

Wireless Sync vs. iTunes Desktop Sync

Ideally, your personal information (contacts, calendar, and notes) is all synced wirelessly and automatically to your iPod touch. With a wireless sync, you don't need to plug your iPod touch into your computer to do the sync—everything happens over the airwaves. Depending on your environment, you may or may not be able to use a wireless sync for all your information. For example, if you use Google, then for a full wireless sync of calendar and contacts, you need to use the Exchange sync option (not iTunes sync).

Setting Up Your iTunes Sync

Now that you've thought about the other options, you're ready to get started setting up your iTunes sync. We show you all the steps for both automated syncs and manual transfers of information to your iPod touch using iTunes.

The iPod touch Summary Screen (Manually Manage Music, Update, Restore, and More)

The **Summary** tab in iTunes is where you see and update your version of your iPod touch operating system software, and it is an important switch related to syncing music, video, and other content. It is also where you can select to automatically open iTunes (to sync) whenever you connect your iPod touch to your computer.

As Figure 3–1 shows, once you connect your iPod touch to your computer, you can see important information, like your iPod touch's memory capacity, installed software version, and serial number. You can also check for updates to the software version, restore data to your iPod touch, and choose from the several options available on this screen.

In particular, you can decide whether you want to **manually manage music and videos** using the check box at the bottom of this screen.

Figure 3–1. *The iPod touch **Summary** screen in iTunes*

To see the **Summary** screen:

1. Start the iTunes software on your computer.

2. Connect your iPod touch to your computer with the white USB cable supplied with the device. Plug one end into the bottom of the iPod touch near the **Home** key and the other end into a USB port on your computer.

3. If you've successfully connected your iPod touch, you should see your iPod touch listed under **DEVICES** in the left nav bar.

4. Click your **iPod touch** in the left nav bar, and then click the **Summary** tab on the top left edge of the main window.

5. If you want to be able to drag and drop music and videos onto your iPod touch, check the **Manually manage music and videos** box.

6. If you want to have iTunes open and sync your iPod touch automatically whenever you connect it to your computer, check the **Open iTunes when this iPod touch is connected** box.

iTunes Navigation Basics

Get a feel for the left nav bar. Click various items in this left nav bar, and notice that the main display window changes.

The top nav bar inside the main window also changes based on what you have selected in the left nav bar. For example, when you click your **iPod touch** in the left nav bar, you'll see tabs across the top of the main window that show information related to your device. When you click the **iTunes store** in the left nav bar, you see tabs related to the store in the main window.

Getting to the Sync Setup Screen (Info Tab)

Your first step is to get to the setup screen for syncing your contacts, calendar, email, and so forth. You follow the same steps described previously for getting to the **Summary** screen, except now you click the **Info** tab at the top to see the Contacts (and other sync settings) in the main iTunes window.

Sync Your Contacts and Calendars

Let's start by setting up syncing of your contacts and calendars.

1. Check the **Sync Contacts with** box and adjust the pull-down menu to the software or service where your contacts are stored. At publication time, on a Windows computer these are Outlook, Google Contacts, Windows Contacts, and Yahoo! Address Book. See Figure 3–2. You can also select **All contacts** or **Selected groups**.

2. To sync Calendars, check the **Sync Calendars with** box and adjust the drop-down list to match the software where you store your calendar on your computer. You may also select **All calendars** or **Selected calendars**.

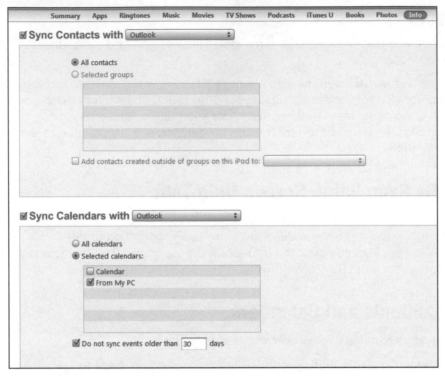

Figure 3–2. *Selecting software for syncing contacts (Windows)*

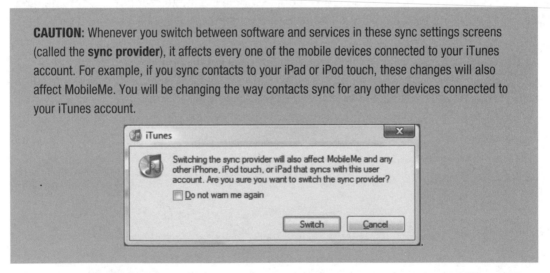

CAUTION: Whenever you switch between software and services in these sync settings screens (called the **sync provider**), it affects every one of the mobile devices connected to your iTunes account. For example, if you sync contacts to your iPad or iPod touch, these changes will also affect MobileMe. You will be changing the way contacts sync for any other devices connected to your iTunes account.

3. If you select Google or Yahoo! sync, you'll be prompted to enter your Google ID or Yahoo! ID and password.

NOTE: The options you see in this and other drop-down boxes on the **Info** tab will vary slightly depending on the software installed on your computer. For example, on a Mac, the contacts sync does not have a drop-down list; instead the other services, such as Google Contacts and Yahoo!, are shown as separate check boxes.

4. To continue setting up your email accounts, bookmarks, and more, scroll down the page. If you don't want to set anything else up for syncing, click the **Apply** button in the lower-right corner of the iTunes screen to start the sync.

TIP: If you're a Mac user who uses Microsoft Entourage, you'll need to enable Entourage to sync with iCal. To do this, go into the **Preferences** settings in Entourage, then go to **Sync Services** and check the boxes for synchronizing with iCal and Address book, as shown in Figure 3–3.

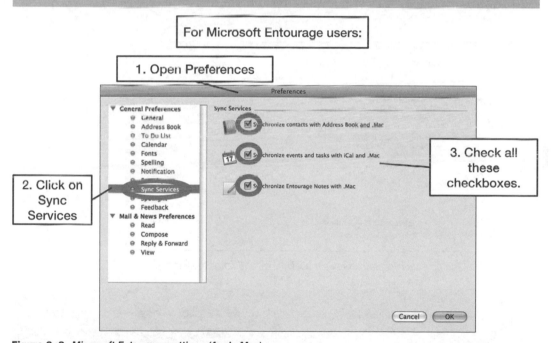

Figure 3–3. *Microsoft Entourage settings (Apple Mac)*

NOTE: As of the writing of this book, Entourage, unlike iCal, can't handle multiple calendars.

Syncing Email Accounts, Browser Bookmarks, and Notes

Scroll down the page to sync email account settings, browser bookmarks, and notes.

> **NOTE:** After syncing the email account settings to your iPod touch, you'll still have to enter your password for each email account in the **Settings -> Mail, Contacts, Calendars** for each email account. You have to do this only once on your iPod touch for each account.

1. Scroll down below the Calendar settings on the same **Info** tab in iTunes to see the **Mail** account settings.

2. Check the **Sync Mail Accounts from** box and adjust the pull-down menu to the software or service that stores your email (Figure 3–4). This might be Outlook on a Windows computer, or Entourage or Mail on a Mac.

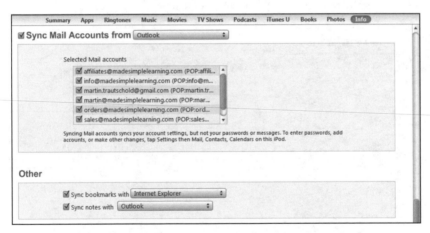

Figure 3–4. *Setting up email accounts, browser bookmarks, and notes to sync*

> **NOTE:** As of publication time, iTunes supports only two web browsers for sync: Microsoft Internet Explorer and Apple Safari. If you use Mozilla Firefox or Google Chrome, you can still sync your bookmarks, but you'll have to install free bookmark sync software (e.g., www.xmarks.com) to sync from Firefox or Chrome to Safari or Explorer. Then you can sync your browser bookmarks in a two-step process.

3. To sync your browser bookmarks, check the **Sync bookmarks with** box and adjust the pull-down menu to the web browser you use (see Figure 3–4). At this time, you can select only Internet Explorer or Safari.

4. To sync your notes, check the **Sync notes with** box and select the software or service where your notes are stored.

5. Click the **Apply** button in the lower-right corner of the iTunes screen to start the sync.

NOTE: Depending on how much information (especially contacts and calendar information) you have, the initial sync could take 15 minutes or more.

Syncing Your iPod touch with iTunes

The syncing is normally automatic when you plug in your iPod touch to your computer's USB port. The only exception is if you have disabled the automatic sync.

Keeping Track of the Sync

At the top of iTunes, inside the Status window, you can see what is happening with the sync. You may see **Syncing contacts with "Martin's iPod"** or **Syncing calendars with "Martin's iPod,"** which lets you see what is currently being synced.

Handling Sync Conflicts

Sometimes, the iTunes sync will detect conflicts between the data in your computer and on your iPod touch, such as the same contact entry with two different company names, or the same calendar entry with two different notes. Handling these conflicts is fairly straightforward.

1. In the **Conflict Resolver** window, click the information that is correct. This turns the background a light blue, while the side not selected is white. See Figure 3–5.

2. If there are any more conflicts, click the **Next** button until you finish resolving all conflicts.

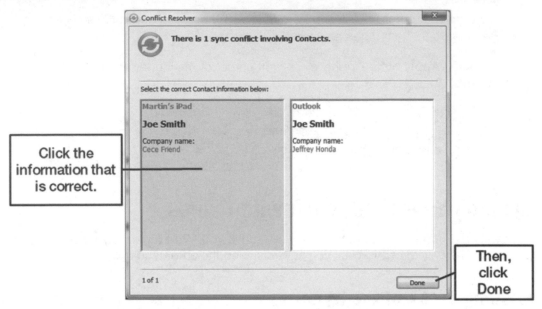

Figure 3–5. *iTunes sync Conflict Resolver*

3. Click **Done** to close the window.

4. All your selections will be applied to the next sync with your iPod touch.
    You are given the choice to **Sync Now** or **Sync Later**.

NOTE: Conflicts can cause the sync to stop in mid-process. Contacts are synced first, then the Calendar. So if a Contacts sync conflict is found, the Calendar will not sync until the Contacts conflict is resolved. Make sure to resync your iPod touch after you resolve conflicts to complete the sync.

Cancelling a Sync in Progress

You can cancel a sync from iTunes or from your iPod touch.

To cancel the sync from iTunes on your computer:

Click the **X** inside the sync status window, as shown in Figure 3–6.

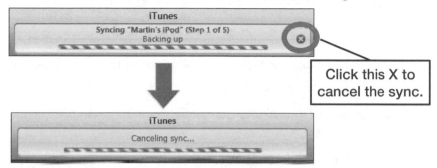

Figure 3–6. *Clicking the X in the status window in iTunes to cancel the sync*

To cancel the sync from the iPod touch:

Slide the slider bar at the bottom of the screen that says **Slide to Cancel.** This is in the same place as the normal **Slide to Unlock** message.

Why Might You Not Want to Use iTunes Automatic Sync?

There could be a few reasons to sync manually instead of automatically:

1. You don't want to fill up your iPod touch with too many music and video files.

2. The sync and backup process takes a long time, so you don't want it to happen every time you connect your iPod touch to your computer.

3. You plug your iPod touch into various computers to charge it up, but don't want to be asked if you want to erase and resync your music every time.

NOTE: If you want to drag and drop music and videos, you need to make sure to check the **Manually manage music and videos** box in the **Summary** tab in iTunes.

Manually Stopping the Auto Sync Before It Starts

There may be times you want to connect your iPod touch to your computer without the auto sync starting up. This could be because you don't have much time and want to quickly drag and drop a few new songs to your iPod touch without syncing everything else.

To stop the normal auto sync of your iPod touch, you can press certain keys on your computer keyboard while connecting your iPod touch to your computer.

On a Windows PC:

>   Press and hold **Shift** + **Ctrl** while connecting your iPod touch to your computer.

On a Mac:

>   Press and hold **Command** + **Option** while connecting your iPod touch.

Turning Off the Auto Sync Permanently

You can turn off the auto sync permanently in iTunes. You might want to do this if you prefer to have manual control over all the sync processes.

> **CAUTION**: Turning off the auto sync also disables the automatic backup of your iPod touch every time you connect it to your computer. This setting is best for a secondary computer, which you might use to charge your iPod touch but would never want to sync.

To turn off the auto sync in iTunes, follow these steps:

1. From the iTunes menu, select **Edit** and then **Preferences**.

2. Click the **Devices** tab at the top.

3. Check the **Prevent iPods, iPhones and iPads from syncing automatically** box (see Figure 3–7).

4. Click the **OK** button to save your settings.

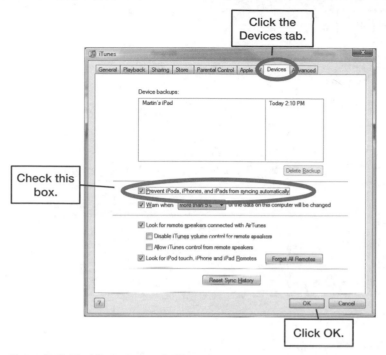

Figure 3–7. *Disabling auto sync in iTunes*

Getting a Clean Start with the Sync

Sometimes you'll have Issues with the sync and just need to get a fresh start. There are a few things you can do in this regard with iTunes: you can erase or reset the sync history so iTunes thinks it is syncing for the first time with your iPod touch, and you can force all information on the iPod touch to be replaced with information from your computer.

Resetting Sync History (Make iTunes Think It Is Syncing for the First Time)

To reset your sync history in iTunes, follow these steps:

1. Select the **Edit** menu and then click **Preferences**.

2. Click the **Devices** tab at the top of the iTunes Preferences window.

3. Click the **Reset Sync History** button at the bottom, as shown in Figure 3–8.

4. Confirm your selection by clicking **Reset Sync History** in the pop-up window.

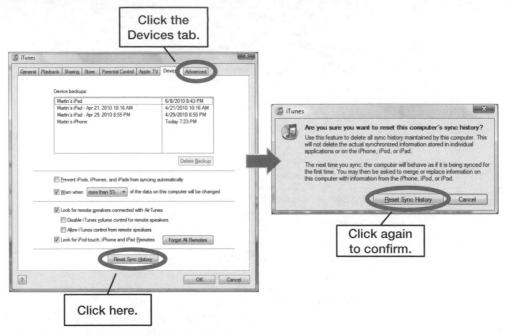

Figure 3–8. *Resetting sync history in iTunes*

Replacing All Information on the iPod touch (Next Sync Only)

Sometimes you may need to get a fresh start with your iPod touch information. For whatever reason, you want to get rid of all the information on your iPod touch in one or all the synced apps and just start over. Follow these steps.

1. As you did to set up the sync previously, connect your iPod touch to your computer, start iTunes, click your **iPod touch** in the left nav bar, and click the **Info** tab at the top of the main window.

2. Scroll all the way down to the **Advanced** section (see Figure 3–9).

3. Check one, some, or all of the boxes as you desire.

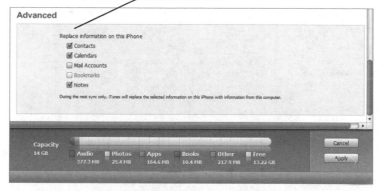

Check any boxes to erase all current information on the iPhone and replace it with the information from your computer.

Figure 3–9. *In the Advanced area, select the information you want to replace.*

4. When you are ready, click the **Apply** button in the lower-right corner. The sync should happen immediately. All of the information for the apps you have checked will be erased from the iPod touch and replaced with the information from your computer.

Apps: Syncing and Managing Them

With iTunes, you can sync and manage your apps on your iPod touch. It's easy to drag and drop your app icons around on a particular **Home** screen page or even between pages on your iPod touch.

Syncing Apps in iTunes

Follow these steps to sync and manage apps:

1. As you did to set up the sync previously, connect your iPod touch to your computer, start iTunes, and click your **iPod touch** in the left nav bar.

2. Click the **Apps** tab on the top of the main window.

3. Check the **Sync Apps** box to see all apps stored on your iPod touch and your **Home** screens, as shown in Figure 3–10.

Figure 3–10. *Sync Apps screen in iTunes*

Moving Apps, Working with Folders, or Deleting App Icons

It is easy to move around and organize your application icons in this screen in iTunes.

**To move an app within a screen:
Click it and drag it around the
screen.**

**To move an app between Home
screen pages: Click and drag it
to the new page in the right
column**. The new page expands—
drop it on the new page.

**To dock an app on the bottom
dock:** Remove one icon if there are
already four icons. Then click and
drag the icon to the dock.

To remove an icon: Hover over it
to see the **X** and then click the **X**.

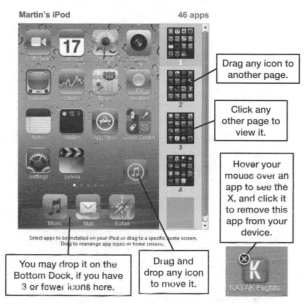

Martin's iPod   46 apps

Drag any icon to another page.

Click any other page to view it.

Hover your mouse over an app to see the X, and click it to remove this app from your device.

Select apps to be installed on your iPod or drag to a specific home screen.
Drag to rearrange app icons or home screens.

You may drop it on the Bottom Dock, if you have 3 or fewer icons here.

Drag and drop any icon to move it.

KAYAK Flights

To create a new folder: Drag and
drop one icon onto another icon.

**To move an app into an existing
folder:** Drag and drop the icon
onto the **Folder** icon.

To move an app out of a folder:
Click the folder to open it. Then
drag and drop the icon outside of
that folder.

**To view another Home screen
page:** Click that page in the right
column.

To delete a folder:
Remove all apps from
that folder (drag them
out) and it will disappear.

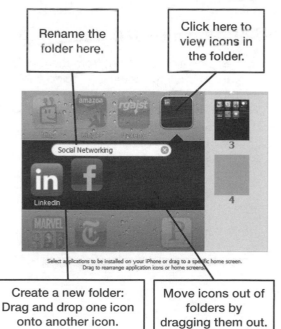

Rename the folder here.

Click here to view icons in the folder.

Social Networking

LinkedIn

Select applications to be installed on your iPhone or drag to a specific home screen.
Drag to rearrange application icons or home screens.

Create a new folder: Drag and drop one icon onto another icon.

Move icons out of folders by dragging them out.

Removing or Reinstalling Apps

To remove an app from your iPod touch, simply uncheck the box next to it and confirm your selection, as shown in Figure 3–11. Don't worry—since you are syncing apps to your computer in iTunes, you still have a copy of the app inside iTunes.

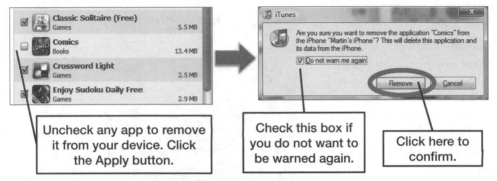

Figure 3–11. *Unchecking an app to delete it from your iPod touch*

> **TIP:** Even if you delete an app from your iPod touch, if you have chosen to sync apps as shown, you can still reinstall that app by rechecking the box next to it. The app will be reloaded onto your iPod touch during the next sync.

Getting Downloaded Items into iTunes to Sync Them

If you buy or download content from the iBookstore, iTunes store, or App Store within iTunes, it automatically appears in your own iTunes library. But how do you get content that you have downloaded from the Web into iTunes? (It does not automatically appear in iTunes.) What happens if something you downloaded is compressed in a .zip file, as is true of some free or paid audiobooks? In this section, we help you understand the basic steps of downloading content from the Web to your computer, then getting it into iTunes so you can sync it to your iPod touch.

Step 1: Download the content to your computer

Go to the web site where you want to download content. In this case, we want a free audiobook from http://librivox.org. We have searched for titles by Mark Twain and want to download the entire set of chapters for *Roughing It*.

Click the link **Zip file of the entire book in the left column of links**. (This 488 MB file will take you between 15 minutes and 4 hours to download depending on the speed of your Internet connection.)

Step 2: Unzip the file, if necessary

Next, locate the file you just downloaded. It will usually be in your Downloads folder. Unzip or uncompress all the files.

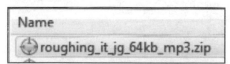

This unzipping process will vary depending on what software you have installed on your PC or Mac. However, it usually involves double-clicking to open the .zip file. Then select Unzip, Unzip All, Extract, or Extract All. **Most often, all these files will be unzipped either directly into the Downloads folder, or a folder within** the D**ownloads** folder **with the name of the zip file.**

Step 3: Drag and drop the content into iTunes

Next, locate the files you extracted and highlight them all. You can select all files in a list by holding the **Shift** key on your computer keyboard and clicking the top file and then the bottom file in the list.

Then, drag the entire highlighted list over to iTunes and drop it on your library in the top of the left column. You can also use the **File -> Add File to Library** menu command instead of the drag-and-drop method.

Step 4: Select content to sync to your device

Use the steps shown in the sections later in this chapter to sync the downloaded content to your iPod touch.

> **NOTE:** If you downloaded a free audiobook from Librivox.org, then the content will not show up in your Audiobooks area in iTunes—it will show up in the Music area. This is because these files are in .mp3 format and iTunes considers them music. So to sync the free audiobook, you need to go to the **Music** tab after you connect your iPod touch to locate these files. Follow the instructions for "Syncing Music" in this chapter.
>
> You can manually change it to be considered an audio book (or podcast, or anything else by hitting CMD/CTRL I (get info), going to the Options Tab, and changing Media Kind.

File Sharing (File Transfer) Between Your iPod touch and Your Computer

As long as you have an app installed that works with files, such as GoodReader or Stanza, you can use iTunes to transfer files between your computer and your iPod touch. You perform this file transfer using the bottom of the **Apps** tab in iTunes—below all the application icon screens.

> **TIP:** Some apps, such as GoodReader, come with wireless methods for transferring and sharing files. Check out the GoodReader section in Chapter 26: "New Media: Reading Newspapers, Magazines, and More," for more information.

Copying Files from Your Computer to Your iPod touch

To copy files from your computer to your iPod touch, follow these steps.

1. As you did to set up the previous sync, connect your iPod touch to your computer, start iTunes, and click your **iPod touch** in the left nav bar.

2. Click the **Apps** tab on the top of the main window.

3. Scroll down to the **File Sharing** section below the apps. See Figure 3–12.

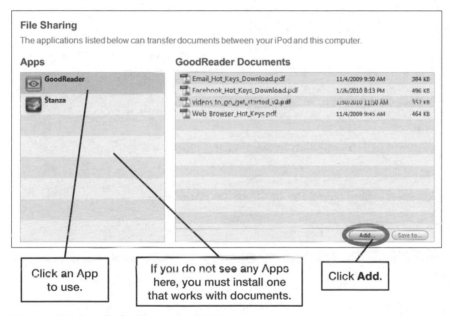

Figure 3–12. *Transferring files to your iPod touch*

4. Click any app to use in the left column, and then click the **Add** button in the lower-right corner.

5. A window will pop up. Select a file to transfer and click the **Open** button. The file will be transferred immediately to your iPod touch.

Copying Files from Your iPod touch to Your Computer

To copy files from your iPod touch to your computer, follow these steps.

1. Connect your iPod touch to your computer, start iTunes, and click your **iPod touch** in the left nav bar.

2. Click the **Apps** tab at the top of the main window.

3. Scroll down to the **File Sharing** section below the apps (see Figure 3–13).

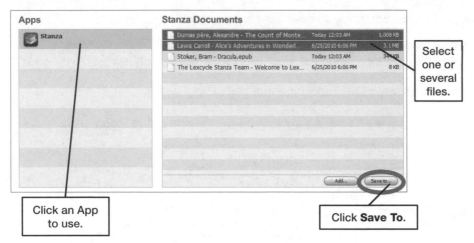

Figure 3–13. *Transferring files from your iPod touch*

4. Click any app from which you want to transfer the files in the left column.

5. Select one or several files using any of these methods:

   a. Click a single file.

   b. Hold the **Control** key (Windows) or **Option** key (Mac) and click any number of files.

   c. Hold the **Shift** key and click the top and bottom file in a list to select all files in that list.

6. After the file(s) are selected, click the **Save To** button in the lower-right corner.

7. A window will pop up asking you to select a folder on your computer to receive the files from your iPod touch. Locate and click the folder, and then click the **Select Folder** button. The file(s) will be transferred immediately to your computer.

Syncing Media and More

Now let's look at how to set up an automatic sync for music, movies, iBooks, iTunes U content, and more.

CAUTION: Make sure you're logged into iTunes with the same iTunes account you want to use on your iPod touch, as Digital Rights Management (DRM)–protected content (music, videos, and more) won't sync unless both accounts match. You can log out and log in to iTunes on both your desktop and your iPod touch if you have to make sure you are logged into the right accounts.

Keeping an Eye on Capacity (Available Space)

As you begin to select ringtones, music, videos, books, podcasts, and more to sync, you will want to keep an eye on the capacity bar at the bottom of each of the iTunes sync screens. If you see that you are nearing or exceeding capacity with any of your selections, you know you need to make a few adjustments. You just can't take it all with you sometimes! Figure 3–14 shows that we currently have 15.6 GB (gigabytes) free on our iPod touch for more content—so we have plenty of free space.

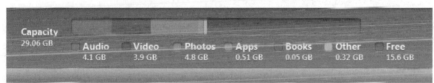

Figure 3–14. *Watching free space available as you make sync selections in iTunes*

Syncing Ringtones

When you click the **Ringtones** tab, you can choose to sync your entire ringtone library or selected items. Ringtones are used for FaceTime calls on the iPod touch.

1. Connect your iPod touch to your computer, start iTunes, and click your **iPod touch** in the left nav bar.

2. Click the **Ringtones** tab at the top of the main window.

3. Check the **Sync Ringtones** box, shown to the right.

4. The default is to sync all ringtones. To sync only specific ones, click the radio button next to **Selected ringtones**.

5. When you are done with your selections, click the **Apply** button to start the ringtone sync.

Syncing Music

When you click the **Music** tab, you can choose to sync your entire music library or selected items.

CAUTION: If you have manually transferred some music, music videos, or voice memos to your iPod touch already, you'll receive a warning message that all existing content on your iPod touch will be removed and replaced with the selected music library from your computer.

To sync music from your computer to your iPod touch, follow these steps.

1. Connect your iPod touch to your computer, start iTunes, and click your **iPod touch** in the left nav bar.

2. Click the **Music** tab on the top of the main window.

3. Check the **Sync Music** box (see Figure 3–15).

4. Click next to **Entire music library** only if you are *sure* your music library will not be too large for your iPod touch.

5. Click next to **Selected playlists, artists, and genres** if you are unsure whether your music library is too large, or if you want to sync only specific playlists or artists.

   a. You can choose whether to include music videos and voice memos by checking those boxes.

   b. You can also automatically fill free space with songs.

CAUTION: We don't recommend checking this option because it will take up all the space in your iPod touch and leave no room for all those cool apps!

   c. Now check off any of the playlists or artists in the two columns on the bottom of the screen. You can even use the search box at the top of the **Artists** column to search for particular artists.

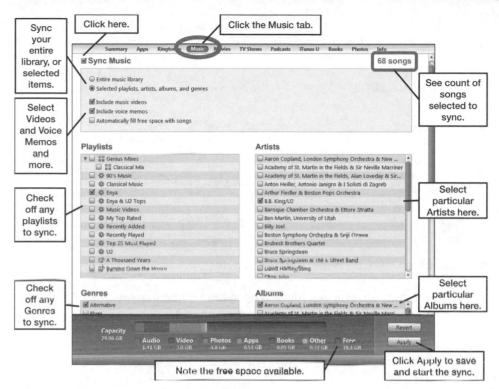

Figure 3–15. *Syncing music with your iPod touch*

Syncing Movies

When you click the **Movies** tab, you can choose to sync specific, recent, or unwatched movies, or all of them.

To sync movies from your computer to your iPod touch, follow these steps.

1. Connect your iPod touch to your computer, start iTunes, and click your **iPod touch** in the left nav bar.

2. Click the **Movies** tab on the top of the main window.

3. Check the **Sync Movies** box (see Figure 3–16).

4. If you'd like to sync recent or unwatched movies, check the **Automatically include** box and use the pull-down to select **All, 1 most recent, All unwatched, 5 most recent unwatched**, etc.

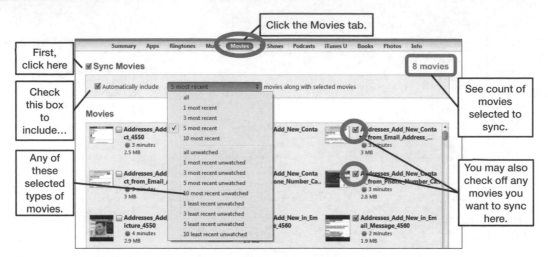

Figure 3–16. *Configuring movie sync to automatically include selections*

5. If you selected any item besides **All**, you have the choice to sync specific movies or videos to your iPod touch. Simply check the boxes next to the movies you want to include in the sync.

Syncing TV Shows

When you click the **TV Shows** tab, you can choose to sync specific, recent, or unwatched TV shows, or all of them.

To sync TV shows from your computer to your iPod touch, follow these steps.

1. Connect your iPod touch to your computer, start iTunes, and click your **iPod touch** in the left nav bar.

2. Click the **TV Shows** tab on the top of the main window.

3. Check the **Sync TV Shows** box (see Figure 3–17).

4. If you'd like to sync recent or unwatched TV shows, check the **Automatically include** box and use the pull-down to select **All, 1 newest, All unwatched, 5 oldest unwatched, 10 newest unwatched**, etc.

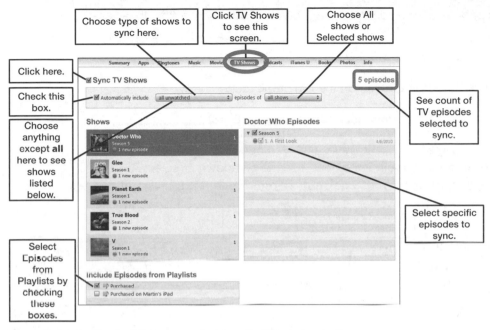

Figure 3–17. *Configuring TV show sync to automatically include selections*

5. Choose **All Shows** or **Selected Shows** next to **episodes of**.

6. If you choose **Selected Shows**, you can choose individual shows and even individual episodes in the two sections in the middle of the screen.

7. If you have playlists of TV shows, you can select those for inclusion by checking the boxes in the bottom section of the screen.

Syncing Podcasts

When you click the **Podcasts** tab, you can choose to sync specific, recent, or unplayed podcasts, or all of them.

> **TIP:** Podcasts are audio or video shows that are usually regularly scheduled (e.g., daily, weekly, or monthly). Most are free to subscribe to in the iTunes store. When you subscribe and set up the auto sync as shown in this section, you'll receive all your favorite podcasts on your iPod touch.
>
> Many of your favorite radio shows are recorded and broadcast as podcasts. We encourage you to check out the **Podcast** section of the iTunes store to see what might interest you. You'll find podcasts of movie reviews, news shows, law school test reviews, game shows, old radio shows, educational content, and much more.

To sync podcasts from your computer to your iPod touch, follow these steps.

1. Connect your iPod touch to your computer, start iTunes, and click your **iPod touch** in the left nav bar.

2. Click the **Podcasts** tab on the top of the main window.

3. Check the **Sync Podcasts** box (see Figure 3–18).

4. If you'd like to sync recent or unplayed podcasts, check the **Automatically include** box and use the pull-down to select **All, 1 newest, All unplayed, 5 newest**, **10 most recent unplayed**, etc.

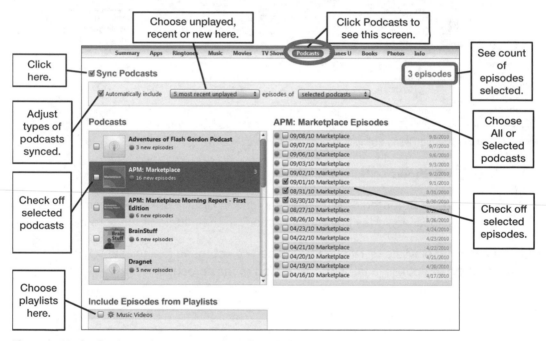

Figure 3–18. *Configuring podcast sync to automatically include selections*

5. Choose **All Podcasts** or **Selected Podcasts** next to **episodes of**.

6. If you choose **Selected Podcasts**, you can choose individual podcasts and even individual episodes in the two sections in the middle of the screen.

7. If you have playlists of podcasts, you can select those for inclusion by checking the boxes in the bottom section of the screen.

> **TIP:** After you sync these podcasts, you enjoy them in the **Podcasts** section of the **Music** app on your device.

Syncing iTunes U

When you click the **iTunes U** tab, you can choose to sync specific, recent, or unplayed iTunes U content, or all content.

> **TIP:** iTunes U podcasts are similar to other audio or video podcasts, except that they focus on educational content and are mostly produced by colleges and universities. Most are free to subscribe to in the iTunes store. When you subscribe and set up the auto sync as shown in this section, you'll receive all your favorite iTunes U podcasts on your iPod touch.
>
> Be sure to check out the **iTunes U** section in the iTunes store. You may find your favorite college or university has shows to teach you biology or astronomy, or a whole lot more. There's even a Stanford University course on how to develop iPod touch apps! Many of the top universities broadcast class lectures from famous professors in iTunes U. Go ahead and check it out—what you'll find is amazing!

To sync iTunes U content from your computer to your iPod touch, follow these steps.

1. Connect your iPod touch to your computer, start iTunes, and click your **iPod touch** in the left nav bar.

2. Click the **iTunes U** tab on the top of the main window.

3. Check the **Sync iTunes U** box (see Figure 3–19).

4. If you'd like to sync recent or unplayed items, check the **Automatically include** box and use the pull-down to select **All, 1 newest, All unplayed, 5 newest**, **10 most recent unplayed**, etc.

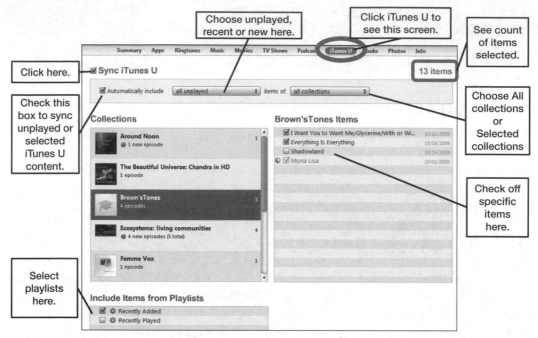

Figure 3-19. *Configuring iTunes U sync to automatically include selections*

5. Choose **All Collections** or **Selected Collections** next to **items of**.

6. If you choose **Selected Collections**, you can choose individual collections and even individual items in the two sections in the middle of the screen.

7. If you have playlists of iTunes U podcasts, you can select those for inclusion by checking the boxes in the bottom section of the screen under **Include Items from Playlists**.

Syncing iBooks, PDF files, and Audiobooks

When you click the **Books** tab, you can choose to sync all or selected books and audiobooks.

TIP: Books on the iPod touch are electronic versions of their paper cousins. They are in a specific electronic format called *ePub*. You can buy them in the iBookstore on the iPod touch or acquire them from other locations and sync them to your iPod touch using the steps described here. Books you acquire elsewhere must be unprotected or "DRM-free" in order to sync them to your iPod touch. You read these books in the **iBooks** app or in other book reader apps on your iPod touch. See Chapter 11: "iBooks and E-Books" to learn more.

To sync books, PDF files, or audiobooks between your computer and your iPod touch, follow these steps.

TIP: You can find free iBooks to download by doing a search for 'project gutenberg' in the iBookstore. You can find free audiobooks to download by going to http://librivox.org from your computer web browser and downloading public domain audiobooks. (These free audiobooks are typically not read by professional actors, but by volunteers, so the quality may vary.) See the section "Getting Downloaded Items into iTunes to Sync Them" in this chapter to see exactly how to download and sync free audiobooks.

1. Connect your iPod touch to your computer, start iTunes, and click your **iPod touch** in the left nav bar.

2. Click the **Books** tab on the top of the main window.

3. Check the **Sync Books** and **Sync Audiobooks** boxes (see Figure 3–20).

4. If you'd like to sync all books, leave the default **All books** selection.

5. Otherwise, choose **Selected books** and make your choices by checking specific books in the window.

TIP: In order to sync iBooks, PDF files, and other similar documents to your iPod touch, you need to first drag and drop your file from your computer into your iTunes library. Grab the file from any folder on your computer, and drag and drop it right on your library in the upper left column in iTunes.

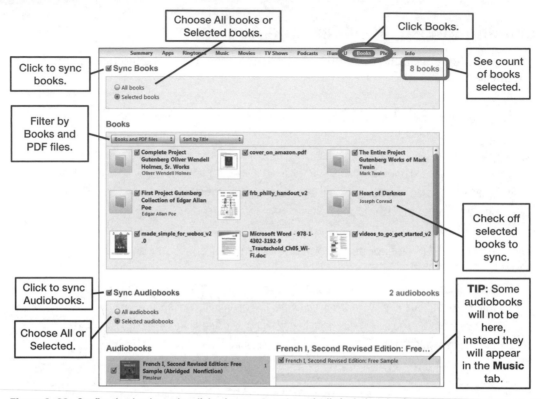

Figure 3–20. *Configuring books and audiobooks sync to automatically include selections*

6. If you would like to sync all audiobooks, leave the default **All audiobooks** selection.

7. Otherwise, choose **Selected audiobooks** and make your choices by checking off specific audiobooks in the window below this selection item.

TIP: After you sync these books, you can enjoy them in the **iBooks** app on your device. You can listen to audiobooks in the **iPod** app, where the **Audiobooks** tab is on the left side.

NOTE: Audiobooks from Audible require that you first authorize your computer with your Audible account before you can sync them to your iPod touch from your computer.

Syncing Photos

When you click the **Photos** tab, you can choose to sync photos from all folders or selected folders and you can even include videos.

> **TIP:** You can create a beautiful electronic picture frame and share your photos on the stunning iPod touch screen (see Chapter 17: "iPod touch Photography"). You can even use your photos to set the background wallpaper and screen-lock wallpaper—see Chapter 7: "Personalize and Secure Your iPod touch" for more information.

To sync photos from your computer to your iPod touch, follow these steps.

1. Connect your iPod touch to your computer, start iTunes, and click your **iPod touch** in the left nav bar.

> **TIP:** Mac users can also sync photos using **iPhoto** or **Aperture**, including Events (time-based sync), Faces (person-based sync), and Places (location-based sync).

2. Click the **Photos** tab on the top of the main window.

3. Check the **Sync Photos from** box. See Figure 3–21.

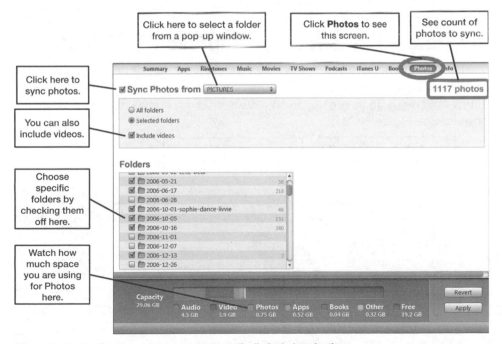

Figure 3–21. *Configuring photo sync to automatically include selections*

4.   Click the pull-down menu next to **Sync Photos from** and select a folder from your computer where your photos are stored. If you want to grab all your photos, go to the highest folder level possible (e.g., **C:** on your Windows computer or "**/**" on your Apple Mac).

5.   If you'd like to sync all photos from the selected folder on your computer, select **All folders**, shown in Figure 3–21.

> **CAUTION:** Because your photo library on your computer may be too large to fit on your iPod touch, be careful about checking **All folders**.

6.   Otherwise, choose **Selected folders** and make your choices by checking specific folders in the window below, shown in Figure 3–21.

7.   You can also include any videos in the folders by checking the **Include videos** box, shown in Figure 3–21.

8.   When you are done choosing your photos to sync, click the **Apply** button to save your settings and start the sync.

9.   When the sync starts, you'll see the status in the middle-top status window in iTunes.

How to Know What Is New or Unplayed in iTunes

You may notice little numbers next to items in the left nav bar of iTunes. There are similar little blue numbers in the upper-right corner of items in the main window. These numbers show how many items are unplayed, unwatched, or, in the case of apps, require updates. See Figure 3–22.

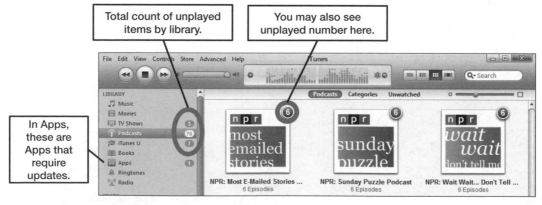

Figure 3–22. *Quickly seeing the number of unplayed items*

Manually Transferring Music, Movies, Podcasts, and More on Your iPod touch (Drag-and-Drop Method)

The auto sync sections showed you how to automatically sync content to your iPod touch. Here you'll learn how to manually transfer songs, videos, books, audiobooks, and more. The process is the same for all types of content, so we'll show you how to do it for just one type.

> **TIP**: Use these same drag-and-drop techniques to add items to a playlist.

To manually transfer content from your computer to your iPod touch, follow these steps.

> **NOTE**: Be sure to check **Manually manage music and videos** on the **Summary** tab in iTunes before you try to drag and drop music or videos. If you've chosen to automatically sync content (e.g., music, movies, podcasts, etc.), you won't be able to use this drag-and-drop method to copy items to your iPod touch.

1. Connect your iPod touch to your computer, and start iTunes.

2. In the left nav bar, click your **iPod touch**. Then click the **Summary** tab at the top. Near the bottom of the screen, make sure the **Manually manage music and videos** box is checked. You may see a warning message if you have previously synced music or videos to your iPod touch, saying that all previously synced music and videos will be replaced with your iTunes library. This is OK.

☑ Manually manage music and videos

3. In the left nav bar, under the **LIBRARY** heading, click the type of content (**Music**, **Movies**, **TV Shows**, **Podcasts**, **iTunes U**, etc.) you'd like to transfer.

4. In the main window, you'll see your library of content. It's usually easiest to select **List View** from the top of iTunes, as shown in Figure 3–23. This allows you to see all the content in a list and easily select a single item or group of items.

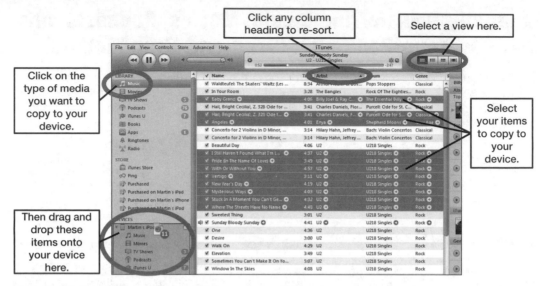

Figure 3–23. *Selecting media to drag and drop onto your device*

5.   Here is how to select content individually, in a list or separated.

a.   To select an individual
item, simply click it to
highlight it.

b.   To select items that are
not in a continuous list,
Windows users press
and hold the **Control**
key while clicking items,
and Mac users press
and hold the **Command**
key while clicking.

c. To select items in a
continuous list, press
and hold the **Shift** key
while clicking first the
top item and then the
bottom item in the list.
All the items in between
will be selected.

▶	Name		Time	Artist
	☑ Hail, Bright Cecilia!, Z. 328 Ode fo...		3:41	Charles Da
	☐ Big Lie Small World	➡	5:05	David Har
	☐ Tomorrow We'll See	➡	4:49	David Har
	☐ Water Music Suite No.2 in D, H...	➡	4:01	English Ba
	☐ Canon and Gigue in D Major: I....	➡	4:32	English Co
	☐ Watermark	➡	2:26	Enya
	☐ Cursum Perficio	➡	4:09	Enya
	☐ On Your Shore	➡	4:00	Enya
	☐ Storms in Africa	➡	4:05	Enya
	☐ Exile	➡	4:22	Enya
	☐ Miss Clare Remembers	➡	2:00	Enya
	☐ Orinoco Flow	➡	4:26	Enya
	☐ Evening Falls...	➡	3:49	Enya
	☐ River	➡	3:12	Enya
	☑ The Longships		3:39	Enya
	☑ Na Laetha Gael M'Óige		3:57	Enya

6. Then, to copy these items to your iPod touch, simply click and drag the
selected item(s) over to your iPod touch and let go of the mouse button.
All selected items will then be copied to your iPod touch in the left
column under **DEVICES**.

Troubleshooting iTunes and the Sync

Sometimes iTunes does not behave exactly as you'd expect it to, so here are a few
simple troubleshooting tips.

Check Out the Apple Knowledgebase for Helpful Articles

The first step when you're having a problem is to check out Apple's support pages,
where you'll find lots of helpful information. On your iPod touch or computer's web
browser, go to this web page and click a topic or device for help.

http://www.apple.com/support/ipod/

iTunes Locked Up and Will Not Respond (Windows Computer)

1. Bring up the **Windows Task Manager** by simultaneously pressing the **Ctrl** + **Alt** + **Del** keys on your keyboard. The **Task Manager** should look something like Figure 3–24.

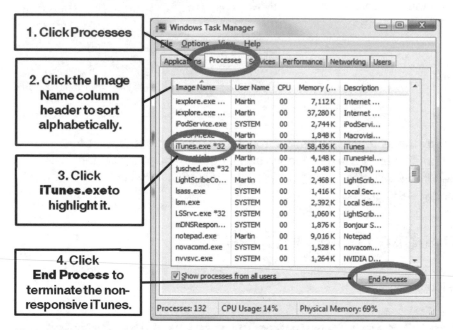

Figure 3–24. *Locating* iTunes.exe *in* **Windows Task Manager** *to terminate it*

2. Then, to end the process, click **End process** from the pop-up window.

3. Now, iTunes should be forced to close.

4. Try restarting iTunes.

5. If iTunes will not start or it locks up again, reboot your computer and try again.

iTunes Locked Up and Will Not Respond (Mac Computer)

If your iTunes ever lock up and the application does not respond on your Mac, press Command + Option + Escape. This is the shortcut to bring up the Force Quit Applications window, shown in Figure 3–25.

1. Go up to the iTunes Menu at the top and click. .

2. Click **Quit iTunes.**

3. If that doesn't work, go to any other program and click the small "Apple" in the upper left-hand corner.

4. Click **Force Quit** and the list of running programs will be displayed.

5. Highlight iTunes and click the **Force Quit** button.

6. If this does not help, try restarting your Mac.

Figure 3–25. *Force Quit Applications window on Mac computers*

Updating Your iPod touch Operating System

You can check for updated software and install updated operating system (iOS) software using iTunes.

> **NOTE:** Do this update when you won't mind being without your iPod touch for 30 minutes or more, depending on the amount of information on your iPod touch and the speed of your computer and Internet connection.

Normally, iTunes will automatically check for updates on a set schedule, about every two weeks. If no update is found, iTunes will tell you when it will check for another update, as shown in Figure 3–26.

1. Start iTunes.

2. Connect your iPod touch to your computer.

3. Click your **iPod touch**, listed under **DEVICES** in the left nav bar.

4. Click the **Summary** tab in the top nav bar.

5. Click the **Check for Update** button in the center of the screen in the **Version** section.

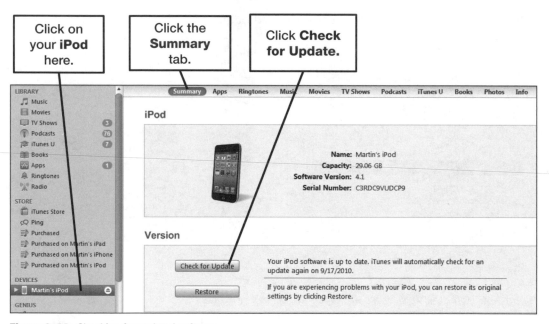

Figure 3–26. *Checking for updated software*

6. If you have the latest version, you'll see a pop-up window saying something like "This version of the iPod touch software (4.1) is the current version." Click **OK** to close the window. You are done with the update process.

7. If you don't have the latest version, a window will tell you a new version is available and ask if you would like to update. Click **Yes** or **Update**.

8. iTunes will take you through a few screens that describe the update and ask you to agree to the software license. If you agree, click **Next** and **Agree** to download the latest iOS software from Apple. This will take about 5–10 minutes.

> **TIP:** We show you all the screens you might see in this update process in the "Reinstalling the iPod touch Operating System" section of Chapter 28: "Troubleshooting."

9. Next, iTunes will back up your iPod touch, which might take 10 minutes or more if your iPod touch is filled with data.

10. Now the new iOS will be installed and your iPod touch erased.

11. Finally, you'll be presented with the screen allowing you to set your iPod up as a new one or restore it from a backup.

    a. Choose **Set up as a new iPod touch** if you want to erase all your data after the update process.

    b. Choose **Restore from the backup of**, and make sure you select the correct backup file (usually the most recent one).

Now your iPod touch will be restored or set up as you selected and your iPod touch OS update is complete.

Chapter 4

Other Sync Methods

In Chapter 3: "Sync Your iPod touch with iTunes," you learned how to connect your iPod touch to your computer and use iTunes to sync your personal information, music, videos, and more. In this chapter, we explore some alternative ways to wirelessly synchronize information to your iPod touch. The benefit of the wireless methods is that you don't need to connect your iPod touch to your computer to have the information updated. Everything happens over the air—automatically. The methods we cover are Apple's Exchange / Google Sync and MobileMe Service.

NOTE: If you use the Gmail account setting instead of Exchange, as we describe in this chapter, to set up your Gmail, you will be able to wirelessly sync your mail, calendar, and notes, but not your Google contacts. So if you do not need Google Contacts synced, you can use the Gmail setting instead of Exchange. Using Gmail, however, you get notes sync over IMAP and Archive instead of Delete.

Wireless Sync of Your Google or Exchange Information

Using the steps we describe here, your iPod touch can wirelessly sync your email, contacts, and calendar from a Microsoft Exchange account or a Google Account.

TIP: For the first time ever, you can now wirelessly sync multiple Exchange accounts on your iPod touch. If you have several Google and Microsoft Exchange or Hotmail accounts, you can wirelessly sync all accounts at the same time to your iPod touch. Before the iPod touch, you had to choose between your accounts. Now you can sync them all!

Why Do We Say Google/Exchange?

We use the words Google and Exchange interchangeably here because you set up your Google sync using the Exchange setting on your iPod touch. Google has licensed Microsoft Exchange ActiveSync so you can now set up your Google account just like an Exchange account and enjoy the same push email, contacts, and calendar functionality. We know it is a little confusing, but you set up both your Google and Exchange accounts in the identical manner, using the Exchange settings on your iPod touch—so we say Google/Exchange.

If You Want a Google Account, Create One

If you do not have a Microsoft Exchange account, but you still want a wireless sync, then you should set up a free Google account to store your contacts and calendar. The account will allow you to start using Google Mail (Gmail), Contacts, and Calendar.

To set up your Google account, follow these steps:

1. From either your computer's web browser or Safari on your iPod touch, type in: www.gmail.com.

2. Press the **Create an account** button.

3. On the next screen, enter the information requested and click the button at the bottom of the page that says **I accept. Create my account.**

4. When that's successful, you'll see a screen that says **Congratulations!** Click the **Show me my account>>** button to get started.

5. To see your Calendar, click the **Calendar** link in the upper left corner.

6. To see your Contacts, click the **Contacts** link in the left side of the Gmail inbox page.

As soon as you set up the sync as shown here, you will begin to see all changes to your contacts and calendar from Google magically appear on your iPod touch. The same goes for any changes or additions from your iPod touch—they will automatically appear in Google in moments.

> **TIP:** It is extremely easy for your Google Contacts list to grow into the thousands because it automatically includes everyone you have ever emailed from your Gmail account. You may want to clean up your list before you set up the sync to your iPod touch.

Setting Up Your Google or Exchange Account on Your iPod touch

Use the following steps to set up the wireless sync for either your Exchange account or your Google contacts and calendar:

1. Touch the **Settings** icon on your iPod touch.

2. Touch **Mail, Contacts, and Calendars**.

3. You'll see a list of your email accounts and, below that, the **Add Account** option.

   If you have no accounts set up, you will see only **Add Account**. In either case, tap **Add Account.**

4. On the next screen, choose **Microsoft Exchange**.

> **NOTE:** You should choose Microsoft Exchange if you want to have the wireless sync with your Google Contacts and Calendar. If you select Gmail, you will not be able to wirelessly sync your Google Contacts. However, with Gmail IMAP you get Notes Sync and Archive.

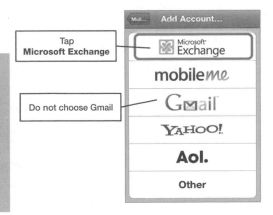

5. Type your email address.

> **TIP:** To type the **.com** (or .net, .edu, .org, etc.) in the email address, press and hold the period key until you see the **.com** key appear above it. Slide over and press **.com**.

> **TIP:** Since your email address is usually also your username, save yourself some time by copying and pasting it.

6. Copy and paste your email address into the **Username** field.

    a. Touch and hold the **email address** until you see the black pop-up appear above it.

    b. Tap **Select All**.

    c. Tap **Copy**.

    d. Touch and hold in the **Username** field until you see the pop-up appear. Tap **Paste**.

Touch and hold your Email address. Tap **Select All**.

Tap **Copy**.

Touch and hold here, then tap **Paste**.

7. Leave the **Domain** blank.
Type your **Password.**
If you want, you can adjust the
Description of the account, which
defaults to your email address.

8. Tap the **Next** button in the upper
right corner.

9. You may see an **Unable to Verify
Certificate** screen as shown. If you
do see it, click **Accept** to continue.

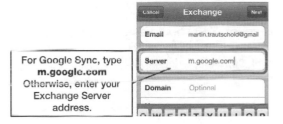

10. In the **Server** field, type
m.google.com to sync to Google.
Otherwise, if you are setting up
your Exchange Server account,
enter that server address.

11. Click **Next** in the upper right
corner.

12. On this screen you have the option
to turn **Mail, Contacts,** and
Calendars wireless sync **On** or **Off**.
For each sync you'd like to turn on,
tap the switch to change it to **On**.

CAUTION: If you already have contacts or calendar items on your iPod touch, you may see a
warning similar to the one shown here.

Your choices are to **Keep on My iPod touch** or **Delete**. If you choose **Cancel**, it stops
setting up your Exchange account.

Select **Keep on My iPod touch** to keep all existing contacts and calendar events on your iPod touch. These items will not end up on your Google or Exchange account—they will stay on your iPod touch.

You may end up with some duplicate contacts or calendar events on your iPod touch if the same ones already exist on your Google or Exchange account.

Select **Delete** if you already have these contacts or calendar items in your Exchange or Google account and do not want to duplicate them.

If you turned on the sync for **Mail**, **Contacts**, and **Calendars**, you'll see a screen similar to the one here. Tap **Save** to save your settings.

You're done with the initial setup of your account. You should see your new account listed under the **Accounts** heading on the **Mail, Contacts, Calendars** screen.

You're done when you see your new account listed here.

Editing or Deleting Your Google or Exchange Account

After you set up your Google or Exchange account on your iPod touch, you may want to adjust some of the default settings, such as which mail folders are synced (only the inbox by default), number of days of mail to sync (default is three days), and other settings. You would also use the steps shown here to remove or delete the account.

1. Get into your Mail settings screen as you did when you first set up your account (tap the **Settings** icon, tap **Mail, Contacts, Calendars**).

2. Tap the mail account you wish to adjust or remove.

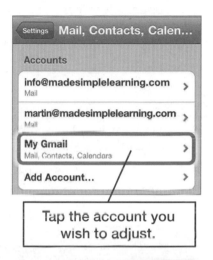

3. In order to change your account username, account name, and password, tap **Account Info** at the top. You will see the information you saw when you first set up this account.

4. If you want to remove this account from your iPod touch, tap **Delete Account** a the bottom and confirm your selection.

5. To enable or disable wireless syncing for **Mail**, **Contacts**, and **Calendar** items, tap the switches to set them **On** or **Off**.

> **NOTE:** If you set any switch to **Off** for these items, they will all be deleted from your iPod touch. For example, all synced contacts would immediately be deleted from your **Contacts** app.

6. To adjust how much mail is synced to your iPod touch, tap **Mail Days to Sync** and adjust to suit your needs (you can go from **1 Day** to **No Limit**, with 3 days as the default).

   Tap the **Email Account Name** in the upper left corner (shown as **My Gmail** in this image) to save your choices and return to the previous screen.

7. Tap **Mail Folders to Push** to specify which mail folders should sync to your iPod touch.

   The default is just the **Inbox**, but you can tap to select any number of folders.

> **TIP:** You can move mail between these folders on your iPod touch only if you have selected them here to sync.

8. Tap the **Email Account Name** in the upper left corner (shown as **My Gmail** in this image) to save your choices and return to the previous screen.

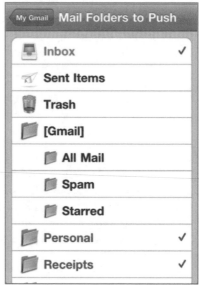

9. Then press the **Mail...** button in the upper left corner to finish with this account and return to your **Settings**.

10. Press the **Home** button to return to the **Home** screen.

Working with Google or Exchange Data on Your iPod touch

Once you set up the wireless sync, your Google and Exchange Contacts and Calendar information will flow quickly into your iPod touch. If you have thousands of contacts, it could take several minutes for the first sync to complete.

You may want to jump ahead and review Chapter 15: "Working with Contacts," and Chapter 16: "Your Calendar," for details about working with both apps.

NOTE: Since the sync with Google or Exchange is wireless, you'll need to make sure you have an active network connection from your iPod touch. Check out Chapter 5: "Wi-Fi Connectivity," to learn more.

New Group for Google/Exchange Contacts

For each Google/Exchange account you add to your iPod touch, you will end up with a separate group in your **Contacts** app. If you've added some contacts to your iPod touch or synced it at least once with iTunes, you may end up with additional groups of contacts, as shown in Figure 4–1.

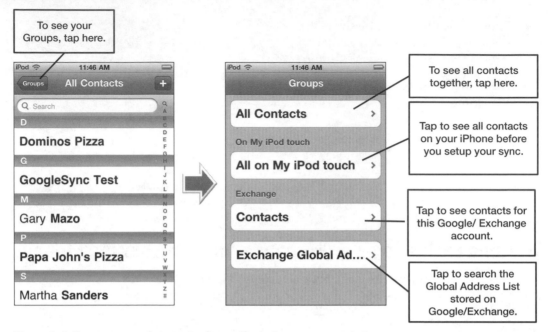

Figure 4–1. *You may see various groups in your Contacts.*

The default view in your **Contacts** list is to see all contacts from all synced accounts. You can selectively view contacts from various accounts. To view your Google or Exchange contacts, follow these steps:

1. Tap the **Contacts** icon.

2. Tap the **Groups** tab in the upper left corner.

3. If you've added new contacts or synced your address book, you'll see a **From My PC** or **From My Mac** group at the top. Under that you will see your Google or Exchange email address or the descriptive name assigned to that account when you set it up. (**MSL** and **MT Gmail** are the two Google/Exchange accounts synced in Figure 4–1.)

4. Tap the **Contacts** listed under your Google or Exchange email address/account name to see all your synced contacts.

Working with Contacts

To add, edit, or delete contacts in your Google or Exchange contacts group, do the following:

1. Follow the steps to view your Google or Exchange contacts group.

2. **To add a contact**: Tap the + button in the upper right corner of the **Contacts** list view. Add contact details as we'll show you in Chapter 15: "Working with Contacts." Touch **Done** in the upper right corner.

3. **To edit a contact**: Locate the contact in the list and tap the **Edit** button at the bottom under the contact details. Make any changes and press the **Done** button.

4. **To delete a contact**: Locate the contact you want to remove. Tap the **Edit** button under the contact details. Scroll to the bottom of the details and tap the **Delete Contact** button.

5. **To search for a contact on your iPod touch**:

    a. If you don't see the search window at the top, drag your finger all the way up the right-side alphabet to the top.

    b. Tap in the **search** window and type a few letters of someone's first name, last name, or company name to find them.

    c. Your **Contacts** list will immediately be filtered by what you type. If you see the name you want, tap it—otherwise, tap the **Search** button in the lower right corner.

6. **To perform a global address list search**:

    a. Tap the **Groups** button in the upper right corner. See Figure 4–1.

    b. Tap the second button under the Google/Exchange contacts group—that is the **Global Address List** search button. If your email address is long, then you will see only your email address on this button; however, if you have a short email address or have provided a short descriptive name, then you will see something like **MSL Global Address List**, as shown in Figure 4–1.

    c. Tap in the **search** window and type a few letters of someone's first name, last name, or company name to find them.

    d. Press the **Search** button to start searching.

The great thing is that any changes you make to your Google or Exchange contacts on your iPod touch are wirelessly communicated and appear in your Google or Exchange account in just a few seconds.

> **NOTE:** To add, edit, or delete contacts in your other group (not the Google or Exchange group), first go to that group (**From My PC** or **From My Mac**), and then make the changes you want. These additions, edits, or deletions will not affect your Google or Exchange contacts—they are kept separate.

Working with the Calendar

After you set up the sync with the Google or Exchange calendar on your iPod touch, all the calendar events will appear on your iPod touch—no wires or sync cable required. You will also be able to invite people to meetings and respond to meeting invitations.

Any event you change or update on your iPod touch will be wirelessly synced with Google or Exchange.

Each Calendar Has a Different Color

You will also notice that every new Google or Exchange account you add to your iPod touch will create a separate calendar with a new color.

To see the color used for each calendar, tap the **Calendars** button in the upper left corner.

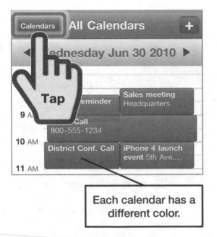

Each calendar has a different color.

On this screen you can see the color for each calendar.

You can selectively show calendars by tapping on the email address.

To hide a calendar, tap the email address to remove the checkmark.

To show a calendar, tap the email address to add the check mark.

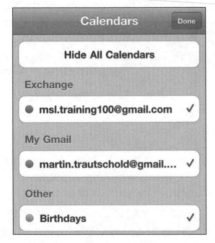

Inviting People to Meetings from Your iPod touch

Now you can invite people to your calendar events if you use Exchange or MobileMe. Here are the steps to follow:

1. Tap your **Calendar** icon to start your calendar.

2. Touch the **+** button in the upper right corner to schedule a new event.

3. On the **Add Event** screen, enter the meeting title and location and adjust the starting and ending time as required.

4. Tap the **Invitees** tab to invite people. (Refer to Figure 4–2.)

5. In order to invite someone, you have a few options.

    a. Type his or her email address (all invitations are sent via email).

    b. Type a few letters of his or her first and last names separated by a space, to instantly locate the person if he or she is in your contact list.

    c. Or, tap the **blue plus sign** to find someone by browsing your contact list.

6. Touch the name and email address you want to use. If someone has more than one email address, you'll need to select one.

7. Add more invitees if you desire, and then tap **Done** to exit the **Add Invitees** window.

8. Adjust any other items in the Add Event screen and tap **Done** to save.

9. The meeting invitation(s) will be sent via email immediately to everyone you invited.

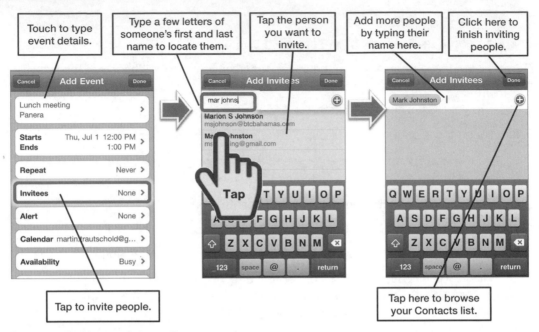

Figure 4–2. *Inviting people to meetings*

Seeing the Status of Invitees on Your Calendar

You can see who has not replied, or who has accepted or rejected your invitations by following these steps. See Figure 4–3.

Tap the meeting in your calendar to view the meeting details.

Tap the invitees to see everyone who was invited.

You will see the status of each person's reply in square brackets in front of their names.

- ■ * = Not responded
- ■ Check mark = Accepted
- ■ ? = Tentative/Maybe
- ■ X = Declined

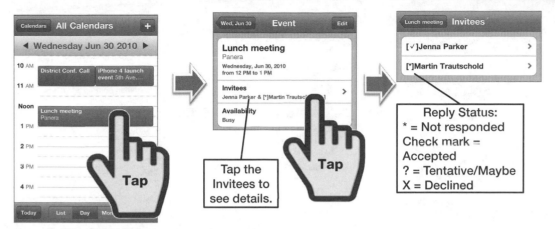

Figure 4–3. *Seeing the status of invitations you have sent*

Responding to Exchange Meeting Invitations from Your iPod touch

When you are connected to an Exchange email server and the person who invited you to a meeting is also on the same Exchange server, you will be able to use the Invitations inbox inside your Calendar app.

You will receive notifications on your **Calendar** icon as shown here. In this image, there are four new meeting invitations.

Follow these steps to work with Exchange meeting invitations in your Calendar invitations inbox.

1. Start your **Calendar** app.

2. Tap the **Invitations** inbox button in the lower right corner. See Figure 4–4.

3. You will see all your invitations listed. Tap the invitation to which you wish to respond.

4. Then you can review the details of the invitation and type a comment to be included in your response by tapping **Add Comments.**

5. To respond to the invitation, tap one of the three buttons at the bottom of the **Event** screen: **Accept**, **Maybe**, or **Decline.**

6. If you select **Accept** or **Maybe**, then the calendar event is added to your iPod touch calendar.

7. The response is sent immediately via email to the meeting organizer. You're done.

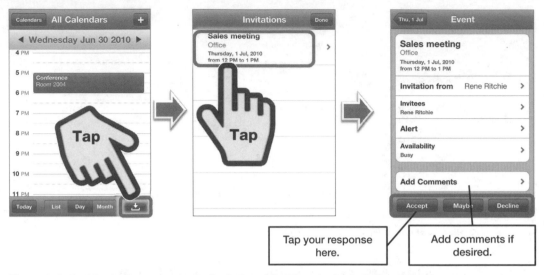

Figure 4–4. *Replying to Exchange meeting invitations using the calendar invitations inbox*

Responding to Google Meeting Invitations from Your iPod touch

If you are using Google Calendar with Exchange sync as we described previously, you will be able to reply to meeting invitations in the **Mail** app on your iPod touch.

> **NOTE:** As of publishing time, only Exchange invitations (not Google invitations) appeared in your Calendar invitations inbox, so you need to reply to these invitations using your **Mail** app. The new version of MobileMe also supports this.

1. Tap your **Mail** icon to start the program.

2. Navigate to the **Inbox**, which has the meeting invitation.

3. Locate the invitation.

Most invitations look something like the image shown here. Usually they start with the word **Invitation**.

> **TIP:** To quickly find all meeting invitations in your inbox, type the word **meet** or **invitation** in the search box. Tap the **Subject** button to search only the message subjects.

4. Tap the Google **Meeting Invitation** to open it.

5. Tap **Yes**, **Maybe**, or **No** next to **Going?** to reply to the invitation.

6. As soon as you tap one of the choices, your reply will be sent. You may be shown a Google Calendar web page to type optional details in your invitation reply.

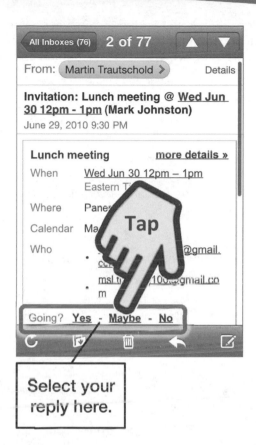

Select your reply here.

Wireless Sync Using the MobileMe Service

Another option if you do not use Google or Exchange and still want to wirelessly sync your information is to use the MobileMe service from Apple. The MobileMe service provides a great service to wirelessly sync your personal information between your computer (PC or Mac) and your iPod touch and other mobile devices, such as an iPad.

The MobileMe Cloud: The MobileMe service uses what is sometimes called a cloud to sync all your information. The MobileMe Cloud is a term used to describe the web servers where all your MobileMe information is stored on the Internet. The servers and the associated software you install on your computer (PC or Mac) and your mobile devices (iPod touch, iPad, etc.) help keep all your mobile devices in sync with your computer. The idea is that changed information (a new calendar event, a new contact name) gets sent from your iPod touch to the cloud. Then the cloud disperses the changed information to all the devices in your MobileMe account. This could be your computer or possibly an iPad or iPod touch.

Once you set up **MobileMe** from your computer and then set up access from your iPod touch, all your personal information (contacts, calendar, even bookmarks) will be shared wirelessly between your computer and your iPod touch.

In addition to the wireless sync of personal information, MobileMe lets you do the following:

- Create a web-based photo gallery that you can access and add to from your iPod touch.

- Create an **iDisk** that allows you to share documents easily between your iPod touch and your computer. You can also use it to share files that are too large to email. Some email systems block files larger than about 5MB.

- Find your lost iPod touch using the **Find My iPod touch** feature.

- Erase all of the personal data on your lost iPod touch remotely using the **Remote Wipe** feature.

- If you have multiple Macs in your home or home and business, MobileMe also allows you to sync **docks**, **settings**, **passwords**, and **other information** between your Macs, and use **Back to my Mac** remote desktop to retrieve files or share screens.

NOTE: As of publishing time, after your 60-day free trial, Apple charges $99/year for individual MobileMe service and $149/year for a family plan.

Check with the MobileMe web site (www.mobileme.com) to find out the latest information.

Signing Up for the MobileMe Service (PC or Mac)

Apple makes it easy for you to learn about MobileMe from iTunes after you register your iPod touch or the first time you connect your iPod touch to your computer. You will most likely see an ad for MobileMe with a **Try It Free** button.

If you use iTunes to sync your iPod touch, you will also see a **Learn More** button at the top of the **Info** tab, as shown in Figure 4–5.

1. Connect your iPod touch to your computer.

2. Click your **iPod touch** in the left nav bar of iTunes.

3. Click the **Info** tab at the top.

4. Click the **Learn More** button in the MobileMe section.

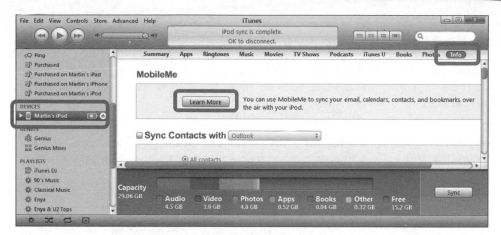

Figure 4–5. *Getting started with MobileMe from the* **iTunes Info** *tab*

You can also sign-up for MobileMe directly from their web site.

1. Type your personal information to set up your account and click the **Continue** button.

Enter your billing information and click the **Sign Up** button at the bottom.

2. If everything was entered correctly, you'll see a **Signup Complete** screen similar to the one shown here.

You have now created your MobileMe account. Now you'll set up MobileMe on your Mac or PC and your iPod touch.

If you are a Windows PC user, skip to the "Set Up MobileMe on Your PC" section.

Setting Up MobileMe on Your Mac

After you have created your MobileMe account, you are ready to set up the software on your Mac. The MobileMe software that runs on your Mac is included in the latest version of the Mac Leopard (v10.5.8 or higher) or Snow Leopard (v10.6.3 or higher) operating systems.

If you don't have the latest version of the Mac system software, you'll have to install it and configure the MobileMe software to sync to the MobileMe "cloud" to get started.

1. Click the Apple menu and select **Software Update** as shown.

   TIP: You'll find extensive step-by-step instructions showing you how to install or upgrade software on your Mac in Chapter 29: "Your iTunes User Guide."

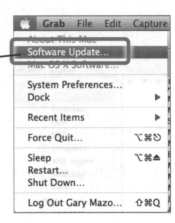

Click here to get the latest software for your Mac.

2. Follow the steps to complete the software update.

3. After you have successfully installed the software update, click the Apple menu and select **System Preferences**.

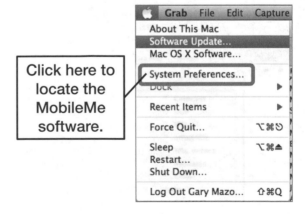

Click here to locate the MobileMe software.

4. Click the **MobileMe** icon in the Internet & Wireless section of System Preferences.

5. Enter your MobileMe **Member Name** and **Password**.

6. Click **Sign In**.

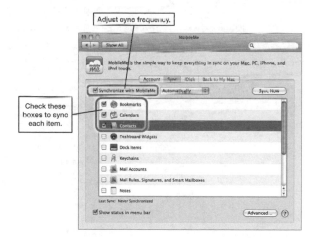

7. Click the **Sync** tab at the top to see the screen shown here.

8. Check the **Synchronize with MobileMe** box.

9. Next to this check box there's a drop-down for configuring the sync frequency. The default is **Automatically**, but you can sync every **Hour**, **Day**, **Week**, or **Manually**.

10. To sync bookmarks, check the **Bookmarks** box and select your computer's web browser.

11. To sync contacts, check the **Contacts** box.

12. To sync calendars, check the **Calendars** box.

13. You can also sync various other items by checking them. After you have set up syncing, you can configure your iDisk by clicking the **iDisk** tab and completing the screen shown in Figure 4–6.

14. When you are done, close the **MobileMe** control panel.

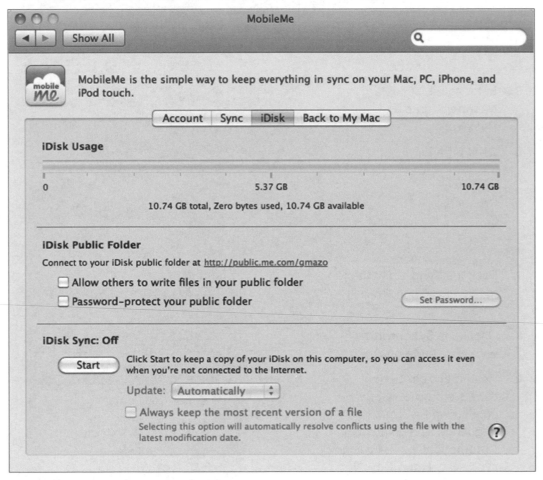

Figure 4–6. *MobileMe control panel showing the **iDisk** tab*

As soon as you close the MobileMe control panel, MobileMe will start sending your selected items—Contacts, Calendars, and Bookmarks— to the MobileMe web site.

Now you can skip to the "Multiple Ways to Access MobileMe" section while we discuss how Windows users configure MobileMe.

Setting Up MobileMe on Your Windows PC

After creating your MobileMe account, you need get the software set up on your PC. You will install the latest version of iTunes and the MobileMe software on your PC and then configure it to sync to the MobileMe "cloud" to get started.

1. On your computer's web browser, go to: www.apple.com/mobileme/setup/pc.html.

2. If you don't have iTunes version 10 or later, click the **iTunes** link to download it.

> **TIP**: We give you extensive step-by-step instructions for installing or upgrading iTunes in Chapter 29: "Your iTunes User Guide."

Click the link to download the MobileMe Control Panel for Windows.

3. Click the **Download** button on this screen to download the installation file.

4. Follow the steps on the screen to install the software on your computer.

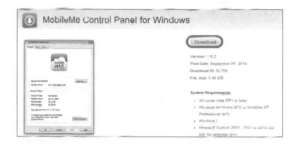

5. Once the software is installed, start it up by:

   - Clicking the **MobileMe** icon on your Windows desktop, or by

   - Searching for and starting it from your **Start** button or **Windows** icon in the lower left corner. Type **MobileMe**, and the icon should appear at the top of the Start menu under **Programs**. Click it.

6. Click the **Sync** tab at the top to see the screen shown here.

7. Check the **Sync with MobileMe** box.

8. Next to this check box you'll find a drop-down for the sync frequency. The default is **Automatically**, but you can choose to sync every **Hour**, **Day**, **Week**, or **Manually**.

9. To sync contacts, check the **Contacts** box and select where your contacts are stored (such as **Outlook**, **Google Contacts**, **Yahoo!**, or **Windows Contacts**). For Google and Yahoo!, you will need to enter your username and password by clicking the **Options** button that appears. See Figure 4–7.

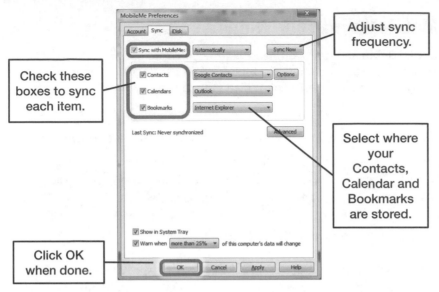

Figure 4–7. *MobileMe for Windows preferences control panel showing the* **Sync** *tab*

10. To sync calendars, check the **Calendars** box and select where your Calendars are stored (e.g., **Outlook** or elsewhere).

11. To sync bookmarks, check the **Bookmarks** box and select your computer's web browser (only Safari and Internet Explorer were supported for syncing bookmarks at publishing time).

12. Click **OK** when done.

As soon as you click **OK**, MobileMe will start sending your selected items—Contacts, Calendars, and Bookmarks—to the MobileMe web site.

Multiple Ways to Access MobileMe

After the first sync, you will have at least three ways to access your synced information:

- The computer where you originally stored your contacts and calendar
- The MobileMe web site
- Your iPod touch (or other mobile device)

Since you already know how to get to the information on your computer, we will focus on how to access information from the MobileMe web site and your iPod touch.

A Quick Tour of the MobileMe Web Site

You can do many useful and amazing things from the MobileMe web site from your computer. You can even locate your iPod touch, send messages to it, make it beep loudly, and remotely lock or erase it. Here we give you a quick tour.

1. Go to the **MobileMe** from a web browser on your computer by typing www.me.com.

2. Type your username and password and click **Log In**.

3. To view your mail, click the **Cloud** icon  in the upper left corner, and then click the **Mail** icon.

This will show your MobileMe inbox for all email going to (membername)@me.com.

4. To view your contacts, click the **Cloud** icon and then click the **Contacts** icon.

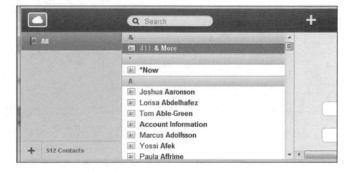

5. To view your calendar, click the **Cloud** icon  and then the **Calendar** icon. Notice there are various buttons at the top for the calendar views: **Day**, **Week**, **Month**, and **List**.

6. To view your photo albums, click the **Cloud** icon 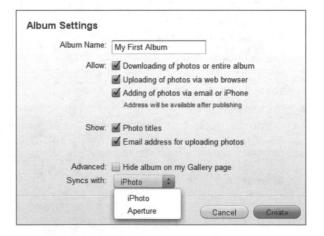 and then the **Gallery** icon.

7. To create a new album, click the **+** in the lower left corner.

8. Enter your **Album Name**, and check the **Allow** and **Show** settings you want. Also, for Mac users, decide whether you want to sync with **iPhoto** or **Aperture**.

9. Click the **Create** button to create your new album.

10. Click the **Upload Arrow** to select photos or videos to upload to your MobileMe album.

11. Navigate to the folder on your computer where your pictures are stored, click the picture or video to select it, and then click the **Open** button.

NOTE: The following image file formats are supported: .png, .gif, .jpg, .jpeg. The following video types are supported: .mov, .m4v, .mp4, .3gp, .3g2, .mpg, .mpeg, .avi.

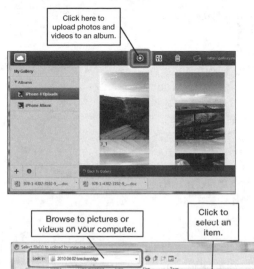

Click here to upload photos and videos to an album.

Browse to pictures or videos on your computer.

Click to select an item.

Then click Open.

12. Click the **Cloud** icon and then the **iDisk** icon to view the files located on the MobileMe iDisk.

TIP: You can easily store and retrieve files on this iDisk from your computer and your iPod touch. You can even share files that are too large to email or that you'd like to print from your iPod touch using the **Public** folder.

13. Click the **Cloud** icon  and then the **Find My iPod touch** icon to locate your iPod touch. You will need to re-enter your password for security purposes. This feature assumes you have already logged into MobileMe from the **Settings** app on your iPod touch.

14. Click your name in the upper right corner, and then select **Account** from the drop-down list. In your account page you can adjust the options, see your account type and trial expiration date (if you are on a free trial), get help, or check whether the MobileMe service is up and running.

Setting Up Your iPod touch to Access Your MobileMe Account

Now that you've set up your MobileMe account, you are ready to sign into it from your iPod touch.

1. Tap your **Settings** icon.

2. Tap **Mail, Contacts, Calendars**.

3. Tap **Add Account**.

4. Tap **MobileMe** for the account type.

5. Enter your **Name** and your MobileMe email **Address** and **Password,** and then tap **Next**.

6. Now you'll see the MobileMe configuration screen showing your sync options.

7. To turn any synced item **On** or **Off**, tap the switch.

8. To turn on **Find My iPod touch**, which will show your iPod touch on a map on the MobileMe web site, move the switch to **On**.

> **NOTE:** If you have any existing contacts, calendars, or other information on your iPod touch, these will be kept separate from your MobileMe contacts and calendars.

9. When you are done, tap **Save.** You should be brought back to the **Settings** screen and see your MobileMe account listed with the selected items turned **On** for syncing. You'll also need the Find My iPhone, iDisk, and MobileMe Gallery Apps (all free) from the App Store to match all the features on MobileMe.com.

Using MobileMe After Setup

Using MobileMe is fairly seamless once you get it set up. You update your contacts and calendar on your iPod touch, and the changes just appear on your computer. And, if you've set up other mobile devices, such as an iPad, on the same account, the changes appear there, too. Everything is kept in sync wirelessly and automatically.

MobileMe has a few very cool features that we will highlight here.

Find My iPod touch, Send Message, and Remote Wipe

From any web browser, you can locate your iPod touch using the **Find My iPod touch** feature in MobileMe. You can send a message and play a loud sound to alert someone on your iPod touch, even if it is locked. You can remotely lock your iPod touch using a 4–digit code and remotely erase all information on your iPod touch.

1. Login to **MobileMe** from any web browser on your computer by going to www.me.com.

2. Type your **username** and **password** and click **Log In**.

3. Click the **Find My iPod touch** icon in the top nav bar to display the current location of your iPod touch.

Find Your iPod touch

4. Re-enter your password for security purposes.

Please re-enter your password

To ensure your location information is viewable only by you, please re-enter the password for **gmazo**.

Cancel   Continue

5. Now you have various options.

    a. You can display a message or play sound on your iPod touch.

    b. You can remote lock your iPod touch with a passcode.

    c. You can completely erase or wipe your iPod touch.

6. Click the **Display a Message** button to display a message on your iPod touch and play a loud sound for up to two minutes or until the screen is tapped.

7. You will see a small alert window pop up on the iPod touch and the sound will play.

8. If you want to lock your iPod touch remotely, tap the **Remote Lock** button on the settings page.

9. Enter a new passcode twice to set it on your iPod touch. Your iPod touch will immediately be locked with this new passcode.

TIP: Since this overrides your existing passcode, you can also use this feature to unlock your iPod touch if you forget your original passcode. Just set a new one using **Remote Lock**.

10. You can also erase all data from your iPod touch by pressing the **Remote Wipe** button.

11. Mark the check box and click **Erase All Data**.

CAUTION: This will erase all data on your iPod touch and cannot be undone. All your data stored on MobileMe will automatically re-sync when you set up the account again. However, applications and other non-MobileMe information will have to be restored from your iTunes backup or from the App store and iTunes.

Canceling Your MobileMe Account

Should you decide that MobileMe is not for you, you can cancel your account. If you cancel your account within the first 60 days, you can avoid the $99.00 charge.

1. To cancel the service, log in to MobileMe from any web browser on your computer by going to www.me.com.

2. Type your username and password and click **Log In**.

3. Click the **Settings** icon in the top row of icons.

4. Notice on the **Summary** tab the date your trial ends. In this image, the trial ends on June 4, 2010.

5. Click **Account Options** in the left column.

6. From the **Account Options** screen, click the **Cancel Account** button.

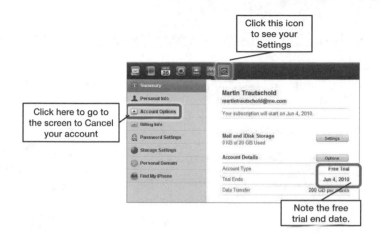

Additional Settings for Google/Exchange or MobileMe

Once you set up the Google/Exchange or MobileMe sync, you may notice a few new options on your Settings screen in addition to the ones shown in Chapter 15: "Working with Contacts," and Chapter 16: "Your Calendar."

1. Tap the **Settings** icon.

2. Tap **Mail, Contacts, Calendars** in the left column.

3. Scroll down the right column to the bottom to see the image shown here.

4. The new option in the Contacts section is the **Default Account**. You can set this to be either your Exchange/Google account or your computer's account.

5. Notice that you can turn your **New Invitation Alerts On** or **Off**.

6. The new option in the Calendars section is **Sync,** which allows you to set how much of your calendar to sync (**2 weeks**, **1 month**, **3 months**, **6 months**, or **All events**).

7. You can also select which is your **Default Calendar** for new events you add to your iPod touch. You can change this calendar when you create a new event.

Chapter 5

Wi-Fi Connectivity

We live in a connected world. Wireless Internet (also known as Wi-Fi) access has become the rule, not the exception—chances are you're already using Wi-Fi at your home or office. Now you can use it to connect your iPod touch.

This chapter covers WLANs (wireless local area networks) and all the ways you can get connected or disconnected from these networks. You will also learn how to prioritize your networks and forget networks you no longer need.

What Can I Do When I'm Connected to a Wi-Fi Network?

Here are some of the things you can do when connected:

- Access and download apps (programs) from the App Store
- Access and download music, videos, podcasts, and more from iTunes on your iPod touch
- Browse the web using Safari
- Send and receive email messages
- Use social networking sites that require an Internet connection, like Facebook, Twitter, etc.
- Play games that use a live Internet connection
- Anything else that requires an Internet connection

Wi-Fi Connections

Every iPod touch comes with Wi-Fi capability built in, so let's take a look at getting connected to the Wi-Fi network. Things to consider about Wi-Fi connections are the following:

- There's no additional cost for network access and data downloads (if you are using your iPod touch in your home, office, or a free Wi-Fi hotspot).

- More and more places, including some airplanes, provide Wi-Fi access, but you may have to pay a one-time or monthly service fee.

NOTE: The newest iPod touch has support for the faster, longer range 802.11n standard. However, it only supports 802.11n on the more crowded 2.4Mhz band, not the less crowded 5Mhz band. If you want to use iPod touch with your 802.11n Wi-Fi router, make sure to set the router to 2.4Mhz. Also, you can leave your Wi-Fi connection on while in sleep mode to receive FaceTime calls or push notifications.

Connecting to a Wi-Fi Network

To set up your Wi-Fi connection, follow these steps:

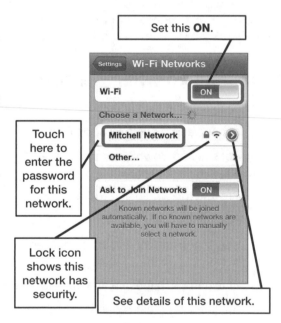

1. Tap the **Settings** icon.

2. Tap **Wi-Fi** near the top.

3. Make sure the **Wi-Fi** switch is set to **On**. If it is currently **Off**, then tap it to turn it **On**.

4. Once Wi-Fi is **On**, the iPod touch will automatically start looking for wireless networks.

5. The list of accessible networks is shown below the **Choose a Network...** option. In this screenshot, you can see that there is one network available.

6. To connect to any of the networks listed, just touch the network name. If the network is unsecure (does not have a lock icon), you will be connected automatically.

Connecting at a Public Wi-Fi Hotspot with Web Login

In locations with free Wi-Fi networks, such as coffee shops, hotels, or restaurants, you will see a pop-up window appear as soon as your iPod touch comes into contact with the network. In these cases, simply tap the network name. You may be brought to a Safari browser screen to complete your login to the network.

1. If you see a pop-up window similar to the one shown, tap the network name you wish to join. In this case, you'd tap the **Panera** network.

2. In some cases, you may see a Safari window pop up, which can be quite confusing because it is so small on your iPod touch screen. You need to use the double-tap or pinch-open gesture (see the Quick Start Guide for help) to zoom in on the web page. You are looking for a button that says **Login** or **Agree** or something similar. Tap that button to complete the connection.

> **NOTE:** Some places, like coffee shops, use a web-based login instead of a username/password screen. In those cases, when you click on the network (or try to use Safari), iPod touch will open a browser screen and you'll see the web page along with login options.

Secure Wi-Fi Networks—Entering a Password

Some Wi-Fi networks require a password to connect. This is set when the network administrator creates the wireless network. You will have to know the exact password, including whether it is case-sensitive.

If the network does require a password, you will be taken to the password-entry screen. Type the password exactly as given to you and press the enter key on the on-screen keyboard (which is now labeled as **Join**).

On the network screen, you'll see a checkmark showing that you are connected to the network.

TIP: You can use the paste function in the password dialog box. So for longer, random passwords, you can transfer them to your iPod touch (in an email message) and just copy and paste them. Just remember to delete the email immediately afterwards to keep things secure. Tap and hold the password in the mail message, select it, and then tap **Copy**. In the Wi-Fi network **Password** field, tap and then select **Paste**.

Switching to a Different Wi-Fi Network

At times you may want to change your active Wi-Fi network. Perhaps the network selected by the iPod touch is not the strongest network, or maybe you want to use a secure network instead of an unsecure one.

To switch from the currently selected Wi-Fi network, tap the **Settings** icon, touch **Wi-Fi**, and then touch the name of the Wi-Fi network you want to join. If that network requires a password, you'll need to enter it to join.

Once you type the correct password (or if you touched an open network), your iPod touch will join that network.

Verifying Your Wi-Fi Connection

It is easy to see if you are connected to a network (and which one) by looking next to Wi-Fi in your main Settings screen.

1. Tap your **Settings** icon.

2. Look next to Wi-Fi at the top.

    ▪ If you see **Not Connected**, you do not have an active Wi-Fi connection.

    ▪ If you see some other name, such as **Panera**, then you are connected to that Wi-Fi network.

Advanced Wi-Fi Options (Hidden or Undiscoverable Networks)

Sometimes you may not be able to see the network you want to join because the name has been hidden (not broadcasted) by the network administrator. This section shows you how to join such networks on your iPod touch. Once you have joined such a network, the next time you come in contact with that network it will join automatically without asking. You can also tell your iPod touch to ask every time it joins a network. And there are times when you may want to erase or forget a network; say you were at a one-time convention and want to get rid of the associated network—you'll learn that here, too.

Why Can't I See the Wi-Fi Network I Want to Join?

Sometimes, for security reasons, people don't make their networks discoverable. If this is the case, you have to manually enter the name and security options to connect.

As you can see in Figure 5–1, your list of available networks includes **Other**. Touch the **Other** button, and you can manually enter the name of a network you would like to join.

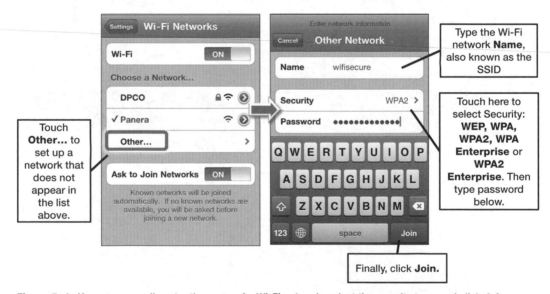

Figure 5–1. *You can manually enter the name of a Wi-Fi network, select the security type, and click* **Join**.

Type in the Wi-Fi network **Name**, touch the **Security** tab, and choose which type of security is being used on that network. If you are unsure, you'll need to find out from the network administrator.

When you have the information you need, enter it along with the proper password, and this new network will be saved to your network list for future access.

Reconnecting to Previously Joined Wi-Fi Networks

The nice thing about the iPod touch is that when you return to an area with a Wi-Fi network you previously joined (whether it was an open or a secure, password-protected network) your iPod touch will automatically join the network without asking you again. However, you can turn off this automatic-joining feature, as described next.

Ask to Join Networks Main Switch

There is a main **Ask to Join Networks** switch, which is set to **ON** by default. Known networks are joined automatically; this only takes effect if no known networks are available. With this switch set to **ON**, you will be asked to join visible Wi-Fi networks. If networks are available that are not known to you, you will be asked before being connected.

If the switch is set to **OFF**, you will have to manually join unknown networks.

Why might you want to turn off automatically joining a network?

This could be a good security measure if, for example, you don't want your kids to be able to join a wireless network on the iPod touch without your knowledge.

Ask to Join and Ask to Login Switch on Each Network

Sometimes, you may find that a particular Wi-Fi network has additional switches that override the main **Ask to Join Networks** switch. Tap the little blue arrow  next to the network name to see details about this Wi-Fi network. **Auto-Join** and **Auto-Login** are set to **ON** by default.

To disable **Auto-Join** or **Auto-Login**, tap each switch to set it to **OFF**.

Forget (or Erase) a Network

If you find that you no longer want to connect to a network on your list, you can **Forget it**—i.e., take it off your list of networks.

1. Tap the **Settings** icon.

2. Tap **Wi-Fi** to see your list of networks.

3. Tap the small blue arrow  next to the network you want to forget in order to see the screen shown here.

4. Tap **Forget this Network** at the top of the screen.

5. You will be prompted with a warning. Just touch **Forget** and the network will no longer show up on your list.

Flying on an Airplane: Airplane Mode

When you fly on an airplane, the flight crew will ask you to turn off all portable electronic devices for takeoff and landing. Then, when you get to a certain altitude, they will say that "all approved electronic devices" can be turned back on. Airplane Mode allows you to use any feature of the iPod that does not required any kind of wireless connection.

If you need to turn off your iPod touch completely, then press and hold the **Power** button on the top right edge, then **Slide to Power Off** with your finger.

In order to enable **Airplane Mode**, follow these steps:

1. Tap the **Settings** icon.

2. Set the switch next to **Airplane Mode** in the top of the left column to **ON**.

3. Notice that the Wi-Fi is automatically turned **Off** and that the phone will not work.

> **TIP:** Some airlines have in-flight Wi-Fi networks. In those flights, you may want to turn your Wi-Fi back **On** at the appropriate time.

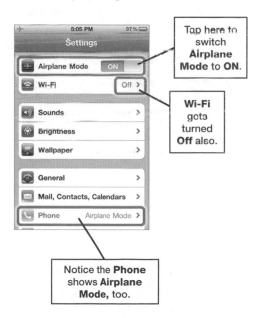

You can turn your Wi-Fi connection **Off** or **On** by following these steps:

1. Tap the **Settings** icon.

2. Tap **Wi-Fi** near the top of the screen.

3. To enable the Wi-Fi connections, set the switch next to **Wi-Fi** in the top of the page to **On**.

4. To disable the Wi-Fi, set the same switch to **Off**.

5. Select the Wi-Fi network and follow the steps given by the flight attendant to get connected.

VPN Connection Set Up on Your iPod touch

Armed with the login instructions and type of VPN connection, you are ready to connect with your iPod touch.

1. Tap the **Settings** icon.

2. Tap **General**.

3. Tap **Network**.

4. Scroll down to the bottom of the screen and tap **VPN**.

Tap here to get started with **VPN** setup.

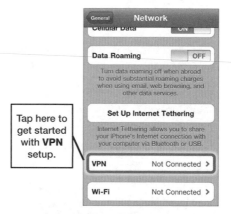

5. On the VPN screen, tap the switch next to VPN to set it to **On**. You should then be taken to the Add Configuration screen. If not, then tap **Add VPN Configuration** at the bottom to set up a new VPN connection.

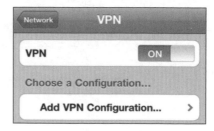

6. The Add Configuration screen is where you set up your VPN login details, using the information from your help desk or VPN administrator.

7. If your VPN is an **L2TP** type, then you would use the screen shown here. Scroll to the bottom and enter the **Proxy** information as required.

8. If your VPN is a **PPTP** type, then you would tap **PPTP** at the top and use the screen shown here. Scroll to the bottom and enter the **Proxy** information as required.

9. If your VPN is an **IPSec** (Cisco) type, then you would tap **IPSec** and use the screen shown here. Scroll to the bottom and enter the **Proxy** information as required.

10. When you are done with your setup, tap the **Save** button in the upper right corner.

11. If you have trouble logging in, make sure you are in a strong wireless coverage area and verify you have typed all your login credentials correctly. It can be difficult when passwords disappear as you type them. You may want to try re-typing passwords and server information before calling the help desk.

Knowing When You Are Connected to a VPN Network

You will see a small **VPN** icon  just to the right of your network connection status display. Only when you see this icon do you know that you are securely connected to the VPN network.

Switching VPN Networks

You may have several VPN networks to which you need to connect. You can select between different VPN configurations on your iPod touch.

1. Tap the **Settings** icon.

2. Tap **General**.

3. Tap **Network**.

4. Scroll down to the bottom of the screen and tap **VPN**.

5. On the VPN screen, tap a different **VPN configuration** to connect to it. Don't tap the blue circle with the > symbol, unless you want to change the login settings for that network.

Chapter 6

Organize Your iPod touch Icons and Folders

Your new iPod touch is very customizable. In this chapter, we'll show you how to move icons around and put your favorites just where you want them. You've got up to 11 pages of icons to work with, and you can adjust the look and feel of those pages so it suits your tastes.

Like a Mac computer or an iPad, the iPod touch has a **Bottom Dock**, where you can put the icons for your favorite apps. Your iPod touch comes with four standard icons in the Bottom Dock, but you can replace these with others so your favorite apps are always available at the bottom of your screen. In the new operating system, iOS4, you can even move an entire folder of apps to the Bottom Dock.

> **TIP:** You can also move or delete icons using iTunes on your computer. Check out Chapter 29: "Your iTunes User Guide" for more information.

Moving Icons to the Bottom Dock—Docking Them

When you turn your iPod touch on, you'll notice the four icons locked to the Bottom Dock: **Music**, **FaceTime**, **Mail,** and **Safari**. It is possible that your icons may be different, but you can easily change them.

Suppose you decide you want to change one or more of these for apps you use more often. Fortunately, moving icons to and from the Bottom Dock is easy.

Keep up to 4 icons that you want to see all the time. These icons will always remain visible even when you slide the other icon screens left/right.

Bottom Dock

Starting the Move

Press the **Home** button to get to your Home screen. Now, touch and hold any icon on the Home screen for a couple of seconds. You'll notice that all the icons start to shake.

Try just moving a couple of icons around at first. You'll see that when you move an icon down, the other icons in the row move to make space for it.

Once you have a feel for how the icons move, you're ready to replace one of the Bottom Dock icons with one of your choosing. While the icons are shaking, take the icon you want to replace from the Bottom Dock and move it up to an area covered by other icons. If you move it to a large blank area, it will jump back to the dock.

> **NOTE:** You can have up to four icons in the Bottom Dock, so if you already have four there, you'll have to remove one to replace it with a new one.

Suppose you want to replace the standard **Music** icon with your **App Store** icon. The first thing to do is just hold the **Music** icon and move it up a row—out of the Bottom Dock, as shown in Figure 6-1.

To stop the icons shaking, tap your **Home** button.

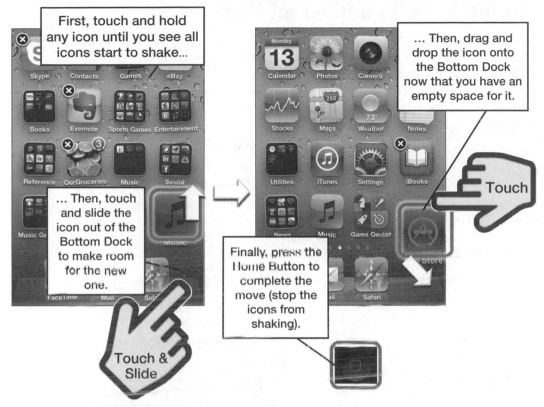

Figure 6-1. *Swapping icons in the Bottom Dock*

Next, locate your **App Store** icon and move it down to the Bottom Dock. As you'll see, the icon becomes sort of transparent until you actually set it into place.

When you are sure you have the icons just where you want them, simply press the **Home** button once and the icons will lock into place. Now, you have the **App Store** icon in the Bottom Dock, where you want it.

Moving Icons to a Different Page

The iPod touch can hold 16 icons on a page (not including the dock) and you can find these pages by swiping (right to left) on your Home screen. With all the cool apps available, it is not uncommon to have five, six, or even more pages of icons. You can have up to 11 pages filled with icons if you're the adventurous type!

> **NOTE:** You can also swipe from left to right on any screen except the Home screen. On the Home screen, swiping left to right takes you to **Spotlight Search**; see Chapter 2: "Typing Tips, Copy/Paste, and Search" for more information.

You may have an icon you rarely use on your first page, and you want to move it way off to the last page. Or you may want to move the icon for an app you often use from the last of the icon pages to the first. Both are very easy to do; it's very much like moving icons to the Bottom Dock, as discussed previously.

1. Touch and hold any icon to initiate the moving process.

2. Touch and hold the icon you wish to move. As shown in Figure 6-2, let's say we want to move the **iBooks** icon to the first page.

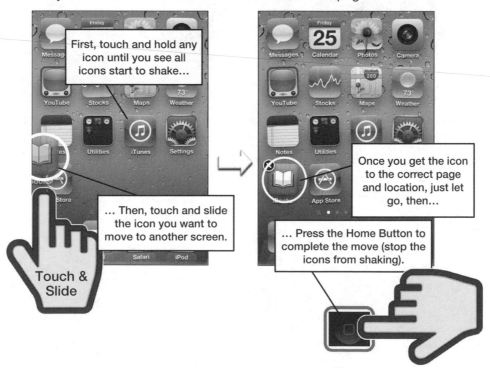

Figure 6-2. *Moving icons from one page to another*

3. Now drag and drop the icon onto another page. To do this, touch and hold the **iBooks** icon and drag it to the left. You'll see all of your pages of icons move by. When you get to the first page, just release the icon and, as you'll see, it will be placed at the very beginning.

4. Press the **Home** key to complete the move and stop the icons from shaking.

Deleting Icons

Be careful—it's as easy to delete an icon as it is to move it, but when you delete an icon on the iPod touch, you are actually deleting the program it represents. This means you won't be able to use the program again without reinstalling it or downloading it again.

Depending on your Application Sync settings in iTunes, the program may still reside in your **Applications** folder in iTunes. In that case, you would be able to easily reinstall the deleted app if you wanted to by checking that application in the list of apps to sync in iTunes. If not, you can always download it again onto your device, from the same account, at no charge

As Figure 6–3 shows, the deleting process is similar to the moving process. Touch and hold any icon to initiate deleting. Just as before, touching and holding makes the icons shake and allows you to move or delete them.

NOTE: You can delete only programs you have downloaded to your iPod touch; the preinstalled icons and their associated programs can't be deleted. You can tell which programs can be deleted because the icons contain a small black **x** in the upper left corner.

Just tap the **x** on the icon you'd like to delete. You'll be prompted to either delete, or cancel the delete request. If you select **Delete**, the icon and its related app are removed from your iPod touch.

First, touch and hold any icon until you see all icons start to shake...

... Then, touch the black (X) on the corner of the icon you want to delete.

Confirm that you have the correct icon selected, and touch "Delete"

Delete "NYTimes"

Deleting "NYTimes" will also delete all of its data.

Delete   Cancel

Touch

NYTimes

Touch

Figure 6-3. *Deleting an icon—and its associated program*

Resetting All Your Icon Locations (Factory Defaults)

Occasionally, you might want to go back to the original factory default icon settings. This might be the case if you've moved too many new icons to your first page and want to see all the basic icons again.

To do this, touch the **Settings** icon. Then touch **General** in the left column and, finally, scroll all the way to the bottom to touch **Reset** in the right column.

Reset   >

NOTE: Built-in apps will get sorted back into the order they were in when Apple shipped the iPod touch. All other apps and their icons that were added will be deleted.

On the **Reset** screen, touch **Reset Home Screen Layout** near the bottom. Now all your icons will be returned to the original positions.

> **CAUTION:** Be careful you don't touch one of the other **Reset** options, as you can inadvertently erase your entire iPod touch if you touch the wrong button. If you do, you'll have to restore data from your iTunes backup, so make sure you backup regularly.

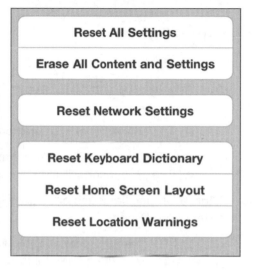

Working with Folders

New to iOS4 is the ability to organize your apps into folders. Previously, each app existed in its spot on your Home page, and once you downloaded many apps, it was hard to keep track of what was where.

Using folders lets you keep your games, your productivity apps, and other like-functioning apps together in folders. Each folder can hold 12 apps—which can really help you organize your iPod touch!

Creating a Folder

Creating folders in iOS4 is intuitive and fun.

1. Hold down an app until all the apps start shaking (as you did in the "Moving Icons" section).

2. Drag an app onto another like-functioning app.

3. For example, drag one "Game" onto another "Game" or one "Utility" onto another "Utility." The iPod touch will initially create a name for the folder.

4. In this example, I dragged one sports-related game onto another and it created a folder called "Sports."

5. Edit the folder name by touching the **Name** field and typing a new name. I typed **Sports Games** as the name of this new folder. See Figure 6-4.

6. Press the **Home** button to set the new folder name.

7. Press the **Home** button again to return to the Home screen, and you will now see the new folder with the new name.

NOTE: You can place up to 12 apps in a given folder. If you try to put more than that, you'll see the new icon continually being "pushed" out of the folder, indicating that the folder is full.

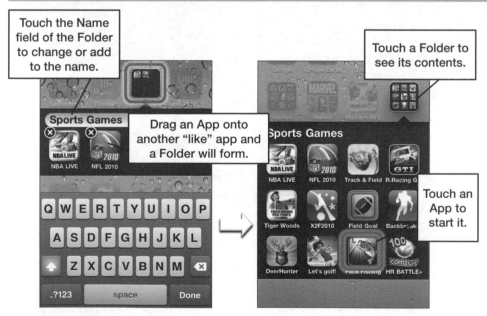

Figure 6-4. *Moving icons to create a folder*

Moving Folders

Just like apps, folders can also be moved from one Home page to another.

1. Press and hold a folder until the folder and icons on the Home screen start to shake.

2. Touch and hold the folder and drag it to the spot on the screen (or to another Home screen) and then let go.

3. When you have the folder in the spot you desire, just press the **Home** button to complete the move.

> **TIP**: You can even move a folder down to the Bottom Dock if you like. This is a very handy way of having lots of apps right at your fingertips. See Figure 6-5.

Move a folder down to the **Bottom Dock** to have access to up to 12 apps at once!

Figure 6-5. *Moving a folder to the Bottom Dock*

Personalize and Secure Your iPod touch

In this chapter, you will learn several easy ways to personalize your iPod touch. We'll show you where you can download free wallpaper to change the look of your **Lock** and **Home** screens. We'll also show you how to personalize the sounds your iPod touch makes by adjusting when and what sound you hear for various activities. Finally, you'll see how to protect your iPod touch with passcode security. Many aspects of the iPod touch can be fine-tuned to meet your needs and tastes—to give your iPod touch a more personal look and feel.

Changing Your Lock Screen and Home Screen Wallpapers

There are actually two screens you can personalize on your iPod touch by changing the wallpaper.

The **Lock Screen** appears when you first turn on your iPod touch or wake it up. The wallpaper for this screen is shown behind the **Slide to Unlock** slider bar.

The **Home Screen** features all of your icons. You can see the wallpaper behind the icons.

You can use the wallpaper pictures that come with the iPod touch or you can use your own images.

> **TIP:** You may want the wallpaper for your **Lock Screen** to be less personal than your **Home Screen** wallpaper. For example, you might choose to put a generic landscape image on your **Lock Screen** and a picture of a loved one on your **Home Screen**. Also, you might want to choose a **Home Screen** wallpaper that's not too busy so it doesn't clash with the icons.

There are a couple of ways to change the wallpaper on the iPod touch. The first way is very straightforward.

Changing Wallpaper from Your Settings App

You can adjust your wallpaper from your **Settings** app.

1. Tap the **Settings** icon.

2. Tap **Wallpaper**.

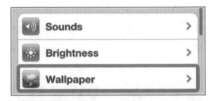

3. Tap the image of your currently selected wallpaper. The Lock screen is shown on the left and the Home screen is on the right.

4. Choose an album.

   - Tap **Wallpaper** to select a pre-loaded wallpaper.

   - Tap **Camera Roll** to select from images you've saved from the Web, screenshots (which you take by pressing and hold the **Home** button and **Power/Sleep** key), or even from wallpaper apps.

   - Tap **Photo Library** to see images in your library.

   - Tap any of the other albums to view pictures you have synced.

5. Once you tap on an album, you'll see the images within that album. Swipe up or down to view all images. The images you have most recently added will be at the very bottom.

6. Tap any image to select it and view it full screen.

7. Unless you have selected an image from the wallpaper album, you can move and scale the image.

- Move the image by touching and dragging your finger.

- Zoom in or out by pinching your fingers open or closed.

- Tap the **Cancel** button to return to the album if you don't like the image.

8. Tap the **Set** button to set the image as your wallpaper.

9. Select where you want this wallpaper to be used.

■ Tap the **Set Lock Screen** button to set the image only for your **Lock Screen**.

■ Tap the **Set Home Screen** button to set the image only for your **Home Screen**.

■ Tap the **Set Both** button to set the image for both your **Lock** and **Home Screens**.

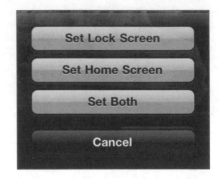

10. Tap the **Home** button to exit out of **Settings** and check out your new Home screen wallpaper. Then press the **Sleep/Power** button on the top right edge of your device to lock it, and tap the **Home** button again to see your Lock screen wallpaper as shown in Figure 7–1.

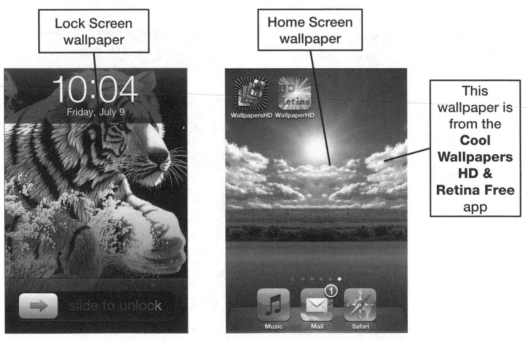

Figure 7–1. *Your Lock screen and Home screen wallpapers*

Using Any Photo as Wallpaper

The second way to change your wallpaper is to view any picture in your **Photos** collection and select it as your wallpaper.

1. Tap the **Photos** icon to get started. To learn more about working with photos, check out Chapter 17: "iPod touch Photography."

2. Touch the photo album you want to look through to find your wallpaper.

3. When you find a photo you want to use, touch it and it will open on your screen.

4. The thumbnail you tap will fill the screen. If this is the image you want to use, tap the **Set as** icon

   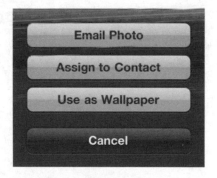 on the lower left corner of the screen.

5. Tap **Use as Wallpaper.**

6. To move, scale, and set as **Home** or **Lock** screen wallpaper, follow steps 7–9 from the previous section. If you decide you'd rather use a different picture, choose **Cancel** and select a different one.

Downloading Great Wallpaper from Free Apps

Go to the **App Store** and do a search for **backgrounds** or **wallpapers**. (See Chapter 20: "The Amazing App Store" for help.) You'll find a number of free and low-cost apps designed specifically for your iPod touch. In this section we highlight one called **Cool Wallpapers HD & Retina Free,** which has hundreds of beautiful background images you can download for free to your iPod touch.

NOTE: With **Cool Wallpapers HD & Retina Free,** as with most wallpaper apps, you'll need a live Wi-Fi Internet connection to view the wallpapers.

Downloading Wallpapers from an App

After you download **Cool Wallpapers HD & Retina Free**, you can get started.

1. Tap the **Cool Wallpapers HD & Retina Free** icon to start it up.

2. The app has a number of categories of backgrounds to choose from (see Figure 7–2).

3. Using the icons on the top bar of the app, you can choose to **Filter** by a category, view **Popular** or **New** backgrounds**,** or **Search** using the search icon**.**

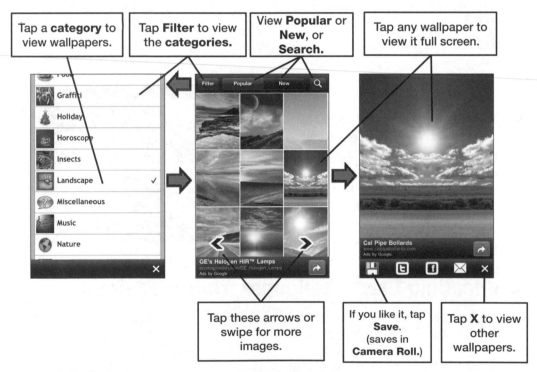

Tap a **category** to view wallpapers.

Tap **Filter** to view the **categories.**

View **Popular** or **New,** or **Search.**

Tap any wallpaper to view it full screen.

Tap these arrows or swipe for more images.

If you like it, tap **Save**. (saves in **Camera Roll.**)

Tap **X** to view other wallpapers.

Figure 7–2. *Previewing free wallpaper from the* **Cool Wallpapers** *app*

4. After touching any wallpaper to bring it to a full-screen preview, tap the **Save** icon in the lower left corner to save a copy into your **Camera Roll** album.

5. Using the other icons on the bottom row, you can send also send as a **tweet**, post the link to **Facebook**, or **Email** a copy of the wallpaper to anyone.

6. Press the **X** in the lower right corner to stop viewing this wallpaper and return to browsing other wallpaper thumbnail images.

> **NOTE:** As with many free apps, you'll see advertisements somewhere in the app; they help the developer pay for the time spent creating the app. In the Cool Wallpapers app, the ads are in the lower bar as you browse the wallpapers.

Using Your Newly Downloaded Wallpaper

Once you've chosen a wallpaper image and saved it to your iPod touch, you need to select it using the steps described in the "Changing Wallpaper from your Settings App" section earlier in this chapter.

Remember that the downloaded wallpaper will be in the **Camera Roll** album. After you tap **Camera Roll** to open it, you'll need to flick all the way to the bottom to see your recent entries.

Adjusting Sounds on Your iPod touch

You can fine-tune your iPod touch so that it does or does not make sounds when certain actions happen, such as an incoming phone call, new mail, or a calendar alert. You can also customize what happens when you send mail or type on the keyboard.

To adjust sounds, follow these steps.

1. Tap your **Settings** icon.

2. Tap **Sounds**.

3. To adjust the volume of the ringtone and other alerts, move the slider bar at the top.

4. To allow the volume keys on the left side of your iPod touch adjust the ringer and alert volumes, set the **Change with Buttons** to **ON**.

5. To change your **Ringtone** or the sound played when you receive a **FaceTime** call, tap **Ringtone**.

6. On the **Ringtone** screen, tap any item to select it.

7. Tap the **Sounds** button in the upper left corner to return to the previous screen.

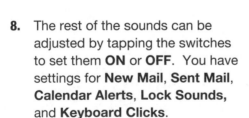

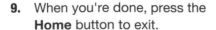

8. The rest of the sounds can be adjusted by tapping the switches to set them **ON** or **OFF**. You have settings for **New Mail**, **Sent Mail**, **Calendar Alerts**, **Lock Sounds**, and **Keyboard Clicks**.

9. When you're done, press the **Home** button to exit.

> **TIP:** On a related note, you can lock the maximum volume playable from the iPod app. Go into Settings ➤ iPod ➤ Volume Limit ➤ Lock Volume Limit. We show you how to do this in Chapter 9: "Playing Music."

Keyboard Options

You can fine-tune your keyboard by selecting various languages and changing settings like **Auto-Correction** and **Auto-Capitalization**. You can even have your iPod touch speak the Auto-Correction suggestions to you as you type. See Chapter 2: "Typing Tips, Copy/Paste, and Search" for keyboard options and how to use the various features.

How to Secure Your iPod touch with a Passcode

Your iPod touch can hold a great deal of valuable and sensitive information. This is especially true if you save information like the Social Security numbers and birth dates of your family members. It's a good idea to make sure that anyone who picks up your iPod touch can't access all that information. Also, if your children are like ours, they'll probably pick up your cool iPod touch and start surfing the Web or playing a game. You might want to enable some security restrictions to keep them safe.

Setting a Simple Four-Digit Passcode

On your iPod touch you have the option of setting a four-digit passcode that prevents unauthorized access to your iPod touch and your information. If the wrong passcode is entered, however, even you won't be able to access your information, so it's a good idea to use a code you'll easily remember.

> **TIP:** If you use Apple's **MobileMe** service described in Chapter 4: "Other Sync Methods," you can use the MobileMe web site to set a passcode on your iPod touch without even touching the iPod touch, by using the remote-lock feature. You can also remotely erase all data on your iPod touch from the MobileMe site with the remote-wipe feature.

To set a passcode to lock your iPod touch, follow these steps.

1. Tap the **Settings** icon.

2. Tap **General.**

3. Scroll down and tap **Passcode Lock.**

4. Tap **Turn Passcode On** to set a passcode.

5. The default is a simple four-digit passcode. Use the keyboard to enter a new four-digit code. You will then be prompted to enter your code once more.

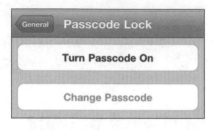

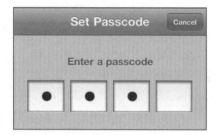

Setting a More Complex Password

If you prefer to have a passcode that is more complicated than just four digits, you can do so by turning **OFF** the **Simple Passcode** on the Passcode Lock screen.

You will then be able to enter a new passcode with letters, numbers, and even symbols.

CAUTION: Be careful! If you forget your passcode, you won't be able to unlock your iPod touch.

Passcode Options: Change Time-Out, Adjusting Passcode Options

Once you have set your passcode, you will be presented with a few options:

- **Turn Passcode Off**

- **Change Passcode**

- **Require Passcode**
  (Immediately, 1 min., 5 min., 15 min., 1 hour, 4 hours)

- **Simple Passcode** (On = four digits, Off = any letters, numbers, or symbols)

- **Erase Data** (On = Erase all data after 10 incorrect password attempts, Off = Do not erase data)

CAUTION: You may want to set **Erase Data** to **OFF** if you have young children who like to bang away at the security to unlock the keyboard when it comes out of sleep mode. Otherwise, you could end up with your iPod touch being frequently erased.

NOTE: Setting a shorter time for **Require Passcode** is more secure. Setting the time as **Immediately**, the default, is most secure. However, using the setting of 1 minute may save you the headache of retyping your passcode if you accidentally lock your iPod touch.

Setting Restrictions

You might decide you don't want your kids listening to explicit song lyrics on your iPod touch. You might also want to block them from visiting YouTube or any other web site. Setting these restrictions is quite easy on your iPod touch.

Restricting Apps

1. Tap **General** in your **Settings** app.

2. Scroll to down the page and tap **Restrictions.**

3. Tap the **Enable Restrictions** button.

4. You will now be prompted to enter a **Restrictions Passcode**—just pick a four-digit code you'll remember.

NOTE: This restrictions passcode is a separate passcode from your main iPod touch passcode. You can certainly set it to be the same to help you remember it. However, this could be problematic if you let your family know the main passcode, but don't want them adjusting the restrictions. You will need to enter this passcode if you want to turn off restrictions later.

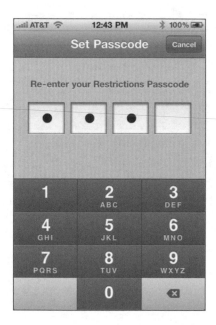

Notice that you can adjust whether to allow certain apps at all: **Safari**, **YouTube**, **iTunes**, **Installing Apps, Camera, FaceTime,** or **Location**.

OFF = RESTRICTED

You might think that **ON** means something is restricted, but it's the opposite. In order to disable or restrict something, you need to touch the slider next to it and change it to **OFF**. If you note the word **Allow** above all the options, it makes sense.

> **NOTE:** For any apps you restrict, their icons will disappear. So if you restrict YouTube, the App Store, and FaceTime, the **YouTube** and **App Store** icons would disappear from the Home screen and the **FaceTime** option would be removed.

Restricting Content

In addition to apps, you can set restrictions for what content can be downloaded and viewed on the iPod touch.   Use this function if you are giving an iPod touch to a child and you don't want him or her to have the ability to download music with explicit lyrics or to watch movies with adult content.

1. Get into the **Restrictions** screen as shown in the previous section.

2. Scroll down to the bottom to see all of the **Allowed Content** settings.

3. To restrict content purchased while inside an app, set **In-App Purchases** to **OFF**. This will include music and videos purchased from the **iTunes** app.

4. Tap **Ratings For** to adjust the ratings based on the country where you live. The set of countries currently supported are: Australia, Austria, Canada, France, Germany, Ireland, Japan, New Zealand, United Kingdom, and the United States.

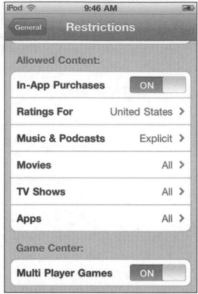

5. Tap **Music & Podcasts** to restrict access to lyrics to non-explicit content. Make sure **Explicit** is set to **OFF** as shown.

6. Tap the **Restrictions** button in the upper left corner to return to the list of options.

7. You can also set the ratings cutoff for **Movies**, **TV Shows,** and **Apps** by tapping each item.

8. When you tap an item such as **Movies**, you see a list of allowed ratings. Tap the highest rating level you want to allow. In this image, we tapped **PG-13.** All movies rated above this (**R** and **NC-17)** are not allowed. The red text and lack of checkmark offer visual clues as to which selections are blocked.

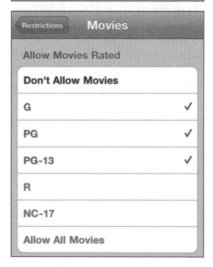

9. Tap **TV Shows** to set those restrictions. Tap the highest rating you want to be allowed. The checkmarks show allowed ratings; the red text is not allowed. In this example, TV-Y, TV-Y7, and TV-G are allowed and higher ratings are not allowed (TV-PG, TV-14, and TV-MA).

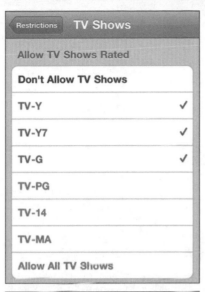

10. Tap **Apps** to set restrictions for apps.

11. In this screen, we are allowing apps with ratings of 4+, 9+, and 12+ to be played. Apps with ratings of 17+ can't be played or downloaded.

12. If you want to disallow playing of **Multi Player Games** in the **Game Center** app, set the switch next to it to **OFF**.

13. Tap the **Restrictions** button in the upper left corner to return to the list of options.

14. Finally, tap the **Home** button to save your settings.

Chapter 8

Multitasking and Voice Control

In this chapter, we describe how to multitask or jump between apps on your iPod touch and control your iPod touch with your voice using the Voice Control feature. Multitasking is a new and very welcome feature on the iPod touch, as it was not available with previous versions. You can leave one app running in the background while you do something else. For example, take a quick break from a game to go and update your status on Facebook or send a tweet on Twitter, then jump back to the game. With Voice Control, you can speak basic commands to control your music. We help you get up and running with this feature as well.

Multitasking or App Switching

With multitasking, also called App Switching, you can leave many of your apps running in the background and switch over to another without stopping the first app.

> **NOTE**: Developers have to implement multitasking on their end, and while more and more multitasking-aware apps and updates are appearing every day, some apps still don't do it or don't do it fully.

Why might you want to use multitasking? Here are a few scenarios when you might want to use multitasking on your iPod touch:

- Copy and paste from one app (**Mail**) to another (**Calendar**).

- Answer a **Skype** call or reply to an **Email** message, and then jump back into the game you were playing without missing a beat.

- Continue listening to Internet radio (such as **Pandora** or **Slacker**) while playing your favorite game or browsing the Web.

- You no longer have to wait for photos to upload to **Facebook** or **Flikr**—they can be running in the background while you go and do other things on your iPod touch.

- You use **Skype** to call people—now you can leave it running in the background to receive incoming calls; this was not possible before.

How to Jump Between Apps

In order to multitask, you need to bring up the **App Switcher** bar at the bottom of the screen.

1. From any app or even the **Home** screen, double-click the **Home** button to bring up the **App Switcher** at the bottom of your screen (see Figure 8–1).

2. All open apps will be shown on the **App Switcher** bar.

3. Swipe right or left to find the app you want and tap it.

4. If you don't see the app you want on the **App Switcher** bar, then press the **Home** button and start it from the **Home** screen.

5. Double-click the **Home** button again and tap the app you just left to jump back to it.

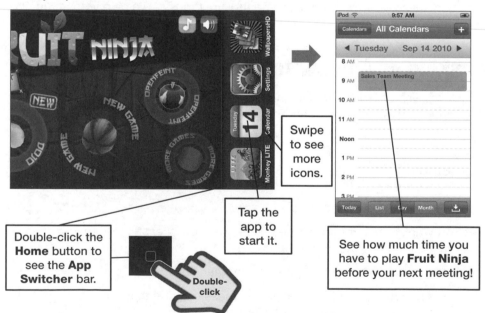

Figure 8–1. *Double-clicking the Home button to bring up the* App Switcher bar *to multitask*

How to Close Apps from the App Switcher

If you exit out of an app using a single click of the **Home** button, that app will stay running in the background, unless it is an active VOIP call, a location/navigation app or some sort of upload. There are times when you want to completely close an app. Sometimes, you may find your iPod touch running a little slower than you might like—it could be time to close apps completely and free up memory.

> **NOTE**: What this does is kill running apps or flush the saved state so the app has to restart the next time you tap it. Built in apps like Mail will restart automatically so you can't miss any emails.

1. Double-click the **Home** button to bring up the **App Switcher** bar.

2. Press and hold any icon in the **App Switcher** bar until they all shake. You will notice that a **red circle** with a minus sign appears in the upper left corner of each icon.

3. Tap the **red circle** 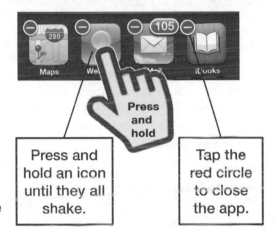 to completely close the app.

4. Keep tapping the red circles to close as many apps as you want.

Press and hold an icon until they all shake.

Tap the red circle to close the app.

Press and hold

iPod Controls and Screen Portrait Orientation Lock

The other thing you can do on the **App Switcher** bar if you swipe from left to right is to see the iPod controls and the screen **Portrait Orientation Lock** icon.

1. From any app or even the **Home** screen, double-tap the **Home** button to bring up the **App Switcher** at the bottom of your screen.

2. Swipe left to right to see the iPod controls and **Portrait Orientation Lock** icon.

3. Tap the **Portrait Orientation Lock** icon to lock the screen in a portrait or vertical orientation, even if you turn the iPod touch on its side. You know it is locked when you see a lock inside the button and a lock in the top status bar.

4. You can also use the **previous track**, **play/pause**, and **next track** buttons in the middle. If you hold down **previous** or **next**, they become **rewind** or **fast forward**.

5. Or, tap the **Music** icon to jump to the iPod.

Voice Control is another feature besides multitasking that makes use of the **Home** button. Voice Control allows you to command some of the features by simply speaking to your iPod touch.

Voice Control

With Voice Control on your iPod touch, you can do a number of things with your iPOd touch, such as play music and even ask your iPod touch the time.

1. Press and hold the **Home** button

    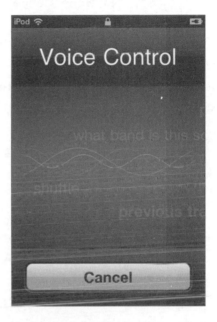 for about two seconds to start **Voice Control**.

2. Speak your command. We show you the various commands you can speak in the next sections.

3. After you speak your command, the iPod touch will repeat it briefly and execute the command it thought it heard you say.

> **TIP: Voice Control** for your music works if your iPod touch is locked—give it a try!

> **TIP**: If you are using your headset microphone for Voice Control, just let the microphone dangle from your ear normally—don't pick it up and hold it closer to your mouth. Holding the microphone too close will distort your voice and Voice Control will not understand you correctly.

List of Voice Commands

There are a number of commands you can use with your iPod touch to control music, tell you the time, and more.

> **TIP**: If you have your iPod touch inside a protective case and you are having trouble with Voice Control, make sure your case is not interfering with the microphone on the iPod touch. Try removing the case and using Voice Control; see if the iPod touch without the case works better than with it.

General Commands

There are a few general commands you can use on your iPod touch.

Say: "**What time is it?**" to hear the current time.

Say: "**No**, **Nope**, **Cancel**, or **Stop**" or tap the **Cancel** button to exit Voice Command.

Say: "**Help**" to get help about how to use Voice Command.

Music and Video Commands

Most of the Voice Commands allow you to control your music and videos on your iPod touch.

Say: "**Pause** or **Play**" to pause or play the currently playing song or video.

Say: "**Play songs by U2**" to play all songs by the band U2.

Say: "**Play artist Enya**" to play songs by Enya.

> **TIP:** If a song or artist has the word "the" in the name, be sure to include it when you say the complete name of the song or artist, including the word "the."

Say: "**Next song**" or "**Next track**" to play the next song.

Say: "**Previous song**" or "**Previous track**" to play the next song.

Say: "**Shuffle**" to turn on shuffle.

Say: "**Genius**" or "**Play more like this**" to turn on the Genius feature and play similar songs.

Say: "**What group plays this song?**" to hear the currently playing artist.

Say: "**Play** (name of album)" to play the entire album.

Say: "**Play** (name of playlist)" to play the playlist.

Changing the Language for Voice Control

You can change the language for **Voice Control** in your **Settings** app.

1. Tap the **Settings** icon.

2. Tap **General.**

3. Scroll down and tap **International**.

4. Tap **Voice Control**.

5. On the next screen, you will see a list of languages. Tap any language to select it. You know a language is selected because it has a check mark next to it. **English (United Kingdom)** is shown as selected.

6. Tap the **International** button in the upper left corner to return to your settings.

Chapter 9

Playing Music

This chapter shows you how to turn your iPod touch into a terrific music player. Since the iPod touch comes from Apple—which popularized electronic music players—you'd expect it to have some great capabilities, and it does. We'll show you how to play and organize the music you buy from iTunes or sync from your computer, how to view playlists in a variety of ways, and how to quickly find songs. You'll learn how to use the Genius feature to have the iPod touch locate and group similar songs in your library—sort of like a radio station that plays only music you like.

> **TIP:** Learn how to buy music right on your iPod touch in Chapter 19: "iTunes on Your iPod touch." And take a look the "iTunes Guide" in Part 4 to find out how to buy music using iTunes on your computer or load your music CDs onto iTunes so you can sync them with your iPod touch.

And you'll learn how to stream music using an app called Pandora. With Pandora, you can select from a number of Internet radio stations, or create your own by typing in your favorite artist's name—and it's all free.

Your iPod touch as a Music Player

Your iPod touch is probably one of the best music players on the market today. The touch screen makes it easy to interact with and manage your music, playlists, cover art, and the organization of your music library. You can even connect your iPod touch to your home or car stereo via Bluetooth, so you can listen to beautiful stereo sound from your iPod touch!

> **TIP:** Check out Chapter 24: "Bluetooth on your iPod touch" to learn how to hook up your iPod touch to your Bluetooth stereo speakers or car stereo.

Whether you use the built-in iPod **Music** app or an Internet radio app like **Pandora**, you'll find you have unprecedented control over your music on the iPod touch.

The Music App

Most music is handled through the **Music** app—the icon is on the **Home** screen, usually in the bottom dock of icons, the first one on the left.

Touch the **Music** icon and, as Figure 9–1 shows, you'll see five soft keys across the bottom:

- **Playlists** lets you see synced playlists from your computer plus playlists created on the iPod touch.

- **Artists** lets you see an alphabetical list of artists, which is searchable like your Address Book.

- **Songs** lets you see an alphabetical list of songs (also searchable).

- **Videos** lets you see a list of videos (also searchable).

- **More** lets you see audiobooks, compilations, composers, genres, iTunes U, and podcasts.

Editing the Soft Keys

One very cool feature on the iPod touch is that you can edit the soft keys at the bottom of the **iPod** app and really customize it to fit your needs and tastes. To do so, first touch the **More** button.

Then touch the **Edit** button at the top left of the screen.

The screen changes to show the various icons that can be dragged down to the bottom dock.

Figure 9–1. *iPod soft keys.*

Let's say you want to replace the **Videos** icon with the one for **Albums**. Just touch and hold the **Albums** icon and drag it to where the **Videos** icon is on the bottom dock (see Figure 9–2). When you get there, release the icon and the **Albums** icon will now reside where the **Videos** icon used to be. You can do this with any of the icons on this **Configure** screen. When you are finished, touch the **Done** button at the top right of the screen.

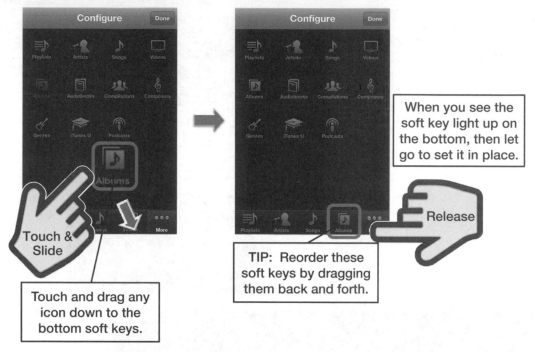

When you see the soft key light up on the bottom, then let go to set it in place.

Release

TIP: Reorder these soft keys by dragging them back and forth.

Touch & Slide

Touch and drag any icon down to the bottom soft keys.

Figure 9–2. *Change the soft keys in the* **Music** *app.*

TIP: You can also reorder the icons across the bottom by dragging and dropping them back and forth along the soft key row.

Playlists View

NOTE: A playlist is a list of songs you create. It can include any genre, artist, year of recording, or collection of songs that interest you.

Add a new playlist here.

Your playlists are listed here.

Many people group together music of a particular genre, like classical or rock. Others may create playlists with fast beat music and call it workout or running music. You can use playlists to organize your music any way you choose.

You can create playlists in iTunes on your computer and then sync to your iPod touch (see the iTunes Guide), or you can create a playlist right on your iPod touch (described in the next section).

Once you've synced a playlist to your iPod touch or created one on your iPod touch, it shows up under **Playlists**.

If you have several playlists listed along the left side, just touch the name of the one you want to listen to.

NOTE: You can edit the contents of some of your playlists on your iPod touch. However, you can't edit **Genius Playlists** on the iPod touch itself.

Creating Playlists on the iPod touch

The iPod touch lets you create unique playlists that can be edited and synced with your computer. Let's say you want to add a new selection of music to your iPod touch playlist. Just create the playlist as we show below and add songs. You can change the playlist whenever you want, removing old songs and adding new ones—it couldn't be easier!

To create a new playlist on the iPod touch, touch the **Add Playlist** tab under **Genius Playlist**.

Give your playlist a unique name (we'll call this one "Bike-riding music"), then touch **Save**.

Now you'll see the **Songs** screen. Touch the name of any song you want to add to the new playlist.

You know a song is selected and will be added to the playlist when it turns gray.

> **NOTE:** Don't get frustrated trying to remove or deselect a song you tapped by mistake. You can't remove or deselect songs on this screen. Instead, you have to click **Done**, then remove them on the next screen.

Select **Done** at the top right and the playlist contents will be displayed.

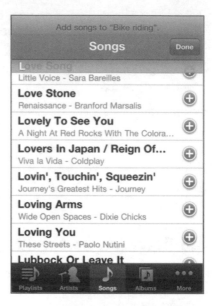

If you tapped a song by mistake or change your mind, after you click **Done** you can remove songs on the next screen.

To delete a song:

1. Touch the **Edit** button at the top (it will disappear once it is touched).

2. Tap the red circle next to the song name.

3. Tap the **Delete** button to the right of the song.

4. Touch the **Done** button.

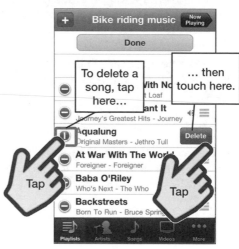

To move a song up or down in a playlist:

1. Touch the **Edit** button as you did above.

2. Touch and hold the three gray bars to the right of the song.

3. Drag the song up or down and then let go.

4. When you're all finished, just touch the **Done** button and your playlist will be set.

To move a song, touch here and drag up or down.

To change the playlist later, touch the **Edit** button and follow the steps above.

Searching for Music

Almost every view from your **Music** app (**Playlists**, **Artists**, **Songs**, etc.) has a search window at the top of the screen, as shown in Figure 9–3. Tap once in the search window and type a few letters of the name of an artist, album, playlist, video, or song to instantly see a list of all matching items. This is the best way to quickly find something to listen to or watch on your iPod touch.

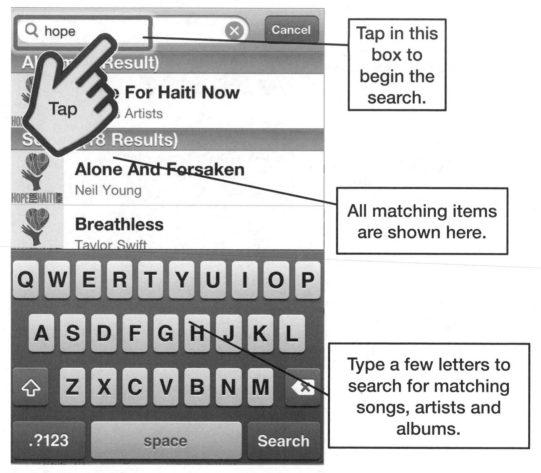

Figure 9–3. *Finding music.*

Changing the View in the Music App

The **Music** app is very flexible when it comes to ways of displaying and categorizing your music. Sometimes you want to look at your songs listed by the artist. Other times you might prefer seeing your library organized by album name. The iPod touch lets you easily change the view to help manage and play just the music you want at a given moment.

Artists View

The **Artists** view lists all the artists on your iPod touch, or, if you are in a playlist, it lists the artists in that playlist.

Flick through the list to move to the first letter of the artist's name.

When you find the artist's name, touch it and all the songs and albums by that artist will be listed, with a picture of the album art to the left.

> **TIP:** Use the same navigation and search features as you do with the **Contacts** app (the address book).

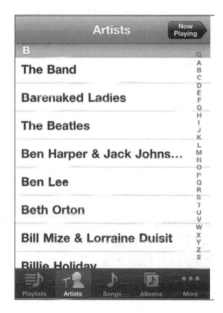

Songs View

Touching the **Songs** button displays a list of every song on your iPod touch.

If you know the name of the song, flick through the list or touch the first letter of the song in the alphabetical list to the right.

Albums View

The music on your iPod touch is also organized by albums, which you'll see when you touch the **Albums** icon.

Again, you can scroll through the album covers or touch the first letter of the album name in the alphabetical list and then make your selection.

When you choose an album, all the songs on that album will be listed.

To go back, just touch the **More** button in the upper left corner.

Genres

The **Genres** tab arranges your music into music types. This can be an easier approach to finding music, as well as a way to have more of a "themed" listening experience.

Thus, if you want to hear a rock or jazz mix, you can select those particular genres and start playing some or all of the songs.

> **NOTE**: The **Genres** tab is usually available in the **More** section, as you can see in Figure 9–1.

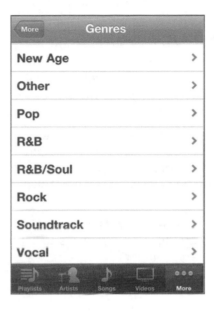

In this image, we touched **Rock**, and the iPod touch shows the list of albums and songs we have in this genre.

Composers

 Composers

As with the other views, touching the **Composers** icon (in the **More** section) lists your music in a specific way.

Suppose you forget the title of the song but you know the composer. Browsing by **Composers** on your iPod touch can help you find just what you are looking for.

Similar to other views, **Composers** shows you how many albums and songs are by each composer.

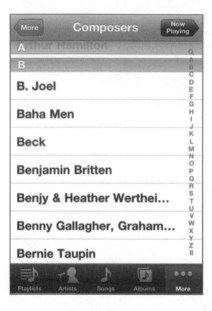

Viewing Songs in an Album

When you're in **Albums** view, just touch an album cover or name and the screen will slide, showing you the songs on that album (see Figure 9–4).

> **TIP**: When you start playing an album, the album cover may expand to fill the screen. Tap the screen once to bring up (or hide) the controls at the top and bottom. You can use these controls to manage the song and screen (described below).

To see the songs on an album that is playing, tap the **List** button. The album cover will turn over, revealing all the songs on that album. The song that is playing will have a small blue arrow next to it.

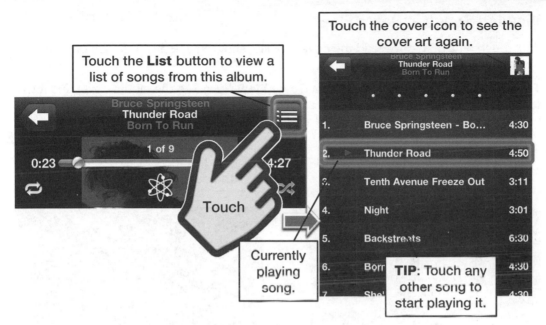

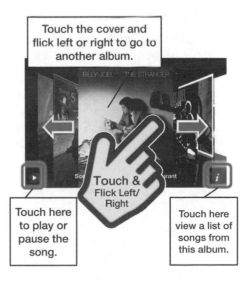

Figure 9-4. *Touch the **List** button to see the songs on a particular album.*

Tap the title bar above the list of songs to return to the album cover view.

Navigating with Cover Flow

Cover Flow is a proprietary and very cool way of looking at your music by album covers. If you're playing a song in the **Music** app and turn your iPod touch horizontal—into landscape mode— your iPod touch will automatically change to **Cover Flow** view.

Viewing Songs in Cover Flow

Just touch an album cover and the cover will flip, showing you all the songs on that album.

To see the song that is playing now (in **Cover Flow** view), tap the album cover and it will turn over, revealing the songs on that album (Figure 9–5). The song that is currently playing will have a small blue arrow next to it.

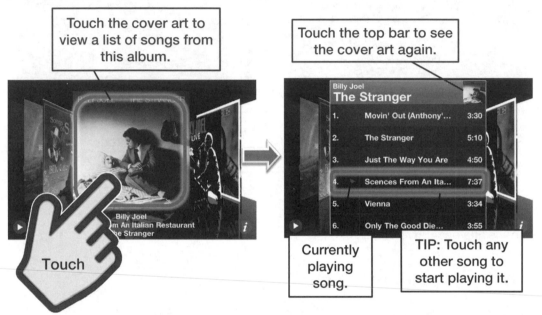

Figure 9–5. *You can look at an album's contents using **Cover Flow**.*

Tap the title bar (above the list of songs) and the album cover will be displayed once more. You can then keep swiping through your music until you find what you are searching for.

> **NOTE**: You can also touch the small "*i*" in the lower right corner and the album cover will flip to show all the songs—just as if you touched the cover.

Playing Your Music

Now that you know how to find your music, it's time to play it! Find a song or browse to a playlist using any of the methods mentioned above. Simply tap the song name and it will begin to play.

This screen shows the name of song at the top, plus a picture of the album cover.

Along the bottom of the screen you'll find the **Volume** slider bar, and the **Previous Song**, **Play/Pause**, and **Next Song** buttons.

To see other songs on the album, just double-tap the album cover and the screen will flip, showing all of the other songs.

You can also touch the **List** button in the upper right corner to view a list of songs on the album.

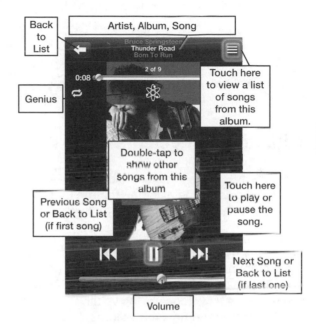

Pausing and Playing

Tap the pause symbol (if a song is playing) or the play arrow (if the music is paused) to stop or resume the song.

To Play the Previous or Next Song

If you are in a playlist, touching the **Next Song** arrow (to the right of the **Play/Pause** button) advances you to the next song in the list. If you are searching through your music by album, touching **Next Song** moves you to the next song on the album. Touching the **Previous Song** button does the reverse.

> **NOTE:** If you're at the beginning of a song, **Previous Song** takes you to the preceding song. If the song is already playing, **Previous Song** goes to the beginning of the current song (and a second tap would take you to the previous song).

Adjusting the Volume

There are two ways to adjust the volume on your iPod touch: using the external **Volume** buttons or using the **Volume Slider** control on the screen.

The external **Volume** buttons are on the upper left side of the device. Press the **Volume Up** key (the top button) or the **Volume Down** key to raise or lower the volume. You'll see the **Volume Slider** control move as you adjust the volume. You can also just touch and hold the **Volume Slider** key to adjust the volume.

> **TIP:** To quickly mute the sound, press and hold the **Volume Down** key and the volume eventually reduces to zero.

Volume Slider

Double-Click the Home Button for iPod Controls

You can play your music while you are doing other things on your iPod touch, like reading and responding to e-mail, browsing the Web, or playing a game. With the iPod touch's new multitasking function, a quick double-tap to the **Home** button on the bottom, followed by a swipe to the right, will bring up the "now playing" **Music** controls in the multitasking window, as shown in Figure 9–6.

NOTE: The widgets show whatever app last played music, so if Pandora was last, you'll see that instead of **Music**—and the widgets will control Pandora instead.

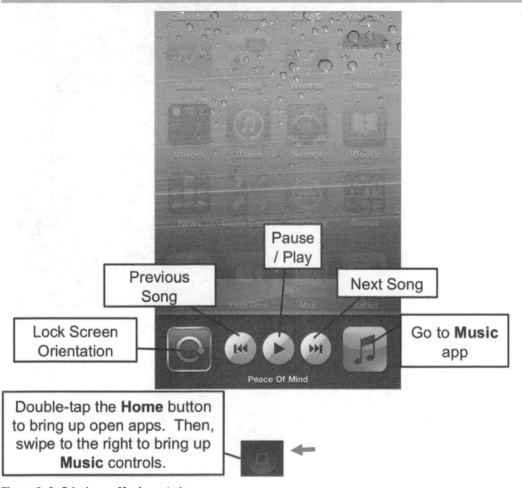

Figure 9–6. *Bringing up **Music** controls.*

TIP: If you hold down the **Previous Song** control, the song will rewind; if you hold down the **Next Song** control, it will fast forward.

Repeating, Shuffling, Moving around in a Song

In play mode, you can activate additional controls by tapping the screen anywhere on the album cover. You'll then see an additional slider (the scrubber bar) at the top, along with the symbols for **Repeat**, **Shuffle,** and **Genius**.

Moving to Another Part of a Song

Slide the scrubber bar to the right and you'll see the elapsed time of the song (displayed to the far right) change accordingly. If you are looking for a specific section of the song, drag the slider, then let go and listen to see if you're in the right place.

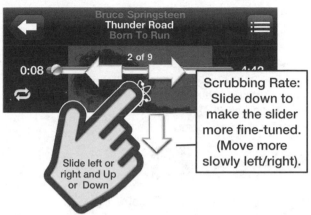

Repeat One Song or All Songs

To repeat the song you're listening to, touch the **Repeat** symbol at the left of the top controls twice until you see it turn blue and display a 1.

To repeat all songs in the playlist, song list, or album, touch the **Repeat** icon until it turns blue (and does not display a 1).

To turn off the **Repeat** feature, press the icon until it turns white again.

Shuffle

If you are listening to a playlist or album or any other category or list of music, you might decide you don't want to listen to the songs in order. You can touch the **Shuffle** symbol so the music will play in random order. You know **Shuffle** is turned on when the icon is blue; when it's white, **Shuffle** is off.

Shake to Shuffle

The **Shake to Shuffle** feature was introduced in the last iPod touch. So, if you've turned on **Shake to Shuffle** mode, all you have to do to change songs is simply give your iPod touch a shake, then shake it again. Every time you shake your iPod touch, you'll skip to the next randomly selected song in the list.

> **TIP**: If you plan on dancing to your tunes while holding your iPod touch, turn off **Shake to Shuffle**!

You can turn on **Shake to Shuffle** in your **Settings** menu.

1. Tap the **Settings** icon.

2. Scroll down and touch the **Music** icon.

3. Move the **Shake to Shuffle** switch to **ON** or **OFF**.

Genius

Apple has a new feature for iTunes called **Genius**. If the **Genius** feature is activated in iTunes, it will show up on your iPod touch with the symbol you see here.

> **NOTE:** You must enable **Genius Playlists** using iTunes on your computer. Check out Chapter 29; "Your iTunes User Guide" to learn how.

Genius Playlist: Tap here to create a new playlist based on this song.

What the **Genius** feature does is create a playlist by finding songs similar to the one you're listening to. Unlike a random "shuffle" of music, **Genius** scours your music library and then creates a new playlist of 25, 50, or 100 songs (you set the **Genius** features in iTunes on your computer).

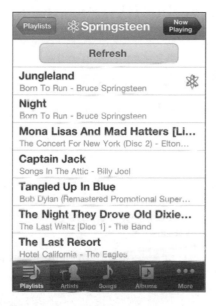

> **TIP**: If you get tired of your **Genius Playlist**, just touch **Refresh** and the list will reset with new songs.

Genius is a great way to mix up your music and keep it fresh—playing the type of music you like but also finding some buried songs that may not be part of your established playlists.

> **TIP:** To create permanent **Genius Playlists**, just create them in iTunes on your computer and sync them to your iPod touch. The **Genius Playlists** you sync from iTunes can't be edited or changed on the iPod touch itself, but you can save, refresh, or delete any **Genius Playlists** created on the iPod touch.

Now Playing

Sometimes you're having so much fun exploring your options for playlists or albums that you get deeply buried in a menu—then find yourself just wanting to get back to the song you're listening to. Fortunately, this is always very easy to do—you can just touch the **Now Playing** icon at the top right of most of the music screens.

Viewing Other Songs on the Album

You may decide you want to listen to another song from the same album rather than going to the next song in the playlist or genre list.

In the upper-right corner of the **Now Playing** screen, you'll see a small button with three lines on it.

Tap that button and the view switches to a small image of the album cover. The screen now displays all the songs on that album.

Touch another song on the list and that song will begin to play.

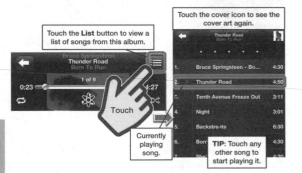

Touch the **List** button to view a list of songs from this album.

Touch the cover icon to see the cover art again.

Currently playing song.

TIP: Touch any other song to start playing it.

> **NOTE:** If you were in the middle of a playlist or a **Genius Playlist** and you jump to another song from an album, you won't be taken back to that playlist. To return to that playlist, you'll need to either go back to your playlist library or tap **Genius** to make a new **Genius Playlist**.

Adjusting Music Settings

There are several settings you can adjust to tweak music-playing on your iPod touch. You'll find these in the **Settings** menu. Just touch the **Settings** icon on your **Home** screen.

In the middle of the **Settings** screen, touch the **iPod** tab to go to the settings screen for **Music**. You'll find five settings you can adjust on this screen: **Shake to Shuffle**, **Sound Check**, **EQ**, **Volume Limit**, and **Lyrics & Podcast Info**.

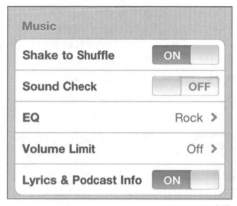

Using Sound Check (Auto Volume Adjust)

Because songs are recorded at different volumes, sometimes a particular song may sound quite loud compared to another. **Sound Check** can eliminate this. If **Sound Check** is set to **ON**, all your songs will play at roughly the same volume.

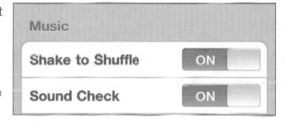

EQ (Sound Equalizer Setting)

Sound equalization is very personal and subjective. Some people like to hear more bass in their music, some like more treble, and some like more of an exaggerated mid-range. Whatever your music tastes, there is an **EQ** setting for you.

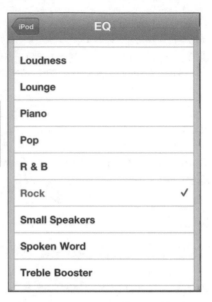

> **NOTE:** Using the **EQ** setting can diminish battery capacity somewhat.

Just touch the **EQ** tab and then select either the type of music you most often listen to or a specific option to boost treble or bass. Experiment, have fun, and find the setting that's perfect for you.

Volume Limit (Safely Listen to Music at a Reasonable Level)

This is a great way for parents to control the volume on their kids' iPod touch. It is also a good way to make sure you don't damage your hearing by listening too loudly through headphones. You just move the slider to a volume limit and then lock that limit.

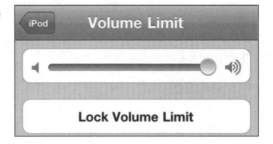

To lock the volume limit, touch the **Lock Volume Limit** button and enter a 4-digit passcode. You will be prompted to enter your passcode once more and the volume limit will then be locked.

Showing Music Controls When Your iPod touch is Locked

You may want to get to your music controls even if your iPod touch is locked. Here's how: Just double-click the **Home** button and the controls for adjusting the music show up on the top of the locked screen. There's no reason to unlock the screen and then go to the Music program to find the controls.

In the image to the right, notice that the screen is still locked—yet the music controls are now visible along the top. You can pause, skip, go to a previous song, or adjust the volume without actually unlocking the iPod touch.

> **NOTE**: You'll only see these controls if there is music playing.

Listening to Free Internet Radio (Pandora)

While your iPod touch gives you unprecedented control over your personal music library, there may be times when you want to listen to some other music.

> **TIP:** A basic **Pandora** account is free. It can save you considerable money compared with buying many new songs from iTunes.

Pandora grew out of the Music Genome Project, a huge undertaking in which a large team of musical analysts looked at just about every song ever recorded and then developed a complex algorithm of attributes to associate with each song.

NOTE: Pandora may have some competition by the time you read this book. Right now there's one other competitor called **Slacker Personal Radio**, but there will probably be more. If you want to find more options, try searching the App Store for "iPod touch Internet Radio." Please also note that Pandora is a US-only application and Slacker is available only in the US and Canada. Spotfly is a similar app for Europe. Hopefully, more options will begin to pop up for international users.

Getting Started with Pandora

With Pandora you can design your own unique radio stations built around artists you enjoy. Best of all, it is completely free!

Start by downloading the Pandora app from the App Store. Just go to the App Store and search for Pandora.

Now just touch the **Pandora** icon to start.

The first time you start Pandora, you'll be asked to either create an account or to sign in if you already have an account. Just fill in the appropriate information—an email address and a password are required—and you can start designing your own music listening experience.

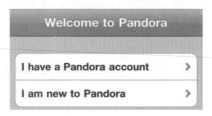

Pandora is also available for your Windows or Mac computer and for most smartphone platforms. If you already have a Pandora account, all you have to do is sign in.

TIP: Remember that you can move apps into folders in iOS4. As you can see in Figure 9–7, we've put three Music apps, including Pandora, into one folder named Music. See more about using folders in Chapter 6: "Organize Icons and Folders."

Figure 9–7. *Put all Music apps, such as Pandora, into one folder for easy retrieval.*

Pandora's Main Screen

Your stations are listed along the left-hand side. Just touch one and it will begin to play. Usually, the first song will be from the actual artist chosen and the next songs will be from similar artists.

Once you select a station, the music begins to play. You'll see the current song displayed, along with album art—very much like when you play a song using the **iPod** app.

You'll also see a small **Now Playing** icon in the upper right corner—very much like the **Now Playing** icon in the iPod music app.

Touch the **Information** icon, just like the one you find in the **Music** app, and you'll see a nice bio of the artist, which changes with each new song.

Thumbs Up or Thumbs Down in Pandora

If you like a particular song, touch the thumbs-up icon and you'll hear more from that artist.

Conversely, if you don't like an artist on this station, touch the thumbs-down icon and you won't hear that artist again.

If you like, you can pause a song and come back later to it, or skip to the next selection in your station.

NOTE: With a free Pandora account, you are limited to a certain amount of skips per hour. Also, you'll occasionally hear advertising. To get rid of these annoyances, you can upgrade to a paid "Pandora One" account.

Pandora's Menu

Between the two thumbs is a **Menu** button. Touch this and you can bookmark the artist or song, go to iTunes to buy music from this artist, or email the station to someone in your **Contacts**.

Creating a New Station in Pandora

Creating a new station couldn't be easier.

Just touch the **New Station** button along the bottom row. Type in the name of an artist, song, or composer.

When you find what you are looking for, touch the selection and Pandora will immediately start to build a station around your choice.

You can also touch **Genre** and build a station around a particular genre of music.

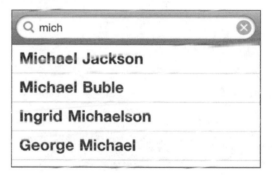

You'll then see the new station listed with your other stations.

You can build up to 100 stations in Pandora.

> **TIP:** You can organize your stations by pressing the **By Date** or **ABC** buttons at the top of the screen.

Adjusting Pandora's Settings—Your Account, Upgrading, and More

You can sign out of your Pandora account, adjust the audio quality, and even upgrade to Pandora One (which removes advertising) by tapping the settings icon in the lower right corner of the screen (see Figure 9–8.)

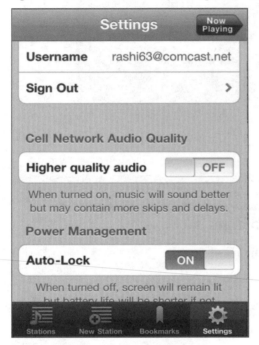

Figure 9–8. *Settings options in Pandora.*

To sign out, tap your account name.

To adjust the sound quality, move the switch under **Cell Network Audio Quality** either **ON** or **OFF**. When you are on a cellular network, setting this to off is probably better, otherwise you may hear more skips and pauses in the playback.

When you are on a strong Wi-Fi connection, you can set this to **ON** for better quality. See Chapter 5: "Wi-Fi Connectivity" to learn more about the various connections.

To save your battery life, you should set the **Auto-Lock** to **ON**, which is the default. If you want the force the screen to stay lit, then switch this to **OFF**.

To remove all advertising, tap the **Upgrade to Pandora One** button. A web browser window will open and you'll be taken to Pandora's web site to enter your credit card information. As of publishing time, the annual account cost is $36.00, but that may be different by the time you read this book.

Chapter 10

Viewing Videos, TV Shows, and More

The iPod touch is an amazing "media consumption" device. Nowhere is this more apparent than in the various video-viewing applications available.

This chapter shows you how to watch movies, TV shows, podcasts, and music videos on your iPod touch. You can buy or download many videos for free from the iTunes store or iTunes University. Now, you can also link your iPod touch to your Netflix account (other video rental services will likely follow soon), allowing you to watch streaming TV shows and movies.

With your iPod touch, you can also watch YouTube videos and videos from the Web on your Safari browser and through various apps such as the **Hulu Plus** app from the App store.

NOTE: As of publishing, Hulu Plus is a U.S.-only app. Netflix is available in the US and Canada. We hope similar apps will make their way to the international market.

Your iPod touch as a Video Player

The iPod touch is not only a capable music player; it is a fantastic portable video playing system. The wide screen, fast processor, incredible pixel density, and great operating system make watching anything from music videos to TV shows and full-length motion pictures a real joy. The size of the iPod touch is perfect for sitting back in a chair or watching on an airplane. It is also great for the kids in the back seat of long car trips. The near ten-hour battery life means you can even go on a coast-to-coast flight and not run out of power! However, if you need more power, you can buy a power inverter for your car to keep the iPod touch charged even longer (see the "Charging Your iPod touch and Battery Tips" section in Chapter 1).

Loading Videos onto Your iPod touch

You can load videos on to your iPod touch just as you did with your music—through iTunes from your computer or right from the iTunes app on your iPod touch.

If you purchase or rent videos and TV shows from iTunes on your computer, then you can manually or automatically sync them to your iPod touch.

Watching Videos on the iPod touch

To watch videos, touch the **Videos** icon, which is usually on the first or second **Home** screen of the iPod touch.

> **NOTE:** You can also watch videos from the **YouTube** icon, the **Safari** icon, and other video-related apps you load from the App store.

Video Categories

Each section of the **Videos** screen is under the **Video** tab in the **iPod** app, separated by horizontal bars: **Movies, TV Shows**, **Podcasts**, and **Music Videos**.

The first category is the **Movies** section, so if you have movies loaded on the iPod touch, they will be visible.

You may see more or fewer categories depending on the types of videos you have loaded on your iPod touch. If you have only **Movies** and **iTunes U** videos, then you would see only those two category buttons. Just touch any of the other categories to show the corresponding videos in each category.

Playing a Movie

Just touch the movie you wish to watch and it will begin to play (see Figure 10–1). Most videos take advantage of the relatively large screen real estate of the iPod touch to play in widescreen or landscape mode. Just turn your iPod touch sideways to watch them.

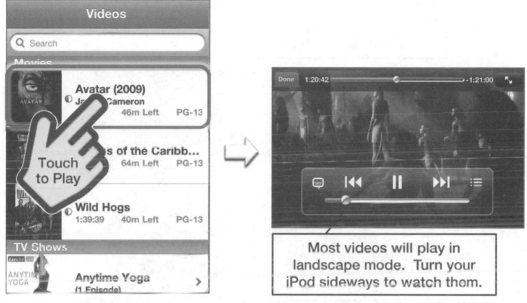

Figure 10–1. *Playing a video.*

When the video first starts, there are no menus and no controls. There is nothing on the screen except for the video.

To Pause or Access Controls

Touch anywhere on the screen and the control bars and options will become visible (see Figure 10–2). Most are very similar to those in the Music player. Tap the **Pause** button and the video will pause.

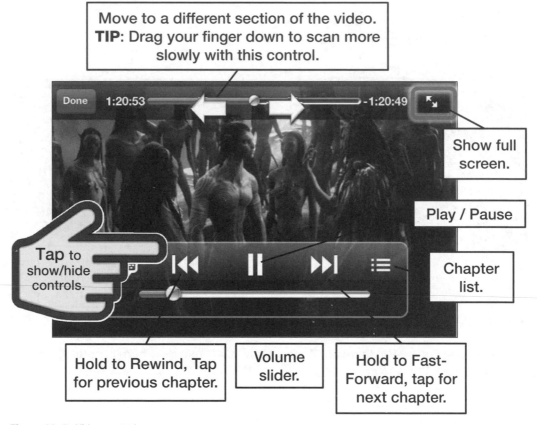

Move to a different section of the video.
TIP: Drag your finger down to scan more slowly with this control.

Show full screen.

Play / Pause

Tap to show/hide controls.

Chapter list.

Hold to Rewind, Tap for previous chapter.

Volume slider.

Hold to Fast-Forward, tap for next chapter.

Figure 10–2. *Video controls.*

Fast-Forward or Rewind the Video

On either side of the **Play/Pause** button are the typical **Fast-Forward** and **Rewind** buttons. To jump to the next chapter-specific part of the video, just touch and hold the **Fast-Forward** button (to the right of **Play/Pause**). When you get to the desired spot, release the button and the video will begin playing normally.

To rewind to the beginning on the video, tap the **Rewind** button. To rewind to a specific part or location, touch and hold like you did while you were fast-forwarding the video.

NOTE: If this is a full-length movie with several chapters, tapping either **Reverse** or **Fast-Forward** will move either back or ahead one chapter.

Using the Time Slider Bar

At the top of the video screen is a slider that shows you the elapsed time of the video. If you know exactly (or approximately) which point in the video you wish to watch, just hold and drag the slide to that location. Some people find this to be a little more exact than holding down the **Fast-Forward** or **Rewind** Buttons.

TIP: Drag your finger down to move the slide more slowly. In other words, start by touching the slider control, then drag your finger down the screen—notice that the further down the screen your finger is, the slower the slider moves left or right. The screen may say "Scrubbing"—which is to lower the sensitivity of how fast the slider moves.

Changing the Size of the Video (Widescreen vs. Full Screen)

Most of your videos will play in widescreen format. However, if you have a video that was not converted for your iPod touch or is not optimized for the screen resolution, you can touch the expand button, which is to the right of the upper Status bar.

You will notice that there are two arrows. If you are in full-screen mode, the arrows are pointing in toward each other. If you are in widescreen mode, the arrows are pointing outward.

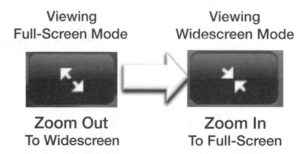

Viewing Full-Screen Mode   Viewing Widescreen Mode

Zoom Out To Widescreen   Zoom In To Full-Screen

In a widescreen movie that is not taking up the full screen of the iPod touch, touching this button will zoom in a bit. Touching it again will zoom out.

NOTE: You can also simply double-tap the screen to zoom in and fill the screen as well. Be aware that, just like on your widescreen TV, when you try to force a non-widescreen video into widescreen mode, sometimes you will lose part of the picture.

Using the Chapters Feature

Most full-length movies purchased from the iTunes store, and some that are converted for the iPod touch, will give you a Chapters feature—very much like if you were watching a DVD on your home TV.

Just bring up the controls for the video by tapping the screen, and then select **Chapters**.

This will bring you back to the main page for the movie.

Touch the **Chapters** button in the upper right corner, and then scroll through to and touch the chapter you wish to watch.

Viewing the Chapters

You can scroll through or flick through quickly to locate the scene or chapter that you wish to watch.

You will also notice that to the far right of each chapter is the exact time (relative to the start of the movie) that the chapter begins.

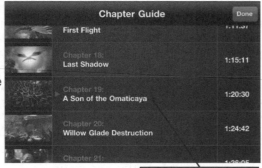

Touch any chapter to jump there.

In addition to the chapter menu mentioned previously, you can also quickly advance to the previous or next chapter in a movie by tapping the **Rewind** or **Fast-Forward** buttons. One tap moves you one chapter in either direction.

NOTE: The Chapters feature usually works only with movies that are purchased from the iTunes store. Movies that are converted and loaded on usually will not have chapters.

Watching a TV Show

The iPod touch is great for watching your favorite TV shows. You can purchase TV shows from the iTunes store, and you can download sample shows from some iPod touch apps, such as the **Hulu Plus** app.

Just scroll down to the **TV Shows** category separator to see the shows you have downloaded on your iPod touch. Scroll through your available shows and touch **Play**. The video controls are the same as those you use when when watching a movie.

Watching Podcasts

We think of podcasts as being audio-only broadcasts that you can download using iTunes. Video podcasts are now quite prevalent and can be found on any number of sites, including many public broadcasting web sites and on iTunes U, a listing of university podcasts and information found within iTunes.

iTunes U Story from Gary Mazo:

> "Recently, I was browsing the **iTunes U** section inside the **iTunes** app on the iPod touch with my son, who was just accepted to CalTech. We were wondering about the housing situation and, lo and behold, we found a video podcast showing a tour of the CalTech dorms. We downloaded it and the podcast went right into the **podcast** directory for future viewing. We were able to do a complete virtual tour of the housing without flying out there from the East Coast."

Watching Music Videos

Music videos are available for your iPod touch from a number of sources. Often, a deluxe album purchased from iTunes will include a music video or two. You can also purchase music videos from the iTunes store. Furthermore, many record companies and recording artists make music videos available for free on their web sites.

Music videos automatically get sorted into the **Music Videos** section of your **Videos** app.

The **Music Videos** are usually right under **TV Shows** in the **Videos** list. The controls work just as they do in all other video applications.

Video Options

As in your music player, there are a few options that you can adjust for the video player. These options are accessed through the **Settings** icon from your **Home** screen.

Touch the **Settings** icon and then scroll down to touch **Videos** and then to the **Video** options.

Start Playing Option

Sometimes you need to stop watching a particular video. This option lets you decide what to do the next time you want to watch—you can either watch the video from the beginning or from where you left off. Just select the option that you desire and that will be the action from now on.

Closed Captioned

If your video has closed captioned capabilities, when this switch is turned to **ON**, closed captioning will be shown on your screen.

TV-Out: Widescreen

There are many third-party gadgets out there that allow you to watch the video from your iPod touch on some external source, either a TV or computer screen, or even an array of video glasses that simulate watching on a very large screen monitor. Most of these require that your TV widescreen setting be set to **ON**. By default, it is set to **OFF**.

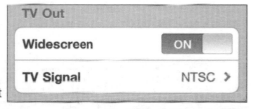

TIP: You can purchase a VGA adapter to plug your iPod touch into a VGA computer monitor to watch movies.

VGA supports video only, requires that the app supports it, and isn't usually compatible with DRM. Apple also makes component video cables that are DRM-compliant and work with most TVs. With iOS 4.2, AirView and Apple TV (2010) will let you stream from iPod touch directly to the TV.

See the "Accessories" section of the Quick Start Guide for more information.

TV Signal

There are some advanced ways of taking content from your iPod touch and playing them on your TV or DVR with the right cable. You also need to have the right TV signal setting. This is typically changed only if you use your iPod touch in another country. If you live in the U.S., your TV works with the NTSC standard.

Most European countries use PAL. If you are not sure which you use, contact your TV, cable, or satellite company.

Deleting Videos

To delete a video (to save space on your iPod touch), just choose the category from which you wish to delete the video—as you did at the start of this chapter (see Figure 10–3).

> **NOTE:** If you're syncing videos from iTunes, make sure to uncheck it there as well, or iTunes just might sync it right back to the iPod touch on the next sync!

Just touch and swipe to the right on a video you wish to delete. Just like deleting an email, a red **Delete** button will appear in the top left-hand corner. Touch the **Delete** button and you will be prompted to delete the video.

Touch the **Delete** button and the video will be deleted from your system.

> **NOTE:** This deletes the video only from your iPod touch—a copy will still remain in your video library in iTunes, assuming that you have synced with your computer after purchasing the video. So you can once again load it back onto your iPod touch. However, if you delete a rented movie from the iPod touch, it will be deleted permanently!

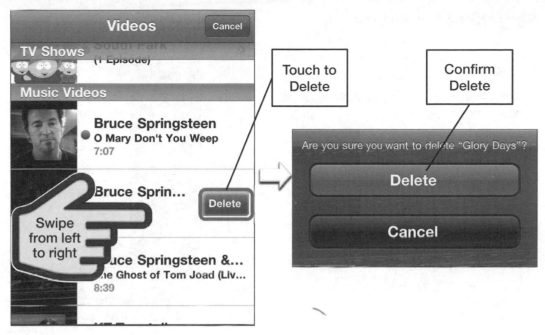

Figure 10–3. *How to delete video.*

YouTube on your iPod touch

Watching YouTube videos is certainly one of the most popular things for people to do on their computers these days. YouTube is as close to you as your iPod touch.

Right on your **Home** screen is a **YouTube** icon. Just touch the **YouTube** icon and you will be taken to the **YouTube** app.

Searching for Videos

When you first start **YouTube**, you usually see the **Featured** videos on YouTube that day.

Just scroll through the video choices as you do in other apps.

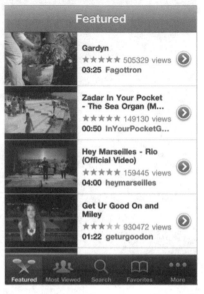

Using the Bottom Icons

Along the bottom of the **YouTube** app are five icons; **Featured**, **Most Viewed**, **Search**, **Favorites** and **More**. Each is fairly self-explanatory.

To see the videos that YouTube is featuring that day, touch the **Featured** icon. To see those videos that are most-viewed online, touch the **Most Viewed** icon.

After you watch a particular video, you will have the option to set it as a favorite on **YouTube** for easy retrieval later on. If you have set bookmarks, they will appear when you touch the **Favorite** icon.

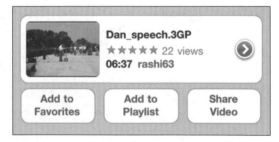

You can search the huge library of YouTube videos. Touch the **Search** box as in previous apps, and the keyboard will pop up. Type in a phrase, topic, or even the name of a video.

In this example, I am looking for the newest Made Simple Learning video tutorial—so I type in "Made Simple Learning" and I see the list of videos to watch.

When I find the video I want to watch, I can touch on it to see more information. I can even rate the video by touching on the video during playback and selecting a rating.

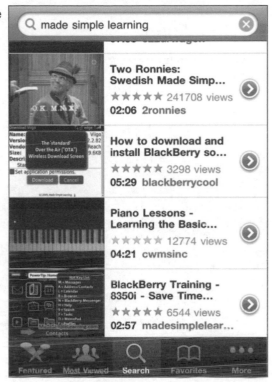

Playing Videos

Once you have made your choice, touch the video you want to watch. Your iPod touch will begin playing the YouTube video in portrait or landscape mode. To force it into portrait mode, just turn the iPod touch so that the screen orientation is vertical (see Figure 10–4).

Figure 10–4 . *Video playing in portrait mode.*

Video Controls

Once the video begins to play, the on-screen controls disappear, so you see only the video. To stop, pause, or activate any other options while the video is playing, just tap the screen (see Figure 10–5).

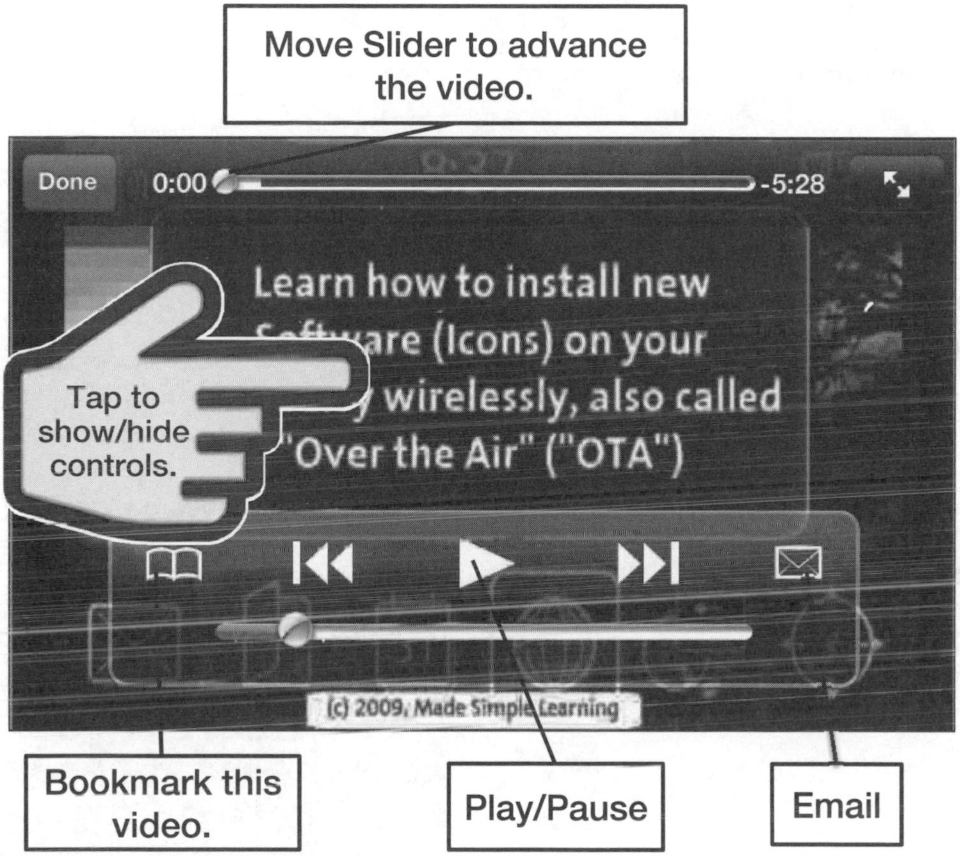

Figure 10–5. *Options within YouTube.*

The on-screen options are very similar to watching any other video. Along the bottom is the slider, which shows your place in the video. To move to another part in the video, just drag the slider.

To fast-forward through the video (in landscape mode,) touch and hold the **Fast-Forward** arrow. To quickly move in reverse, touch and hold the **Reverse** arrow. To advance to the next video in the YouTube list, tap the **Fast-Forward/Next** arrow. To watch the previous video in the list, tap the **Reverse/Back** arrow.

To set a favorite, touch the **Favorite** icon farthest to the left.

To email the video, touch the **Share** icon and your email will start with the link to the video in the body of the email. Type the recipient's name (see Chapter 17: "iPod touch Photography" for more on how to send content via email).

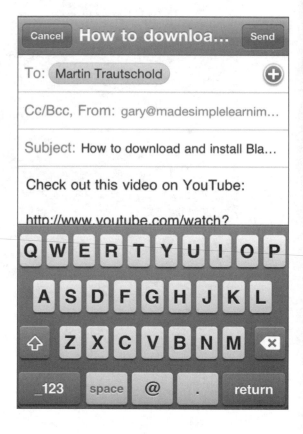

Checking and Clearing your History

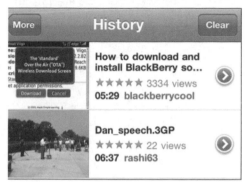

Touch **More** and then **History** and your recently viewed videos appear.

If you want to clear your history, just touch the **Clear** button in the upper right corner.

To watch a video from your history, just touch it and it will start to play.

Netflix on the iPod touch

In recent years, Netflix has grown to become a leading source of video rentals for consumers. Most recently, Netflix added video streaming of content delivered wirelessly to computers and other set-top boxes for your TV.

Now, Netflix is available to iPod touch users through the Netflix app in the App store.

Go to the App store and search for the Netflix app. See Chapter 20: "The Amazing App Store" for more information on the App store.

Choose the **Download** button (the app is free) and you are on your way.

You need an active Netflix account, so either create one when you start up the app or sign into your Netflix account if you already have one.

The beauty of the Netflix app is that you can add DVDs to your queue and have them sent out to you, and you can also watch TV shows and movies instantly—streaming them right to the iPod touch.

Navigating Netflix is very easy and similar to using Netflix on your computer. You have soft keys at the bottom with buttons for **Home**, **Genres**, **Search**, and your **Instant Queue.**

As you scroll down, there are separators for **Television**, **Movies**, **New Arrivals**, **Recently Watched** and more.

Usually, at the top of the list is the last movie or TV show you were watching. You can just touch **Resume** to continue watching. As you scroll down, you should see video categories based on the preferences you selected when you established your Netflix account.

Use the **Genres** button to narrow down your search. If you don't find what you are looking for, touch the search window and type in the name of a movie, actor, director, or genre.

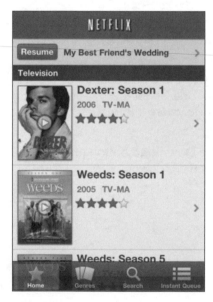

Once you find the movie or TV show you want to watch, touch **Play** and the movie will begin to stream to your iPod touch. The video controls are exactly like those in all the other iPod touch video-playing apps.

> **CAUTION:** Netflix uses a great deal of data, so make sure you have a strong Wi-Fi signal. Also, not all Netflix content is available for streaming.

Hulu on the iPod touch

In recent years, Hulu has grown to become a leading source of video streaming of content delivered wirelessly to computers and other set-top boxes for your TV.

Just after launch of the iPod touch, the **Hulu Plus** app was released in the App Store. Hulu Plus is a subscription-based service of $10.00 a month, but there is also free content available.

Essentially, with the full subscription, pretty much every episode of every TV show you watch or have ever watched is now available to stream to your iPod touch.

Launch the app and you will five icons at the bottom: **Free Gallery**, **Featured**, **Popular**, **Search**, and **More**.

Scroll through the **Free Gallery** to see which shows are available now for free viewing.

Touch a show and it immediately begins playing. Hold the iPod touch in landscape mode to have the video fill up the screen.

Searching for Videos

Touch the **Search** icon at the bottom and type in the name of a particular TV show. You can also just browse the **Featured** or **Popular** categories. When you find your show, all the videos available will be available to watch.

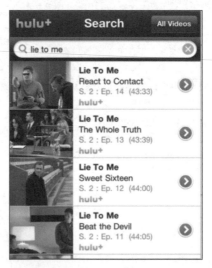

NOTE: if you do not have a Hulu Plus subscription, you will not be able to view the videos.

Watching Movies and Viewing Queue and History

Touch the **More** button and you will be taken to a screen that allows you to see available **TV** shows, **Movies**, **Recently Added** content, your **Queue**, your **History**, and your **Subscriptions** to **Hulu Plus**.

Just touch the appropriate tab to go to a particular section of the app.

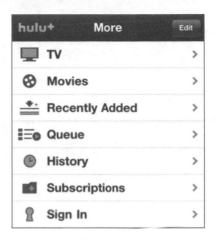

Video Controls in Hulu Plus

The video controls are a bit different in the **Hulu Plus** app. Touch the screen, as in any other video, and the video controls appear.

There is a **Play/Pause** button at the left and then a timeline for the video. Simply drag your finger along the timeline to advance to another part of the video.

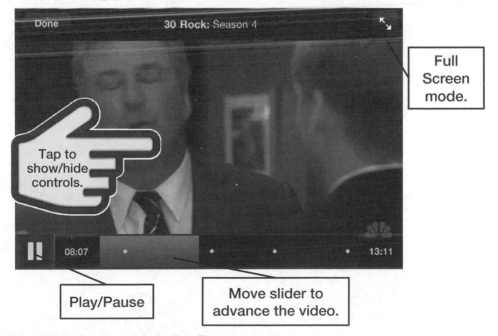

Figure 10–6. *Video controls in the Hulu Plus app.*

NOTE: You cannot advance through commercials in **Hulu Plus**. During a commercial, an icon will appear in the upper right-hand corner that resembles the **Share** icon, but if you touch it you will go to the web site of the advertiser.

CAUTION: Hulu Plus and **Netflix** use a great deal of data, so make sure you have a strong Wi-Fi signal.

iBooks and E-Books

Ever since the new screen resolution for the iPhone and iPod touch was announced, one of the features touted has been its ability as an e-book reader. In this chapter, we will show you that what emerged was an unparalleled book-reading experience. We will cover iBooks, how to buy and download books, and how to find some great free classic books. We will show you other e-book reading options using the third-party Kindle and Kobo (formerly Shortcovers) readers on your iPod touch.

The iPod touch uses Apple's proprietary e-book reader, iBooks. In this chapter, we will show you how to download the iBooks app, how to shop for books in the iBooks store, and how to take advantage of all the iBooks features.

With iBooks, you can interact with a book like never before. Pages turn like a real book, and you can adjust font sizes, look up words in the built-in dictionary, and search through your text.

In the App store, you can also find apps for Amazon's Kindle reader, a Barnes and Noble reader, the Stanza reader, and the Kobo reader. Both the Kindle reader and the Kobo reader offer a great reading experience on the iPod touch.

Downloading iBooks

Search the App store for "iBooks" or "Apple." Among the selections available for download will be iBooks.

> **NOTE**: On a brand new iPod touch, you should get a notice asking you "do you want to download iBooks now?"

Select the **iBooks** app and touch the **Free** button to download.

Select **Install** and iBooks will be downloaded and installed on the iPod touch.

The iBooks Store

Before you can start enjoying your reading experience, you need to load up your iBooks library with titles. Fortunately, many books can be found for free in the iBooks store, including the nearly complete Gutenberg Collection of classics and public domain titles.

> **NOTE**: Paid iBooks content is not available in all countries. Free content, however, is.

Just touch the **Store** button in the upper right-hand corner of your bookshelf, and you will be taken to the iBooks store.

The iBooks store is arranged much like the App store. There is a **Categories** button in the top left, opposite the **Library** button. Touch this to see all the available categories from which you can choose your books.

Featured books are highlighted on the front page of the store, with **New** and **Notable** titles displayed for browsing.

At the bottom of the store are five soft keys: **Featured**, **Charts**, **Browse**, **Search**, and **Purchases**.

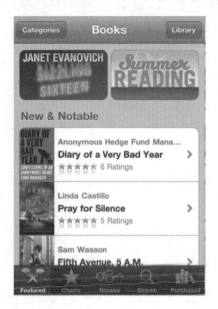

Touch the **Charts** button 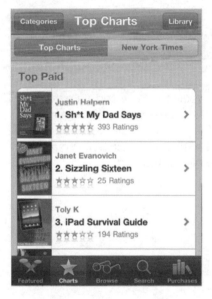 to see all the top charts and New York Times bestselling books. Touch the **Purchases** button to see all the books you have purchased or downloaded for your library.

Purchasing a book is much like purchasing an app. Touch the book title in which you are interested and browse the description and customer reviews. When you are ready to purchase the title, touch the price button.

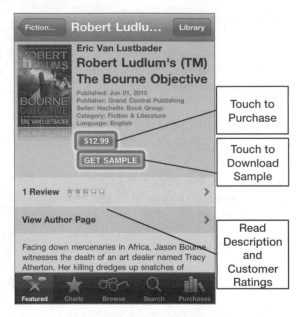

Touch to Purchase

Touch to Download Sample

Read Description and Customer Ratings

NOTE: Many titles have a sample download. This is a great idea if you are not sure that you want to purchase the book. Just download a sample, and you can always purchase the full book from within the sample.

Once you decide to download a sample or purchase a title, the view shifts to your bookshelf and you can see the book being deposited onto your bookshelf. Your book is now available for reading.

Using the Search Button

Just like iTunes and the App store, iBooks gives you a search window in which you can type virtually any phrase. You can search for an author, title, or series. Just touch **Search** at the bottom of the screen, and the onscreen keyboard pops up. Type in an author, title, series, or genre of book.

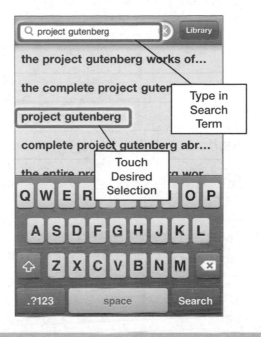

TIP: To search for lots of free books, do a search for "Project Gutenberg" to see thousands of free public domain titles.

You will see suggestions pop up that match your search; just touch the appropriate suggestion to go to that title.

Reading iBooks

Touch any title in your library to open it for reading. The book will open to the very first page, which is often the title page or other "front matter" in the book.

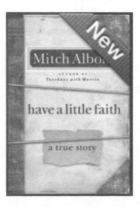

In the upper left-hand corner, next to the **Library** button, is a **Table of Contents** button, as you can see in Figure 11–1. To jump to the table of contents, either touch the **Table of Contents** button or simply turn the pages to advance to the table of contents.

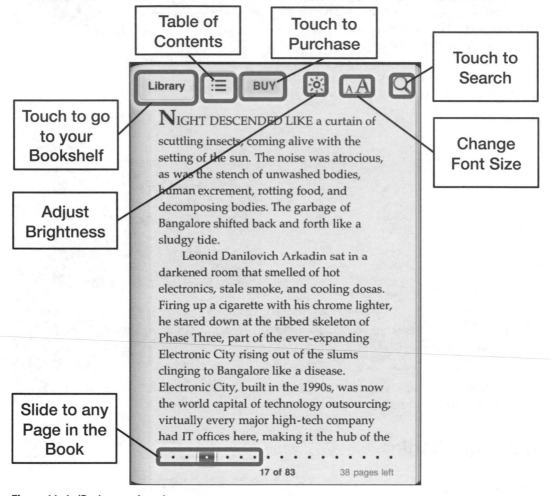

Figure 11–1. *iBooks page layout.*

Pages can be turned in one of three ways. You can either touch the right-hand side of the page to turn to the next page, or slowly touch and hold the screen on the right-hand edge of the page, and, while continuing to touch the screen, gently and slowly move your finger to the left.

Touch the right-hand side of the Page and "Turn," just like a Book

TIP: If you move your finger very slowly, you can actually see the words on the back of the page as you "turn" it—a very cool visual effect.

The last way to turn pages is to use the slider at the bottom of the page. As you slowly slide from left to right, you will see the page number on top of the slider. Release the slider and you can advance to that particular page number.

444 of 843

Customizing Your Reading Experience: Brightness, Fonts, and Font Sizes

In the upper center of the book, there are three icons available (brightness, size, and search) to help make your reading experience that much more immersive (see Figure 11–2).

Touch the **Brightness** icon and you can adjust the brightness of the book.

If you are reading in bed in a very dark room, you might want to slide it all the way down to the left. If you are out in the sunlight, you may need to slide it all the way up to the right. However, remember that the screen brightness consumes more battery power than most other features, so turn it back down when you don't need it so bright anymore.

NOTE: This adjusts the brightness only within iBooks. To adjust the global brightness of the iPod touch, use the control in the Settings app. (Go to the **Settings** icon -> **Brightness & Wallpaper**.)

Figure 11-2. *iBooks adjusting font sizes.*

The next icon is the **Font Size and Type** adjustment.

To Increase the Font Size:

Tap the large "A" multiple times.

To Decrease the Font Size:

Tap the small "A" multiple times.

There are six available font styles. (There may well be more fonts when you read this book.)

Have fun and try out some of the various fonts. The default selection is the Palatino font, but all of the fonts look great, and the larger font size can make a difference for some. The goal is to make this as comfortable and as enjoyable a reading experience as possible.

Growing Your Vocabulary Using the Built-In Dictionary

iBooks contains a very powerful built-in dictionary, which can be quite helpful when you run across a word that is new or unfamiliar.

NOTE: The first time you attempt to use the dictionary, the iPod touch will need to download it. Follow the onscreen prompts to download the dictionary.

Accessing the dictionary could not be easier. Just touch and hold any word in the book. A pop-up will appear with the options of using the dictionary, highlighting a word, creating a note, or searching for other occurrences of this particular word.

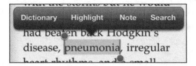

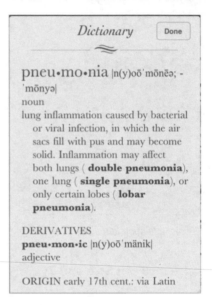

Touch **Dictionary**, and a pronunciation and definition of the word will be displayed. Touch **Done** to leave the dictionary and go back to the book.

Setting an In-Page Bookmark

There may be times when you wish to set an in-text bookmark for future reference.

In the upper right-hand corner is a **Bookmark** icon. Touch the **Bookmark** icon and it will change to a red bookmark on the page.

To view your bookmarks, just touch the **Table of Contents** icon at the top left of the screen (next to the **Library** icon) and then touch **Bookmarks**. Touch the bookmark highlighted and you will jump to that section in the book.

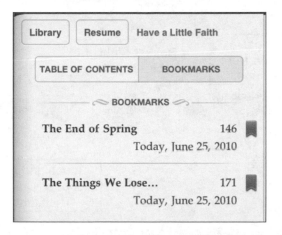

TIP: You do not need to set a bookmark every time you leave iBooks. iBooks will automatically remember where you left off in your book. Even if you jump to another book, when you return to the book you were just reading, you will return to exactly where you left off. iBooks will now also sync with your iPad iBooks so you can move back and forth between devices and keep your place.

Using Highlighting and Notes

There are some very nice "added touches" to the **iBooks** app. There may be times that you want to highlight a particular word to come back to at another time. There may be other times you want to leave yourself a note in the margin.

Both of these are very easy to do in iBooks. This feature is not yet available when viewing PDF files in iBooks.

Highlighting Text

To highlight text, do the following:

1. Touch and hold any word to bring up the menu options.

2. Choose **Highlight** from the menu options.

3. To remove the highlight, just touch and hold, and then select **Remove Highlight**.

To change the color of the highlight, do the following:

1. Touch and hold the highlighted word.

2. Choose **Colors** from the menu.

3. Choose a new color (see Figure 11–3).

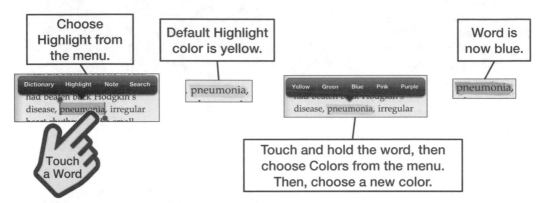

Figure 11–3. *Using the highlighting feature in iBooks.*

Adding Notes

To add a note in the margin, just do the following:

1. Touch and hold any word, as you did previously.

2. Choose **Note** from the menu.

3. Type in your note and then touch **Done**.

4. The note now appears on the side of the page in the margin (see Figure 11–4).

> **TIP**: Your notes will also appear under your bookmarks on the title page. Just touch the **Title Page** button and then touch **Bookmarks**. The notes you write will be at the bottom of the page.

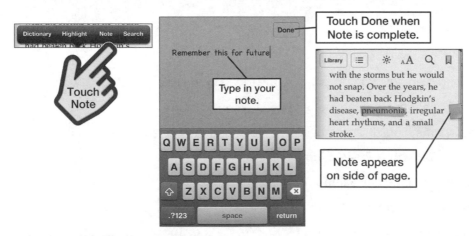

Figure 11–4. *Using the **Notes** feature in iBooks.*

Using Search

iBooks contains a powerful search feature built right in. Just touch the **Search** icon and then (as in other programs on the iPod touch) the built-in keyboard will pop up. Type in the word or phrase for which you are searching, and a list of chapters is shown where that word occurs.

Just touch the selection desired and you will jump to that section in the book. You also have the option of jumping right to Google or Wikipedia by touching the appropriate buttons at the bottom of the search window.

> **NOTE:** Using the Wikipedia or Google search will take you out of iBooks and launch Safari.

Deleting Books

Deleting books from your **iBooks** library is very similar to deleting applications from the iPod touch.

In the "Library" view, just touch **Edit** in the

top right-hand corner.

Once you touch the **Edit** button, you will notice a small black "x" in the upper left-hand corner of each book.

Just touch the "x" and you will be prompted to delete the book. Once you touch **Delete**, the book will disappear from the shelf.

Reading PDF Files in iBooks

One very cool feature of iBooks is the ability to read PDF files that are sent to you via email or synced via iTunes (See Chapter 3: "Sync your iPod touch with iTunes.")

In this example, a PDF file has arrived in our email, and we want to save it and view it in **iBooks.**

1. Open the PDF file from the email.

2. In the upper right-hand corner choose **Open in...** and then choose **iBooks**. The PDF file will now go into the PDF category of iBooks.

3. The PDF is saved in the PDF section. Just touch to open and read like any other iBook.

4. To delete, follow the preceding instruction for deleting an iBook.

NOTE: When you select **Open in...** in the upper right-hand corner of the PDF from the email, all available PDF reading apps will be listed. Choose **iBooks** from the list to open in iBooks or choose another reader to open in that app.

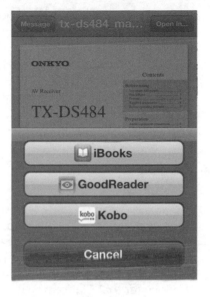

Until you save your first PDF file, you will see only "Books" listed in your bookshelf. After you save your first PDF file, you will now have a button marked **PDFs** next to the **Books** button.

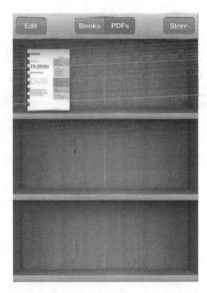

Other E-Book Readers: Kindle and Kobo

iBooks, as we have shared, offers an unparalleled e-book reading experience. There are, however, other e-book reader apps available for the iPod touch that are worth checking out.

Many users already have a Kindle and have invested in their Kindle library. Others use Kobo e-reader software (formerly Shortcovers) and have invested in a library of books for that platform.

Fortunately, both e-book platforms have apps in the iPod touch App store. When either program is downloaded and installed, you can sign in and read your complete library on your iPod touch.

NOTE: No matter which of these other e-readers you choose, you can always just "sign in," see your complete library, and pick up just where you left off in your last book—even if you started reading on a different device.

Download E-Reader Apps

Go to the App store, touch **Categories,** and, from there, touch **Books**. There you will find the Kindle app and the Kobo app. Both are free apps, so just touch the **Free** button and the downloads will initiate.

TIP: It is usually faster to just "search" by the name of the app if you know which one you are looking for.

Once the e-reader software is installed, just touch the icon to start the app.

Kindle Reader

Amazon's Kindle reader is the world's most popular e-reader. Millions of people have Kindle books, so the Kindle app allows you to read your Kindle books on your iPod touch.

The Kindle app has just been updated to support audio/video on iPod touch and iPad, making it even more advanced than on Kindle hardware itself.

TIP: If you use a Kindle device, don't worry about signing in from your IPod touch. You can have several devices tied to your single account. You will be able to enjoy all the books you purchased for your Kindle right on the Kindle app on the iPod touch. In some books, the publisher might limit this capability.

Just touch the Kindle app and either sign in to your Kindle account or create a new account with a user name and password.

Once you sign in, you will see your Kindle books on the home page. You can touch either a book to start reading, or **Get Books** to start shopping in the Kindle store.

NOTE: Touching **Get Books** will start up your Safari browser. From there you can purchase Kindle books. Once you are done, you will need to exit Safari and start up the Kindle app once again.

To read a Kindle book, touch the book cover. The book will open.

To see the options for reading, just touch the screen, and they will be along the bottom row of icons.

You can add a bookmark by touching the plus (+) button. Once the bookmark is set, the plus (+) turns to a minus (-).

You can go to the cover, table of contents, or beginning of the book (or specify any location in the book) by touching the **Book** button.

The font, as well as the color of the page, can be adjusted. One very interesting feature is the ability to change the page to "**Black**," which is great when reading at night.

To advance pages, either swipe from right to left, or touch the right-hand side of the page. To go back a page, just swipe from left to right or touch the left-hand side of the page.

Tap the screen and a slider appears at the bottom, which you can move to advance to any page in the book.

To return to your list of books, just touch the **Home** button.

Kobo Reader

Like the Kindle reader, the Kobo reader asks you first to sign in to your existing Kobo Books account. All of your existing Kobo Books will then be available for reading.

Kobo uses a "bookshelf" approach, similar to iBooks. Tap the book cover for whichever book you wish to open.

Or, touch the **List** tab to see your books organized in a list format.

You can also directly go to the Kobo store to purchase books by touching the **Discover** or **Browse** buttons at the bottom.

Open any book, and along the top of the Kobo reader are two buttons: **I'm Reading** and **Settings**.

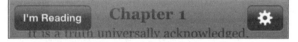

Touch the **I'm Reading** button, and a bookmark is placed where you left off in the book and the screen goes back to your bookshelf.

Touch the **Settings** button, and along the bottom will be buttons for viewing bookmarks, seeing information about the book, and adjusting the page transition style and font. Under those buttons are four icons: **Font**, **Brightness**, **Screen Lock**, and **Nighttime Reading**. Touch any of the buttons to make adjustments to your viewing.

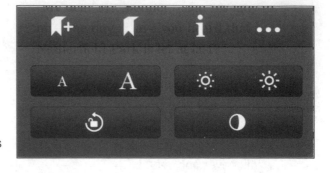

To advance pages in the Kobo reader, touch the right-hand side of the page. To go back a page, just touch the left-hand side of the page. You can also use the slider at the bottom to advance through the pages.

Chapter 12

Surfing the Web with Safari

Now, we'll take you through a very fun thing to do on your iPod touch: surfing the Web. You may have heard web surfing on the iPod touch is a more intimate experience than ever before—we agree! We'll show you how to touch, zoom around, and interact with the Web like never before with Safari on your iPod touch. You'll learn how to set and use bookmarks, quickly find things with the search engine, open and switch between multiple browser windows, and even easily copy text and graphics from web pages.

Web Browsing on the iPod touch

You can browse the Web to your heart's content via your iPod touch's Wi-Fi connection. Like its larger cousin, the iPad, your iPod touch has what many feel is the most capable mobile browsing experience available today. Web pages look very much like web pages on your computer. With the iPod touch's ability to zoom in, you don't even have to worry about the smaller screen size inhibiting your web browsing experience. In short, web browsing is a much more personal experience on the iPod touch.

Choose to browse in portrait or landscape mode, whichever you prefer. Quickly zoom into a video by double-tapping it or pinching open on it, which is natural to you because those are the motions to zoom in text and graphics.

Why Do Some Videos and Sites Not Appear? (Flash Player Required)

This content requires Flash

To view this content, JavaScript must be enabled, and you need the latest version of the Adobe Flash Player.

Download the free Flash Player now!

Some web sites are designed with Adobe Flash Player, and at the time of this writing, the iPod touch does not support Adobe Flash. Apple has made a decision to not support the Flash Player. If you tap a video and the video does not play, or you see something like "Flash plugin required," "Download the latest Flash plugin to view this video," or "Adobe Flash required to view this site," you will not be able to view the video or web page.

The only way to see these Flash videos is to view them from a computer that does support Adobe Flash. Remember, you can send the web address to yourself in an email message (see our section on emailing links to web pages for instructions).

More and more sites are now starting to use HTML5 video instead of Flash, including YouTube, Vimeo, TED, the *New York Times*, and *Time* magazine, which will play on your iPod touch.

An Internet Connection Is Required

You do need a live Internet connection on your iPod touch via Wi-Fi to browse the Web. Check out Chapter 5: "Wi-Fi Connectivity" to learn more.

Launching the Web Browser

You should find the Safari (web browser) icon on your **Home** screen. Usually, the **Safari** icon is in the **Bottom Dock**.

Touch the **Safari** icon, and you will be taken to the browser's home page. Most likely, this will be Apple's iPod touch page.

Just turn your iPod touch on its side to see the same page in wider landscape mode. As you find web sites you like, you can set bookmarks to easily jump to these sites. We will show you how to do that later in this chapter.

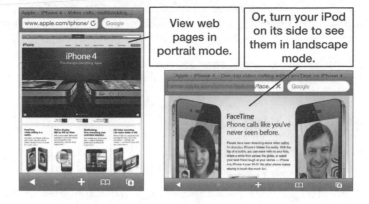

Layout of Safari Web Browser Screen

Figure 12–1 shows how a web page looks in Safari and the different actions you can take in the browser.

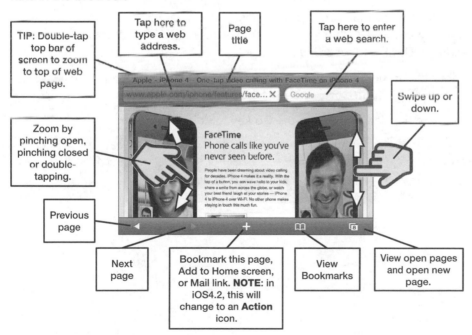

Figure 12–1. *Safari web browser page layout.*

As you look at your screen, notice that the **Address Bar** is in the upper left side of the screen. This displays the current web address. To the right is the **Search** window. By default, this is set to Google search, but you can change that if you want.

At the bottom of the screen are five icons: **Back**, **Forward**, **Add Bookmark**, **Bookmarks**, and **Pages view**.

Typing a Web Address

The first thing you'll want to learn is how to get to your favorite web pages. Just like on your computer, you type the web address (URL) into the browser.

1. To start, tap the **Address Bar** at the top of the browser as shown in Figure 12–2. You'll then see the keyboard appear and the window for the address bar expand.

2. If there is already an address in the window and you want to erase it, press the ⊗ at the right end of the bar.

3. Start typing your web address (you don't need the **www.**).

4. When you start typing, you may see suggestions appear below—just tap any of those to go to that page. The suggestions are very complete because they are pulled from your browsing history, bookmarks, the web address (URL), and web page titles.

5. Remember the **.com** key at the bottom of the page. If you press and hold it, you will see **.edu**, **.org**, and other common domain types.

6. When you are finished typing, tap the **Go** key to go to that page.

> **TIP:** Don't type the **www.** because it's not necessary. Remember to use the **colon**, **forward slash**, **underscore**, **dot**, and **.com** keys at the bottom to save time.

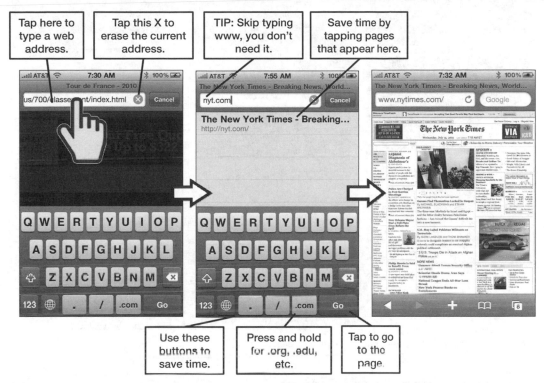

Figure 12–2. *Typing a web address.*

TIP: Press and hold the **.com** key to see all the options: **.org, .edu, .net, .de**, and so on.

Moving Backward or Forward Through Open Web Pages

Now that you know how to enter web addresses, you'll probably be jumping to various web sites. The **Forward** and **Back** arrows make it very easy to go to recently visited pages in either direction, as Figure 12–3 shows. If the **Back** arrow is grayed out, the "Using the **Open Pages** Button" section can help.

Let's say you were looking at the news on the *New York Times* web site, and you jumped to ESPN to check sports scores. To go back to the *New York Times* page, just tap the **Back** arrow. To return to the ESPN site again, touch the **Forward** arrow.

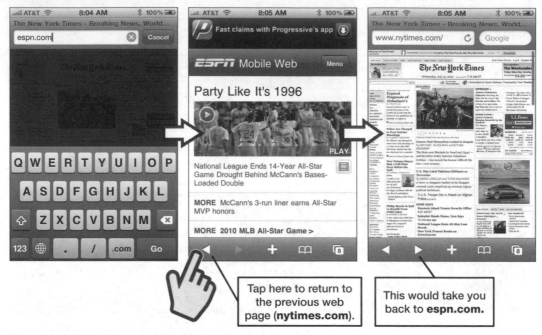

Figure 12–3. *Returning to a previously viewed web page.*

Using the Open Pages Button

Sometimes, when you click a link, the web page you were viewing moves to the background and a new window pops up with new content (another web page, a video, etc.). You will see the page you were on move to the background and a new page being opened. In such cases, the **Back** arrow in the new browser window will not work.

Instead, you have to tap the **Open Pages** icon in the lower right corner to see a list of open web pages and then tap the one you want. In the example shown in Figure 12–4, we touched a link that opened a new browser window. The only way to get back to the old one was to tap the **Open Pages** icon and select the desired page.

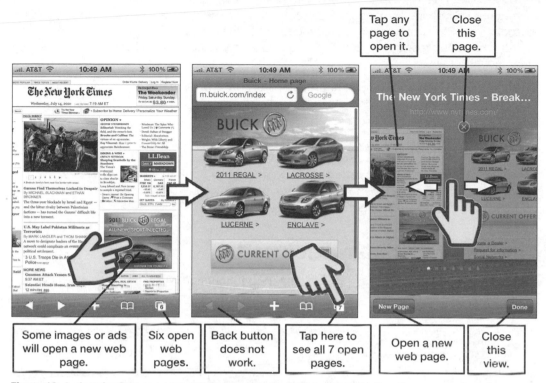

Tap any page to open it.

Close this page.

Some images or ads will open a new web page.

Six open web pages.

Back button does not work.

Tap here to see all 7 open pages.

Open a new web page.

Close this view.

Figure 12–4. *Jumping between open web pages when the* **Back** *button doesn't work.*

Zooming In and Out in Web Pages

Zooming in and out of web pages is very easy on the iPod touch. There are two primary ways of zooming—double-tapping and pinching.

Double-Tapping

If you tap twice on a column of a web page, the page will zoom in on that particular column. This lets you home in on exactly the right place on the web page, which is very helpful for pages that aren't formatted for a mobile screen.

To zoom out, just double-tap once more. See graphically how this looks in the "Quick Start Guide" earlier in this book.

Pinching

This technique lets you zoom in on a particular section of a page. It takes a little bit of practice but will soon become second nature. Take a look in the "Quick Start Guide" to see graphically how it looks.

Place your thumb and forefinger close together at the section of the web page you wish to zoom into. Slowly pinch out, separating your fingers. You will see the web page zoom in. It takes a couple of seconds for the web page to focus, but it will zoom in and be very clear in a short while.

To zoom out to where you were before, just start with your fingers apart and move them slowly together; the page will zoom out to its original size.

Activating Links from Web Pages

When you're surfing the Web, often you'll come across a link that will take you to another web site. Because Safari is a full-function browser, you simply touch the link and you will jump to a new page.

Working with Safari Bookmarks

As soon as you start browsing a bit on your iPod touch, you will want to quickly access your favorite web sites. One good way to do this is to add bookmarks for one-tap access to web sites.

> **TIP:** You can sync your bookmarks from your computer's web browser (Safari or Internet Explorer only) using iTunes on your computer. Check out Chapter 3: "Sync Your iPod touch with iTunes" for more details.

Adding a New Bookmark

Adding new bookmarks on your iPod touch is just a few taps away.

1. To add a new bookmark for the web page you are currently viewing, tap the **plus sign** ✛ at the bottom of the screen.

2. Choose **Add Bookmark**.

Add Bookmark

3. We recommend that you edit the bookmark name to something short and recognizable.

4. Tap **Bookmarks** if you want to change the folder where your bookmark is stored.

5. When you're finished, tap the **Save** button.

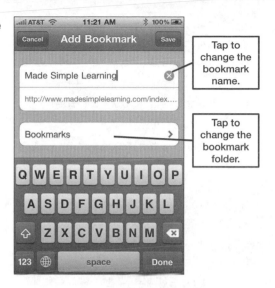

Tap to change the bookmark name.

Tap to change the bookmark folder.

Using Bookmarks and History

Once you have set a few bookmarks, it is easy to view and work with them. In the same area, you can also see and use your web browsing history. A very useful tool on your iPod touch is the ability to browse the Web from your **History**, just as you would on a computer.

1. Tap the **Bookmarks** icon at the bottom of the page.

2. Swipe up or down to view all your bookmarks.

3. Tap any bookmark to jump to that web page.

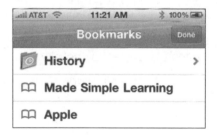

4. Tap the **History** folder to view your recent history of visited web pages.

5. Notice that, at the bottom of the list, you see additional folders for **Earlier Today** and previous days.

6. Tap any history item to go to that web page.

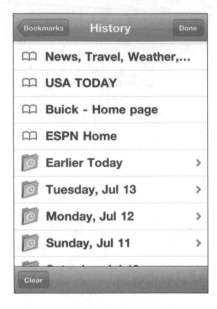

> **TIP:** To clear your history, tap the **Clear** button in the lower left corner. You can also clear your history, cookies, and cache in the **Settings** app. Tap **Settings**, tap **Safari**, scroll to the bottom, and tap **Clear History, Clear Cookies,** or **Clear Cache.**

Managing Your Bookmarks

It is very easy to accumulate quite a collection of bookmarks, since setting them up is so easy. You may find you no longer need a particular bookmark, or you may want to organize them by adding new folders.

If you have organized your **Phone Favorites** list, you already know how to organize your bookmarks; you use the same steps.

Like other lists on your iPod touch, you can reorder your **Bookmarks** list and remove entries.

1. View your **Bookmarks** list as you did previously.

2. Tap the **Edit** button in the lower left corner.

3. To reorder the entries, touch and drag the right edge with the three gray bars up or down the list. In this case, we are dragging the bookmark to the **iPad Made Simple** book page on amazon.com up to the top.

4. To create a new folder for bookmarks, tap the **New Folder** button in the lower right corner.

5. To delete a bookmark, tap the red circle to the left of the entry to make it turn vertical.

6. Then tap the **Delete** button.

7. When you are finished reordering and deleting entries, tap the **Done** button in the upper left corner.

8. To edit a bookmark name, folder, or web address, tap the bookmark name itself.

9. Then, you can make any adjustments to the name, web address, or folder.

10. To change the folder where the bookmark is stored, tap the button below the web address. In this image, it says **Bookmarks**, but in your iPod touch, it may be different. This bookmark points to the iPod touch Made Simple page on amazon.com.

11. Tap **Done** when you're finished.

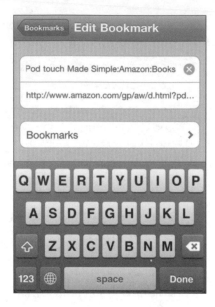

Safari Browsing Tips and Tricks

Now that you know the basics of how to get around, we will cover a few useful tips and tricks to make web browsing more enjoyable and fast on your iPod touch.

Jumping to the Top of the Web Page

Sometimes, web pages can be quite long, which can make scrolling back to the top of the page a bit laborious. One easy trick is to just tap the gray title bar of the web page; you'll automatically jump to the top of the page, as shown in Figure 12–5.

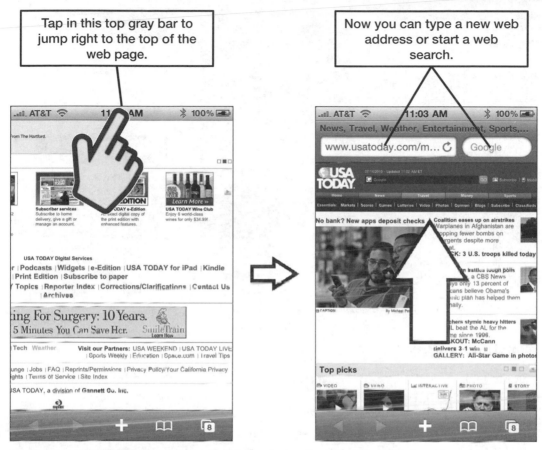

Figure 12–5. *Jumping quickly to the top of a web page by tapping at the top.*

Emailing a Web Page

Sometimes while browsing, you find a page so compelling you just have to send it to a friend or colleague. Touch the **plus sign** ➕ in the middle of the bottom bar, and select **Mail Link to this Page** (see Figure 12–6). This creates an email message with the link that you can send.

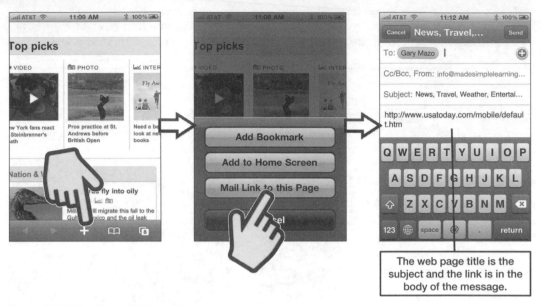

Figure 12–6. *Emailing a link to a web page.*

Printing a Web Page

The iPod touch (at the time of this writing) does not have a built-in **Print** command. You have a couple of options, but neither is very simple. When iOS 4.2 is released in November, a **Print** option will be available.

- *Option 1:* Email yourself or a colleague the web page link and print it from a computer. If you are traveling and staying at a hotel with a business center, you may be able to send it to someone at the business center or front desk to print the page.

- *Option 2:* Buy a network printing app from the **App Store** that allows you to print to a networked printer. Of course, this works only if you have access to a networked printer. It's usually best if you do this from your home or office network and can get help setting up, as doing so can be challenging.

Watching Videos in Safari

You will find videos in web sites. You will be able to play many but not all videos. Those formatted with Adobe Flash will not be playable on your iPod touch (see our note at the beginning of this chapter).

When you tap the **Play** button, you will be taken out of **Safari** into the iPod video player.

You can then turn your iPod touch on its side to view the video in landscape, or wide-screen, mode.

Tap the screen to bring up the player controls if they have disappeared.

When you are finished watching the video and want to return to the web page, tap the **Done** button in the upper left corner.

> **TIP:** Check out all the video player tips and tricks in Chapter 10: "Viewing Videos, TV Shows, and More."

Saving or Copying Text and Graphics

From time to time, you may see text or a graphic you want to copy from a web site. We tell you briefly how to do this in this section, but to see graphically how to get it done, including using the **Cut** and **Paste** functions, please see the "Copy and Paste" section in Chapter 2: "Typing Tips, Copy/Pate and Search." Here's a quick look:

To copy a single word, touch and hold the word until you see it highlighted and the **Copy** button appears. Then tap **Copy.**

To copy a few words or entire paragraph, touch and hold a word until it is highlighted. Then drag the blue dots left or right to select more text. You can flick up or down to select an entire paragraph. Then tap **Copy**.

> **TIP:** Selecting a single word puts the copy feature in word-selection mode, where you can drag to increase or decrease the number of words selected. If you go past a single paragraph, it will typically switch to element-selection mode where, instead of corners, you get edges that you can drag out to select multiple paragraphs, images, and so on.

To **Save** or **Copy** a graphic, touch and hold the picture or image until you see the pop-up asking if you would like to **Save** or **Copy** the image.

Saving Time with AutoFill

AutoFill is a great way to save time typing your personal information including usernames and passwords on web sites. The AutoFill tool can remember and fill in information required in web forms. You will save a lot of time by enabling AutoFill.

Check out the steps we show you later in this chapter in the "Enabling AutoFill" section to set up AutoFill to work on your iPod touch.

Once **AutoFill** is enabled, just go to any web page that has a field to fill out. As soon as you touch the field, the keyboard will come up at the bottom of the screen. At the top of the keyboard, you will see a small button that says **AutoFill**. Touch it, and the web form should be filled out automatically.

> **CAUTION:** Having your name and password entered automatically means that anyone who picks up your iPod touch will be able to access your personal sites and information. You may want to use passcode security as we show you in Chapter 7: "Personalize and Secure Your iPod touch."

For Usernames and Passwords

The first time you go to a web site where you have to enter a username and password, you type them and press **Submit** or **Enter**. At that time, AutoFill will ask if you want to remember them.

Tap **Yes** if you want them to be remembered and next time automatically entered.

The next time you visit this login page, your username and password will be automatically filled in.

For Personal Information

There are many times on the web where you have to enter your name, email address, home address, and more. With AutoFill set up and tied to your contact record on the iPod touch, filling in these forms just takes a single tap of your finger.

You will go to many sites with web forms that need to be completed. Take this example of a web form on www.madesimplelearning.com for free iPod touch tips. It would take a while to manually type your email address, and first and last name.

As soon as you tap the first field to type, in this case **Email**, you see the AutoFill bar appear just above your keyboard.

Tap the **AutoFill** button, and your email address and name are immediately filled in from your contact record.

Adding a Web Page Icon to Your Home Screen

If you love a web site or page, it's very easy to add it as an icon to your **Home** screen. That way, you can instantly access the web page without going through the **Safari ➤ Bookmarks** bookmark selection process. You'll save lots of steps by putting the icon on your **Home** screen (see Figure 12–7). This is especially good for quickly launching web apps, like **Gmail** or **Buzz** from Google, or web app games.

Here's how to add the icon:

1. Touch the **plus sign**  at the bottom of the browser.

2. Touch **Add to Home Screen**.

3. Adjust the name to shorten it to about ten or fewer characters, because there's not much room for the name of the icon on your **Home** screen.

4. Tap the **Add** button in the upper right corner.

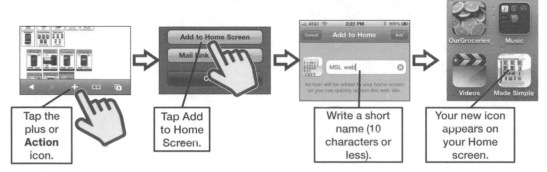

Figure 12–7. *Adding an icon for a web page to your **Home** screen.*

Adjusting the Safari Browser Settings

As with other settings we've adjusted so far, the settings for Safari are found in the **Settings** app.

1. To access settings for **Safari**, tap the **Settings** icon.

2. Tap **Safari**

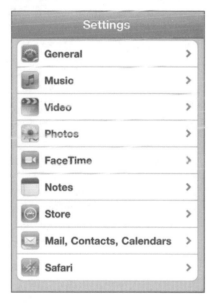

Changing the Search Engine

By default, the search engine for the Safari browser is **Google**. To change this to **Yahoo** or **Bing**, just touch the **Search Engine** button and then choose the new search engine.

Adjusting Security Options

Under the **Security** heading, **Fraud Warning**, **JavaScript**, and **Block Pop-ups** should, by default, be set to **ON**. You can modify either of these by just sliding the switch to **OFF**.

> **NOTE:** Many popular sites like Facebook require JavaScript to be **ON**.

Tap the **Accept Cookies** button to adjust to accept cookies **Always**, **Never**, or **From visited**. We recommend keeping it as **From visited**. If you make it **Never**, some web sites will not work properly.

Speeding Up Your Browser by Clearing History and Cookies

On the bottom of the Safari settings screen, you can see the **Clear History**, **Clear Cookies,** and **Clear Cache** buttons.

If you notice your web browsing getting sluggish, it's probably a good time to clear out all three of these by tapping them and confirming your choices.

TIP: Clearing the history, cookies, and cache is also a good privacy measure, as it prevents others from seeing where you've been browsing.

Enabling AutoFill

As we showed you earlier in this chapter, AutoFill is a convenient way to have Safari automatically fill out web page forms that ask for your name, address, phone number, or even username and password. It can save you a tremendous amount of time typing and retyping your name and other information.

To enable **AutoFill**, follow these steps:

1. From the **Safari** menu in the **Settings** app, tap **AutoFill**.

2. Set the switch next to **Names & Passwords** to **ON**.

3. Set the switch next to **Use Contact Info** to **ON**.

4. After setting **Use Contact Info** to **ON**, you will be brought to your **Contacts** list to select a contact to use.

5. Swipe up and down to find someone, or double-tap the top bar that says **Contacts** to bring up the search window.

6. Once you find the contact you want to use, tap it to be returned to the Safari settings screen.

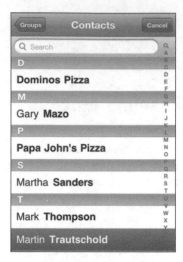

Chapter 13

FaceTime Video Messaging and Skype

Your iPod touch brings many new capabilities to your life, some of which seemed like science fiction just a few years ago. For example, video calling is now not only possible, but extremely easy to use with the new **FaceTime** app.

As long as you and your caller are on iOS device and you're both on a Wi-Fi network, you can have unlimited video calls. In this chapter, we will show you how to enable and use the **FaceTime** program, as well as how to start having fun with this great new feature.

Making calls over Wi-Fi is also possible with Skype, the popular video calling and chat program that many of us use on our computers. We will also show you how you can use the **Skype** app.

Video Calling

For many years, we have watched TV episodes and movies debut future technology like this. For example, many of these episodes and movies have shown people talking on small, portable phones and having video conversations. Even *The Jetsons* cartoon in the 1970s had this as a future concept.

The iPod touch makes that future thinking a reality today.

Setting up FaceTime

FaceTime needs to be set up the first time you use it on your iPod touch. The process is usually pretty painless. Because the iPod touch is not a phone, **FaceTime** needs to be associated with an email address to work. Follow these steps to associate **FaceTime** with an email address:

1. Touch the **FaceTime** icon (it's usually located in the bottom dock of the iPod touch).

2. Either sign into your Apple account using your Apple ID or your MobileMe user name and password. If you don't have an account or if you want to create new one specifically for **FaceTime** purposes, just touch the **Create New Account** button (see Figure 13–1).

3. Once the account is set up, you can choose the email address you want to use for placing **FaceTime** calls. You can also add other email addresses to use with your FaceTime account.

> **NOTE:** Once **FaceTime** is set up, you can always make adjustments or add additional email addresses by going to **Settings** and then to the **FaceTime** tab. From this tab, you can choose to add more email addresses or change your caller ID for **FaceTime** calls.

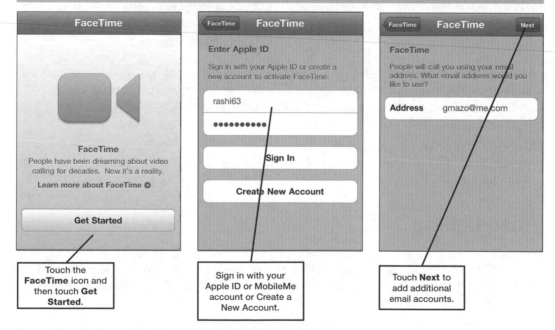

Figure 13–1. *Setting up FaceTime on your iPod touch.*

Video Calling with FaceTime

FaceTime is the featured app highlighted in many of Apple's iPhone and iPod touch commercials. Essentially, **FaceTime** is free over Wi-Fi calling that allows you to see the caller on the other end of the conversation through the phone's front-facing camera.

> **NOTE:** For now **FaceTime** is only available on the New iPhone 4 and the newest iPod touch devices running iOS 4.1 and higher, and it's only available over a Wi-Fi network.

Enabling FaceTime Calling on your iPod touch

When you first use your iPod touch, **FaceTime** is not yet enabled. To enable the iPod touch to receive and make **FaceTime** calls, follow these steps:

1. Go to your **Settings** icon and touch it.

2. Scroll down to the **FaceTime** option tab.

3. Toggle the **FaceTime** switch to the **ON** position.

Using FaceTime

Once **FaceTime** is enabled, you can place a **FaceTime** call from the **FaceTime** app or from the **FaceTime** button at the bottom of a contact page. **FaceTime** will only work, however, if the other caller is on an iPod touch or iPhone 4, and the **FaceTime** feature is enabled on both devices.

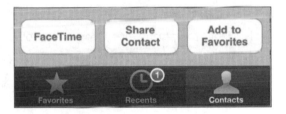

To initiate a **FaceTime** call, follow these steps:

1. Touch the **FaceTime** icon (initially in the bottom dock) on your iPod touch.

2. Choose a **Favorite**, a **Recent**, or a **Contact** who is capable of a **FaceTime** call. The app will ask the caller on the other end to **Accept** the **FaceTime** call.

Accepting a call from someone else is also easy. Simply **Accept** the **FaceTime** call from the other caller by touching **Accept** button or by **Sliding to Answer** if the iPod is in sleep mode (see Figure 13–2).

Figure 13–2. *Accepting a FaceTime call.*

Once a **FaceTime** call is initiated, follow these steps to conduct a video conference:

1. Hold the phone away from you a bit.

2. Make sure you are *framed* properly in the window.

3. You can move the small image of yourself around the screen to a convenient spot.

4. Touch the **Switch Camera** button to show the **FaceTime** caller you are looking at. The **Switch Camera** button will now use the standard camera on the back of the iPod touch. In Figure 13–3, I get to see the beautiful vistas of Colorado from Martin's vacation with his family, and he gets to see my dog on the couch!

5. Touch the **End** button to end the **FaceTime** call.

6. Touch the **Mute** button to temporarily mute the call.

Touch "Switch Camera" Button to Show What you See using the Main Camera

Figure 13–3. *Switching camera views on a FaceTime call.*

Setting Favorites in FaceTime

Just as when using an iPhone, you can set **Favorites** for **FaceTime** calling on your iPod touch. The favorites that you set need to be individuals who have an iPod touch or an iPhone 4. These people also need to set up their device for FaceTime calls. Follow these steps to add people to your **Favorites**:

1. Start the **FaceTime** app as you did previously.

2. Touch the **Favorites** soft key at the bottom (see Figure 13–4 below).

3. Touch the "**+**" sign and then choose a contact to add to your **Favorites**.

NOTE: When choosing a contact, choose either the person's iPhone number or the email address associated with the person's FaceTime account.

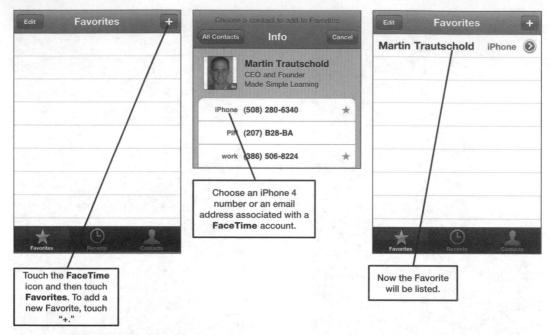

Touch the **FaceTime** icon and then touch **Favorites**. To add a new Favorite, touch "+."

Choose an iPhone 4 number or an email address associated with a **FaceTime** account.

Now the Favorite will be listed.

Figure 13–4. *Adding a Favorite in FaceTime.*

Multitasking Using FaceTime

One of the great features of your new iPod touch is that it uses the latest iOS software from Apple, which allows you to multitask (see Chapter 8: "Multitasking and Voice Control;" to learn more about how to switch between apps.

When you are in a **FaceTime** call, just double-click the **Home** button to see other apps that are running. Go to another app and you will see a bar at the top of the screen that says, "Touch to resume FaceTime."

Simply touch that bar to go back to the call.

Making Phone Calls and More with Skype

Social Networking is all about keeping in touch with our friends, colleagues, and family. Passive communication through sites such as www.facebook.com and www.myspace.com is nice; however, sometimes there is just no substitute for hearing someone's voice.

Amazingly, you can make phone calls using the **Skype** app from any iPod touch. Calls to other Skype users anywhere in the world are free. A nice thing about Skype is that it works on computers and many mobile devices, including iPhone 4s, iPod touches, some BlackBerry smartphones, and other mobile devices. You will be charged for calls to mobile phones and landlines, but the rates are reasonable.

NOTE: Skype currently supports iOS 4 multitasking.

Downloading Skype to Your iPod touch

You can download the free **Skype** app from the App Store by searching for *Skype* and installing it. If you need help getting this done, please check out Chapter 20: "The Amazing App Store."

Creating Your Skype Account on Your iPod touch

If you need to set up your Skype account and have not already done so from your computer (see the "Using Skype on your Computer" section later in this chapter), then follow these steps to set up **Skype** on your iPod touch:

1. Tap the **Skype** icon from your **Home** screen.

2. Tap the **Create Account** button.

3. Tap **Accept** if you accept the **No Emergency Calls** pop-up warning window.

4. Enter your **Full Name**, **Skype Name**, **Password**, and **Email**, and then decide whether you want to **Get News and Offers** by setting the switch at the bottom.

5. Tap the **Done** button to create your account.

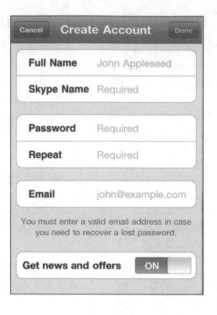

Log in to the Skype App

After you create your account, you're ready to log in to **Skype** on your iPod touch. To do so, follow these steps:

1. If you are not already in **Skype**, tap the **Skype** icon from your **Home** screen.

2. Type your **Skype Name** and **Password**.

3. Tap the **Sign In** button in the upper-right corner.

4. You should not have to enter this log in information again; it is saved in **Skype**. The next time you tap **Skype**, it will automatically log you in.

Finding and Adding Skype Contacts

Once you have logged into the **Skype** app, you will want to start communicating with people. To do so, you will have to find them and add then to your **Skype** contacts list:

1. If you are not already in **Skype**, tap the **Skype** icon from your **Home** screen and log in, if asked.

2. Tap the **Contacts** soft key at the bottom.

3. Tap the **Search** window at the top, and then type someone's first and last name or **Skype Name**. Tap **Search** to locate that person.

4. Once you see the person you want to add, tap his name.

5. If you are not sure whether this is the correct person, tap the **View Full Profile** button.

6. Tap **Add Contact** at the bottom.

7. Adjust the invitation message appropriately.

8. Tap the **Send** button to send this person an invitation to become one of your **Skype** contacts.

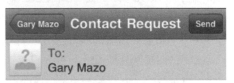

9. Repeat the procedure to add more contacts.

10. When you are done, tap the **Contacts** soft key at the bottom.

11. Tap **All Contacts** from the **Groups** screen to see all new contacts you have added.

12. Once this person accepts you as a contact, you will see him listed as a contact in your **All Contacts** screen.

TIP: Sometimes you want to get rid of a **Skype** contact. You can remove or block a contact by tapping her name from the contact list. Tap the **Settings** icon (upper right corner) and select either **Remove from Contacts** or **Block**.

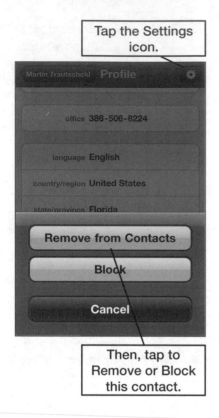

Tap the Settings icon.

Then, tap to Remove or Block this contact.

Making Calls with Skype on Your iPod touch

So far you have created your account and added your contacts. Now you are ready to finally make that first call with **Skype** on your iPod touch:

1. If you are not already in **Skype**, tap the **Skype** icon from your **Home** screen and log in, if asked.

2. Tap the **Contacts** soft key at the bottom.

3. Tap **All Contacts** to see your contacts.

4. Tap the contact name you wish to call (see Figure 13–5).

5. Tap the **Call** button.

6. You may see a **Skype** button and a **Mobile** or other phone button. Press the **Skype** button to make the free call. Making any other kind of call requires that you pay for it with *Skype Credits*.

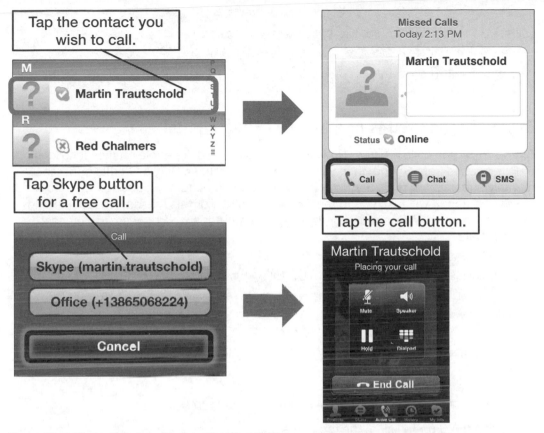

Figure 13–5. *Placing Calls from Skype on Your iPod touch.*

NOTE: You can call toll free numbers for free using **Skype Out** on your iPod touch. The following notice comes from the Skype web site at www.skype.com:

"The following countries and number ranges are supported and are free of charge to all users. We're working on the rest of the world. France: +33 800, +33 805, +33 809 Poland: +48 800 UK: +44 500, +44 800, +44 808 USA: +1 800, +1 866, +1 877, +1 888 Taiwan: +886 80."

Receiving Calls with Skype on your iPod touch

Apple's iOS4 innately supports background *voice over Internet protocol* (VoIP) calls. With the latest version of **Skype**, you can have **Skype** running in the background and still be able to receive a **Skype** call when it comes in. You can even (theoretically) be on a voice call and then answer your **Skype** call!

> **TIP:** Skype is a huge battery drain. If you want to call someone you know who uses **Skype** on her iPod touch, just send her a quick email or give her a quick call to alert her to the fact you would like to talk to her using the **Skype** app.

Buying Skype Credits or a Monthly Subscription

Skype-to-**Skype** calls are free. However, if you want to call people on their landlines or mobile phones from **Skype**, then you will need to purchase Skype Credits or purchase a monthly subscription plan. If you try to purchase the credits or a subscription from within the **Skype** app, it will take you to the Skype web site. For this reason, we recommend using **Safari** on your iPod touch or using your computer's web browser to purchase these credits.

> **TIP:** You may want to start with a limited amount of Skype Credits to try out the service before you sign up for a subscription plan. Subscription plans are the way to go if you plan on using the **Skype** app to talk to a lot for non-Skype callers (e.g., regular landlines and mobile phones).

Follow these steps to use **Safari** to buy Skype Credits:

1. Tap the **Safari** icon.

2. Type www.skype.com in the top address bar and tap **Go**.

3. Tap the **Sign In** link at the top of the page.

4. Enter your **Skype Name** and **Password**, and then tap **Sign me in**.

5. If you are not already on your **Account** screen, tap the **Account** tab in the right side of the Top Nav Bar.

6. At this point, you can choose to buy credits or a subscription:

   - Tap the **Buy pre-pay credit** button to purchase a fixed amount of credits.

   - Tap the **Get a subscription** button to buy a monthly subscription account.

7. Finally, complete the payment instructions for either type of purchase.

Chatting with Skype

In addition to making phone calls, you can also chat via text with other **Skype** users from your iPod touch. Starting a chat is very similar to starting a call; follow these steps to do so:

1. If you are not already in **Skype**, tap the **Skype** icon from your **Home** screen and log in if asked.

2. Tap the **Contacts** soft key at the bottom.

3. Tap **All Contacts** to see your contacts.

4. Tap the name of the contact you wish to chat with (see Figure 13–6).

5. Tap the **Chat** button.

6. Type your chat text and press the **Send** button. Your chat will appear in the top of the screen.

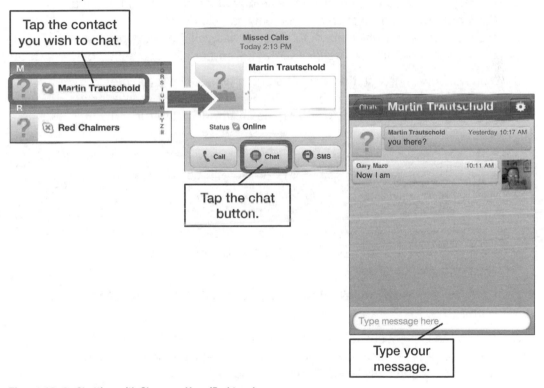

Figure 13–6. *Chatting with Skype on Your iPod touch*

Adding Skype to Your Computer

You can use the **Skype** app on your computer, as well. We will show you how this works next. You can also use **Skype** to make video calls on your computer if you also have a web cam hooked up.

NOTE: When you call from your computer to an iPod touch, you will not be able to do a video call.

To create a Skype account and download **Skype** software for your computer, follow these steps:

1. Open a web browser on your computer.

2. Go to: www.skype.com.

3. Click the **Join** link at the top of the page.

4. Create your account by completing all required information and clicking the **Continue** button. Notice that you only have to enter information in the required fields, which are noted with an asterisk. For example, you do not need to enter your gender, birthdate, and mobile phone number.

5. You are now done with the account setup process. Next, you are presented with the option of buying Skype Credits; however, this is not required for free **Skype**-to-**Skype** phone calls, video calls, or chats.

TIP: You only need to pay for **Skype** if you want to call someone who is not using **Skype**. For example, calls to phones on landlines or mobile phones (not using **Skype**) will cost you. At publishing time, pay-as-you-go rates were about US 2.1 cents per minute; monthly subscriptions ranged from about US $3 - $14 for various calling plans.

6. Next, click the Get Skype link in the Top Nav Bar of the site to download **Skype** to your computer.

7. Click the **Get Skype for Windows** button or the **Get Skype for Mac** button.

8. Follow the instructions to install the software. For more information on downloading and installing software, see the "Getting iTunes Software" section in Chapter 29: "Your iTunes User Guide.'

9. Once the software is installed, launch it and log in using your Skype account.

10. You are ready to initiate (or receive) phone calls, video calls, and chats to anyone else using **Skype**, including all your friends with **Skype** on their iPod touches.

Chapter 14

Email on Your iPod touch

In this chapter, we will help you explore the world of email in the **Mail** app on your iPod touch. You will learn how to set up multiple email accounts, check out all the various reading options, open attachments, and clean up your **Inbox**.

If you had an earlier version of the iPod touch before your new iPod touch, you will be pleased with the new **Unified Inbox** feature that lets you see all your email in a single inbox. You will also enjoy the new threaded message feature where all messages related to a single topic (replies, forwards, and so on) are kept together in a single group.

And for cases when your email is not working quite right, you will learn some good troubleshooting tips to help you get back up and running.

Getting Started with Mail

Setting up email on your iPod touch is fairly simple. You can sync email account settings from **iTunes** (see the "Sync Email Account Settings" section in Chapter 3: "Sync Your iPod touch with iTunes"), or you can set up email accounts directly on your iPod touch. You do need a network connection to get email up and running.

A Network Connection Is Required

Mobile email is all the rage today. You can view, read, and compose replies to emails already synced to your iPod touch without a network connection; however, you will need to have Wi-Fi network connectivity to send and/or receive email from your iPod touch. Check out Chapter 5: "Wi-Fi Connectivity" to learn more about this topic. Also check out the "Reading the Top Connectivity Status Icons" section in the Quick Start Guide in Part 1.

TIP: If you are taking a trip, simply download all your email before you get on the airplane; this lets you read, reply, and compose your messages while offline. All emails will be sent after you land and re-establish your connection to the Internet.

Setting up Email on the iPod touch

You have two options for setting up your email accounts on the iPod touch:

1. Use iTunes to sync email account settings.

2. Set up your email accounts directly on the iPod touch.

If you have a number of email accounts that you access from an email program on your computer (e.g., **Microsoft Outlook** and **Entourage**), then the easiest approach is to use **iTunes** to sync your accounts. See the "Sync Email Account Settings" section in Chapter 3: "Sync Your iPod touch with iTunes" for help.

If you only have a few accounts, or you do not use an email program on your computer that **iTunes** can sync with, then you will need to set up your email accounts directly on the iPod touch.

Entering Passwords for Email Accounts Synced from iTunes

In the "Sync Email Account Settings" section of Chapter 3: "Sync Your iPod touch with iTunes," we showed you how to sync your email account settings to your iPod touch. After this sync completes, you should be able to view all of the email accounts on your iPod touch by opening the **Settings** app. All you will need to do is enter the password for each account.

To enter your password for each synced email account, follow these steps (see Figure 14–1):

1. Tap the **Settings** icon.

2. Tap the **Mail, Contacts, and Calendars** option.

3. Under **Accounts**, you should see all your synced email accounts listed. Tap any listed email account, type its password, and click **Done**.

4. Repeat for all listed email accounts.

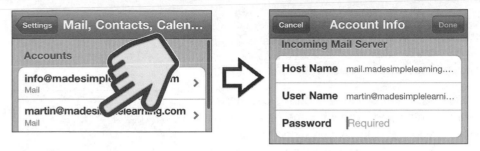

Figure 14-1. *Entering passwords for each email account synced from iTunes.*

Adding a New Email Account on the iPod touch

To add a new email account on your iPod touch, follow these steps:

All accounts you have set up will be listed here.

1. Tap the **Settings** icon.

2. Tap **Mail, Contacts, and Calendars**.

3. Tap **Add Account** below your email accounts.

> **TIP:** To edit any email account, just touch that account.

4. Choose which type of email account to add on this screen:

   - Tap **Microsoft Exchange** if you use a **Microsoft Exchange** email server or use Google and want to sync your **Google Contacts** and **Google Calendar** wirelessly.

   - Tap **Gmail** if you use **Gmail** and do not want your contacts synced wirelessly.

   - Tap **MobileMe, Yahoo, or Aol** if you use these services.

   - Tap **Other** to setup a different account.

> **TIP:** Learn more **Google/Microsoft Exchange** and **MobileMe** in Chapter 4: "Other Sync Methods."

5. If you select **Other** from the account type, then you will see the screen shown to the right. This screen lets you can add various types of mail, contact, and calendar accounts. Follow these steps to add the various types of accounts:

   - To add a mail account, tap **Add Mail Account**.

   - To add contact accounts, tap **Add LDAP Account** or **Add CardDAV Account**.

   - To add calendar accounts, tap **Add CalDAV Account** or **Add Subscribed Calendar**.

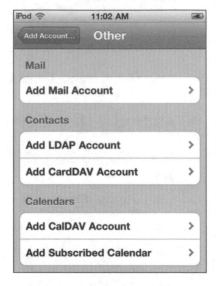

6. Now you will be able to enter your login credentials. Type your name as you would like others to see it when they receive mail from you into the **Name** field. If you selected a **Contacts** or **Calendars** type of account, then you would need to enter the **Server Name**, **User Name**, **Password**, and **Description**.

7. Next, add the appropriate information into the **Address**, **Password**, and **Description** fields.

8. Tap the **Next** button in the upper-right corner.

Specifying Incoming and Outgoing Servers

Sometimes, the iPod touch will not be able to automatically set up your email account. In these cases, you will need to type in a few more settings manually to enable your email account.

> **TIP:** You may be able to find the settings for your email provider by doing a web search for your email provider's name and "email settings." For example, if you use **Windows Live Hotmail** (formerly known as **Hotmail**), then you might search for "POP or IMAP email settings for Windows Live Hotmail." If you cannot find these settings, then contact your email provider for assistance.

If the iPod touch is unable to log in to your server with only your email address and password, then you see a screen similar to the one shown to the right.

Under **Incoming Mail Server**, type the appropriate information into the **Host Name**, **User Name**, and **Password** fields. Usually, your incoming mail server is something like **mail.*name_of_your_isp*.com**.

To adjust the name of your outgoing server, tap **Outgoing Mail Server.** You can adjust the outgoing mail server on the following screen. These server names usually look like either **smtp.*name_of_your_isp*.com** or **mail.*name_of_your_isp*.com**.

You can try to leave the **Server Name** and **Password** fields blank. If that doesn't work, you can always go back and change them.

You may be asked if you want to use SSL (*secure socket layer*), a type of outgoing mail security that may be required by your email provider. If you don't know whether you need it, just check the mail settings with your email provider.

> **TIP:** The authors recommend that you use SSL security whenever possible. If you do not use SSL, then your login credentials, messages, and any private information is sent in plain text (unencrypted), leaving it open to snoopers.

Verifying that Your Account Is Set Up

Once all the information is entered, the iPod touch will attempt to configure your email account. You may get an error message; if that happens, you need to review the information you input.

If you are taken to the screen that shows all your email accounts, look for the new account name.

If you see it, your account was set up correctly.

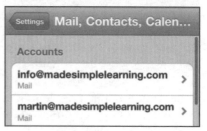

Fixing the "Cannot Get Mail" Error

If you tap **Mail** icon and you receive an error that says "Cannot Get Mail – No password provided for (your account)," you will need to enter your password.

Review this chapter's "Enter Passwords for Email Accounts Synced from iTunes" section for help.

A Tour of Your Mail Screens

Now that you have set up your email accounts on your iPod touch, it's time to take a brief tour of the **Mail** app. To better understand how to get around your **Mail** program, it helps to have a picture of how all the screens fit together (see Figure 14–2).

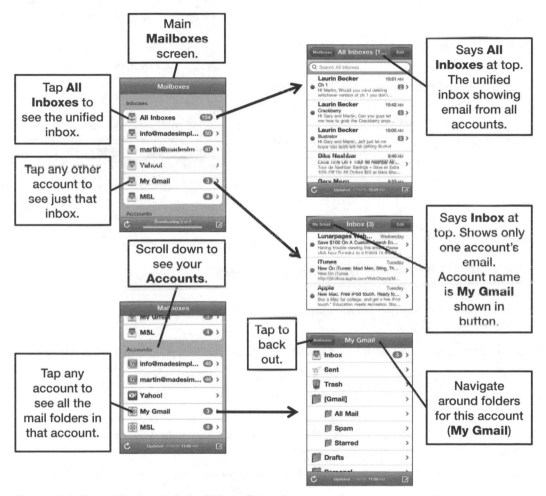

Figure 14–2. *How all the screens in the Mail app fit together.*

Mailboxes Screen - Inboxes and Accounts

The top-level screen is your **Mailboxes** screen. You can always get to it by tapping the button in the upper-left corner. Keep tapping this upper-left button until you see no more buttons. When that happens, you are in the **Mailboxes** screen.

From the **Mailboxes** screen you can access the following items:

- **The Unified Inbox**: Do so by tapping **All inboxes**.

- **The inbox for each individual account**: Do this by tapping that email account name in the **Inboxes** section.

- **The folders for each email account in the Accounts section**: Do so by tapping the account name to see all folders.

Inbox and Threaded Messages Views

You will notice that any unread messages are marked with a blue dot ● to the left of the message (see Figure 14–3).

You will also notice that some messages show a number and a right-facing arrow (>) to the right of the message, like this: **2** > This shows that there are two related messages (replies and forwards) to the message shown.

Tap any message to open it. The only time it will not open is if there are related messages. In that case, you will first see a screen with all the related messages. Tap any of those messages to open and view them.

To leave the **Inbox** view, tap the button in the upper-left corner.

You can tell which email account you are viewing by looking at the button in the upper-left corner.

- If the button says **Mailboxes**, you know you are looking at all your inboxes together.

- If the button says an account name, such as **martin@madesimplelearning.com**, then you know you are only looking at the inbox for that account.

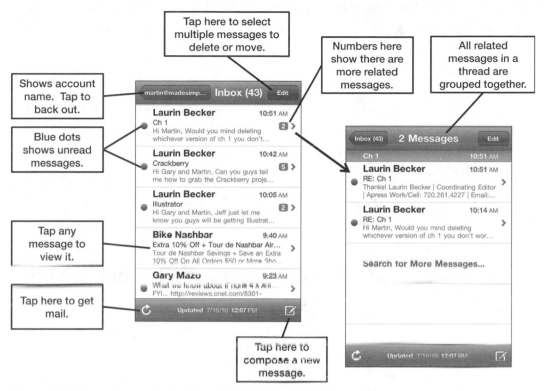

Figure 14–3. Inboxes on your iPod touch and threaded message views.

Moving Around in Mail Folders

You can get around your mail folders for each individual account by starting from the **Mailboxes** screen shown in Figure 14–4:

1. Swipe down to the bottom of the **Mailboxes** screen to see your accounts.

2. Tap any account to view all folders synced in that account.

> **NOTE:** You will only see those mail folders you have chosen to sync during the mail set up process. For example, you might have 20 mail folders on your main mail account, but you might only see a few folders on your iPod touch. The default synced mail folders are **Inbox**, **Sent**, **Draft**, and **Deleted Items**.

3. You may need to swipe to the bottom to see all your synced email folders.

4. Tap any folder to view the mail items in that folder.

5. To get back to the mail folders, tap the button in the upper-left corner.

6. To return to the **Mailboxes** screen, tap the **Mailboxes** button in the upper-left corner.

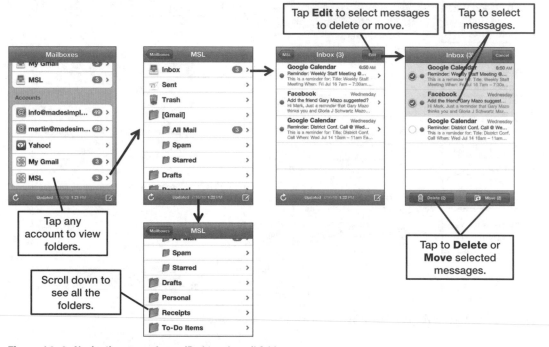

Figure 14–4. *Navigating around your iPod touch mail folders.*

Move or Delete Multiple Messages

If you want to move or delete several messages at once, you can do so from the **Inbox** screen (see the right-most two images in Figure 14–4). Follow these steps to delete multiple messages at once:

1. Tap the **Edit** button in the upper-right corner while you are viewing an **Inbox** screen.

2. Tap to select the desired messages; a red check mark next to a message indicates it is selected. Scroll up or down in your inbox to select as many messages as you want.

3. To delete the messages, tap the **Delete** button at the bottom.

4. To move the messages to another folder, tap the **Move** button and select the folder.

> **TIP:** Using the **Edit** feature in your **Mail** app is a fantastic way to quickly clean up your **Inbox**. Simply tap **Edit**, tap to select all the messages, and then tap **Delete** at the bottom. You have a clean **Inbox** in just a few taps!

Viewing an Individual Message

When you tap a message from the **Inbox** screen, you see the **Main** message view.

Portrait View

Holding your iPod touch in **Portrait** (vertical) orientation gives you the image shown in Figure 14–5. We will describe the various buttons and functions shown on this screen later in this chapter.

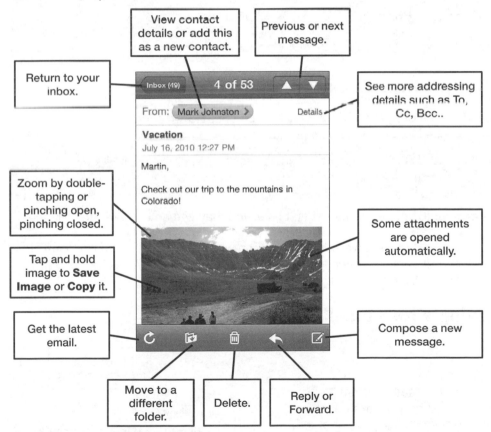

View contact details or add this as a new contact.

Previous or next message.

Return to your inbox.

See more addressing details such as To, Cc, Bcc..

Zoom by double-tapping or pinching open, pinching closed.

Some attachments are opened automatically.

Tap and hold image to **Save Image** or **Copy** it.

Get the latest email.

Compose a new message.

Move to a different folder.

Delete.

Reply or Forward.

Figure 14–5. *Buttons and actions available while viewing an email message.*

Landscape View

You may prefer to use the wider screen view, especially when enjoying pictures. To do this, just turn your iPod touch on its side to get the **Landscape** orientation.

TIP: If you are setting your iPod touch down on a desk or holding it in your lap, then you may want to use the **Portrait Lock** icon to lock your view in **Portrait** (vertical) mode. This will prevent the image from flipping around unnecessarily. To lock the view, follow these steps:

1. Double-tap the **Home** button and swipe left to right.

2. Tap the **Portrait Lock** button to lock the screen in **Portrait** mode.

Composing and Sending Emails

To launch the email program, tap the **Mail** icon on your **Home** screen.

TIP: If you left the **Mail** app while viewing a particular email, list of folders, or an account, then you will be returned directly to that same location when you return to the **Mail** app.

If you are going into your email for the first time, you may see an empty **Inbox**. Hit the

Refresh button in the lower-left corner of the window to retrieve the latest email. The iPod touch will begin to check for new mail and then display the number of new messages for each account.

Composing a New Email Message

When you start the **Mail** program, your first screen should be your **Accounts** screen. At the bottom-right corner of the screen, you will see the **Compose** icon. Touch the **Compose** icon to get started creating a new message.

Tap to compose a new message.

Addressing Your Message - Choose the Recipients

You have a few options for selecting recipients, depending on whether the person is in your **Contact List** on your iPod touch:

Option 1: Type a few letters of someone's first name, hit the **Space** key, and then type a few letters of that person's last name. The person's name should appear in the list; tap that person's name to select that contact.

Option 2: Type an email address. Notice the **@** and **Period** (**.**) keys on the keyboard, which help your typing.

> **TIP:** Press and hold the **period** key to see `.com`, `.edu`, `.org`, and other email domain name suffixes.

Option 3: Hit the **+** sign to view your entire **Contact List** and search or select a name from it.

If you want to use a different contact group, tap the **Groups** button in the upper left of the screen.

Deleting a Recipient

If you need to delete a name from the recipient list (e.g., from the **To:**, **Cc:**, or **Bcc:** fields), tap a name to select it To: martha@abcco.com and hit the **Backspace** key [⌫].

TIP: If you want to delete the last recipient you typed (and the cursor is sitting next to that name), hit the **Delete** key once to highlight the name and hit it a second time to delete it.

Adding a Cc or Bcc Recipient

 To add a carbon copy (**Cc:**) or blind carbon copy (**Bcc:**) recipient, you need to tap the **Cc:/Bcc:** just under the **To:** field at the top of the email message. Doing so opens up the tapped field.

Changing the Email Account to Send From

If you have more than one email account set up, the iPod touch will use whichever account is set as the default account. (This is set in **Settings** > **Mail, Contacts, Calendars** > **Default Account** at the bottom of the **Mail** section.)

Follow these steps to change the email account you send from:

1. Tap an email's **From:** field to highlight it.

2. Tap the **From:** field again to see a list of your accounts in a scroll wheel at the bottom of the screen.

3. Scroll up or down, and then tap a new email account to select it.

4. Tap the **Subject** field to finish changing the sending email address.

Type Your Subject

Now you need to enter a subject for your email. Follow these steps to do so:

1. Touch the **Subject:** line and enter text for the **Subject:** field of the email.

2. Press the **Return** key or tap the **Body** section of the email to move the cursor to the **Body** section.

Typing Your Message

Now that the cursor is in the body of the email (under the subject line), you can start typing your email message.

Email Signatures

The default email signature is shown in the image to the right: **Sent from my iPod**.

> **TIP:** You can change this signature to be anything you want; see the "Changing Your Email Signature" section later in this chapter for more information on this topic.

Keyboard Options

While you are typing, remember you have two keyboard options: the smaller **Portrait** (vertical) keyboard and the larger **Landscape** (horizontal) keyboard (see Figure 14–6).

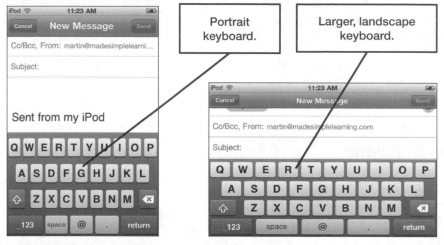

Figure 14–6. *You have two built-in keyboards for typing.*

TIP: If you have larger hands, it might be easier to type when the keyboard is larger. Once you get the hang of typing on the larger keyboard with two hands, you will find that it is much faster than typing with one finger. Also, you will see auto-capitalization and auto-correction happening. Learn more typing tips in Chapter 2: "Typing Tips, Copy/Paste, and Search."

Send Your Email

Once you have typed your message, tap the blue **Send** button in the top-right corner. Your email will be sent, and you should hear the iPod touch's sent mail sound, which confirms that your email was sent. You can learn how to enable or disable this sound in the "Adjusting Sounds on your iPod touch" section of Chapter 7: "Personalize and Secure your iPod touch."

Save As Draft to Send Later

If you are not ready to send your message, but want to save it as a draft message to send later, follow these steps:

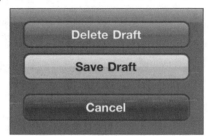

1. Compose your message, as described earlier.

2. Press the **Cancel** button in the upper-left corner.

3. Select the **Save Draft** button at the bottom of the screen.

Later, when you want to locate and send your draft message, follow these steps:

1. Open the **Drafts** folder in the email account from which you composed this message. See the "Moving Around in Mail Folders" section earlier in this chapter for help getting into the **Drafts** folder.

2. Tap an email message in the **Drafts** folder to open it.

3. Tap anywhere in the message to edit it.

4. Tap the **Send** button.

Checking Sent Messages

Follow these steps to confirm that the email was sent correctly:

1. Tap the **Email account name** button in the upper-left corner to see the mail folders for the account you just used to send your message.

2. Tap the **Sent** folder.

3. Verify that that the top email you see in the list is the one you just composed and sent.

NOTE: You will only see the **Sent** and **Trash** folders if you have actually sent or deleted email from that account on the iPod touch. If your email account is an IMAP account, you may see many folders other than those described in this chapter.

Reading and Replying to Mail

Follow these steps to read your email:

1. Navigate to the **Inbox** of the email account you want to view using the steps described earlier in this chapter.

2. To read any message, just touch it from your **Inbox**.

3. New, unread messages are shown with a small blue dot to the left of the message.

4. Flick your finger up or down in the **Inbox** to scroll through your messages.

5. When you are reading a message, swipe up or down to scroll through it.

Tap here to reply or forward.

Zooming In or Out

As when browsing the Web, you can zoom in to see your email in larger text. You can also double-tap, just as you do on the Web; and you can also **Pinch** to zoom in or out (see the "Zooming" section in our Quick Started Guide in Part 1 of this book for more information on these features).

Email Attachments

Some email attachments are opened automatically by the iPod touch, so you don't even notice that they were attachments. Examples of these include Adobe's portable document format (**PDF**) files (used by **Adobe Acrobat** and **Adobe Reader**, among other apps) and some types of image, video, and audio files. You may also receive documents such as Apple **Pages**, **Numbers**, **Keynote**, Microsoft **Word**, **Excel**, and **PowerPoint** files as attachments. You will need to open these.

Knowing When You Have an Attachment

Any email with an attachment will

have a little **Paperclip** icon next to the sender's name, as shown to the right. When you see that icon, you know you have an attachment.

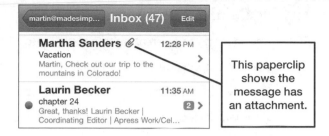

Receiving an Auto-open Attachment

Now assume you received a one-page **PDF** file or an image. (Multipage **PDF** files require that you tap to open them.) Once you open a mail message with this kind of attachment, you will see it directly below the message (see Figure 14–7).

Figure 14–7. *Some attachments will open automatically, while others will need to opened.*

> **TIP:** If you want to save or copy an auto-opened attachment, simply press and hold until you see the pop-up window. At this point, you can select **Copy** or **Save Image**. When you save an image, it will be placed in your **Photos** app in the **Camera Roll** album.

Opening Email Attachments

Instead of immediately opening in the body of the email as we just described, other types of attachments will need to be opened manually. Such attachments include spreadsheets, word processing documents, and presentation files.

Tap for Quick Look Mode

Follow these steps to open attachments in **Quick Look** mode:

1. Open the message with an attachment (see Figure 14–8).

2. Quickly tap the attachment to instantly open it in **Quick Look** mode.

3. You can navigate around the document. Remember you can zoom in or out and swipe up or down.

4. If you open a spreadsheet with multiple tabs or spreadsheets, you will see tabs across the top. Touch another tab to open that spreadsheet.

5. When you are done looking at the attachment, tap the document once to bring up the controls, and then tap **Done** in the upper-left corner.

6. If you have apps installed that can open the type of attachment you are viewing (in this case a spreadsheet), then you will see an **Open In** button in the upper-right corner. Tap the **Open In** button to open this file in another app.

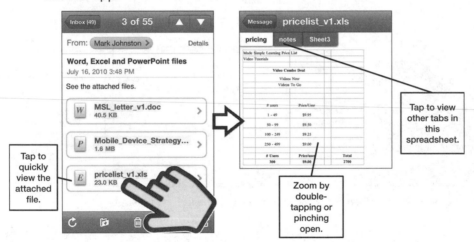

Figure 14–8. *Quickly viewing attachments by tapping them.*

Opening Docs in Other Apps

You may want to open the attachment in another application. For example, you might want to open a **PDF** file in **iBooks, Stanza,** or **GoodReader.** Follow these steps to do so:

1. Open the email message.

2. Press and hold the attachment until you see the pop-up window.

3. Select the **Open In** option.

4. Select the application you would like to use from the list (Figure 14–9 shows a user choosing **Stanza**).

5. Finally, you can edit the document, save it, and email it back to the sender.

> **TIP:** We have heard rumors that the Apple word processor, spreadsheet, and presentation software (**Pages**, **Numbers**, and **Keynote**) is coming soon to the iPod touch. Our *iPad Made Simple* book (Apress, 2010) includes descriptions of these apps because they are already available for the iPad.

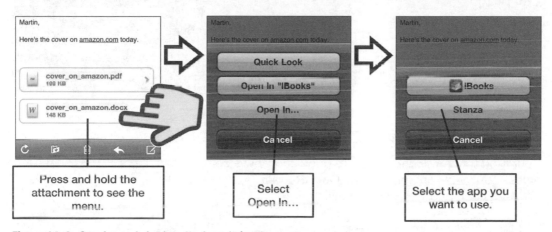

Figure 14–9. *Opening and viewing attachments in other apps.*

Viewing a Video Attachment

You may receive a video as an attachment to an email. Certain types of videos can be viewed on your iPod touch (see the "Supported Email Attachment Types" section later in this chapter for a list of supported video formats). Follow these steps to open a video attachment:

1. Tap the video attachment to open it and view it in the video player.

2. When you are done viewing the video, tap the screen to bring up the player controls.

3. Tap the **Done** button in the upper-left corner to return to the email message.

Opening and Viewing Compressed .zip Files

Your iPod touch will not be able to open and view a compressed file of .zip format unless you install an app such as **GoodReader**. At publishing time, **GoodReader** was still a free app and well worth installing.

> **TIP:** Learn how to install and use **GoodReader** it in Chapter 26: "New Media: Reading Newspapers, Magazines, and More."

1. Install the free **GoodReader** from the App Store.

2. Open up the email message with the .zip file attachment.

3. Touch and hold the .zip attachment until you see a pop-up window at the bottom with a button that says **Open in "GoodReader."** Tap that button to open the .zip in **GoodReader**.

> **CAUTION:** Do not just quickly tap the attachment to open it. At publishing time, this resulted in a blank white or black screen with nothing happening. Make sure to touch and hold the attachment until you see the button pop up.

4. **GoodReader** should now open and your .zip file should be at the top of the list of files. To open or uncompress the .zip file, tap the file and select the **Unzip** button.

5. Now you should see the uncompressed file, which in this case is an Adobe .pdf file in the list of files above the .zip file.

6. Tap that uncompressed file to view it.

7. When you are done reading the attachment, double-click your **Home** button and tap the **Mail** icon to return to your reading your email.

Issues When Opening Email Attachments

Some types of attachments cannot be opened on your iPod touch. Such attachments show up with a **Question Mark (?)** icon. In the image to the right, we tried to click an attachment of the type winmail.dat, which failed.

Supported Email Attachment Types

Your iPod touch supports the following file types as attachments:

- .doc and .docx (**Microsoft Word** documents)

- .htm and .html (web pages)

- .key (a **Keynote** presentation document)

- .numbers (an **Apple Numbers** spreadsheet document)

- .pages (an **Apple Pages** document)

- .pdf (Adobe's portable document format, used by programs such as **Adobe Acrobat** and **Adobe Reader**)

- .ppt and .pptx (**Microsoft PowerPoint** presentation documents)

- .txt (a text file)

- .vcf (a contact file)

- .xls and .xlsx (**Microsoft Excel** spreadsheet documents)

- .mp3 and .mov (audio and video formats)

- .zip (compressed files -these are only readable if you have an app installed that can read them such as **GoodReader**; see the "Opening and Viewing Compressed .zip Files" section earlier in this chapter.

- Audio formats supported:

    - HE-AAC (V1)

    - AAC (16 to 320 Kbps)

    - Protected AAC (from iTunes Store)

    - MP3 (16 to 320 Kbps)

    - MP3 VBR

    - Audible (formats 2, 3, and 4)

    - Apple Lossless

    - AIFF

    - WAV

- Video formats supported:

    - H.264 video up to 720p at 30 frames per second

    - Main Profile level 3.1 with AAC-LC audio up to 160 Kbps, 48kHz

- Stereo audio in `.m4v`, `.mp4`, and `.mov` file formats

- MPEG-4 video, up to 2.5 Mbps, 640 by 480 pixels, and at 30 frames per second

- Simple Profile with AAC-LC audio up to 160 Kbps, 48kHz, stereo audio in `.m4v`, `.mp4`, and `.mov` file formats

- Motion JPEG (M-JPEG) up to 35 Mbps, 1280 by 720 pixels, 30 frames per second, and audio in ulaw

- PCM stereo audio in `.avi` file format

Replying, Forwarding, or Deleting a Message

At the bottom of your email-reading pane is a toolbar.

From this toolbar, you can move the message to a different mailbox or folder; delete it; or reply, reply all, or forward it.

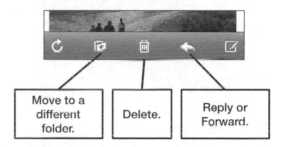

Move to a different folder.

Delete.

Reply or Forward.

Touch the **Small Arrow** icon  to see these option buttons appear: **Reply**, **Reply All**, and **Forward**.

> **NOTE:** The **Reply All** button appears only if there was more than one recipient for the email message.

You can reply, reply all or forward messages

Reply

Reply All

Forward

Cancel

Replying to an Email

You will probably use the **Reply** command most frequently. Follow these steps to respond to an email on your iPod touch:

1. Touch the **Reply** button.

    You will see that the original sender is now listed as the recipient in the **To:** line of the email. The subject will automatically state: "Re: *(Original subject line)*."

2. Type your response.

3. When you are done, just touch the blue **Send** button at the top-right corner of the screen.

Using Reply All

Using the **Reply All** option is just like using the **Reply** function, except that all of the original recipients of the email and the original sender are placed in the address lines. The original sender will be in the **To:** line, while all other recipients of the original email will be listed on the **Cc:** line. You will only see the **Reply All** option if more than one person received the original email.

> **CAUTION:** Be careful when you use **REPLY ALL**. This can be dangerous if some of the recipients are not shown on the original email because they stretch off the edge of the screen. If you do use **REPLY ALL**, then make sure you check the **To:** and **Cc:** lists to make sure everyone should be receiving your reply.

Using the Forward Button

Sometimes you get an email that you want to send to someone else. The **Forward** command will let you do that (see the "Email Attachments" section earlier in this chapter for more about working with attachments.)

> **NOTE:** You need to forward attachments to send them to others. If you want to send someone an attachment from an email you receive, you must choose the **Forward** option. (Note that choosing the **Reply** and **Reply All** options will not include the original email attachment(s) in your outgoing message.)

When you touch the **Forward** button, you may be prompted to address whether you want to include attachments (if there were any) from the original message.

At this point, you follow the same steps described previously to type your message, add addressees, and send the message.

Cleaning up and Organizing Your Inbox

As you get more comfortable with your iPod touch as an email device, you will increasingly find yourself using the **Mail** program. It will eventually become necessary to occasionally do some email housecleaning. You can delete or move email messages easily on your iPod touch.

Deleting a Single Message

To delete a single message from your **Inbox**, follow these steps:

1. Swipe right or left on a message in the **Inbox** to bring up the **Delete** button.

2. Tap **Delete** to remove the message.

> **NOTE:** for Gmail IMAP accounts it will say **Archive** instead of **Delete**.

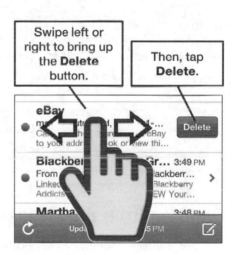

Swipe left or right to bring up the **Delete** button.

Then, tap **Delete**.

Deleting or Moving Several Messages

It's easy to delete several messages on the iPod touch. Follow these steps to do so:

1. View any mail folder on your iPod touch.

2. Tap the **Edit** button in the upper-right corner.

3. Select one or more messages by tapping them. You will see a red check mark for each selected message.

4. Once the messages are selected, you can delete or move them.

5. To delete the selected messages, tap the **Delete** button at the bottom.

6. To move the selected messages, tap the **Move** button and select the folder to which you want to move the messages.

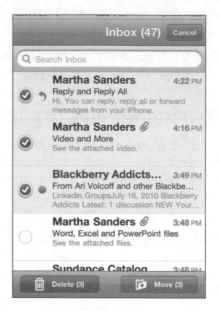

> **TIP:** You do not get another prompt before the messages are moved to the **Trash** or **Archived** folder. If you need to restore any of these messages, navigate to your **Trash** folder and move the messages back to your **Inbox** folder. Exchange and IMAP email accounts will sync these folder moves to your email server, POP3 accounts will not.

Deleting from the Message Screen

The **Message** screen includes another way to delete messages. Follow these steps to do so:

1. Open any message to read it.

2. Tap the **Trash Can** icon in the bottom middle of the screen.

    You will see the email shrink and fly into the **Trash Can**, so it can be deleted.

> **TIP:** You can use the **Settings** app to make your iPod touch ask you before deleting email. To do so, tap **Mail, Contacts, Calendars** and set the switch next to **Ask Before Deleting** to **Yes**.

You can organize your mail by moving it into other folders. Email messages can be moved out of your **Inbox** for storage or for reading at another time.

> **NOTE:** To create folders in addition to the default **Inbox** and **Trash** folders, you need to set them up in your main email account and sync them to your iPod touch. We will show you how to do this in this chapter's "Fine Tune Your Email Settings" section.

Moving an Email to a Folder While Viewing It

Sometimes, you may want to organize your email for easy retrieval later. For example, you might receive an email about an upcoming trip and want to move it to the **Travel** folder. Sometimes you receive emails that require attention later, in which case you can move them to the **Requires Attention** folder. This can help you remember to work on such emails later.

Follow these steps to move an email message:

1. Open the email message.

2. Tap the **Move** icon in the upper-right corner.

3. Choose a new folder, and the message will be moved out of the **Inbox**.

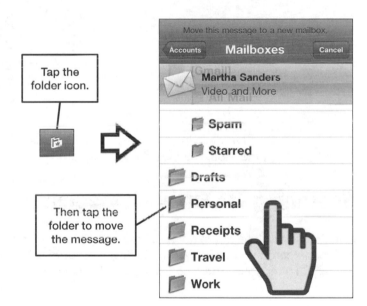

Tap the folder icon.

Then tap the folder to move the message.

Copy-and-Paste from an Email

Here are a few tips to select text or pictures and copy them from an email message:

- Double-tap text to select a word, then drag the blue handles up or down to adjust the selection.

  Next, select **Copy**.

- Press and hold text, and then choose **Select** or **Select All**.

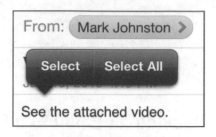

- Press and hold an image, and then select **Save Image** or **Copy**.

For a more complete description, please check out the "Copy and Paste" section in Chapter 2: "Typing Tips, Copy/Paste and Search."

Searching for Email Messages

The iPod touch has some good built-in search functionality to help you find your emails. You can search your **Inbox** by the **From:**, **To:**, **Subject**, or **All** fields. This functionality helps you filter your **Inbox**, so you can find exactly what you are searching for.

Activating Email Search

You initiate an email search by going to the **Inbox** of the account you wish to search. If you scroll up to the top, you will see the familiar **Search** bar at the top of your **Inbox** (see Figure 14–10).

If your email account supports the feature, you can also search the server for email messages. At the time of writing, a few of the supported types of searchable email accounts include **Exchange**, **MobileMe**, and **Gmail IMAP**. Follow these steps to search through your email on a server:

1. Touch the **Search** bar to see a new menu of soft keys under the **Search** bar.

2. Type the text you wish to search for.

3. Touch one of the soft keys under the search window:

    a. **From**: Searches only the sender's email addresses.

    b. **To**: Searches only the recipients' email addresses.

    c. **Subject**: Searches only message **Subject** fields.

    d. **All**: Searches every part of the message.

For example, assume I want to search my **Inbox** for an email I received from Martin. I would type Martin's name into the **Search** box and then touch **From**. My **Inbox** would then be filtered to show only the emails from Martin.

> **NOTE:** If you have multiple email accounts, you can search al particular inbox or search all of your inboxes at the same time. For a more global search on your iPod touch, use the **Spotlight Search** feature shown in the "Finding Things with Spotlight Search" section of Chapter 2: "Typing Tips, Copy/Paste, and Search."

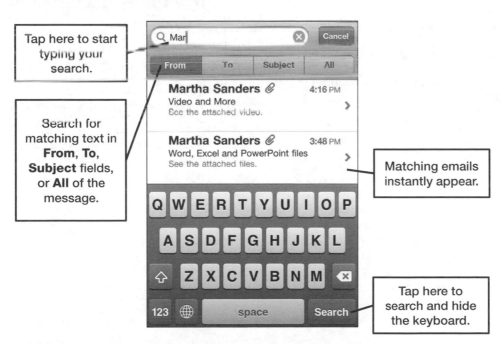

Figure 14–10. *Searching for email using the From, To, Subject, or All fields.*

Fine Tuning Your Email Settings

You can fine tune your email accounts on your iPod touch with the myriad options available in the **Settings** app.

Follow these steps to change these settings:

1. Tap the **Settings** icon.

2. Tap **Mail, Contacts, Calendars**.

The sections that follow explain the adjustments you can make.

Automatically Retrieve Email (Fetch New Data)

In addition to the options under **Advanced**, you can use the **Email** settings to configure how often your email is fetched or pulled to your iPod touch. By default, your iPod touch automatically receives mail or other contact or calendar updates when they are *pushed* from the server.

You can adjust this setting by taking the following steps:

1. Touch the **Settings** icon.

2. Touch **Mail, Contacts, Calendars**.

3. Touch **Fetch New Data** under the email accounts listed.

4. Set **Push** to **ON** (default) to automatically have the server push data. Turn It **OFF** to conserve your battery life.

5. Adjust the timing schedule to pull data from the server. This is how frequently applications should pull new data from the server.

> **NOTE:** If you set this option to **Every 15 Minutes**, you will receive more frequent updates, but sacrifice battery life compared to a setting of **Hourly**.

Having automatic retrieval is very handy if you just want to turn on your iPod touch and see that you have messages; otherwise, you need to remember to check.

Advanced Push Options

At the bottom of the **Fetch New Data** screen, below the **Hourly** and **Manually** settings, you can touch the **Advanced** button to see a new screen with all your email accounts listed.

Tap any email account to adjust its settings.

Most accounts can be **Fetched** on the schedule you set or set to **Manual**. The **Manual** option requires that you retrieve data using the **Update** button. This screen gives you the ability to adjust **Fetch**, **Manual**, or in some cases **Push** settings for each account you have set up.

Adjusting Your Mail Settings

Under the **Accounts** section, you can see all the email settings listed under **Mail**. The **Default** settings may work well for you; however, if you need to adjust any of these settings, you can follow these steps:

Show: This sets how many emails are pulle from the server. You can specify anywhere 25 to 200 messages (the default is 50 recen messages).

Preview: This option lets you set how man) lines of text in addition to the **Subject** are s in the **Inbox** preview. You can adjust this va from **None** to **5 Lines** (the default is **2 Lines**

Minimum Font Size: This is the default font size shown when opening an email the first time. It is also smallest font size that you are allowed to zoom out to when viewing an email. Your options are **Small**, **Medium**, **Large**, **Extra Large**, and **Giant** (the default is **Medium**).

Show To/Cc Label: With this option set to **ON**, you will see a small **To** or **Cc** label in your **Inbox** before the subject. This label shows which field your address was placed in (the default state of this option is **OFF**).

Ask Before Deleting: Change this option to **ON** to be asked every time you try to delete a message (the default is **OFF**).

Load Remote Images: This option allows your iPod touch to load all the graphics (remote images) that are placed in some email messages (the default value for this option is **ON**).

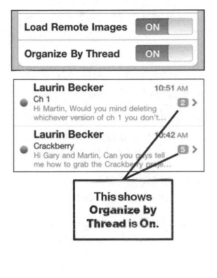

Organize by Thread: This option groups related emails together. It shows only one message, with a number next to it. That number indicates how many related emails exist. This feature gives you a good way to keep all discussions together in one place (the default value of this option is **ON**).

Always Bcc Myself: This option sends a blind carbon copy (**Bcc:**) of every email you send from your iPod touch to your email account (the default value of this option is **OFF**).

Changing Your Email Signature

By default, emails you send will say "Sent from my iPod." Follow these steps to change the **Signature** line of the email:

1. Tap the **Signature** tab and type in the new email signature you want at the bottom of emails sent from your iPod touch.

2. When you are done editing the **Signature** field, tap the **Mail, Contacts...** button in the upper-left corner. This will return you to the **Mail** settings screen.

Changing Your Default Mail Account (Sent From)

If you have multiple email accounts set up on your iPod touch, you should set one of them – usually, the one you use most – as your **Default Account**. When you select **Compose** from the **Email** screen, the default account is always chosen. Follow these steps to change the email account you send from by default:

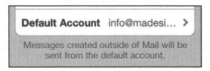

1. Tap the **Default Account** option, and you will see a list of all your email accounts.

2. Tap the one you wish to use as your **Default Account** choice.

3. When you are done, touch the **Mail, Contacts...** button to return to the **Mail** settings menu.

Toggling Sounds for Receiving and Sending Email

You may notice a little sound effect every time you send or receive email. What you hear is the default setting on your iPod touch.

If you want to disable this or change it, you do so in the **Settings** program:

1. Tap your **Settings** icon.

2. Tap **Sounds**.

3. You will see various switches to turn sound effects on or off. Tap **New Mail** and **Sent Mail** to adjust the **ON** or **OFF** options.

Advanced Email Options

NOTE: Email accounts set up as **Exchange**, **IMAP**, or **MobileMe** will not have this **Advanced** email settings screen. This only applies to POP3 email accounts.

To get to the **Advanced** options for each email account, follow these steps:

1. Touch the **Settings** icon.

2. Touch **Mail, Contacts, Calendars**.

3. Touch an email address listed under **Accounts**.

4. At the bottom of the mail settings popup window, tap the **Advanced** button to bring up the **Advanced** dialog.

Removing Email Messages from iPod touch After Deletion

You can select how frequently you want email removed completely from your iPod touch once it is deleted.

Touch the **Remove** tab and select the option that is best for you; the default setting is **Never**.

Using SSL/Authentication

These features were discussed previously, but this option supplies another location to access these features for a particular email account.

Deleting from Server

You can configure your iPod touch to handle the deletion of messages from your email server. Usually, this setting is left at **Never**; typically, this function is handled on your main computer. If you use your iPod touch as your main email device, however, you might want to handle that feature from the phone itself. Follow these steps to use your iPod to remove deleted emails from the server:

1. Touch the **Delete from Server** tab to select the feature that best suits your needs: **Never**, **Seven Days**, or **When removed from Inbox**.

2. The default setting is **Never**. The **Seven Days** option should give you enough time to check email on your computer, as well as your iPod touch, and then decide what to keep and what to get rid of.

Changing the Incoming Server Port

As you did with the **Outgoing Server Port** earlier, you can change the **Incoming Server Port** if you are having trouble receiving email. It is very rare that your troubles will be related to the port you receive mail on, which means that you will rarely need to change this number. If your email service provider gives you a different number, just touch the numbers and input a new port. The value for an **Incoming Server Port** is usually 995, 993, or 110; however, the port value could also be another number.

Troubleshooting Email Problems

Usually, your email works flawlessly on your iPod touch. Sometimes, whether it is a server issue, a network connectivity issue, or an email service provider requirement; email may not work as flawlessly as you would hope.

More often than not, there is a simple setting that needs to be adjusted or a password that needs to be re-entered.

If you try out some of the troubleshooting tips that follow and your email is still not working, then your email server may just be down temporarily. Check with your email service provider to make sure your mail server is up and running; you might also check whether your provider has made any recent changes that would affect your settings.

TIP: If these tips that follow do not solve the problem, please check out Chapter 28: "Troubleshooting" for more helpful tips and resources.

Email Isn't Being Received or Sent

If you can't send or receive email, your first step should be to verify you are connected to the Internet. Look for Wi-Fi or 3G connectivity in the upper-left corner of your **Home** screen (see the "How Do I Know When I'm Connected?" section of the "Quick Start Guide" for details.

Sometimes, you need to adjust the outgoing port for email to be sent properly. Do so by following these steps.

1. Tap **Settings**.

2. Touch **Mail, Contacts and Calendars**

3. Touch your email account that is having trouble sending messages under **Accounts**.

4. Touch **SMTP** and verify that your outgoing mail server is set correctly; also check that it is set to **On**.

5. Touch **Outgoing Mail Server** at the top and verify all the settings, such as **Host Name**, **User Name**, **Password**, **SSL**, **Authentication**, and **Server Port**. You might also try 587, 995, or 110 for the **Server Port** value; sometimes that helps.

6. Click **Done** and the email account name in the upper-left corner to return to the **Email** settings screen for this account.

7. Scroll down to the bottom and touch **Advanced**.

8. You can also try a different port setting for the server port on this screen, such as 587, 995, or 110. If those values don't work, contact your email service provider to get a different port number and verify your settings.

Verifying Your Mail Account Settings

Follow these steps to verify your account settings:

1. Tap the **Settings** icon.

2. Tap **Mail, Contacts, Calendars**.

3. If you received an error message from a particular email account, touch that that account.

4. Verify that the **Account** is set to **ON**.

5. Verify that your email **Address** is correct in the **POP Account Information** section.

6. Verify that the information in the **Host Name**, **User Name**, and **Password** fields is all correct.

7. If you received an error message while trying to send an email, the issue will be most likely in the **SMTP** settings in your **Outgoing Mail Server** area.

8. Tap **SMTP** to adjust more settings.

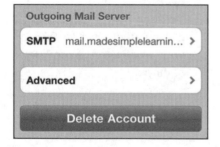
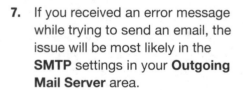

9. Touch the **Primary Server** tab and make sure that it is set to **On**.

10. Underneath the **Primary Server** tab, you will see other SMTP servers that are used for your other email accounts. One option is to use one of the other SMTP servers that you know is working. In that case, just touch the tab for that server and turn that switch to **On**.

11. Tap the **Primary Server** address to view and adjust more settings.

12. Verify that the **Primary Server** is **ON**.

13. Contact your email service provider to verify other settings, such as **Host Name**, **User Name**, **Password**, **SSL**, **Authentication**, and **Server Port**. We will share more details and some tips about these settings in the sections that follow.

14. Tap the **Done** button when finished and then tap the button with your email account listed in the upper-left corner to return to previous screens. Or, you can tap the **Home** button to exit to your **Home** screen.

Using SSL

Some SMTP servers require the use of *secure socket layer* (SSL) security. If you are having trouble sending email and the **Use SSL** switch is set to **OFF**, try setting it to **ON** to see if that helps.

Changing the Method of Authentication

Under the SSL switch is an **Authentication** tab. Usually, **Password** is the correct setting for this switch. We don't recommend that you change this setting unless you have specific directions from your email service provider to make a change.

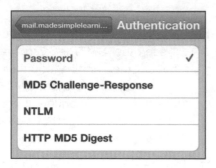

Changing the Server Port

Most often, when you configure your email account, the server port is set for you. Sometimes there are tweaks that need to be made that are specific to your ISP.

If you have been given specific settings from your ISP, you can change the server port to try to alleviate any errors you might be seeing. Follow these steps to change the **Server Port** settings:

1. Go back to the specific **SMTP** settings for your account.

2. Touch the tab for the **Primary Server**, as you did in the "Verify Mail Account Settings" section.

3. Scroll down to **Server Port** and touch the screen on the number indicated.

4. This causes a keyboard to pop up, which you can use to input a new port number (the one given you by your ISP). Most often, the number provided by your ISP will be 995, 993, 587, or 110; however, if you're given a different number, just input it.

5. When you are done, touch the **SMTP** tab in the upper-left corner to return to the previous screen.

Chapter 15

Working with Contacts

Your iPod touch gives you immediate access to all your important information. Just like your computer, your iPod touch can store thousands of contacts for easy retrieval. In this chapter, we'll show you how to add new contacts (including from an email address), customize your contacts by adding new fields, organize your contacts into groups, quickly search or scroll through contacts, and even show a contact's location with the iPod touch **Maps** app. We will also show you how to customize the **Contacts** view so it is sorted and displayed just the way you like it. Finally, you will learn a few troubleshooting tips

The beauty of the iPod touch is how it integrates all of the apps so you can email and map your contacts right from the contact entry.

Loading Your Contacts onto the iPod touch

Chapter 3: "Sync Your iPod touch with iTunes" covers how to load your contacts onto the iPod touch using iTunes on your Mac or Windows computer. You can also use the Google Sync or MobileMe services described in Chapter 4: "Other Sync Methods."

> **TIP:** You can add new contact entries from email messages you receive. Learn how in Chapter 14: "Email on Your iPod touch."

When Is Your Contact List Most Useful?

The **Contacts** app is most useful when two things are true:

1. You have many names and addresses in it.

2. You can easily find what you need.

Two Simple Rules to Improve Your Contact List

Here are a couple of basic rules to help make your contact list on your iPod touch more useful.

Rule 1: Add anything and everything to your contacts.

> You never know when you might need that obscure restaurant name or that plumber's number.

Rule 2: As you add entries, make sure you think about how to find them in the future (by first name, last name, or company name).

> This chapter offers many tips and tricks to help you enter names so that they can be instantly located when you need them.

> **TIP:** Here's a good way to find restaurants. Whenever you enter a restaurant into your contacts list, put the word "restaurant" into the company name field, even if it's not part of the name. Then when you type the letters "rest," you'll instantly access all your restaurants!

Adding a New Contact Right on Your iPod touch

You can always add your contacts right into your iPod touch. This is handy when you're away from your computer—but have your iPod touch —and need to add someone to your contacts. It's very easy to do. Here's how!

Start the Contacts App

From your Home screen, touch the **Contacts** icon and you'll see the **All Contacts** list. Tap the **+** in the upper right corner to add a new contact, as shown in Figure 15–1.

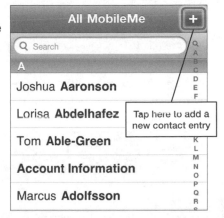

Touch the **First Last** button and enter the new contact's first and last names. You can also add a company name.

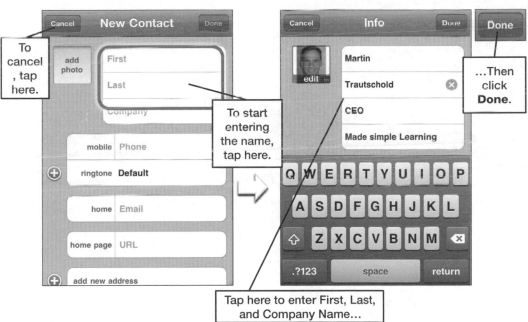

Figure 15–1. *Entering a new contact name.*

Touch the **First Last** button and enter the new contact's first and last names. You can also add a company name.

> **TIP:** Keep in mind that the contacts search feature uses first, last, and company names. When you add or edit contacts, adding a special word to the company name can help you find a particular contact later. For example, adding the words "Cece friend" to the **Company** field can help you find all of Cece's friends quickly using the search feature.

Under the **First Last** button are five more buttons, as shown in Figure 15–2. Each is activated by touching either the green "**+**" to the left of the button (when available) or the button itself.

Figure 15–2. *Available contact fields.*

Adding a New Phone Number

Touch the **Phone** button and use the number keyboard to input the phone number.

> **TIP:** Don't worry about parentheses, dashes, or dots—the iPod touch will put the number into the correct format. Just type the digits of the area code and number. If you know the country code, it's a good idea to put that in as well.

Next, choose which type of phone number this Is—mobile, home, work, or other type. There are nine fields you can choose from, and there's also a **Custom** field if you find that none of the built-in fields apply.

Adding an Email Address and Web Site

Touch the **Email** tab and enter the email address for your contact. You can also touch the tab to the left of the email address and select whether this is a home, work, or other email address.

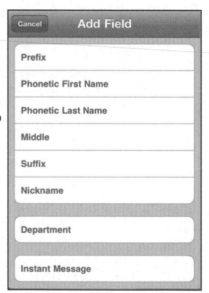

Under the **Email** field, you'll also find a **home page** field in which you can enter the address of your contact's web site.

NOTE: If you used MobileMe to sync your contacts, MobileMe will automatically look for a Facebook homepage to integrate into the contact info if you have the **Facebook** app installed and set it to sync contacts.

The iPod touch gives you the option to include only the fields that are relevant for a particular contact. Just touch the **add field** tab and select any of the suggested fields to add to that particular contact.

For example, to add a **Birthday** field to this contact, just touch **Birthday**.

When you touch **Birthday**, you're presented
with a wheel. Spin the wheel to the
corresponding date to add the birthday to
the contact information.

TIP: Suppose you meet someone at the bus stop—someone you want to remember. Of course,
you should enter your new friend's first and last names (if you know it), but you should also enter
the words "bus stop" in the **Company name** field. Then when you type the letters "bus" or
"stop," you'll instantly find everyone you met at the bus stop, even if you can't remember their
names!

Adding the Address

Below the **home** field are the fields for adding
the address. Input the **Street**, **City**, **State,** and
Zip Code. You can also specify the **Country**
and whether this is a home or work address.

When you are done, just touch the **Done** button
in the upper right corner of the **New Contact**
form.

Adding a Photo to Contacts

From the New Contact screen you've been working in, just touch the **Add Photo** button next to the **First Last** tab.

If you are changing a photo, when you are in edit contact mode, you'll see **edit** at the bottom of the existing photo.

After you touch the **add photo** button, you'll see that you can

- Take a Photo
- Choose a Photo

If there's a photo already in place, you can

- Edit a Photo
- Delete a Photo

To choose an existing photo, select the photo album where the picture is located and touch the corresponding tab. When you see the picture you want to use, just touch it.

You'll notice that the top and bottom of the photo become grayed out and that you can manipulate the picture by moving it, pinching to zoom in or out, and then arranging it in the picture window.

Once the picture is sitting where you want it, just touch the **Choose** button in the lower right corner and that picture will be set for the contact.

TIP: If you just moved into a new neighborhood, it can be quite daunting to remember everyone's name. A good practice to follow is to add the word "neighbor" into the **Company name** field for every neighbor you meet. To instantly call up all your neighbors, simply type the letters "neigh."

Searching Your Contacts

Let's say you need to find a specific phone number or email address. Just touch your **Contacts** icon as you did previously. You'll see a search box at the top of your **All Contacts** list, as shown in Figure 15–3.

Figure 15–3. *The contacts search box.*

Enter the first few letters of any of these three searchable fields:

- First Name
- Last Name
- Company Name

The iPod touch begins to filter immediately and displays only those contacts that match the letters typed.

> **TIP:** To further narrow the search, hit the space key and type a few more letters.

When you see the correct name, just touch it and that individual's contact information will appear.

Quickly Jump to a Letter by Tapping and Sliding on the Alphabet

If you hold your finger on the alphabet on the left edge of the screen and drag it up or down, you can jump to that letter.

Search by Flicking

If you don't want to manually input letters, you can just move your finger and flick from the bottom up, and you'll see your contacts move quickly on the screen. Just continue to flick or scroll until you see the name you want. Tap the name and the contact information will appear.

Search Using Groups

If you have your contacts sorted by groups on your PC or Mac and you sync your iPod touch 4 with the computer or over the air using MobileMe, those groups will be synced to your iPod touch 4. When you start your **Contacts** app, you will see **Groups** at the top. Under the Groups heading, you will see **All Contacts**.

Choose **All Contacts** to search all the available contact information on the iPod touch.

If you have multiple accounts synced, you will see a tab for each individual account and one for **All Contacts** at the top.

This example shows two groups— one is a Microsoft Exchange account (i.e., a company email account) and the other is my **MobileMe** contacts.

If you have an Exchange ActiveSync account and your company has enabled it, your Exchange Global Address List shows up here under Groups. You can use it to search for anyone in your company.

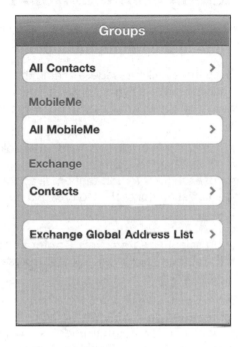

NOTE: You can't create groups in the **Contacts** app on the iPod touch — they must be created on your computer or synced when you add contact accounts to your iPod touch.

Adding Contacts from Email Messages

What happens when you receive an email message from someone who is not yet a contact in your address book? Adding a new contact from an email message is easy.

Open the email message. Then, in the email message's **From** field, just touch the name of the sender next to the **From:** tag.

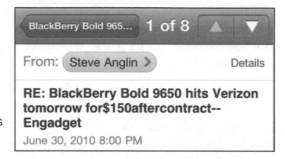

If the sender is not in your address book, you'll be taken to a screen that lets you choose whether to add that email address to an existing contact or to create a new one.

If you select **Create a New Contact**, you'll be taken to the same New Contact screen you saw earlier in Figure 15–1.

But suppose this is someone's personal email address and you already have an entry for that person with a work email address. In that case, you would select **Add to Existing Contact** and choose the correct person. Then you'd give this email address a new tag—"personal," in this case.

Linking Contact to Another App

You might have contact information for the sender of the email message in another app on the phone. With the iPod touch, it's easy to link these contacts together.

In this example, Steve, the sender of the email message, is one of my LinkedIn contacts, but he's not a contact on my iPod touch. Here's how I can link his contact information in my iPod touch to the information I have in LinkedIn:

1. I add him to my contacts, as shown previously.

2. I start up my LinkedIn app—see Chapter 22: "Social Networking" for more information on the topic.

3. I find my contact information for Steve to verify that he is in my **LinkedIn** app.

4. I go to the **Connections** icon.

5. I choose **Download All** in the top right-hand corner.

6. The LinkedIn app then informs me that this will add the photo, current company and title, email addresses, and web sites associated with this contact (see Figure 15–4).

7. This is exactly what I want in my iPod touch contacts, so I choose **Download All New Connections**.

8. Steve's picture and updated information are then brought Into his contact information on my iPod touch.

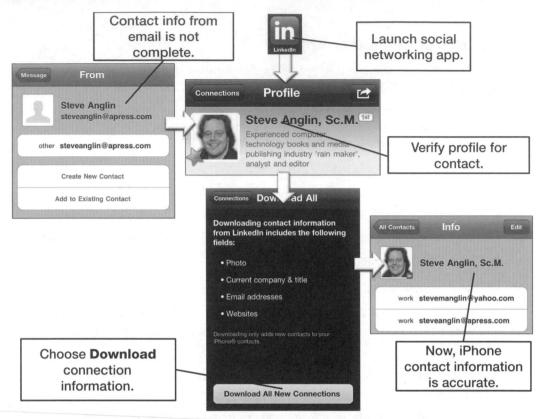

Figure 15–4. *Linking new contact from an email message to an existing social networking contact profile.*

TIP: Learning the names of the parents of your school-age children's friends can be fairly challenging. In the **First** field, however, you can add not just your child's friend's name but the parents' names as well (e.g., **First: Samantha (Mom: Susan, Dad: Ron)**). Then in the **Company** field, add in the name of your child and "school friend" (e.g., **Cece school friend**). Then, by just typing your child's name in your **All Contacts** list's search box, you'll find every person you've met at your child's school. Now you can say, "Hello, Susan, great to see you again!" without missing a beat. *Try your best to covertly look up the name.*

Sending a Picture to a Contact

If you want to send a picture to a contact, you will need to do that from the **Photos** app (see Chapter 17: "iPod touch Photography").

Sending an Email Message from Contacts

Since many of the core apps (**Contacts**, **Mail**, and **Messages**) are fully integrated, one app can easily trigger another. So, if you want to send an email message to one of your contacts, open the contact and tap the email address. The **Mail** app will launch and you can compose and send an email message to this person.

Start your contacts by touching the **Contacts** icon. Either search or flick through your contacts until you find the contact you need.

> home **martin@madesimplelearni...**

In the contact information, touch the email address of the contact you'd like to use.

You'll see that the **Mail** program launches automatically with the contact's name in the **To:** field of the email message. Type and send the message.

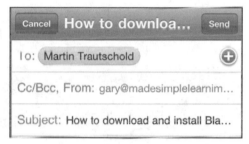

Showing Your Contacts Addresses on the Map

One of the great things about the iPod touch is its integration with Google Maps. This is very evident in the **Contacts** app. Let's say you want to map the home or work address of any contact in your address book. In the old days (pre- iPod touch), you'd have to use Google, MapQuest, or some other program and laboriously retype or copy and paste the address information. Happily, you don't have to do this on the iPod touch.

Simply open the contact as you did earlier. This time, touch the address at the bottom of the contact information.

> work **25 Forest View Way**

Your **Maps** app (which is powered by Google Maps) immediately loads and drops a push-pin at the exact location of the contact. The contact name will appear above the push-pin.

Touch the tab on the top of the push-pin to get to the info screen.

Now you can select **Directions To Here** or **Directions From Here**.

Type the correct start or end address and touch the **Route** button in the lower right corner. If you decide you don't want the directions, just tap the **Clear** button in the top left.

What if you had just typed the address in your **Maps** app instead of clicking from your contact list? In that case, you might want to touch **Add to Contacts** to add this address.

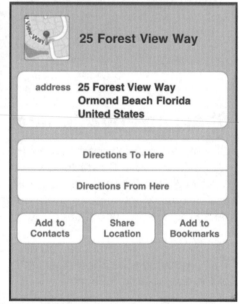

TIP: To return to your contact information, tap the **Map** button, and then exit **Maps** and start up **Contacts**. You can also use multi-tasking (see Chapter 8: "Multitasking and Voice Control") and double-click the **Home** button and choose the **Contacts** app.

Changing Your Contact Sort Order and Display Order

Like other settings, the Contacts options are accessible via the **Settings** icon.

Touch the **Settings** icon, scroll down to **Mail, Contacts, Calendars**, and touch the tab.

Scroll down and you'll see **Contacts** with two options underneath. To change the sort order, touch the **Sort Order** tab and select whether you want your contacts sorted by first name or last name.

You may want to change how your contacts are displayed. Here's where you get it done; you can choose **First, Last** or **Last, First**. Tap the **Display Order** tab and choose whether you want your contact displayed in first-name or last-name order. Tap the **Mail...** button in the upper left corner to save your settings changes.

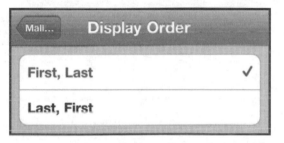

Searching for Global Address List (GAL) Contacts

If you have an Exchange account configured, you should have an option for a Global Address List. This gives you access to your Global Address List if you are connected to your organization's server.

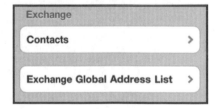

Open your **Contacts** app and look under Exchange for a tab that says **Exchange Global Address List**.

Contacts Troubleshooting

Sometimes your **Contacts** app might not work the way you expect. If you don't see all your contacts, review the steps in the Chapter 3: "Sync Your iPod touch with iTunes" or Chapter 4: "Other Sync Methods" on how to sync with your address book application. Make sure you have selected **All Groups** in the settings in iTunes.

> **TIP:** If you are syncing with another contact application, such as **Contacts** in Gmail, make sure you select the option closest to **All Contacts** rather than a subset like a particular group.

When Global Address List Contacts Don't Show Up (For Microsoft Exchange Users)

First, make sure you are connected to a Wi-Fi network.

Next, check your Exchange settings and verify you have the correct server and login information. To do so, tap the **Settings** button, and then scroll to and touch **Mail, Contacts, and Calendar**. Find your Exchange account on the list and touch it to look at the settings. You may need to contact technical support at your organization to make sure your Exchange settings are correct.

Chapter 16

Your Calendar

The iPod touch makes the old calendar that used to hang on the fridge obsolete. In this chapter, we will also show you how to utilize the **Calendar** app of the iPod touch to its full potential. We will show you how to schedule appointments, how to manage multiple calendars, how to change views on your calendar, and even how to deal with meeting invitations.

NOTE: For most of this chapter, we will talk about syncing your iPod touch calendar with another calendar because it is nice to have your calendar accessible on your iPod touch and other places. If you choose, you can also use your iPod touch in a *standalone* mode, where you do not sync to any other calendar. In the latter case, all the steps we describe for events, viewing, and managing events still apply equally to you. If you go with the standalone calendar, it is important that you use the **iTunes** automatic backup feature to save a copy of your calendar. This will help you recover your calendar in case something happens to your iPod touch.

Manage Your Busy Life on Your iPod touch

The **Calendar** app is a powerful and easy-to-use application that helps you manage your appointments, keep track of what you have to do, set reminder alarms, and even create and respond to meeting invitations (for **Exchange** users).

Today's Day and Date Shown on Calendar Icon

The **Calendar** icon is usually right on your iPod touch **Home** screen. You will quickly notice that your **Calendar** icon changes to show today's date and the day of the week. The icon to the right shows that it is a Friday, the 16th day of the month.

> **TIP:** If you use your iPod touch's **Calendar** app often, you might want to think about pinning or moving it to the **Bottom** dock; you learned how to do this in the section on docking icons in Chapter 6: "Organize Your iPod touch."

Syncing or Sharing Your Calendar(s) with Your iPod touch

If you maintain a calendar on your computer or on a web site such as **Google Calendar**, you can synchronize or share that calendar with your iPod touch either by using **iTunes** and your sync cable or by setting up a wireless synchronization (see Chapter 3: "Sync Your iPod touch with iTunes" and Chapter 4: "Other Sync Methods" for more information on syncing).

After you set up the calendar sync, all of your computer's calendar appointments will be synced with your iPod touch calendar automatically, based on your sync settings (see Figure 16–1).

If you use **iTunes** to sync with your calendar (e.g., **Microsoft Outlook**, **Entourage**, or Apple's **iCal**), your appointments will be transferred or synced every time you connect your iPod touch to your computer.

If you use another method to sync (e.g., **MobileMe**, **Exchange**, or similar), this sync is wireless and automatic, and it will most likely happen without you having to do anything after the initial setup process.

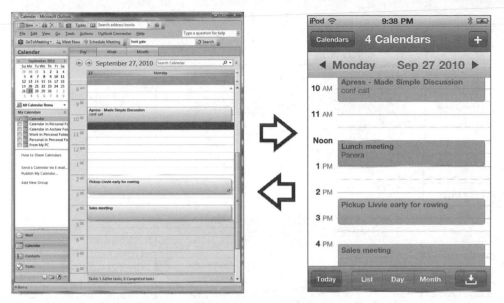

Figure 16–1. *Syncing a PC, Mac, or online calendar to an iPod touch.*

Viewing Your Schedule and Getting Around

The default view for the **Calendar** app shows your **Day** view. This view shows you at a glance any upcoming appointments for your day. Appointments are shown in your calendar (see Figure 16–2). If you happen to have multiple calendars set up on your computer, such as **Work** and **Home**, then appointments from the different calendars will display as different colors on your iPod touch calendar.

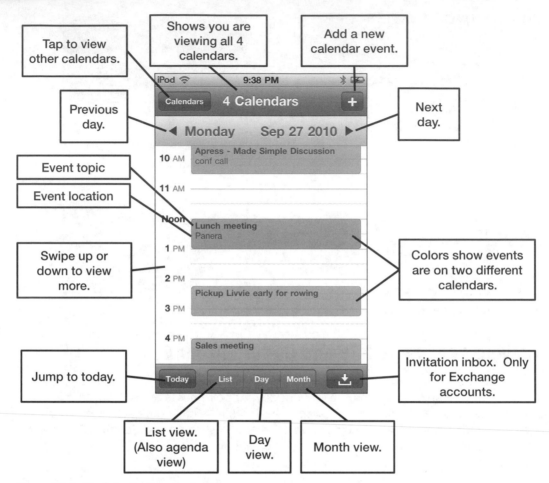

Figure 16–2. *The Calendar Day view layout.*

You can manipulate the calendar in various ways:

- **Move a day at a time**: If you tap the triangles next to today's date at the top, you move forward or backward a day.

TIP: Touch and hold the triangles next to the date to advance quickly through days.

- **Change views**: Use the **List**, **Day**, and **Month** buttons at the bottom to change the view.

- **Jump to today**: Use the **Today** button located in the bottom-left corner of the screen.

The Three Calendar Views

Your **Calendar** app comes with three views: **Day**, **Month**, and **List**. You can switch views by tapping the name of the view at the bottom of the screen. Here's a quick overview of the three views.

Day view: When you start the iPod touch's **Calendar** app, the default view is usually the **Day** view. This allows you to quickly see everything you have scheduled for the day. You can find buttons to change the view at the bottom of the **Calendar** app.

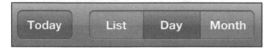

List view (also known as **Agenda** view): Touch the **List** button at the bottom, and you can see a list of your appointments.

Depending on how much you have scheduled, you could see the next day or even the next week's worth of scheduled events.

Swipe up or down to see more events.

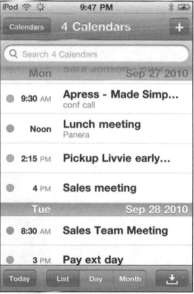

Month view: Touch the **Month** button at the bottom, and you can see a layout of the full month. Days with appointments have a small dot in them. Dots for the current day will show up highlighted in blue.

TIP: To return to the **Today** view, just touch the **Today** button at the bottom left of the screen.

Go to the next month: Tap the triangle to the right of the month shown at the top.

Go to the previous month: Tap the triangle to the left of the month.

NOTE: While you can scroll in the **Calendar** app, you cannot swipe through your days; this runs counter to what you might expect.

Working with Several Calendars

The **Calendar** app can view and work with more than one calendar. The number of calendars you see depends on how you set up your synchronization using the **iTunes** program or other sync methods. The example that follows categorizes personal appointments in the **Home** calendar and work appointments in a separate **Work** calendar.

The **Calendar** app displays the **Home** calendar appointments in red and the **Work** appointments in orange or green.

When you configured your **Sync** settings, you were able to specify which calendars you wanted to sync with your iPod touch. You can customize your calendar further by following these instructions:

Changing the colors: You need to change the color of the calendar in the program on your computer that is synced to your iPod touch; doing so changes the colors on your iPod touch. Sometimes you cannot change colors, such as when syncing a **Google** calendar using the **Exchange** setting.

Adding a new calendar: It takes two steps to create and sync a new calendar with your iPod touch:

1. Set up your new calendar on your computer's calendar program.

2. Adjust your **Sync** settings to ensure this new calendar syncs to your iPod touch.

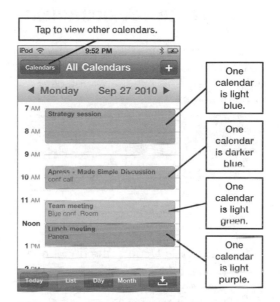

Viewing only one calendar: To view just one calendar at a time, tap the **Calendars** button at the top and select only the calendar you wish to see.

Adding New Calendar Events

You can easily add new events or appointments right on your iPod touch. These new events and appointments will be synced (i.e., shared with) your computer the next time the sync takes place.

Adding a New Appointment

Your instinct will most likely be to try to touch the screen at a particular time to set an appointment; unfortunately, this is not how you set appointments.

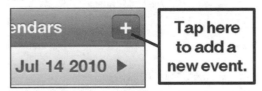

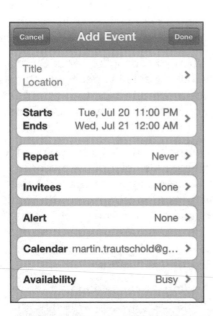

To add a new calendar event from any **Calendar** view, follow these steps:

1. Tap the "**+**" icon at the upper right corner of the screen to see the **Add Event** screen.

2. Next, touch the box marked **Title & Location**.

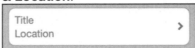

Type in a title for the event and the location (optional). For example, you might type "Meet with Martin" as the title and input the location as "Office." Or, you might choose to type "Lunch with Martin" and then choose a very expensive restaurant in New York City.

3. Touch the blue **Done** button in the upper-right corner to return to the **Add Event** screen.

4. Touch the **Starts** or **Ends** tab to adjust the timing of the event. To change the start time, touch the **Starts** field to highlight it in blue. Next, move the rotating dials at the bottom to reflect the correct date and start time of the appointment.

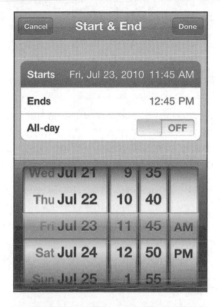

5. Alternatively, you can set an all-day event by touching the switch next to **All-day**; this sets the switch to **ON**.

NOTE: You will see a tab labeled **Invitees** before the **Repeat** tab only if your event is set up on an **Exchange/Google** or **MobileMe** calendar (see Chapter 4: "Other Sync Methods" to learn how to invite people to a meeting and reply to invitations.

Recurring Events

Some of your appointments happen every day, week, or month at the same time. Follow these steps if you are scheduling a repeating or recurring appointment:

1. Touch the **Repeat** tab and then select the correct time interval from the list.

2. Touch **Done** to return to the main **Event** screen.

3. If you set a **Repeat** meeting, then you will also have to say when the recurring meeting ends. Tap the **End Repeat** button to set this.

4. You can select **Repeat Forever** or set a date.

5. Tap **Done** when finished.

Calendar Alerts

You can have your iPod touch 4 give you an audible reminder, or *alert*, about an upcoming appointment. Alerts can help you keep from forgetting an important event. Follow these steps to create an alert:

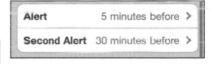

1. Touch the **Alert** tab and then select the option for a reminder alarm. You can have no alarm at all or set a reminder anytime from five minutes before the event all the way to two days before it, depending on what works best for you.

2. Touch **Done** to get back to the main **Event** screen.

Second Alert

In most cases, you will see a tab for a **Second Alert** once you set your first alert.

> **NOTE:** You will see a **Second Alert** if the calendar you are using is synced using iTunes or **MobileMe**. However, you will not see a second alert if your event is tied to a **Google Calendar** synced using the **Exchange** setting.

You can set this additional alert to another time before or after the first alert. Some people find a second alert very helpful for remembering critical events or appointments.

> **TIP:** Here's a practical example that illustrates when you might want to set up two calendar alerts.
>
> If your child has a doctor or dentist appointment, then you might want to set the first event to go off the night before. This will remind you to write a note to the school and give it to your child.

You can then set the second event for 45 minutes prior to the appointment time. This will leave you enough time to pick up your child from school and get to the appointment.

Choosing which Calendar to Use

If you use more than one calendar in **Outlook**, **Entourage**, **iCal**, or some other program, then you will have various calendars available to you when you sync your iPod touch with that program.

> **NOTE:** If you create an event and choose an **Exchange** or **MobileMe** calendar, then you'll see an option to invite other users to the event.

Touch the **Calendar** button in the upper-left corner to see all your calendars. Tap the calendar you want to use for this particular event. The default calendar selected is usually the one you selected the last time you used your iPod touch to schedule an event.

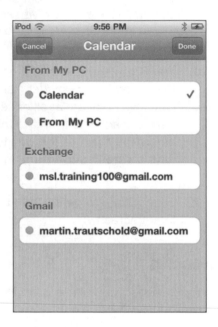

Availability

You can choose your availability from the following options: **Busy** (default), **Free**, **Tentative**, or **Out of Office**.

> **NOTE:** You will only see the **Availability** field if the calendar you are using for this event is synced with the **MobileMe**, **Exchange**, or **Exchange/Google** settings.

Adding Notes to Calendar Events

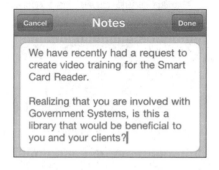

Follow these steps if you want to add some notes to this calendar event:

1. Tap **Notes** and type or copy-and-paste a few notes.

2. Tap **Done** to finish adding notes.

3. Tap **Done** again to save your new calendar event.

> **TIP:** If this is a meeting somewhere new, you might want to type or copy-and-paste some driving directions.

Using Copy-and-Paste Text in the Calendar

The iPod touch 4's new **App Switcher** program means you can now easily jump between any two apps. There may be times when you want to jump between your **Email** and your **Calendar** apps to copy-and-paste information. The information to copy-and-paste could be anything, such as driving directions or critical notes you need at your fingertips for a meeting. Follow these steps to copy-and-paste information between your **Email** and **Calendar** programs:

1. Create a new calendar event or edit an existing one, as explained previously in this chapter.

2. Scroll down to the **Notes** field and tap it to open it up.

3. Double-tap the **Home** button to bring up the **App Switcher.**

4. If you see the **Mail** icon, tap it. If you don't see **Mail** icon, swipe left or right to look for it. Once you find it, tap it to open the **Mail** app.

5. Double-tap a word, then use your fingers to drag the blue handles to select the text you want to copy.

6. Tap the **Copy** button.

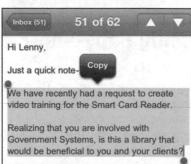

7. Double-tap the **Home** button to bring up the **App Switcher.**

8. Tap the **Calendar** icon. It should be the first icon on the left, since you just jumped out of it.

9. Now tap and hold in the **Notes** field. When you let go, you should see the **Paste** pop-up field. If you don't see it, then hold your finger down a bit longer until you do see it.

10. Tap **Paste**.

11. Now you should see the text you copied pasted into the **Notes** field. Tap **Done** to save your changes.

Editing Appointments

Sometimes, the details of an appointment may change and need to be adjusted (see Figure 16–3). Fortunately, it's easy to revise an appointment on your iPod touch:

1. Tap the appointment that you want to change.

2. Tap the **Edit** button in the upper-right corner to see the **Edit** screen showing the appointment details.

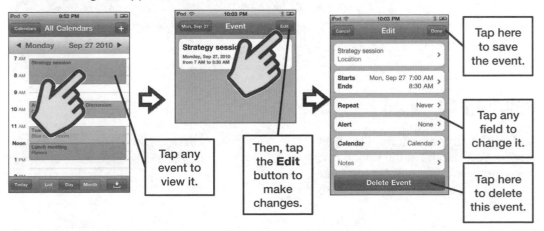

Figure 16–3. *Editing an appointment.*

Now just touch the tab in the field you need to adjust. For example, you can change the time of this appointment by touching the **Starts** or **Ends** tab, and then adjusting the time for the event's starting or ending time.

Editing a Repeating Event

You edit a recurring or repeating event in exactly the same manner as any other event. The only difference is that you will be asked a question after you finish editing the event. You need to answer this question and tap the **Done** button.

Tap **Save for this event only** if you want to make changes to only this instance of the repeating event.

Tap **Save for future events** if you want to make changes to all instances of this repeating event.

Switching an Event to a Different Calendar

If you mistakenly set up an event on the wrong calendar, then go ahead and tap the **Calendar** button to change the calendar. Next, select one of the different calendars you have synced to your iPod touch.

> **NOTE:** Different fields may appear or disappear, depending on the calendar you choose to use.
>
> If you change your event from a calendar synced using **iTunes** to one synced with **Exchange**, you will see the **Second Alert** field disappear. Also, you will see two new fields appear in an **Exchange**, **Google**, or **MobileMe** calendar: **Invitees** and **Availability**.

Deleting an Event

Notice that, at the bottom of the **Edit** screen, you also have the option to delete this event. Simply touch **Delete Event** button at the bottom of the screen to do so.

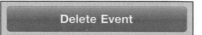

Meeting Invitations

For those who use **Microsoft Exchange**, **Microsoft Outlook**, or **Entourage** regularly, meeting invitations become a way of life. You receive a meeting invitation in your email, you accept the invitation, and then the appointment gets automatically placed in your calendar.

On your iPod touch, you will see the invitations you accept placed into your calendar immediately.

> **NOTE:** If you use an **Exchange** calendar or a **Google** calendar, you can invite people and reply to meeting invitations on your iPod touch (see the "Working with the Google or Exchange Calendar" section of Chapter 4: "Other Sync Methods" to learn more about this subject).

If you touch the meeting invitation in your calendar, you can see all the details that you need: the dial in number, the meeting ID, and any other details that might be included in the invitation.

> **NOTE:** At the time of writing, you can accept meeting invitations on your iPod touch from your **Exchange** account. You can also create meetings for your **Exchange** account if you choose the **Exchange** calendar. Invitations will also transfer automatically from **Entourage**, **iCal**, or **Outlook** if you have **iTunes** set to sync with those programs.

Calendar Options

There are only a few options to adjust in your **Calendar** app; you can find these in the **Settings** app. Follow these steps to adjust these options:

1. Tap the **Settings** icon from your **Home** screen.

2. Scroll down to the **Mail**, **Contacts**, **Calendars** option and tap it.

3. Scroll down to **Calendars** (it's at the very bottom!) to see a few options.

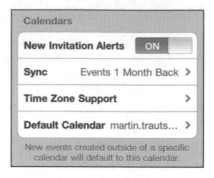

4. The first option is a simple switch that notifies you about **New Invitation Alerts**. If you receive any meeting invites, it is good to keep this option set in the default **ON** position.

5. Next, you may see the **Sync** option if you sync your **Calendar** program using **Exchange** or **MobileMe**. You can adjust the setting to sync events to **2 weeks back, 1 month, 3 months, 6 months**, or **All Events**.

6. Next, you can choose your time zone. This setting should reflect your **Home** settings from when you set up your iPod touch. If you are traveling, however, and want to adjust your appointments for a different time zone, you can change the **Time Zone** value to whatever city you prefer.

Changing the Default Calendar

We mentioned earlier that you can have multiple calendars displayed on your iPod touch. This option allows you to choose which calendar will be your **Default** calendar.

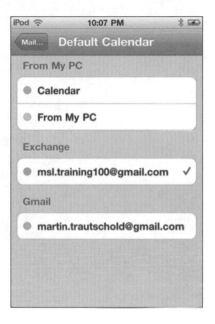

> **NOTE:** You will only see the **Default Calendar** option if you have more than one calendar syncing to your iPod touch.

Specifying a calendar as the default means that this calendar will be selected by default when you go to schedule a new appointment.

If you wish to use a different calendar – say, your **Work** calendar – then you can change that when you actually set the appointment, as shown earlier in this chapter.

iPod touch Photography

While no previous versions of the iPod touch have included a camera, there is camera on the new iPod touch. The iPod touch comes with not one, but two cameras: a 0.7-megapixel camera on the back and a 0.3-megapixel VGA camera on the front for video chats and self-portraits. Learn more about using the front-facing camera in the new **FaceTime** app in Chapter 13: "FaceTime Video Messaging and Skype."

NOTE: The resolution on the iPod touch makes pictures look beautiful. However, it's nowhere near the quality of the camera on the new iPhone 4, so pictures will lose some quality when you sync them and view them on your computer.

Viewing and sharing your pictures on the iPod touch is truly a joy, due in large part to the beautiful high-resolution screen. In this chapter, we discuss the many ways to get pictures onto your iPod touch . We also show you how you to use the touch screen to navigate through your pictures, how to zoom in and out, and how to manipulate your photos.

TIP: Did you know that you can take a picture of the entire screen of your iPod touch 4 by pressing two keys simultaneously? Now you can prove that you got the high score on Tetris!

Here's how to get it done: press both the **Home** button and the **On/Off/Sleep** key on the top right edge (you can press one, hold it, and then press the other). If you have done this correctly, the screen should flash and you'll hear a camera sound. The screen capture you have taken will be in your Camera Roll album in the **Photos** app.

Using the Camera App

The **Camera** app (Figure 17–1) should be on your home page—usually on the first screen at the top. If you don't see it, then swipe left or right until you find it.

Touch the **Camera** icon and the shutter of the camera opens with an animation on your screen.

Switch between the two cameras

Touch screen to see Zoom Control Slider.

Thumbnail of previous picture taken. Touch to launch **Photo** app.

Toggle between Camera and Video Camera

Touch to take picture

Figure 17–1. *Layout of* ***Camera*** *app.*

Geo-Tagging

Geo-tagging is a feature that puts your GPS (geographic positioning system) coordinates into the picture file. If you upload your pictures to programs like Flickr, the coordinates of your picture can help your friends to locate where the picture was taken. The iPod touch supports geo-tagging over Wi-Fi, so you need to be connected to a Wi-Fi network and uses Wi-Fi triangulation for GPS coordinates to be embedded in the image.

NOTE: For Mac users, iPhoto uses geo-tagging to put photos into the Places category of iPhoto.

If you have Location Services turned on (see Chapter 1: "Getting Started") when you start the camera, you will be asked if it is OK to use your current location.

To double-check, do the following:

1. Start your **Settings**.

2. Go to **General**.

3. Then touch **Location Services**. You will see a screen like the one here.

4. Make sure the switch next to **Camera** is toggled to **ON**.

Taking a Picture

Taking a picture is as simple as pointing and shooting, yet there are some adjustments that you can make if you choose.

Once your camera is on, center your subject in the screen of your iPod touch.

When you are ready to take a picture, just touch the **Camera** button along the bottom. You will hear a shutter sound, and the screen will show an animation indicating that the picture is being taken.

Once the picture is taken, it will drop down into the window in the lower left-hand corner. Touch that small thumbnail, and the Camera Roll album of your **Photos** app will load.

Using the Zoom

The iPod touch camera includes a 5x digital zoom.

NOTE: A digital zoom is never as clear as an analog zoom, so be aware that picture quality is usually degraded slightly when using the zoom.

To use the zoom, just touch the screen and move the Zoom slider, as shown in Figure 17–1.

Switching Cameras

As mentioned, the iPod touch comes with two cameras: a .7-megapixel camera for most photography and a VGA camera for self-portraits or for use in **FaceTime** video calls (see Chapter 13: "FaceTime Video Messaging and Skype").

To switch between the cameras, do the following:

1. Touch the **Switch Camera** icon from the **Camera** app.

2. Wait for the camera to switch to the front-facing camera, and line up the shot.

3. Touch the **Switch Camera** icon again to switch back to the standard camera.

TIP: Because of the placement of the front-facing camera, faces can look somewhat distorted. Try moving your face back a bit and adjusting the camera angle to get a better image.

Viewing Pictures You Have Taken

Your iPod touch stores pictures you take in what is called your Camera Roll. You can access the Camera Roll from inside both the **Camera** and **Photos** apps. In the Camera app, touch the **Pictures** icon in the bottom left corner of the camera screen.

Once you touch a picture to view, you can swipe through your pictures to see all the pictures in the Camera Roll.

To get back to the Camera Roll, press the **Camera Roll** button in the upper left corner.

To take another picture, touch the **Done** button in the upper right corner.

Getting Photos onto Your iPod touch

You have many options for loading photos onto your device.

Sync using iTunes: Probably the simplest way is to use iTunes to sync photos from your computer. This is described this in detail in Chapter 3: "Sync Your IPod touch with iTunes."

Receive as email attachments: While this is not useful for large numbers of pictures, it works well for one or a few photos. Check out Chapter 14: "Email on your iPod touch" for more details about how to save attachments. (Once saved, these images show up in the Camera Roll album.)

Save images from the Web: Sometimes you'll see a great image on a web site. Press and hold it to see the pop-up menu and then select **Save Image**. (Like other saved images, these end up in the Camera Roll album.)

Download images from within an app: A good example of this is the Wallpaper image shown in Chapter 7: "Personalize and Secure your iPod touch."

Sync with iPhoto (for Mac users): If you use a Mac computer, your iPod touch will most likely sync automatically with **iPhoto** or **Aperture**.

Here are a few steps to get iPhoto sync up and running:

1. Connect your iPod touch and start **iTunes**.

2. Go to the **Photo** tab along the top row of Sync Options.

3. Choose the **Albums**, **Events**, **Faces**, or **Places** you want to keep in sync with the iPod touch (see Figure 17–2).

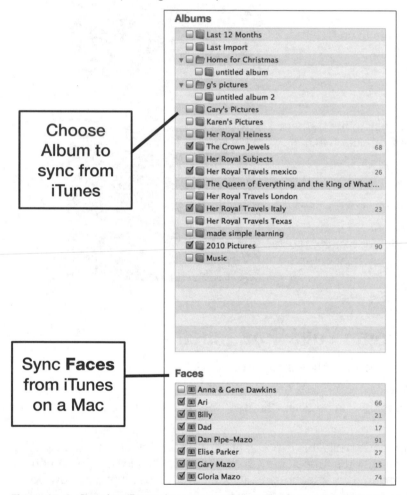

Choose Album to sync from iTunes

Sync Faces from iTunes on a Mac

Figure 17–2. *Choosing albums, faces, or events from iTunes to sync with the iPod touch.*

Drag and drop (for Windows users): Once you connect your iPod touch to your Windows computer, it will appear in Windows Explorer as a Portable Device, as shown in Figure 17–3. Here are the steps to follow to drag and drop photos between your iPod touch and computer:

Figure 17–3. *Windows Explorer showing the iPod touch as a portable device (connected with USB cable).*

1. Double-click on the iPod touch image under Portable Devices to open it.

2. Double-click on **Internal Storage** to open it.

3. Double-click on **DCIM** to open it.

4. Double-click on **100APPLE** to open it.

5. You will see all the images in the Saved Photos album on your iPod touch.

6. To copy images to your iPod touch, select and then drag and drop images from your computer into this folder.

7. To copy images from your iPod touch, select and then drag and drop images out of this folder onto your computer.

> **TIP:** Here's how to select multiple images in Windows.
>
> Draw a box around the images, or click on one image and then press **Ctrl+A** to select them all. Hold down the **Ctrl** key and click on individual pictures to select them. Right-click on one of the selected pictures and choose **Cut** (to move) or **Copy** (to copy) all of the selected images. To paste the images, press and click on any other disk or folder, such as **My Documents**, and navigate to where you want to move or copy the files. Then right-click again and select **Paste**.

Viewing Your Photos

Now that your photos are on your iPod touch , you have several cool ways to look through them and show them to others.

Launching from the Photos Icon

If you like using your **Photos** icon, you might want to place it in your Bottom Dock for easy access if it's not already there (see Chapter 6: "Organize your Icons and Folders.")

To get started with photos, touch the **Photos** icon.

The first screen shows your photo albums, which were created when you set up your iPod touch and synced it with iTunes. Chapter 3: "Sync Your iPod touch with iTunes" showed you how to choose which photos to sync with your iPod touch. Any changes to the library on your computer will be automatically updated on your iPod touch.

Choosing a Library

From the Photo Albums page, touch one of the library buttons to show the photos in that album. The screen will immediately change to show you thumbnails of the pictures in this library.

Tap and drag your finger up and down to view all the pictures. You can flick up or down to quickly move throughout the album.

Working with Individual Pictures

Once you locate the picture you want to view, just tap on it. The picture then loads into the screen.

NOTE: If your photos were shot in landscape mode, they will not take up the full screen on your iPod touch.

TIP: The picture here was shot in landscape mode, so to see it in a full screen, you have to turn your iPod touch on its side or just double-tap it to fill the screen.

Moving Between Pictures

The swipe gesture is used to move from one picture to the next. Just swipe your finger left or right across the screen, and you can move through your pictures.

> **TIP:** Drag your finger slowly to move more gradually through the picture library.

When you reach the end of an album, tap the screen once and you'll see a tab in the upper left corner that has the name of the photo album. Touch that tab and you'll return to the thumbnail page of that particular album.

To get back to your main photo album page, touch the button that says **Albums** in the top left corner.

Zooming In and Out of Pictures

There are two ways to zoom in and out of pictures on your iPod touch: double-tapping and pinching.

Double-Tapping

As the name describes, this is a quick double-tap on the screen to zoom in on the picture, as shown in Figure 17–4. You will be zoomed in to the spot where you double-tap. To zoom out, just double-tap once more.

See Chapter 1: "Getting Started" for more help on double-tapping.

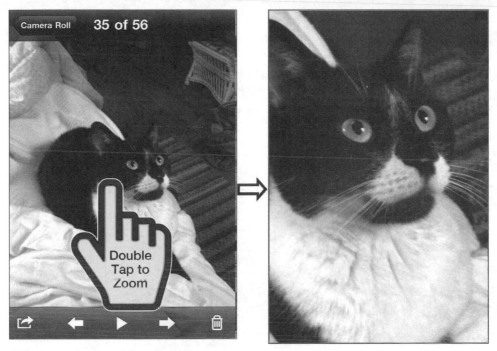

Figure 17–4. *Double-tapping on a picture to zoom.*

Pinching

Also described in Chapter 1: "Getting Started," pinching is a much more precise form of zooming in. While double-tapping zooms in or out only to one set level, pinching really allows you to zoom in or out just a little bit or quite a lot.

To pinch, hold your thumb and forefinger close together and then slowly (while touching the screen) separate them, making the picture larger. To zoom out, start with your thumb and forefinger apart and move them together.

> **NOTE:** Once you have activated the zoom using either method, you will not be able to easily swipe through your pictures until you return the picture to its standard size.

Viewing a Slideshow

You can also view the pictures in your photo album as a slideshow. Just tap the screen once to bring up the on-screen soft keys. In the center is a **Slideshow Play** button— touch once to start the slideshow. You can start the slideshow from any picture in the album.

Slideshow Options let you adjust how long each picture remains on the screen. You can also choose transitions and other settings (see Figure 17–5). To end the slideshow, tap the screen.

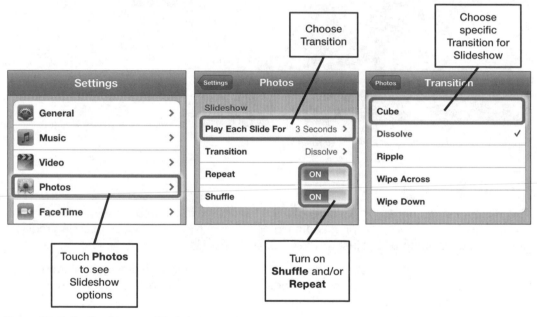

Figure 17–5. *Configuring your slideshow.*

Adjusting Slideshow Options

To configure a slideshow, you will need to change your settings. To do so, touch the **Settings** icon on the Home screen.

Scroll down to the **Photos** tab and touch the screen. You will then see the various options you can use, including four options for adjusting for slideshows.

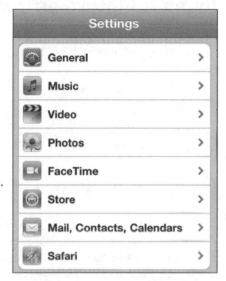

To specify how long to play each slide, touch the **Play Each Slide For** tab. You can choose a range between 2 and 20 seconds.

If you want pictures to repeat in a slideshow, just move the **Repeat** switch to **ON**.

If you want the pictures to move in an order different from the way they are listed, choose **Shuffle**, and, just like the Shuffle command on the music player, the pictures will play in a random order.

Using a Picture as Your iPod touch Wallpaper

For information on how to select and use a picture as your iPod touch wallpaper (and more wallpaper options), please go to Chapter 7: "Personalize and Secure your iPod touch."

> **NOTE:** You can have different pictures for your Home screen and Lock screen or use the same picture for both.

Emailing a Picture

As long as you have an active Internet connection (see Chapter 5: "Wi-Fi Connectivity"), you can send any picture in your photo collection via email. Tap the **Options** button on the thumbnail bar—the one furthest to the left of the bottom row of soft keys. If you don't see the icons, tap the screen once.

Choose the **Email Photo** option and the **Mail** app will automatically launch (Figure 17–6).

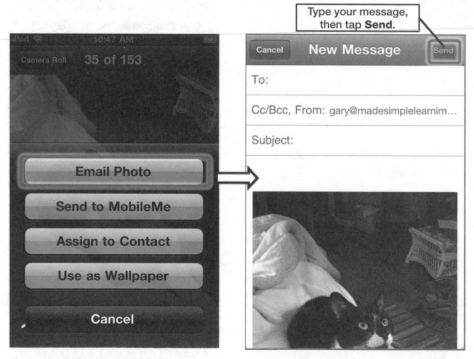

Figure 17–6. *Emailing a photo.*

Touch the **To** field as you did in Chapter 14: "Email on your iPod touch," and select the contact to receive the picture. Tap the blue **+** button to add a contact.

Type in a subject and a message, and then touch **Send** in the upper right corner. That's all there is to it.

Email, Copy, or Delete Several Pictures At Once

If you have several pictures you want to email, copy, or delete at the same time, you can do it from the thumbnail view, as shown in Figure 17–7.

NOTE: The **copy** function allows you to copy and paste multiple pictures into an email message or other app. **Share** renames the image to photo.png; **copy**-and-**paste** leaves it with the DCIM folder file name.png. When you select **Share**, a pop-up will ask you if you want to send them in small, medium, large, or original size with size of attachment in MB.

At publishing time, you could share or email a maximum of five pictures. This may change with future software.

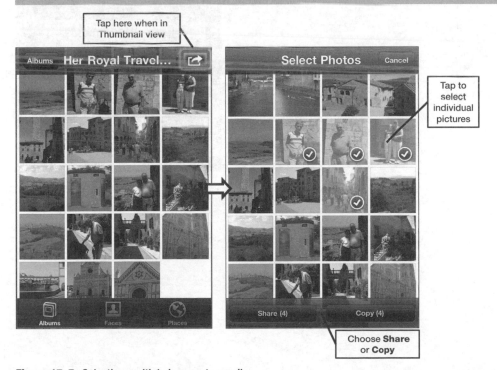

Figure 17–7. *Selecting multiple images to email.*

Assigning a Picture to a Contact

Chapter 15: "Working with Contacts" covers how to add a picture when editing a contact. You can also find a picture you like and assign it to a contact. First, find the photo you want to use.

As you did with wallpaper and emailing a photo, tap the **Options** button—the one furthest to the right of the upper row of soft keys. If you don't see the icons, tap the screen once.

When you touch the **Options** button, you'll see a drop-down of choices: **Email Photo**, **Assign to Contact**, **Use as Wallpaper**, and **Copy Photo**.

Touch the **Assign to Contact** button.

Select a Picture, then choose **Assign to Contact.**

You will see your contacts on the screen. You can either perform a search using the search bar at the top or just scroll through your contacts.

Once you find the contact to which you would like to add the picture, touch the name.

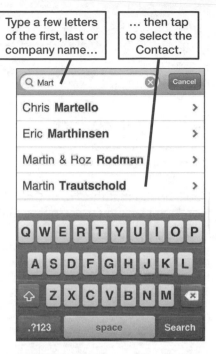

Type a few letters of the first, last or company name...

... then tap to select the Contact.

You will then see the **Move and Scale** screen. Tap and drag the picture to move it; use pinch to zoom in or out.

When you have it just as you want, touch the **Set Photo** button to assign the picture to that contact

... then tap here

> **NOTE:** You will return to your Photo Library, not to the contact. If you want to check that the picture did get set to your contact, exit the **Photo** app, start the **Contact** app, and then search for that contact.

Deleting a Picture

Why can't you delete certain pictures from your iPod touch? (In other words, why is the **Trash Can** icon missing?)

You'll notice that the **Trash Can** icon is not visible for any photo that is synced from iTunes. You can delete such pictures only from your computer library. Then, the next time you sync your iPod touch , they will be deleted.

Trash Can icon is **only** Visible in **Camera Roll**.

When you are looking through pictures in your Saved Photos (which is not synced with iTunes, but is comprised of pictures you save from an email message or download from the Web), you'll see the **Trash Can** icon in the bottom icon bar. This **Trash Can** icon does not appear when you are viewing pictures from your Photos Library or other synced albums.

If you don't see the bottom row of icons, tap the photo once to activate them. Then tap the **Trash Can** icon. You will be prompted with the option to delete the picture.

Touch **Delete Photo** and the picture will be deleted from your iPod touch.

Downloading Pictures from Web Sites

You now know how to transfer pictures from your computer to your iPod touch and save them from email messages. You can also download and save pictures right from the Web onto your iPod touch.

> **CAUTION:** We strongly encourage you to respect image copyright laws as you download and save images from the Web. Unless the web site indicates an image is free, you should check with the web site owner before downloading and saving any pictures.

Finding a Picture to Download

The iPod touch makes it easy to copy and save images from web sites. This can be handy when you are looking for a new image to use as wallpaper on your iPod touch.

First, tap the **Safari** web browser icon and type a search for iPod touch wallpaper to locate a few sites that might have some interesting possibilities. (See Chapter 12: "Surf the Web with Safari" for help.)

Once you find a picture you want to download and save, tap and hold it to bring up a new menu of options that includes **Save Image** (among others), as shown in Figure 17–8. Choose this option to save the picture in your Camera Roll album.

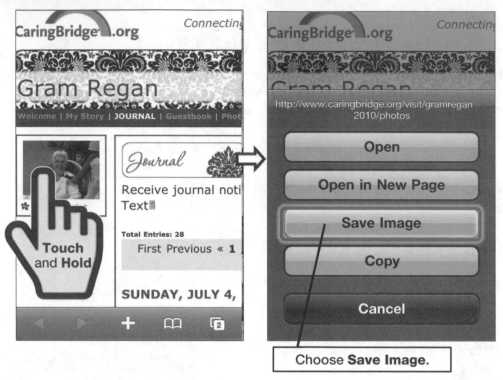

Figure 17–8. *Saving an image from a web site.*

Now touch your **Photo** icon and you should see the picture in the **Camera Roll** album.

Chapter 18

Recording and Editing Videos

Your iPod touch is a very capable video recorder. You can record and export HD video up to 720p. You can then publish that video straight to YouTube or **MobileMe** or even send it to an email recipient. In this chapter, we will also show you how to shoot and quickly *trim* your videos, as well as upload them.

Video Recording

New to the iPod touch this year is the **iMovie** app that Mac users have been using for some time. With iMovie, you can actually create movies by joining movie clips, adding pictures and transitions, and then adding your own audio track. When you're finished, you can upload the movie to the Web.

In the next section, you will learn how to add video clips, audio, pictures, and transitions. You will also learn how to produce a high quality, high definition video right on your iPod touch.

Starting the Video Recorder

The software for the video recorder is actually part of the **Camera** app (see Figure 18–1). Follow these steps to use the built-in video recorder.

1. Start up the **Camera** app (see Chapter 17: "iPod touch Photography" for more information on how to do this).

2. Move the slider in the lower-right corner from the **Camera** icon to the **Video Recorder** icon.

3. Try to keep the iPod touch steady as you record your scene.

4. Touch the **Stop** button when you are done recording.

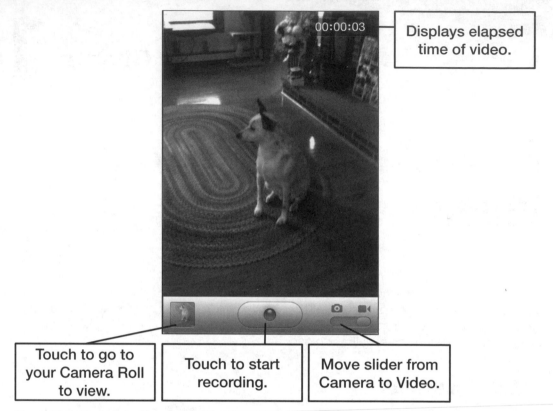

00:00:03

Displays elapsed time of video.

Touch to go to your Camera Roll to view.

Touch to start recording.

Move slider from Camera to Video.

Figure 18–1. *The layout and controls of the video recorder.*

Adjust Point of White Balance

The iPod touch video camera is fixed focused. You can adjust the point of white balance of the video based on the subject. Follow these steps to take advantage of this feature:

1. To focus on something in the foreground of the video, touch the screen in the foreground. This brings up a small box appears to show the area of white balance.

2. To switch the white balance to a subject in the background, touch another part of the screen. The box will temporarily display the new area of white balance.

Trimming the Video

The iPod touch allows you to perform edits on your video right on the phone. Once the video has been recorded and you press the **Stop** button, the video immediately goes into your **Camera Roll**.

Touch the small image of the video in the lower-left corner to bring up the video. At the top of the screen, you will see a timeline with all the frames of your video at the top of the screen (see Figure 18–2). Follow these steps to edit your just recorded video.

1. Drag either end of the timeline and you will see that the video goes into **Trim** mode.

2. Drag the ends of the video on either end until it is the length you desire.

3. When the video is the correct length, touch the **Trim** button in the upper-right corner.

4. Next, select either **Trim Original** or **Save as New Clip**. The latter option saves another version of the newly trimmed video.

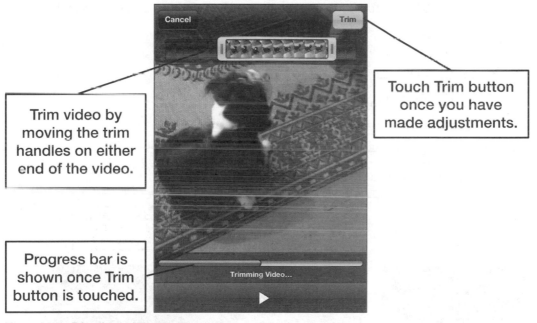

Figure 18–2. *Trimming a video.*

> **NOTE**: If you touch and hold on an end bar, it will "zoom" out and let you do more precise editing. Let go and it will "zoom" back out for grosser editing.

Sending the Video

As with photos, you have several options for using your iPod touch to send recorded video to others. Follow these steps to send a video from your iPod touch:

1. Touch the **Send** icon 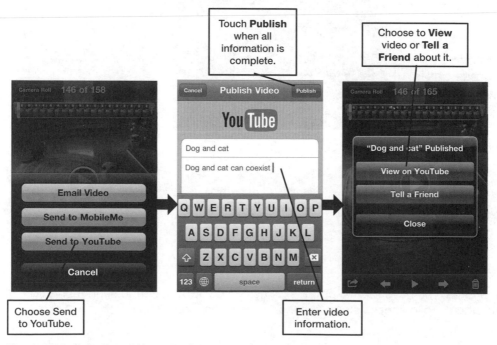 in the lower-left corner.

2. Choose your preferred option for sending the video: **Email**, **MMS**, **MobileMe**, or **YouTube**.

3. The next screen you see will depend on the choice you made in Step 2. If you selected **Email**, your **Email** app will launch.

Uploading to YouTube

The iPod touch allows you to upload an HD (720p) video right to your YouTube account. You just need to be connected to a Wi-Fi network. Follow these steps to upload a video to YouTube:

1. Locate the video you wish to upload in your **Camera Roll**.

2. Touch the **Send** icon.

3. Choose **Send to YouTube**.

4. Enter a title, description, and *tags* for the video.

5. Choose Standard Definition or HD.

6. Choose a Category for the video.

Figure 18–3. *Uploading a video to YouTube.*

NOTE: To upload a video to MobileMe or YouTube, you need to have an account with the site you want to upload to (see Chapter 4: "Other Sync Methods" to learn more about MobileMe).

Using iMovie

Mac users have been enjoying the **iMovie** app for years. This app lets you combine movie clips with pictures and music, enabling you to add fancy transitions between scenes to make a professional-looking movie.

One great feature of the new iPod touch is that users can enjoy the power of **iMovie** right on their iPod touch. The **iMovie** app is a US $4.99 download from the App Store. It is usually listed under either the **Featured** apps or the **Awesome iOS4** apps sections. You can also just search the App Store for "iMovie" to go straight to the download page (see Chapter 20: "The Amazing App Store" for more information on searching the App Store for content).

Getting Started with iMovie

The **iMovie** app works with *projects*. If you have stored projects, they appear on the **Projects** page. This will most likely be your first time using the app, so you won't have any projects. Follow these steps to start an **iMovie** project:

1. Tap the **Plus sign** icon ![plus icon] to start a new project.

2. Select a theme for the project. Current themes include **Modern**, **Bright**, **Travel**, **Playful**, and **News**.

3. Select **Theme Music ON** if you want to use specific music designed for that theme.

4. Tap the **Insert Media** icon to choose media for your movie. To choose a video, touch the **Video** soft key at the bottom. To choose photos, touch the **Photos** soft key. Finally, to choose a sound track from your own music files, touch the **Audio** soft key and navigate to the song desired (see Figure 18–4).

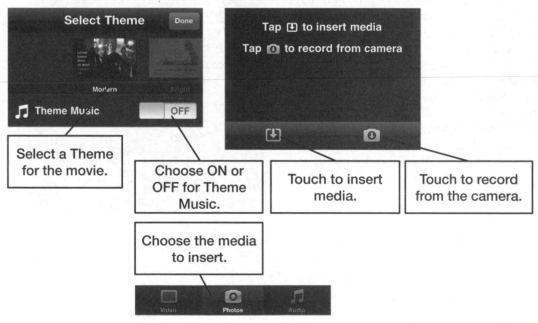

Figure 18–4. *Choosing media to add to your iMovie project.*

Constructing Your Movie

Creating a movie in **iMovie** is as simple as adding new content, transitions, and audio. Follow these steps to build your movie:

1. Tap the **Insert Media** button again and choose another movie clip or photo from your **Photos** app.

2. There is now a small **Double Arrow** icon between the different media in the project. This is the **Transition** icon. Double-tap the **Transition** icon to bring up the **Transitions Settings** menu (see Figure 18–5).

3. Choose a transition (currently there are only three choices: **None**, **Cross Dissolve**, and **Theme**).

4. Choose a transition length. These can range from .5 seconds to 2.0 seconds.

5. Touch the **Done** button.

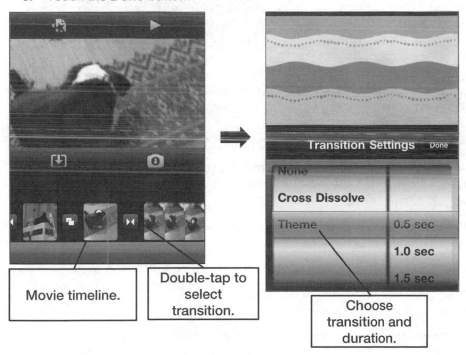

Figure 18–5. *Adding transitions to the iMovie project.*

Follow these steps to preview the movie:

1. Slide the timeline at the bottom to the beginning, and then touch the **Play**

 button.

2. When you are done, touch the **Projects** 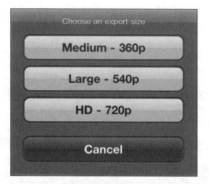 button in the top left of your screen. This will return you to the **Projects** screen.

Sharing Your Movie

Touch the **Share** button and **iMovie** gives you an option screen that lets you choose the export size of the movie. You can choose to export your movie as an HD (720p), large (540p), or medium (360p) movie file.

> **NOTE**: HD 720p movies have the best quality; however, these can be quite large, depending on the length of the movie. Obviously, it will take longer to email or upload an HD movie than an equivalent large- or medium-sized movie.

The **Export** screen marks the progress of the movie export. The iPod touch tells you that the movie was exported to the **Camera Roll** feature of your **Photo** app. Follow these steps to share a project from your **Camera Roll**:

1. Go to your **Camera Roll** (see Chapter 17: "iPod touch Photography" for more information on how to do this).

2. Find the new movie in the **Camera Roll**. You will see a **Video** icon at the bottom of the picture; the image will also show the length of the video.

3. Touch the video from the **Camera Roll**.

4. Choose **Share** from the soft keys at the bottom.

5. Choose to send your project through one of the following methods: **Email**, **MobileMe**, or **YouTube**.

> **NOTE**: To maintain your high quality 720p video, you should sync it back to your computer. Manual uploads over Wi-Fi will possibly let you share your movie at the highest quality. Syncing your movies to iTunes will ensure that the original quality is preserved.

iTunes on Your iPod touch

In this chapter, you will learn how to locate, buy, and download media using the **iTunes** app right on your iPod touch. With iTunes, you will be able to download music, movies, TV shows, podcasts, audiobooks, and free educational content from leading universities with iTunes U. You will also learn how to redeem iTunes gift cards.

Some of us still remember going to the record store when that new single or album came out. It was an exciting feeling, browsing through all the vinyl albums, then tapes and CDs, and looking at all the music we wanted.

Those days are pretty much long gone with the iPod touch. All the music, movies, TV shows, and more are available right from the iPod touch itself.

iTunes is a music, video, TV, podcast, and more store—virtually every type of media you can consume on your iPod touch is available for purchase or rent (and often for free) right from the iTunes store.

Just released for iTunes is a new sort of music social networking component called Ping. Follow artists, see what your friends are listening to, and more.

Getting Started with iTunes on the iPod touch

Earlier in this book, we showed you how to get your music from iTunes on your computer into your iPod touch (see Chapter 3: "Sync Your iPod touch with iTunes"). You can also learn more about using iTunes on your computer in Chapter 29: "Your iTunes User Guide." One of the great things about iTunes is that it is very easy to buy or obtain music, videos, podcasts, and audiobooks, and then use them in minutes right on your iPod touch.

The iPod touch allows you to access iTunes (the mobile version) right on your device. After you purchase or request free items, they will be downloaded to your **iPod** app on the iPod touch. They will also be automatically transferred to your iTunes library on your computer the next time you perform a sync, so you can also enjoy the same content on your computer.

A Network Connection Is Required

You do need an active Internet connection via Wi-Fi in order to access the iTunes store. Check out Chapter 5: "WiFi Connectivity" to learn more about network connectivity.

Starting iTunes

When you first received your iPod touch, **iTunes** was one of the icons on the first Home screen page. Touch the **iTunes** icon, and you will be taken to the mobile iTunes Store.

NOTE: The **iTunes** app changes frequently. Since the **iTunes** app is really a web site, it is likely to change somewhat between the time we wrote this book and when you are looking at it on your iPod touch. Some of the screen images or buttons may look slightly different than the ones shown in this book.

Navigating iTunes

iTunes uses icons similar to other programs on the iPod touch4, so getting around is quite easy. There are three buttons at the top and seven icons or soft keys at the bottom to help you. Look at Figure 19–1 to see the soft keys and features. Scrolling is just like scrolling in any other program; move your finger up or down to look at the selections available.

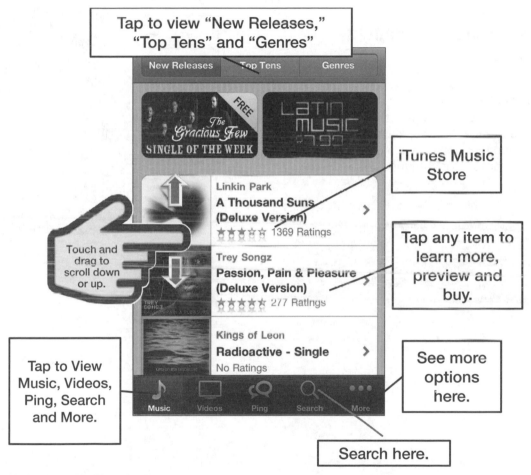

Figure 19–1. *The iTunes layout.*

Finding Music with New Releases, Top Tens, and Genres

Along the top of the iTunes music store screen are three buttons: **Featured**, **Top Charts**, and **Genius**. By default, you are shown the **Featured** selections when you start iTunes.

Top Tens: The Popular Stuff

If you like to see what is popular in a particular category, you will want to browse the **Top Tens** category. Tap **Top Tens** at the top, and then tap a category or genre to see what is popular for that category.

> **CAUTION:** These songs or videos are selling well, but that doesn't mean that they will appeal to you. Always give the item a preview and check out the reviews before you pay for it.

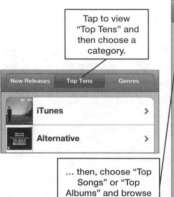

Tap to view "Top Tens" and then choose a category.

... then, choose "Top Songs" or "Top Albums" and browse the top of the charts

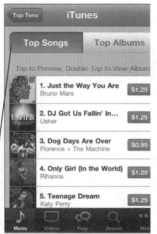

Genres: Types of Music

Touch the **Genres** button to browse music based on a genre. This is particularly helpful if you have a favorite type of music and would like to browse just that category.

There is quite an extensive list of genres to browse; just scroll down the list as you would in any other iPod touch app.

Go ahead and browse through the music until you see something that you would like to preview or buy.

Browsing for Videos (Movies)

Touch the **Videos** icon and then Touch the **Movies**, **TV Shows** or **Movie Videos** buttons on the top to browse all the video-related items (see Figure 19–2).

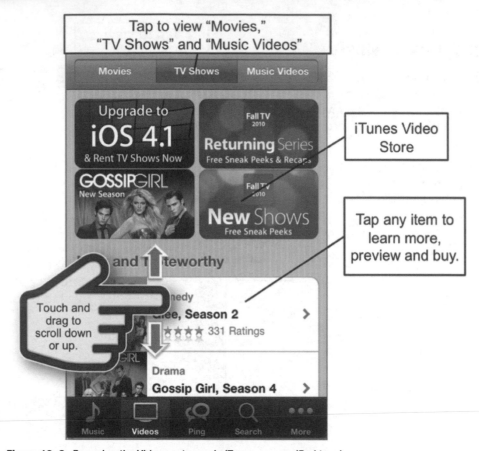

Figure 19–2. *Browsing the Videos category in iTunes on your iPod touch.*

You can also use your finger to scroll all the way to the bottom of the page to check out the links there, including these links in particular:

- **Top Tens**
- **Genres**

Tap any movie or video to see more details or preview the selection. You have the option to rent or buy some movies and TV shows.

Rentals: Some movies are available for rent for a set number of days.

> **NOTE:** The rental period in the US is 24 or 48 hours, and the rental period in Canada is 48 hours. Other countries may vary slightly.

Buy: This allows you to purchase and own the movie or TV show forever.

Finding TV Shows

When you're done checking out the movies, tap the **TV Shows** button at the top to see what is available from your favorite shows (see Figure 19–3).

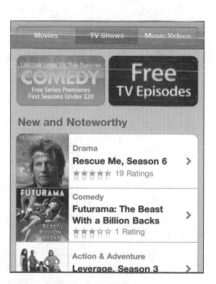

When you tap a TV series, you will see the individual episodes available. Tap any episode to check out the 30-second preview. See Chapter 10: " Viewing Videos, TV Shows and More " for more on watching videos. When you're finished with the preview, tap the **Done** button.

Figure 19–3. *Buying a TV season or episode.*

When you are ready to buy, you can choose to buy an individual episode or the entire TV series. Many, but not all TV series allow you to purchase individual episodes.

Maybe you want to get your fix of *Modern Family* and see the pilot episode that you missed. You can do this quickly and easily on your iPod touch.

NOTE: There is also a **Free TV Episode** category, where you can get samples and bonus content.

Audiobooks in iTunes

Audiobooks are a great way to enjoy books without having to read them. Some of the narrators are so fun to listen to that it is almost like watching a movie. For example, the narrator of the *Harry Potter* series can do dozens of truly amazing voices. We recommend that you try out an audiobook on your iPod touch; audiobooks are especially great when you are on an airplane and want to escape from the rest of the passengers, but don't want to have the light on.

TIP: If you're a big audiobook listener, getting an Audible.com subscription can get you the same content at cheaper prices.

 **Audiobooks**

If you are an audiobook aficionado, be sure to check out the audiobooks in iTunes.

You can use the top three buttons to browse the audiobooks in iTunes:

- **Featured**
- **Top Tens**
- **Categories**

Touch "More" then touch the "Audiobooks" tab then touch Featured, Top Tens or Categories.

iTunes U: Great Educational Content

If you like educational content, then check out **iTunes U**. You will be able to see whether your university, college, or school has its own section.

One good example we discovered in just a few minutes of browsing around was a panel discussion with three Nobel Prize–winning economists moderated by Paul Solman (Economic correspondent for PBS *News Hour*). You can find the podcast in **iTunes U ➤** Universities & Colleges **➤** Boston University **➤** BUNIVERSE - Business **➤** Audio. Like much of the content in **iTunes U**, it was free!

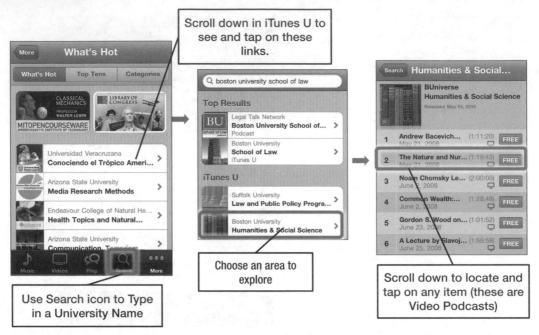

Figure 19–4. *You can search for a particular university, then browse iTunes U by that university.*

If you are in a location with a good Wi-Fi signal, you can tap the title of the audio or video item, and then listen to or watch it streaming (see Figure 19–4). If your signal gets interrupted, however, you will lose your place in the video. There are many advantages to actually downloading the file (if possible) for later viewing, not least of which is that you get more control of the video-watching experience.

> **NOTE**: iTunes audio streaming, like audio podcasts, uses the new background audio multitasking API in iOS4 and allows you to back out of a streaming podcast to check email and then go right back to it.

Download for Offline Viewing

If you know you are going to be out of wireless coverage for a while, such as on an airplane or in the subway, you will want to download the content for later, offline viewing or listening. Tap the **Free** button to change it to a **Download** button, and then tap it again. You can then monitor the download progress (some larger videos may take ten minutes or more to complete) by tapping the **Downloads** button at the bottom right of the screen. When the download is complete, the item will show up in the correct area in your **Music** app.

Searching iTunes

Sometimes you have a good idea of what you want, but you are unsure where it is located or perhaps you don't feel like browsing or navigating all the menus. The Search tool is for you.

Up in the top right-hand corner of the **iTunes** app, as in virtually every other iPod touch app, you have a search window.

Touch **Search**, and the search window and the on-device keyboard will pop up. Once you start typing, the iPod touch will begin to match your entry with possibilities.

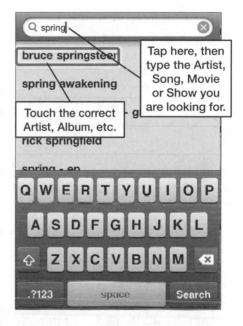

Tap here, then type the Artist, Song, Movie or Show you are looking for.

Touch the correct Artist, Album, etc.

Type in the artist, song name, video name, podcast name, or album you are searching for, and the iPod touch will display detailed matches. Be as general or as specific as you would like. If you are just looking to browse all particular songs by an artist, type the artist's name. If you want a specific song or album, enter the full name of the song or album.

When you locate the song or album name, simply touch it and you will be taken to the purchase page.

Purchasing or Renting Music, Videos, Podcasts, and More

Once you locate a song, video, TV show, or album, you can touch the **Buy** or (if you see it) **Rent** button. This will cause your media to start downloading. (If the content is free, then you will see the **Free** button, which you tap to turn into a **Download** button.)

We suggest you view or listen to the preview, as well as check out the customer reviews first, unless you are absolutely sure you want to purchase the item.

Previewing Music

Touch either the title of the song or its track number to the le
of the song title; this will flip over the album cover and launch
the preview window.

You will hear a representative clip of 30 seconds of the song

Touch the **Stop** button and the track number will again be
displayed.

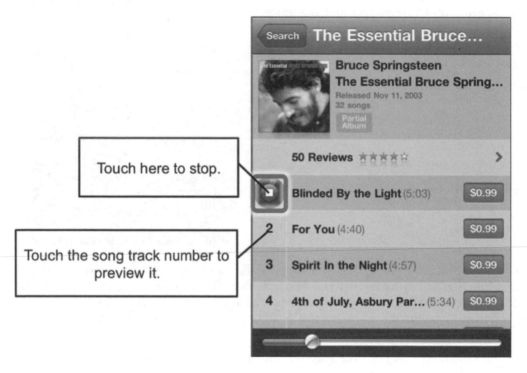

Checking Out Customer Reviews

Many items in iTunes offer customer reviews. The reviews range from a low of one star to a high of five stars.

> **CAUTION:** *Be aware that the reviews can have explicit language.* Many of the reviews are clean; however, some do contain explicit language that may not be caught by the iTunes store right away.

Reading the reviews might give you a fairly good idea of whether you would like to buy the item.

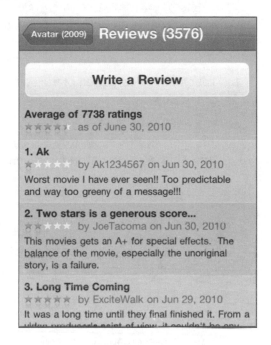

Previewing a Video, TV Show, or Music Video

Pretty much everything on iTunes offers a preview. Sometimes you will see a **Preview** button, as with music videos and movies. TV shows are a little different; you tap the episode title in order to see the 30-second preview.

We do highly recommend checking out the reviews, as well as trying the preview before purchasing items on iTunes.

Typical movie previews or trailers will be longer than 30 seconds. Some are two and a half minutes or longer.

Purchasing a Song, Video, or Other Item

Once you are sure you want to purchase a song, video, or other item, follow these steps to buy it.

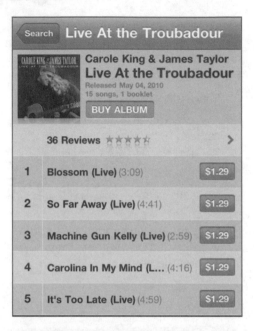

1. Touch the **Price** button of the song or the **Buy** button.

2. The button will change and turn into a green **Buy Now**, **Buy Song**, **Buy Single**, or **Buy Album** button.

3. Tap the **Buy** button.

4. You will see an animated icon jump into the shopping cart. Type in your iTunes password and touch **OK** to complete the sale.

Touch the **More** button in the lower right-hand corner to see the download progress for each song on the album.

The song or album will then become part of your music library, and it will be synced with your computer the next time you connect your iPod touch to iTunes on your computer.

After the download is complete, you will see the new song, audiobook, podcast, or iTunes U podcast inside the correct category within your **iPod** icon.

> **NOTE:** Purchased videos and iTunes U videos go into the **Vidcos** app on your iPod touch.

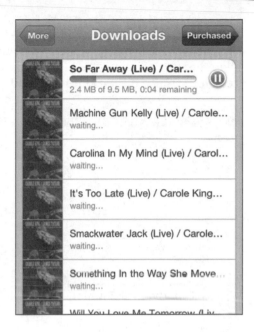

Podcasts in iTunes

Podcasts are usually a series of audio segments; these may be updated frequently (such as hourly news reports from National Public Radio) or not updated at all (such as a recording of a one-time lecture on a particular topic).

 Podcasts

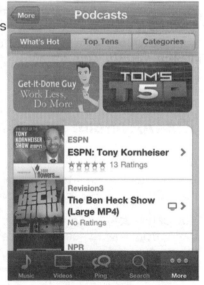

You can use the top three buttons to browse the podcasts in iTunes:

- **What's Hot**
- **Top Tens**
- **Categories**

Downloading a Podcast

Podcasts are available in video and audio varieties. When you locate a podcast, just touch the title of the podcast (see Figure 19–5). Luckily, most podcasts are free. If it is free, you will see a **Free** button instead of the typical **Buy** button.

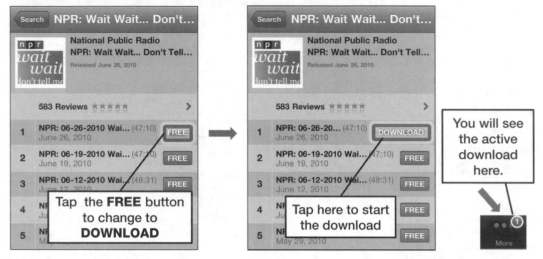

Figure 19–5. *Downloading an NPR podcast.*

When you touch the button, it turns into a green button that says **Download**. Touch **Download**, and an animated icon jumps into your **Downloads** icon at the bottom bar of soft keys. A small number displayed in red reflects the number of files downloading.

The Download Icon: Stopping and Deleting Downloads

As you download items, they appear in your Downloads screen. This behavior is just like the behavior of iTunes on your computer.

You can touch the **Downloads** icon along the bottom row to see the progress of all your downloads.

Where the Downloads Go

All of your downloads will be visible in either your **iPod** icon or your **More** icon, organized by category. In other words, if you download a podcast, you will need to go into your **iPod** icon, touch **More**, and then the **Podcasts** tab to see the downloaded podcast.

Sometimes, you decide that you do not want the all downloads you selected. If you want to stop a download and delete it, swipe your finger over the download to bring up the **Delete** button, and then tap **Delete** (see Figure 19–6).

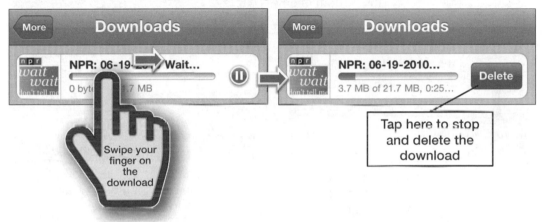

Figure 19–6. *Deleting a file while downloading.*

Redeeming an iTunes Gift Card

One of the cool things about iTunes on your iPod touch4 is that, just as with iTunes on your computer, you can redeem a gift card and receive credit in your iTunes account for your purchases.

At the bottom of the **iTunes** screen, you should see the **Redeem** button (see Figure 19–7).

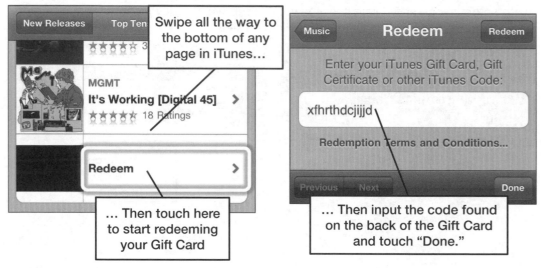

Figure 19–7. *Redeeming an iTunes gift card.*

Tap the **Redeem** button to start the process of entering your iTunes gift card number for an iTunes store credit.

Ping: Apples Music Social Networking App

Just recently, Apple introduced Ping as part of iTunes 10. You can read more about the desktop version in Chapter 29: "Your iTunes User Guide." Ping is also built into the **iTunes** app on the iPod touch.

Ping gives you the opportunity to follow your favorite music artists and view videos, pictures, or content the artist might choose to post. Ping also allows you to follow friends and see what they are listening to and make comments to their posts.

Using Ping on the iPod touch

Ping is located along the bottom soft keys of the **iTunes** app. Set up Ping from your desktop iTunes app as we show you in Chapter 29: "Your iTunes User Guide," and then you will find that it will already be set up on your iPod (or any other iOS device you have).

NOTE: If it doesn't show up, you might need to sync once after you've enabled it on iTunes desktop in order for it to appear on iTunes app.

You will notice three soft keys across the top: Activity, People, and My Profile. When Ping launches, it displays the Activity screen, which shows the artists and friends you are following and their recent activity.

Touching the **People** soft key at the top will show you the people you are following as well as those who are following you.

Touch the **My Profile** soft key, and you can also see who you are following and add comments to be seen by those who are following you.

Touch the **My Info** button at the bottom, and you can see your picture and the music that you like, which you chose when you set up your Ping account in iTunes 10.

Ping is in its infancy now, but it promises to become a more full-featured social networking site devoted exclusively to music in the not-too-distant future.

Chapter 20

The Amazing App Store

You have just seen how easy it is download music, videos, and podcasts from iTunes right to your iPod touch. We have also shown you how to download iBooks from the iBooks store.

It is just as easy to download new applications from Apple's amazing App Store. Apps are available for just about any function: games, productivity tools, social networking, and anything else you can imagine. As the advertising says, *There's an app for that*.

In this chapter, you will learn how to navigate the **App Store** program (and its tightly integrated web site, as well as how to search for and download apps. You will also learn how to maintain and update your apps once they are downloaded onto your iPod touch.

NOTE: If you purchase a new iPod touch while travelling and bring it home to a country where it's not yet sold, then there's a good chance you may not be able to use your iPod touch to purchase apps specifically designed for the iPod touch in your home country from the App Store. The work-around is to buy iPod touch apps on the desktop version of **iTunes** (which does work) and sync them over.

Learning More About Apps and the App Store

In this chapter, we will focus on the App Store that you can access on your iPod touch. However, you should remember that you can also shop at the App Store using the **iTunes** program on your Mac or PC (see Figure 20–1).

Figure 20–1. *Accessing the App Store from the iTunes program on your computer or the App Store icon on your iPod touch.*

In a very short amount of time, the App Store has exploded in popularity. There are apps for just about anything you can imagine. Apps come in all prices; in many cases, the apps are even free!

The following interesting App Store statistics are provided courtesy of the www.148apps.biz web site. These stats were copied from the web page at http://148apps.biz/app-store-metrics/ when it was updated on September 14, 2010:

In September 2010, there were more than 450 apps submitted every day! (*Author's note:* By the time you read this, there will likely be more than 300,000 apps in the store.)

- COUNT OF ACTIVE APPLICATIONS IN THE APP STORE
    - Total Active Apps (currently available for download): 259,475
    - Number of Active Publishers in the U.S. App Store: 52,281
- APPLICATION PRICE DISTRIBUTION
    - Current Average App Price: $2.86 (down from $3.05 in July 2010)
    - Current Average Game Price: $1.22 (was $1.28 in July 2010)
    - Current Average Overall Price: $2.63 (was $2.79 in July 2010)

Where to Find News and Reviews for Apps

You can find reviews for many apps in the App Store itself, and we recommend you check out the App Store reviews. However, sometimes you will probably want more information from expert reviewers. If so, blogs are a great place to find news and reviews.

Here is a list of Apple iPhone and iPod touch-related blogs with reviews of apps:

- **The iPod touchBlog**: www.tipb.com
- **Touch Reviews**: www.touchreviews.net
- **Touch My Apps**: www.touchmyapps.com
- **The Unofficial Apple Weblog**: www.tuaw.com
- **Cult of Mac**: www.cultofmac.com
- **App Smile**: www.appsmile.com

Many lists of apps can also be found from these links:

- **PC Magazine**: www.pcmag.com/article2/0,2817,2366274,00.asp
- **Mobile Clues**: www.mobileclues.com/10-best-iphone-apps-for-business
- **iPhone Daily**: http://iphonedaily.net/iphone-software/top-100-free-iphone-application-on-appstore.html
- **iLounge**: www.ilounge.com/index.php/news/comments/download-now-ilounges-2010-ipod-iphone-buyers-guide/
- **Best Applications**: http://bestapplications.net/

A Few Cool Apps

With more than 250,000 apps in the store and hundreds of new ones added daily, it is impossible to give you a top 10 list of apps. Instead, we've listed a number of apps that we like or have heard are really cool. Table 20–1 lists of a number of fun, cool, useful, or simply entertaining apps. The table also shows whether an app is free, but it does not otherwise include pricing because prices change frequently in the App Store.

Table 20–1. *Cool iPod touch Apps*

App Name	Type	What it does	Free / Paid
Pandora Radio	Music	Create your own customized radio station to listen to your favorite artists for free. (Learn more in Chapter 9.)	Free
Slacker Radio	Music	Create your own customized radio station to listen to your favorite artists for free. (Learn more in Chapter 9.)	Free
Google Earth	Mapping	Zoom around the world with a birds-eye view. Swipe, rotate, and zoom to see the world at an amazing level of detail.	Free
Skype	Phone & Chat	Turn your iPod touch into a speakerphone. Call anyone else in the world who also has a Skype account - for free. (Learn more in Chapter 13.)	Free
IM+	Instant Messaging	Connect to a variety of instant messaging networks, including the following: Google Talk, Windows Live Messenger, Yahoo! Jabber, MySpaceIM, ICQ, MSN, iChat, and AIM.	Free
Text+ 4	Text Messaging	Send free text and multimedia messages to anyone with a mobile phone.	Free
Flashlight	Lighting	Turn your iPod touch into a flashlight or strobe light to help you when it's dark.	Free
Words with Friends	Games	Lets you play a Scrabble-like game with your friends or just anyone.	Free
Angry Birds	Games	Shoot birds across the screen to knock down buildings.	Paid

App Name	Type	What it does	Free / Paid
ESPN Fantasy Football	Games	Manage your favorite teams and leagues. Follow games in real-time to see how you're doing.	Paid
Evernote	Note	Take notes, store pictures, and create voice notes. Categorize and sort your notes. (Learn more in Chapter 23.)	Free
Facebook	Social Networking	Stay up-to-date with all your friends on Facebook. (Learn more in Chapter 22.)	Free
Kindle	Ebook Reader	An alternative to iBooks, this reader allows you to read Kindle books from www.amazon.com. (Learn more about Kindle in Chapter 11.)	Free
GoodReader	Ebook Reader	Lets you read PDFs and Ebooks, as well as unzip compressed .zip files and more. (Learn more about GoodReader in Chapter 11.)	Free
iMovie	Video Editor	Edit movies you take with your iPod touch right on the device! (Learn more in Chapter 18.)	Paid
Weather Bug	Weather	See forecasts for the weather anywhere. It lets you see radar maps, 10-day and hourly forecasts, and more.	Free
Remote	Remote Control	Control music on your computer (iTunes) or your Apple TV. (Learn more in Chapter 29.)	Free

App Store Basics

After only a little time on the site, you should find the App Store to be quite intuitive to navigate. We'll cover some of the basics for getting the most out of the App Store, so that your experience will be as enjoyable and productive as possible.

> **NOTE:** App availability varies by country. Some apps are only available in some countries, and some countries may not have certain games sections due to local ratings laws.

A Network Connection Is Required

After you set up your **App Store** (**iTunes**) account, you still need to have the right network connectivity via Wi-Fi to access the **App Store** and download apps. Check out Chapter 5: "Wi-Fi Connectivity" to learn how to tell whether you are connected.

Starting the App Store

The **App Store** icon should be on your first page of icons on the **Home** screen. Tap the icon to launch the **App Store** program.

The App Store Home Page

We'll look at several parts of the App Store home page: the top bar of the page, its middle content, and its bottom soft keys.

We'll look at the top bar of the page first. At the top of the page shown in Figure 20–2, you will see three buttons: **New**, **What's Hot**, and **Genius**. Tap any of these to change the view.

> **TIP: Genius** is a fairly new feature in the App Store. Once you enable it and agree to the terms and conditions, the **Genius** feature suggests apps you might like based on apps you have already downloaded and installed on your iPod touch. It can be quite a nice way to filter through the hundreds of thousands of apps to find the ones that might interest you.

The middle of the page is your main content area. This main content area shows you a list of apps or the details of a specific app when you are viewing one app. You can swipe up or down to view more apps in a list or details for a specific app. You can swipe left or right when viewing screen shots. On this **Featured** apps page, you will notice that there are a few large icons at the top. Clicking these icons will show you either types of apps or individual apps. Swipe down to see a number of featured apps below the larger icons.

The bottom of the App Store page has five soft key buttons, which are listed here:

- **Featured**: Shows apps that have been highlighted by the App Store or by the app developers.

- **Categories**: Shows a list of categories used to organize the apps, so you can browse by category.

- **Top 25**: Shows the top-selling or top-downloaded apps.

- **Search**: Finds an app using entered search terms.

- **Updates**: Lets you update any apps you have installed.

You can tell that Figure 20–2 is showing **Featured** apps because the **Featured** soft key is highlighted on the bottom row of soft keys. Also, scrolling is handled the same way as in **iTunes** and in other programs—just move your finger up and down to scroll through the page.

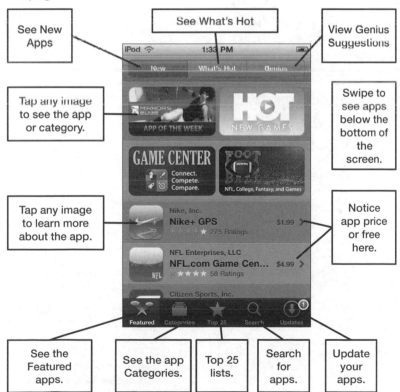

Figure 20–2. *The layout of the App Store home page.*

NOTE: The App Store is essentially a web site, so it changes frequently. Some of the details and nuances of the App Store might be a bit different after this book goes to print.

Viewing App Details

If you see an app in a list that looks interesting, tap it to learn more. The **Details** screen for the app shows its price, a description, screen shots, and reviews (see Figure 20–3). You can use this information to help you determine whether the app will be a good choice for you.

Swipe down to read more details about the app on the **Info** page. Swipe left or right to view more screen shots of the app. Tap the **Rating** button near the bottom to read all the reviews for an app.

You can also see other details about the app, such as its file size, its version number, and developer information near the bottom of the **Info** page.

You can also **Tell a Friend** or **Report a Problem** using the buttons at the bottom of the screen.

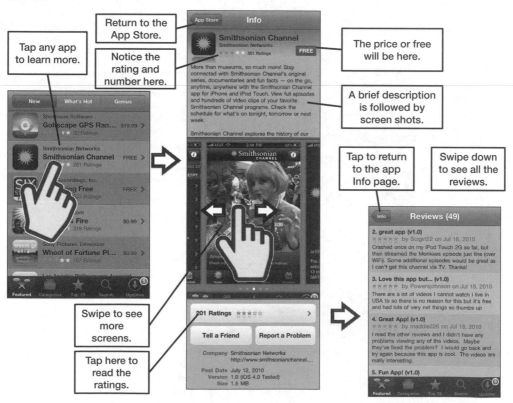

Figure 20–3. *Viewing details about an app.*

Finding an App to Download

If you want to search for an app to download, begin by looking around in the default view, which shows the **Featured** apps. Scroll down the page to see all the featured apps.

Viewing the New Apps

The default view in the **App Store** program shows new and featured apps. This is the view shown back in Figure 26–2. You can tell that this view shows new featured apps because the **Featured** soft key  is highlighted at the bottom of the screen, and the **New** button at the top of the page is highlighted.

Viewing What's Hot

Touch the **What's Hot** button at the top of the screen, and the "hottest" apps in the store will be shown on the screen. Again, just scroll through the hottest apps to see if something catches your eye.

> **NOTE:** The fact that an app is in the **What's Hot** category does not necessarily mean you will also believe it is useful or fun. Check out the app descriptions and reviews carefully before you purchase anything.

Genius

The third button at the top of the **Featured** apps section is the **Genius** feature. This feature works like the identically named feature in **iTunes** used on your computer for music. For example, it displays apps you might like based on apps you already have installed on your iPod touch.

> **NOTE:** The first time you use the **Genius** feature, you will have to accept the terms and conditions presented before the feature will be enabled.

Based On

Notice that there is a **Based on (app name)** label above each app. This label shows you that the suggested app was based on a specific app you've installed on your iPod touch. For example, the **CBS Radio** suggestion was based on the fact that **Pandora Radio** is installed. It's possible you don't know about CBS Radio, but maybe you'll give it a try based on this recommendation.

Swipe to Remove

If you do not like a **Genius** suggestion, then you can swipe left or right on it to bring up the **Delete** button, just as you would to remove email or other items from lists on your iPod touch. Tap the **Delete** button to remove that app from the list.

Disable the Genius Feature

To disable the **Genius** feature, you need to go into your **App Store** settings (see the "App Store Settings" section later in this chapter to learn how to disable this feature).

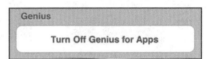

Categories

Sometimes, all the choices presented can be a bit overwhelming. If you have a sense of what type of app you are looking for, touch the **Categories** button along the bottom row of soft keys (see Figure 20–4).

The current categories available are shown in Table 20–2.

Table 20–2. *The List of App Store Categories*

■ Games	■ Reference	■ Finance
■ Entertainment	■ Travel	■ Education
■ Utilities	■ Sports	■ Weather
■ Social Networking	■ Navigation	■ Books
■ Music	■ Healthcare & Fitness	■ Medical
■ Productivity	■ News	
■ Lifestyle	■ Photography	

NOTE: The categories listed are fluid and change over time, so it is possible that the categories you see will have changed by the time this book finds its way into your hands.

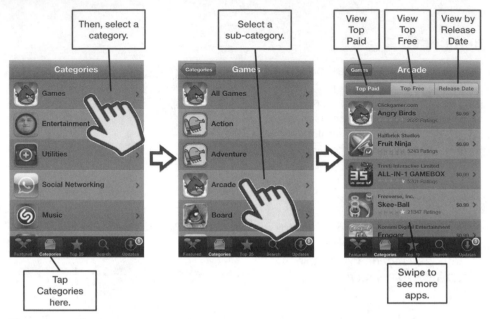

Then, select a category.

Select a sub-category.

View Top Paid

View Top Free

View by Release Date

Tap Categories here.

Swipe to see more apps.

Figure 20–4. *Viewing apps by category – Games, in this example.*

Looking at the Top 25 Charts

Touch the **Top Charts** soft key along the bottom row, and the **App Store** program will change the view again. This time, it will show you the top 25 paid, free, and top-grossing apps. Just touch one of the **Top Paid, Top Free**, or **Top Grossing** buttons at the top to switch between the views.

NOTE: The Top Grossing category refers to the highest money-making apps, which is sales volume times selling price. This view will help more expensive apps place higher in the charts. For example, a $4.99 app that sells 10,000 units will rank much higher on the **Top Grossing** chart than a $0.99 app that sells the same number of units.

Searching for an App

Let's say you have a specific idea of the type of app you want to find. Touch the **Search** soft key and type in either the name of the program or the type of program.

So, if you are looking for an app to help you with rowing, just type in *rowing* to see what comes up.

You may see some suggested search terms appear; tap these to narrow your search.

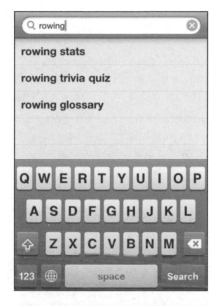

In this example, tapping **Rowing Stats** in the suggested search terms yielded only one result.

We want to see all the rowing-related apps, so we tap in the **Search** bar and use the **Backspace** key to erase the word *Stats*. Next, we tap the **Search** button in the lower-right corner to see a broader list of rowing-related results.

> **TIP:** If you row on the water (instead of only on a rowing machine), you might want to check out **SpeedCoach Mobile**, which sells for $64.99. There is also a free (at the time of writing) alternative called **iRowPro**.

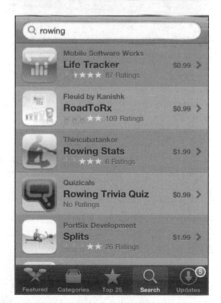

Downloading an App

Once you find an app that interests you, you can download it right to your iPod touch, as shown in Figure 20–5.

After locating the app you want to buy, notice the small button that says either Free or $0.99 (or whatever the price is).

Just touch that button, and it will change to say **Install** if it is a free program or **Buy Now** if it is a paid program.

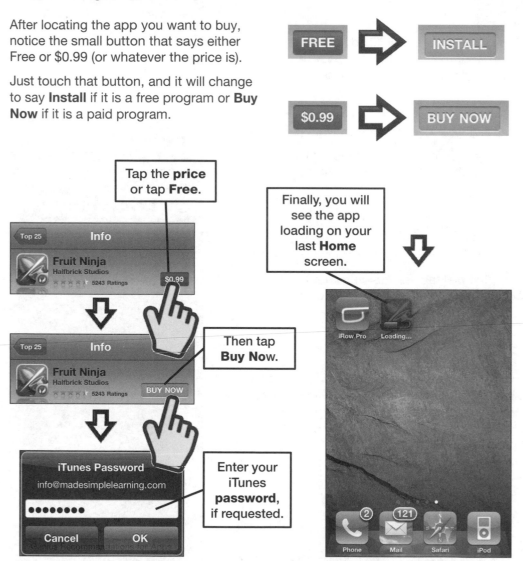

Figure 20–5. *Buying an app or downloading a free app.*

Once you have read the reviews and the app description (and perhaps visited the developer support site), go ahead and download or purchase the app. Once you tap the **Download App** button, you will be prompted to input your **iTunes** password.

Input your password and tap **OK**; the app will be downloaded to your iPod touch, as shown in Figure 20–5.

Finding Free or Discounted Apps

After browsing around the App Store, you will notice a couple of things. First, there are lots of *free* apps. Sometimes, these are great applications. Other times, they are not so useful—but they can still be fun!

Second, you will notice that there will be sales for some of the apps, and other apps will become less expensive over time. So, if you have a favorite app and it costs $6.99, it is likely that waiting a few weeks or a month might result in a lower price.

Maintaining and Updating Your Apps

Often, developers will update their apps for the iPod touch. You don't need to use your computer to perform the update—you can do it right on your iPod touch.

You can even tell if you have updates, and how many, by looking at the **App Store** icon. The one shown here has five app updates available for you to download.

Once you enter the App Store, tap the right-most icon on the bottom row. This is the **Updates** icon.

If you have apps with updates available, there will be a small number indicated in red. This number corresponds to the number of apps with updates.

When you touch the **Update** button, the iPod touch shows you which apps have updates.

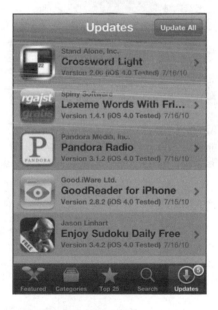

To get your updates, you could touch an individual app. However, it is easier to touch the **Update All** button

in the upper-right corner to have all your apps updated at once. The iPod touch will leave the **App Store** program, and you can see the progress of the updates in little status bars. All apps updating will have icons that look grayed out.

Some status messages will show **Waiting**, while others will show **Loading** or **Installing**. When the update is complete, all your icons will return to their normal colors.

> **NOTE:** You will need to relaunch the **App Store** program to get back in. The update process takes you completely out of the store.

App Store Settings

As with other apps, your settings for the **App Store** program are located in the **Settings** app. You can check which account is logged into the store, log out, turn off the **Genius** feature, view your iTunes account, and work with your newsletter subscriptions.

> **TIP:** If you want to prevent someone from buying apps on your iPod touch using your iTunes account, you can **Sign Out** of iTunes using the steps below.

Follow these steps to change a setting for the **App Store** program:

1. Tap the **Settings** icon.

2. Scroll down and tap **Store**. Notice that you can see the account you are logged in with at the top of this screen.

3. Tap **Sign Out** if you wish to log out of **iTunes**. For example, you might be giving this iPod touch to someone you do not want to buy apps using your iTunes account.

4. Tap **View Account** to see details of your account (you will need to sign in).

The figure to the right shows your account information. Tap **Payment Information** to adjust your billing information (e.g., credit card type and number).

5. Tap **Billing Address** to update your address.

6. Tap **Change Country** to change your country.

7. Scroll down to see more settings.

8. You can toggle the **Genius** feature off or on by tapping the **Turn Off Genius for Apps** or **Turn On Genius for Apps** button, respectively. Or, you can **Subscribe** or **Unsubscribe** to the iTunes newsletter from this dialog.

9. Tap **Done** in the upper-right corner when finished.

Chapter 21

Games and Fun

Your iPod touch excels at many things. It is a multimedia workhorse, and it can keep track of your busy life. Your iPod touch particularly excels in two areas: as a gaming device and for displaying iPod touch iOS4-specific apps that take advantage of the beautiful, high-resolution touch screen. You can even find versions of popular games for the device that you might expect to find only on dedicated gaming consoles.

The iPod touch brings many advantages to portable gaming: the high definition (HD) screen delivers realistic visuals; the high quality audio provides great sound effects; and the gyroscope and the accelerometer allow you to interact with your games in a way that many PCs and dedicated gaming consoles (outside of the Wii) don't. For example, in racing games, the last feature lets you steer your car by turning the iPod touch as you hold it.

The iPod touch is also great for lots of other fun stuff such as following your local baseball team. You can even using the iPod touch as a musical instrument with great apps like Ocarina (which we will show you later in the chapter.)

> **NOTE:** We have written many books on the BlackBerry smartphones, and we have many BlackBerry devices lying around the house. The BlackBerry smartphones don't disappear into our children's rooms; rather, the iPod touch is the device that our children (and our spouses) have decided is fun enough to grab. We routinely discover that the iPod touch has disappeared from its charger and have to yell out, "Where is my iPod touch? I need to finish this book!"

Using the iPod touch As a Gaming Device

The iPod touch includes a built-in accelerometer and *gyroscope*, which is essentially a device that detects movement (acceleration) and tilt.

Combine the accelerometer with a fantastic screen, lots of memory, and a fast processor, and you have the makings of a great gaming platform. With literally thousands of gaming titles to choose from, you can play virtually any type of game you wish on your iPod touch.

With iOS 4, if a game supports multitasking, you can even take a phone call and come back to the exact place you left off when the call ends. This means no more restarts!

> **NOTE:** Some games do require that you have an active network connection through Wi-Fi to engage in multiplayer games.

With the iPod touch, you can play a driving game and use the iPod touch itself to steer. You do this simply by turning the device. You can touch the iPod touch to brake or tilt it forward to accelerate.

The game on the right, **Real Racing HD**, is so realistic that it might make you car sick!

"Real Racing HD"

Tap to Brake

Tilt the iPad left/ right to steer the Car

Lean forward to accelerate

Or, you can try a fishing game, where you case and reel in fish from the perspective of being on a boat!

"Flick Fishing"

Wind with your finger to reel in your fish

If music/rhythm games are your thing, then you will find many such programs in the App Store. Popular console games such as **Rock Band**, **Guitar Hero**, and others have been ported to the iPhone.

On some games, such as the new **Guitar Hero**, you really have to "strum" to keep pace and score points.

The iPod touch also has a very fast processor and a sophisticated graphics chip. Bundling these together with the accelerometer gives you a very capable gaming device.

Acquiring Games and Other Fun Apps

As is the case for all iPod touch apps, games can be found at the App Store (see Figure 21-1). You can get them either through iTunes on your computer or through the device's built-in **App Store** program.

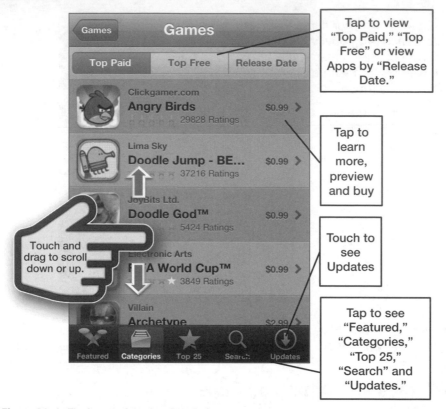

Figure 21–1. *The layout of the App Store's Games section.*

To get a game, fire up the **App Store** program, as you did in the previous chapter. Next, use the **Categories** icon to go to the **Games** tab. You will also find many games in the **Featured** section of the App Store, as well as in the **New and Notable** section. Figure 21–2 shows the app purchase page for a game available for the iPod touch.

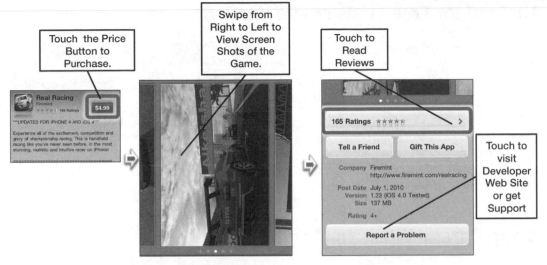

Figure 21-2. *The layout of the App Purchase page.*

Reading Reviews Before You Buy

Many of the games have user reviews that are worth perusing. Sometimes, you can get a good sense of the game before you buy it. If you find a game that looks interesting, don't be afraid to do a simple Google search to see whether any mainstream media outlets have performed a full review.

Looking for Free Trials or Lite Versions

Increasingly, game developers are giving users free trials of their games to see if they like them before they buy. You will find many games have both a *lite* version and a *full* version in the App Store.

Some "free" games are supported by the inclusion of ads within the game. Other games are free to start, but require in-app purchases for continued play or additional features.

Being Careful When You Play

You might use the iPod touch to cast your line in a fishing game, as you would in real life. You can also move around a bit in driving and first-person shooter games. So be mindful of your surroundings as you play! For example, make sure you have a good grip on your device, so it doesn't slip out of your hand; we recommend a good silicone case to help with this.

> **CAUTION:** Games such as **Real Racing HD** can be quite addictive!

Two-Player Games

The iPod touch really opens up the possibility for two-player gaming. In this example, we are playing checkers against one another, using the iPod touch as a game board.

You can find similar two-person gaming apps for other board games, such as chess or checkers.

Online and Wireless Games

The iPod touch also allows online and wireless, peer-to-peer gaming (if the game supports it). Many new games are incorporating this technology. In **Scrabble**, for example, you can play against multiple players on their own devices. You can even use the iPod touch as your game board and up to four individual iPhones as wireless "racks" to hold the letters of all the players. Just flick the letters off the rack, and they go onto the board – very cool!

The example to the right shows the screen presented when a user chooses the **Online** option from the **Real Racing HD** menu. At this point, the user now has the option to either play against another opponent through Wi-Fi or to join an online league race.

NOTE: If you just want to play against a friend who is nearby, select Wi-Fi mode for multiplayer games. If you just want to play against new people, try going online for a league race or game.

Playing Music Games with Your iPod touch

The iPod touch's relatively large screen means that you can even install a piano keyboard on your iPod touch 4and play music. There are a number of music-related games available; check out the **Music** subcategory of the **Games** category in the iTunes Store to see what's available.

One of the apps that was in the Top 5 of the **Paid iPod touch** apps category when we were writing this book was **Ocarina** , which turns your iPod touch into a flute-like instrument for just US $0.99.

Download the app and just have fun with it!

If you have children, they might enjoy it, as well.

NOTE: This app wants to know your location, so it can tell people around the world where you are when they hear you play. You can always refuse when it asks you for permission to share your location.

Playing Songs from the Songbook

To use Ocarina, begin by tapping the **Menu** button in the center and select **Info**. You can find out where to go to get music to play. You can visit http://Ocarina.smule.com to acquire tutorials and music. With Ocarina, you blow into your microphone and place your fingers on the circles, just as you would for a recorder (see Figure 21–3).

TIP: Begin by trying out the tutorial that teaches the notes of the scale. Next, you can try playing a song or just "freestyle."

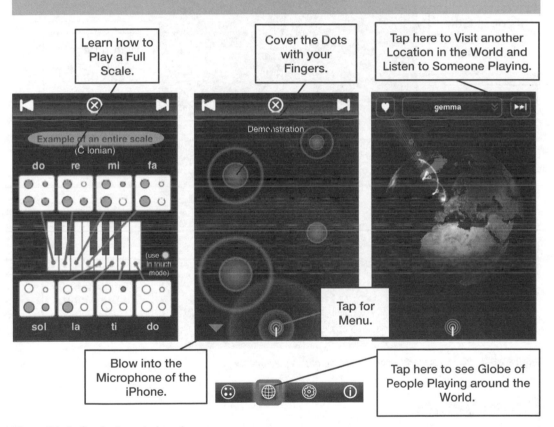

Figure 21–3. *Ocarina's controls and menu.*

The World View

Tap the **Menu** button and select **World** (see Figure 21–4). This shows you a globe with people happily "making music" in various places around the world.

If you like the way someone is playing, then hit the **Heart** icon. If you do not like the music you're hearing, then hit the **Next** icon (the two right arrows).

> If you do not like the way someone plays, click here to skip to the next person.

> If you like the way someone plays, click here.

> Watch people playing Ocarina and their locations.

gemma

World

Region

Top Melodies

My Loved

My Melodies

> Click here to go to the Menu.

Figure 21–4. *Ocarina's world view – watching others play Ocarina.*

Game Center

With the new iPod touch, Apple has introduced a new concept to portable gaming: the **Game Center**. **Game Center** is a place for you to meet up with friends, invite friends to play a game or to share accomplishments from games you and your friends both play.

Setting up Game Center

The first time you start up **Game Center** from your iPod touch, you will be asked to either sign in using your Apple ID and password or your **MobileMe** ID and password. Input your biographical information and then input an email address (or several email addresses) to authenticate **Game Center** use.

Make sure that the **Allow Game Invites** and **Find me By Email** buttons are turned **ON** so that your friends can ask you to play.

Using Game Center

Once you have set up **Game Center**, the fun begins. Start up **Game Center**, and you will see how many friends you have, how many **Game Center** games you have, and how

many achievements you have earned. All this is visible from the **Me** tab at the bottom.

Touch the **Friends** tab, and you will see how many **Game Center** friends you have. Itt seems as thoug this maxes out at 500 friends.

Touch the **Games** tab, and you will see how many **Game Center** games are on your device.

> **NOTE**: Once you have a **Game Center** account, you can log in from any iOS device to see your games, friends, and achievements.

Touch the **Requests** tab to either see pending requests or touch the **+** sign to invite contacts (through email addresses) to become your **Game Center** friends.

Playing a Multiplayer Game

Some **Game Center** games allow you to play (and invite) a **Game Center** friend to a one-on-one game. Some games will match you up with other players online, while others only allow you to share your achievements with your friends.

The screenshot tyup – I fixed it.o the right shows the **Game Center** with two games enabled: **Real Racing HD**, which only allows the user to share achievements; and **Adrenaline Golf**, which allows the user to play against friends or to get matched up online.

2 Games
0 of 0 achievements **Adrenaline Golf Online** › #0 of 619
1 of 21 achievements **Real Racing** › #3280 of 6199

In a multiplayer game (like **Adrenaline Golf**), you can start the game either from within **Game Center** or from the game's icon on the iPod touch.

The screenshot to the right displays your options when a user chooses **Play Multiplayer** in **Adrenaline Golf**. Doing so brings up options for **Automatic Match Making** or **GameCenter Invite**.

Choosing **Automatic Match Making** prompts the iPod touch to find opponents for the user to play against.

Other Fun Stuff: Baseball on the iPod touch

There are many great apps that can provide you with endless hours of entertainment on the iPod touch. The iPod touch was released on opening day of the Major League Baseball season, so it is appropriate to highlight an app that was honored as the first "App of the Week" in the iPod touch App Store.

At Bat 2010 for iPod touch is a US $14.99 application that is well worth the entry fee for any baseball fan. It also highlights the iPod touch's capabilities.

The main view of the app changes based on whether there are baseball games currently being played. When you first register the app, you pick your favorite team. The favorite team on the iPod touch in this example is set to the Red Sox. So, if this team is playing, then the view automatically goes to that team's game first. If this team is not playing, then the app displays a recap of the team's previous game. Alternatively, it might list the details of the team's next game.

The main view during game time shows a batter at the plate (see Figure 21–5). This batter represents the real batter. Batters will switch sides of the plate, depending on whether the batter currently up hits from the left or right side of the plate. The current pitch count is shown above the plate, and the score is displayed at the top of the screen.

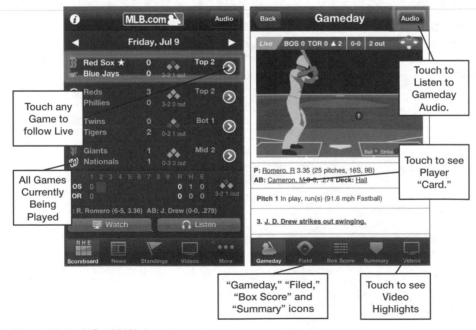

Figure 21–5. *At Bat 2010's layout.*

When you see a player at the plate or on base, you can touch the player's image to bring up his baseball card and view his stats.

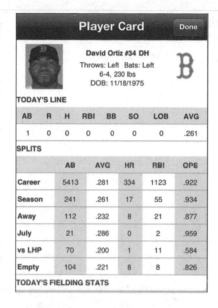

If the game is being televised, there will be a **Watch** button at the lower left of the **Home** screen.

Touch the **Watch** button, and you will be taken to the MLB TV **Login** screen to watch the game.

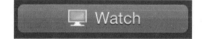

NOTE: You need to have a separate MLB TV account to be able to watch live games.

You can touch the **Listen** icon to listen to the game day audio from either of the two cities playing a particular game.

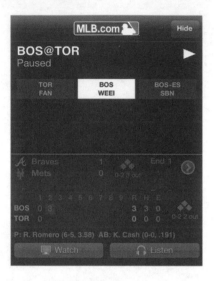

You can also touch the **Information** icon to adjust your favorite team, input your MLB TV subscription information (if you have one), or jump right to the MLB web site.

> **TIP**: You can even allow notifications to be sent when something newsworthy occurs related to your favorite team. To do this, touch the **Information** icon and turn **Notifications** to **ON**.

To see video highlights of key plays of the game, just touch the **Videos** box in the lower-right corner.

Touch any of the listed videos, and it will begin to play in the iPhone's **Video** player.

To jump to any other game that is being played, touch the **Back** button from the **Gameday** view, and then touch the **Scoreboard** icon on the main page.

The options in this app are quite extensive, and the experience is immersive. This is a great way to follow your favorite teams, wherever you might be.

Chapter 22

Social Networking

Some of the most popular places to "connect" these days are those sites that are often referred to as social networking sites—places that allow you to create your own "page" to broadcast your interests and to connect with friends and family to see what is going in their lives. Some of the biggest web sites for social networking are Facebook, Twitter, and LinkedIn. Apple just introduced its own sort of music social networking site called Ping, which is part of iTunes; you can read more about it in Chapter 19: "iTunes on your iPod Touch" and Chapter 29: "Your iTunes User Guide." Apple also introduced Game Center, which has a social networking component to it, which we talk about in Chapter 21: "Games and Fun."

In this chapter, we will show you how to access several social networking sites from your iPod touch. You will learn how to update your status, "tweet," and keep track of those who are important or simply of interest to you.

Facebook

Facebook was founded in February of 2004. Since then, it's become the premier site for users to connect, re-connect, and share information with friends, family, and co-workers. Today, over 400 million people use Facebook as their primary source of catching up with the people who matter most to them.

> **NOTE: You cannot play Facebook games such as FarmVille and Mafia Wars inside the Facebook app on your iPod touch.** This may disappoint you if you are a big Facebook game player. However, you can often get the same games, including FarmVille, from the App Store and connect them to your Facebook computer version to keep your place.

On your iPod touch, you have three primary ways of accessing your Facebook page as of publishing time:

1. Use **Safari** to go to the standard (full) web site: www.facebook.com

2. Use **Safari** to go to the mobile site: touch.facebook.com

3. Use the iPod touch **Facebook** app.

NOTE: The iPod touch app is a bit more limited than the full web site, but it's much easier to navigate and you can upload pictures right from the device.

Different Ways to Connect to Facebook

You can access Facebook by using the iPod touch app or by using one of two Facebook web sites in your Safari browser. For our purposes, we will focus on the **Facebook** app for the duration of this chapter.

Downloading and Installing the Facebook App

In order to find the app, use the **Search** feature in the App Store and type in **Facebook**.

You can also go to the Social Networking category in the App Store and find the official **Facebook** app as well as many other Facebook-related apps.

NOTE: Some of the apps may look like official Facebook apps and they do cost money. The only official app is the iPhone/iPod app mentioned.

In order to connect to your account on Facebook, you will need to locate the icon you just installed and click on it. We use the example of Facebook here, but the process is very similar for the rest of the apps.

Once Facebook is successfully downloaded, you should see the icon shown here:

The Facebook App

To get the **Facebook** app installed on your iPod touch, start up the **App Store** and search for Facebook. Tap the **Install** button from the **Facebook** app listing.

Facebook App Basics

Once Facebook is downloaded and installed, the first thing you will see is the login screen. Input your account information—your email address and password.

After you log in the first time, you will see a **Push Notifications** warning message.

Click **OK** if you want to allow these messages, which can be pokes from other Facebook friends, notes, status update notifications, and more.

Once you log in, you will see the Facebook screen shown in Figure 22–1. Tap the **Facebook** logo to navigate around the app.

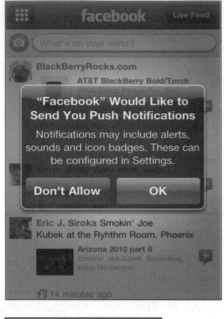

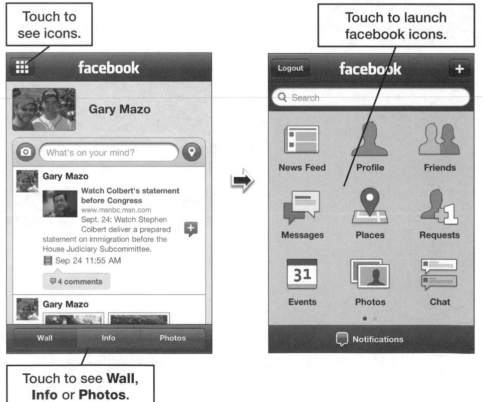

Figure 22–1. *Using the Facebook app.*

Navigating Around Facebook

Toggle between the **Navigation** icons and your current location by tapping the word **Facebook** at the top of the page.

For example, if you are in the **News Feed** and tap **Facebook**, you will see all the icons. Tap **Facebook** again and you will return to the **News Feed**.

From the icons page, you can access your **News Feed**, **Profile**, **Notifications**, **Upload a Photo**, **Friends**, **Requests**, **Events**, **Chat**, or **Inbox**.

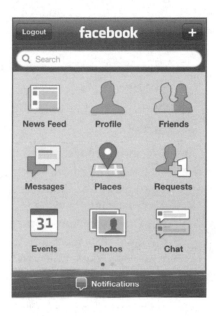

Communicating with Your Friends

1. Tap **Facebook** at the top to see all the icons.

2. Tap the **Friends** icon and your list of friends is displayed.

3. Touch the friend and you will go to his or her Facebook page, where you can then write on the **Wall** and see your friend's **Info** and **Photos**.

Uploading Pictures with the Facebook App

An easy and fun thing to do with Facebook is to upload pictures. Here's how to upload pictures in the **Facebook** app:

1. From the Facebook main icons, tap **Photos**.

2. Choose an album, such as Mobile Uploads.

3. Tap the **Camera** next to the *What's on your mind?* box. Then tap the **Take Photo or Video** to snap a picture or take a video to upload. Or, tap **Choose From Library** to navigate through the pictures on your iPod touch until you find the picture you wish to upload.

4. Next, tap **Write a caption...** to write a caption, if so desired.

5. To finish the upload, tap the blue **Upload** button and the photo will go into your Mobile Uploads folder.

> **NOTE**: When you upload a photo, the image quality won't be the same as it was originally on your iPhone.

 Gary Mazo Went to get the mail and a huge hawk was having lunch.

🗓 9 minutes ago

Facebook Notifications

Depending on your settings for Facebook push notifications, you can be inundated by updates, wall posts, and invitations. If you don't have too many Facebook friends and you want to know when someone is writing something on your wall or commenting on a post or picture, just set your push notification to **On**.

When a notification comes in, it will appear on your screen—even if your phone is locked.

In this example, Gary's daughter posted on his wall while his phone was locked. The message appeared on his screen and the **slide to unlock** button was replaced by a **slide to view** button.

Sliding the button to the right launched the **Facebook** app, and Gary could respond to the message.

Sara's message is now at the top of Gary's wall. The notification of her post is also highlighted at the bottom of the screen.

Settings to Customize Your Facebook App

Here's how to adjust settings for the **Facebook** app:

1. Tap the **Settings** icon.

2. Tap **Facebook** in the left column.

3. You can now adjust various options:

    Shake to Reload feature, which reloads or updates the page when you shake your iPod touch.

    Vibrate feature, which alerts you when notifications are sent.

    Push Notifications, which have simple **On/Off** toggle switches. Touch **Push Notifications** to see the detailed switches on the next screen.

Push Notifications settings screen for the **Facebook** app:

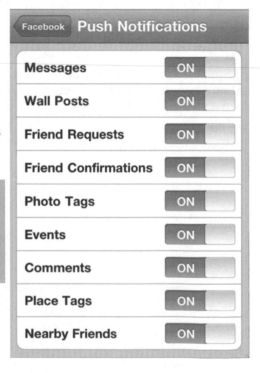

Touch each switch to set it **ON** or **OFF**.

For each switch that is in the **ON** position, you will receive Push Notifications when something changes—for example, when you receive a message that somebody has confirmed you as a friend, tagged you in a photo, or commented on your Wall.

> **TIP:** The **Facebook** app has a new **Places** feature, which allows you to "check in" and then see **Nearby Friends** as shown in the settings screen to the right.

LinkedIn

LinkedIn has core functionality very similar to Facebook, but it tends to be more business and career focused. With LinkedIn, you can connect and re-connect with current and past business associates, send messages, see what people are up to, have discussions, and more.

As of publishing time, the status of LinkedIn was very similar to Facebook. You can go to the regular LinkedIn site on the Safari browser or download the **LinkedIn** app for the iPhone.

Which is better? We like the **LinkedIn** app for the iPod touch slightly better than the mobile LinkedIn.com site in Safari. It's easier to navigate using the **LinkedIn** app with the large buttons, but you can see more on the screen in the Safari version. We recommend giving both options a try to see which you like better—it is really a personal preference.

Downloading the LinkedIn App

Start up the App Store on your iPod touch. Type **LinkedIn** in the search window and locate the app. It's free, so tap the **FREE** button to install it.

Logging In to LinkedIn App

Once the app is installed, click on the **LinkedIn** icon and enter your login information.

Navigating Around the LinkedIn App

LinkedIn has an icon-based navigation similar to Facebook. Tap any icon to move to that function, and then tap the **Home** icon in the upper left corner to return to the Home screen. See Figure 22–2.

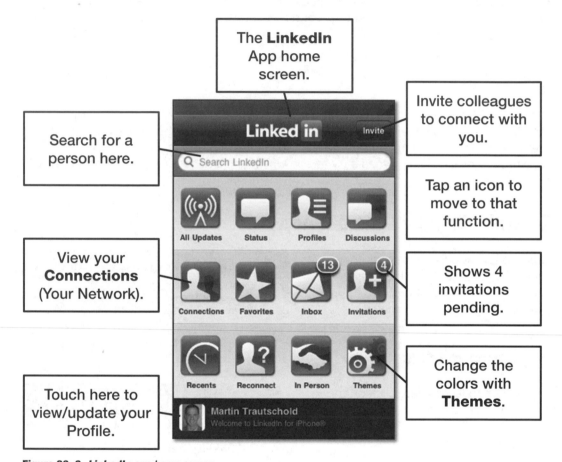

The **LinkedIn** App home screen.

Invite colleagues to connect with you.

Search for a person here.

Tap an icon to move to that function.

View your **Connections** (Your Network).

Shows 4 invitations pending.

Change the colors with **Themes**.

Touch here to view/update your Profile.

Figure 22–2. *LinkedIn* app home screen

Communicating with LinkedIn Connections

One of the things you will most likely do the most with the **LinkedIn** app is communicate with your connections. Here's the easy way to do so:

1. Touch the **Connections** icon.

2. Scroll through your connections or type in a connection name in the search box.

3. Touch the contact you are looking for.

4. Touch the **Send** icon ![send icon] in the upper right-hand corner and then choose **Send Message**.

Twitter

Twitter was started in 2006. Twitter is essentially an SMS (text message)–based social networking site. It is often referred to as a "micro-blogging" site where the famous and not-so-famous share what's on their mind. The catch is that you have only 140 characters to get your point across.

With Twitter, you subscribe to "follow" someone who "tweets" messages. You might also find that people will start to "follow" you. If you want to follow us, we are @garymadesimple on Twitter.

Making a Twitter Account

Making a Twitter account is very easy. We do recommend that you first establish your Twitter account on the Twitter web site, www.twitter.com. When you establish your account, you will be asked to choose a unique user name—we use @garymadesimple— and a password.

You will receive an email confirmation. Click on the link in your email message and you will be taken back to the Twitter web site. You can choose people to follow, make tweets on the web site, and also read tweets from your friends.

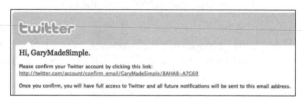

Twitter Options for the iPod touch

There are many options for using Twitter on the iPod touch. The easiest way to follow others and to tweet is to use one of the Twitter apps from the App Store.

There are many Twitter apps from which to choose. For purposes of this book, we are highlighting two specific Twitter apps, **TweetDeck** and **Twitter**. Both are very well designed and easy to use.

NOTE: Twitter has recently purchased the makers of **Tweetie** and **Tweetie 2**. The official **Twitter** app for iPod touch has a strong resemblance to these apps.

Downloading a Twitter App

Go to the App Store, touch **Categories**, and choose **Social Networking**. You should see both **TweetDeck** and **Twitter** in the **Featured** section. If not, simply touch the **Search** window and type in either app name.

Download the app as you would any other app to the iPod touch.

Starting Any Twitter App for the First Time

Touch the appropriate app icon and the program will start. The first time you use a Twitter app, you will be required to sign in to Twitter. Your user name is the one you picked when you first signed up for Twitter.

Using TweetDeck

TweetDeck gives you a very clean Home screen. It uses a **Column** view so you can easily scroll through the **Friends**, **Mentions**, and **Direct Message** screens. To make one screen the **Active** screen, just touch it.

Usually the second screen contains the **Mentions**, which are responses to your tweets—almost like a text message conversation.

> **NOTE**: You can have more than three columns. Just touch the **Add Column** button at the bottom and scroll the available columns to add to your Twitter home page.

The controls for TweetDeck are along the bottom. There are five icons available to you, as shown in Figure 22–3.

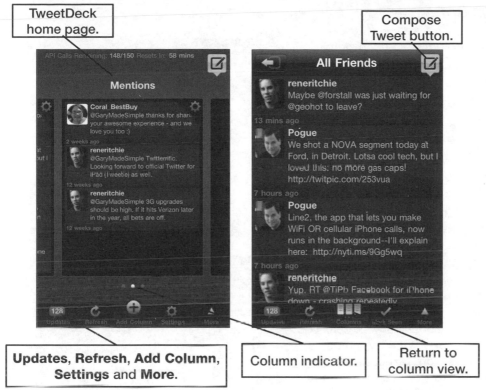

Figure 22-3. *Layout of TweetDeck home page.*

Accounts and Settings

There are several adjustable fields in the **Accounts and Settings** section of the app. Touch the **Manage Accounts** tab to add or edit your Twitter account.

Touch the **Sign into an Account** to sign in to another Twitter account. Just touch the tab and input your username and password.

Touch the **Settings** tab to adjust auto correction, auto capitalization, and sound options. You can also choose your picture service if you have a specific service for uploading pictures to Twitter.

Refresh Button

Touching the **Refresh** button simply
refreshes your tweets.

> **NOTE**: If you select the **Shake Refresh**
> option in the settings, you can just shake
> your iPod touch to refresh tweets.

Add Column Button

The **Add Column** button adds another
column onto your Twitter Home screen.
Just slide from right to left to advance from
one column to the next. The dots at the
bottom indicate how many screens you
have to move through. You can add a
column for **Search**, **Direct Messages**,
Mentions, **Favorites**, **Twitter Trends**,
Twitter Lists, **Twitter Search**, and **All
Friends**.

Composing a Tweet

Touch the **Compose Tweet** icon
and the tweet composition screen is
displayed. Your Twitter ID is in the "From"
line and you have 140 characters to
express what's on your mind.

When you are done, just touch the **Send**
button in the upper right-hand corner.

Reading and Replying

Touch a tweet to bring it to the main
screen. In addition to the tweet being nice
and large, you can touch on a link within
the tweet to launch the web view. If you
want to view the link in Safari, just touch

the **Safari** button.

> **NOTE:** When you view the link in Safari, you can quickly jump back to **TweetDeck** by double-clicking your **Home** button and using the App Switcher bar.

Along the top and the bottom of the tweet window, you will see six icons: **@Reply/all**, **send DM**, **retweet**, **email tweet**, **send RE:** and **+favorite**.

Each will bring up an additional window and the onscreen keyboard for you to type your reply, send a direct message to the author, retweet, email the tweet, forward the tweet, or set it as a favorite.

Using Twitter

The official **Twitter** app takes a streamlined approach to using Twitter. The Home screen shows you the tweets from those you are following. The full message is nice and large.

Along the bottom are five icons, the first being the main **Twitter** feed. The other icons are **Mentions**, **Direct Messages**, **Search**, and the **More** button, which takes you to your **Profile**, **Favorites**, **Drafts**, **Lists**, and **Accounts and Settings**.

The **Compose Tweet** icon is in the top left-hand corner. See Figure 22–4.

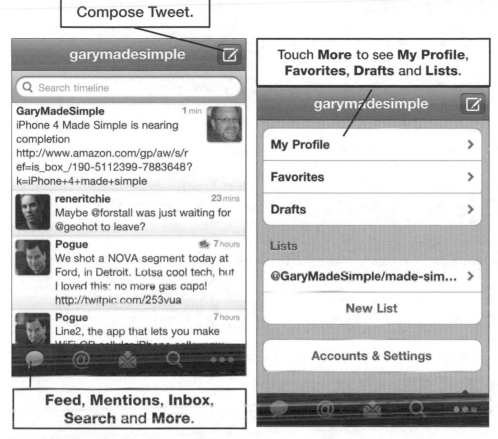

Compose Tweet.

Touch **More** to see **My Profile**, **Favorites**, **Drafts** and **Lists**.

Feed, Mentions, Inbox, Search and More.

Figure 22–4. *Layout of Twitter home page.*

Refreshing Your List of Tweets

To refresh your list of tweets, pull down the main page and you will see the **Pull down to refresh** notification at the top. Once the page is pulled down, you will see a **Release to refresh** note. Release the page and it will refresh the tweets.

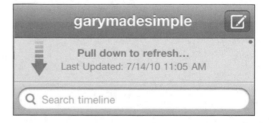

Your Twitter Profile

Touch the **More** button and then touch **My Profile** to display your Twitter profile.

To see your tweets, just touch **Tweets**.

To see those tweets you have labeled as favorites, touch the **Favorites** button.

To see those individuals whom you are following, touch the **Following** button.

> **NOTE**: The numbers corresponding to your followers, those you are following, your favorites, and your tweets are displayed above the title of the button.

Scroll down the page to see your **Retweets**, **Lists**, and the **Services** to which you can subscribe.

Compose Button

Touch the **Compose** button  and the **New Tweet** screen pops up. The character counter will count down from 140 as you type your message.

Options within Tweet

From your Twitter Home screen, just touch one of your tweets for options. You can **Reply**, **Retweet**, **Set as Favorite**, **Send Link**, or **Email the Tweet**. Just touch the corresponding button to the action.

Details for the **Link** and **Mail** options shown in Figure 22–5.

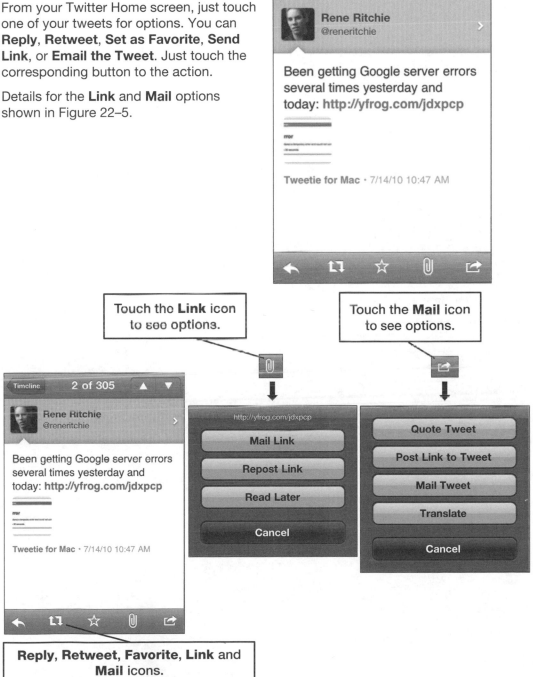

Figure 22–5. *Options within a tweet in the launch **Twitter** app.*

Chapter 23

Eliminate Your Paper Notes

This chapter provides an overview of the **Notes** app, which you can use to write notes, make grocery lists, and make lists of movies you'd like to watch or books you'd like to read. We will show you how to organize and even email notes to yourself or others. Ideally, we hope that Notes will become so easy on the iPod touch that you can eventually get rid of most, if not all, of your paper sticky notes!

There are various free or low-cost notes apps in the App Store. Later in this chapter we will also give you a view of an excellent—and free—alternative to the **Notes** app called **Evernote**. With Evernote, you can tag and organize your notes, add pictures to notes, add voice notes, and show the location where you originally wrote your note. Another nice thing about Evernote is that it will auto-synchronize your notes with the Evernote web site (so you can manage notes from your computer) and many other mobile devices.

TIP: The **Notes** app that comes with the iPod touch is pretty basic and utilitarian. If you need a more robust notes application that can sort, categorize, import items (PDF, Word, and so on), use folders, search, and more, you should check out the App Store on your iPod touch. Do a search for "notes," and you will find at least a dozen notes-related apps ranging from free to $0.99 and up.

The Notes App

Like many people, your desk or wall is probably filled with little yellow sticky notes—reminders concerning everything imaginable. Even with our computers, we still tend to write ourselves little notes. One of the great things about the iPod touch is that you can write your notes on familiar yellow notepaper, and then keep them neatly organized and sorted. In the upcoming iOS version 4.2, you will even be able to change the font of your notes. You can even email them to yourself or someone else to make sure that the information is not forgotten. You can also backup your notes using iTunes and, if you choose, sync notes to your computer or web sites such as Google.

The **Notes** app on the iPod touch gives you a convenient place to keep your notes and to-do lists. You can also keep shopping lists, such as grocery lists or items you need from the hardware or pet store. If you have your iPod touch with you, you can add items to these lists as soon as they occur to you, and they can be accessed and edited at any time.

Sync Notes

You can sync notes with your computer or other web site using the methods shown in Chapter 3: "Sync Your iPod touch with iTunes" and Chapter 4: "Other Sync Methods." Figure 23–1 shows how to sync using iTunes from the notes stored in Microsoft Outlook to the **Notes** app on your iPod touch. The nice thing about syncing notes is that you can add a note on your computer and have it just appear on your iPod touch. Then when you are out and about, you can edit that note and have it synced back to your computer. No more re-typing or remembering things! You always have your iPod touch with you, so taking notes anywhere and anytime can be a great way never to forget anything important.

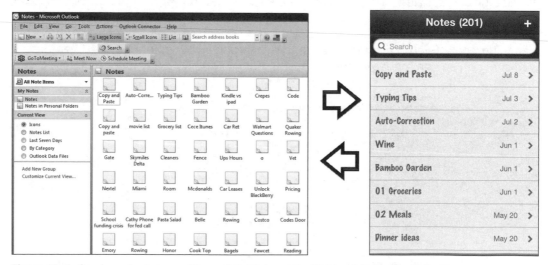

Figure 23–1. *Syncing notes between Microsoft Outlook and the iPod touch **Notes** app using iTunes.*

Getting Started with Notes

Like all other apps, simply tap the **Notes** icon to start it (see Figure 23–2).

After starting the **Notes** app, you see what looks like a typical yellow note pad.

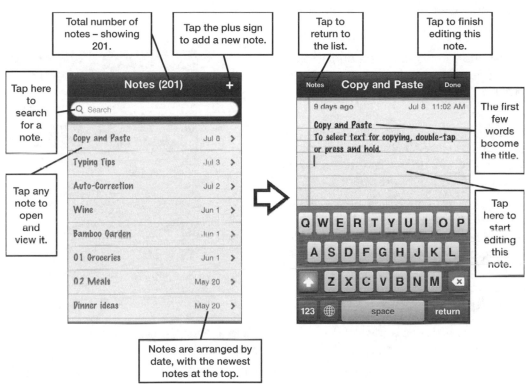

Figure 23–2. *Notes app basic navigation.*

Multiple Notes Accounts

If you happen to be syncing at least one IMAP email account and your computer using iTunes, then you will see that your notes from each of these accounts are kept separate. This is very much like how your contacts are kept in separate groups by email account and how your calendars are kept separate by email account.

In order to see multiple notes accounts, you have to set a switch in the account setup screen.

When you setup your IMAP email account, in **Settings** > **Mail,Contacts,Calendars**, you will see options to turn Notes syncing on or off. In order to see these Notes accounts, you have to set the **Notes** switch to **On**, as shown for this Gmail account.

To view the various notes accounts, tap the **Accounts** button in the upper left corner of the **Notes** app.

Then, on the next screen, you can tap selections to view **All Notes** or your notes for each account. In this image, the **Gmail** or **MobileMe** account are options.

Notes you add to an individual account will be kept with that account. For example, if you add notes to Gmail, then those would show up only on your **Gmail** account.

How Are My Notes Sorted?

You see that all notes are listed in reverse chronological order, with the most recently edited notes at the top and the oldest at the bottom.

The date that is shown is the last time and date that the particular note was edited, not when it was first created. So you will notice the order of your notes moving around on the screen.

This sorting can be a good thing because your most recent (or frequently edited) notes will be right at the top.

> **TIP:** If you want a nice app to keep track of your to-do lists, **Things for iPod touch** (US $9.99 in the App Store) is a good choice.

Adding a New Note

To start a new note, tap the plus sign 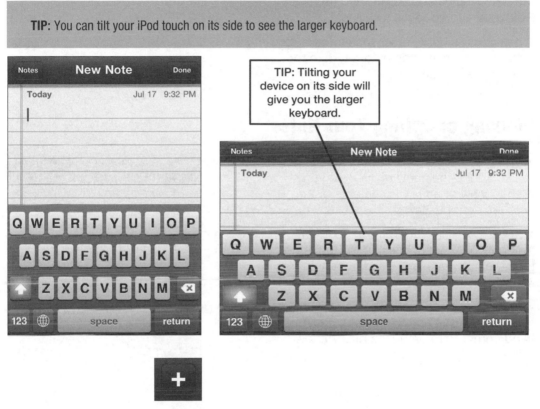 in the upper right-hand corner (see Figure 23–3).

The notepad is blank, and the keyboard pops up for you to begin typing.

TIP: You can tilt your iPod touch on its side to see the larger keyboard.

Figure 23–3. *Adding a new note and using the larger keyboard.*

Adding a Title to the Note

The first few words you type before you hit the **Return** key will become the title of the note. So think about what you want as the title, and type that first. In the image shown, **Grocery list** becomes the title of the note.

Put a new item on each line, and tap the **Return** key to go to the next line.

When you are done, touch the **Notes** button in the top left-hand corner to return to the main Notes screen.

Viewing or Editing Your Notes

Your notes appear in the list as tabs to touch. Touch the name of the note you wish to view or edit. The contents of the note are then displayed.

You can scroll in Notes as you do in any program. You will notice that the date and time the note was last edited appear in the upper right-hand corner.

When you are done reading the note, just touch the **Notes** button in the top left-hand corner to return to the main Notes screen.

To advance through multiple notes, just touch the arrows at the bottom of the screen. Touch the **Forward** arrow. The page turns, and you can see the next note. To go back, just hit the **Back** arrow.

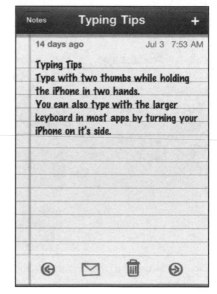

Editing Your Notes

You can easily edit or change the contents of a note. For example, you might keep a "Things to Do" note and quickly edit it when you think of something else to add to the list (or when your family reminds you to get something from the store).

Touch any note in the list to open it.

Then tap the screen anywhere; the cursor moves to that spot for editing.

If you double-tap a word, the blue handles used to copy and paste appear. Just drag the handles to select text.

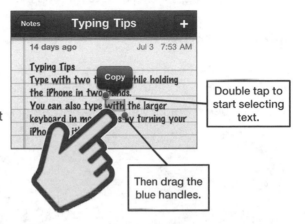

If you touch and hold your finger on a word, a magnifying glass appears so you can find the exact spot you are looking for (see Figure 23–4). Release your finger, and the **Select** menu appears. Choose **Select** or **Select All**.

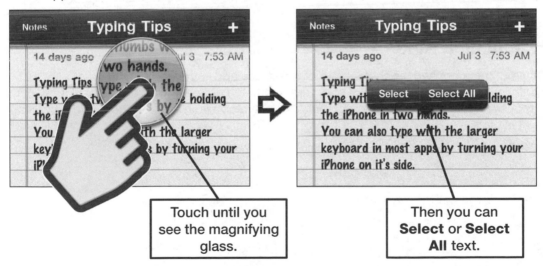

Figure 23–4. *Selecting text in a note.*

You can also use the **Delete** key to delete a word or a line after selecting it—this is the fastest way to delete a number of words or lines of text.

TIP: Using the copy handles is the best way to select a large amount of text; it is faster and more precise.

When done editing, touch the **Notes** button to return to the list.

Deleting Notes

To delete a note, tap it to open it from the main Notes screen and then touch the **Trash Can** icon at the bottom (see Figure 23–5).

The iPod touch prompts you to **Delete Note** or **Cancel**.

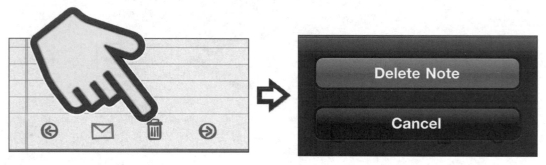

Figure 23–5. *Deleting a note.*

Emailing a Note

One of the most convenient features of the **Notes** app is the ability to email a note, as shown in Figure 23–6. Let's say you wrote a grocery note and wanted to email it to your spouse. From the text of the note, touch the **Envelope** icon at the bottom of the screen.

Figure 23–6. *Emailing a note.*

Now you see the Compose New Mail screen, with the subject as the title of the note and the body of the message as the contents of the note. Address and send the note as you

would any other email message. Touch the **To** line of the email, touch the ⊕ sign, and find the contact you wish to use. You can also start typing someone's name or email address and then choose from the pop-up list of names.

Once you're done typing, tap **Send** to send the note on its way.

> **TIP**: Hitting space twice automatically inserts a period. Holding down a character gives you accent/variant options. Tapping the numbers toggle puts you in numbers entry mode and leaves you there. Sliding from the number toggle to the character you want and then letting go inserts the character. It also automatically switches you back to alphabet mode.

Creating a New Calendar Event from an Underlined Day and Time

If you type in the words "tomorrow morning" in a note and save it, the next time you open that note, you will see that the words have been underlined. If you touch and hold the underlined words, you will see a button asking if you want to **Create Event**. Tap the button to create a new calendar event for tomorrow morning.

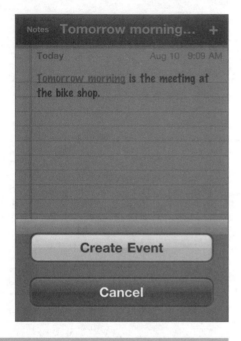

TIP: Whenever date and time words are underlined, the iPod touch recognizes them as potential calendar events. This works in notes, email messages, and other places on your iPod touch.

An Alternative Note App: Evernote

A visit to the App Store will show you several note-taking and organizing apps designed for the iPod touch. Prices range from free to about US $20.00.

A good free notes app is called **Evernote**. Evernote is great because you can track just about anything with it: text notes, pictures you snap, voice notes, copies of Safari web pages, documents—almost anything you can imagine. Also, when you enter a note in Evernote on your iPod touch, you can automatically synchronize it with your Mac, PC, iPad, BlackBerry, or other mobile device. The same goes for notes you enter on your Mac, PC, or other devices—they all sync to your iPod touch. All text is searchable, and you can even "geo-locate" (have your iPod touch tie your GPS location to where you originally created each note) using Evernote.

Getting Started with Evernote

Start by going to the App Store and downloading Evernote. See Chapter 20: "The Amazing App Store" for help getting apps.

Once Evernote is downloaded and installed, touch the **Evernote** icon to start the application.

The first time you use Evernote, you will be prompted to sign up for a free account. Type in your email address and set a password, and you are ready to start.

Adding and Tagging Notes

After logging in, you see the **New Note** screen (you know you are on this screen because the New Note soft key is highlighted in the lower left corner).

The **New Note** screen of Evernote gives you various options for adding a new note.

- **Text** (type a text note)
- **Snapshot** (take a picture with your iPod touch camera)
- **Camera roll** (select a picture from your saved pictures to add as a note)
- **Voice** (record a voice note)

Just tap the type of note you want to add.

Text Notes

Tap the **Text** icon to start typing a text note.

Give your note a unique title and then add some tags to the note. These tags are used to help organize your notes, and they can be useful when searching through your notes.

You can add tags by typing them, separated by commas.

> **TIP:** If you are consistent about your tags, you can easily sort and find notes by these tags.

Or, if you already have typed a few tags on other notes, you can tap the  next to the tags and select from existing ones.

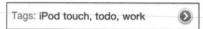

Selecting tags from the list is easier, and it helps you avoid making new typing mistakes.

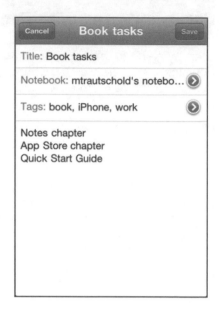

Snapshot

Tap **Snapshot** to bring up your camera so you can grab a picture and save it as a note. The picture is also geo-tagged with your current GPS location to track where you took it. You can even take a picture of a document and have Evernote find words in the image of the document (see the "Searching for Notes" section in this chapter).

TIP: Remember that you can flip your camera around to the front-facing camera on your iPod touch so you can snap a picture of yourself—or a picture of you and a friend!

Camera Roll

Tap **Camera roll** from the New Note screen to select an image from your camera roll to add as a new note.

Voice Notes

Tap **Voice** to record a voice note and add it to your list of notes. Remember, you can record your voice or any sounds around you, such as the sounds of the ocean, a running river, the wind, or even your niece's piano recital.

When you tap the **Voice** icon, you are given a 3-second countdown before the voice recorder starts recording. When you are done recording, you press the green triangle button to save It as a new note.

To erase the note and start over, press the red X button (**Discard**).

To stop recording, press the square **Stop** button.

You don't name the note when you record it—this is so you can do it completely hands-free.

As you can see, each voice note is titled as an **Untitled audio note.** To name the voice note and give it tags, go into your Notes list view in Evernote and edit the voice notes. See the "Editing Rich Text" section for more on editing an audio or voice note.

Refresh, Email, Delete, or Edit a Note

When you are viewing a note, you have four options, shown as soft keys along the bottom of each note.

Tap the **Refresh** icon at the left end of the soft keys to make sure you have the most up-to-date version of this note from the server.

To delete the note, tap the **Trash Can** icon.

You can also email your notes by touching the **Envelope** icon at the bottom of the screen, just as you can in the **Notes** app.

To edit a note, just touch the **Pencil** icon at the bottom of the screen. This brings up the editing screen.

When you are done editing, tap the **Save** button in the upper right corner.

Editing Rich Text Notes (Voice and Picture)

When you edit a rich text note, such as a picture or voice note, you will receive a warning message about rich text notes, which is shown here.

This warning applies only if you want to type text in the body of the note.

If you are only adding a title and assigning tags, you don't need to worry about it.

However, if you are typing text, we recommend selecting **Append**, which will add your changes to your existing note.

Note Grouping

You have various options for customizing the way you group your notes in Evernote on your iPod touch.

1. To view your notes, tap the **Notes** soft key along the bottom.

2. In order to change the way your notes are grouped, tap the information button ⓘ in the upper right corner (see Figure 23–7).

3. On the **Note Grouping** screen, you can group the notes by date created, updated, title, notebook, city, and country (using their geographic location).

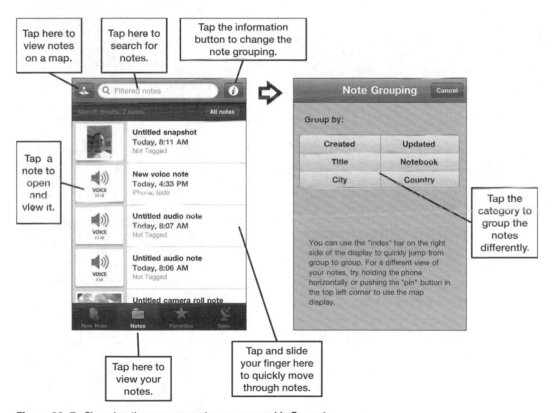

Figure 23–7. *Changing the way your notes are grouped in Evernote.*

Searching for Notes

Evernote offers extensive and flexible searching features. You can even search for text contained in images. To wit, here's how to find the word **Client** in a picture taken with by the iPod touch of a fax cover page:

1. Tap the **New Note** soft key, and then tap **Snapshot** to take a picture of any document with text on it. In this case, we took a picture of a fax cover page.

2. Tap the **Notes** soft key and tap the search notes field at the top of the page.

3. Press the **Search** key at the bottom right.

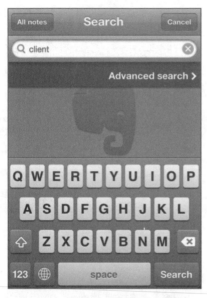

> **TIP:** If you are searching for text in an image, and your basic search did not work the first time, you may need to tap **Advanced search >** under the search window. Then tap **Other** at the very bottom and select **Images** under the **Contains** heading near the bottom of the page.

4. Evernote should then scan all your notes, including text in images, to find your results. In this case, we were presented with a single result—the picture of the fax cover page that contained the word **Client**. Notice that the search word is highlighted in the image.

The Evernote Places View

One cool Evernote view is the **Places View**. If you allow Evernote to use your location, Evernote will tag all your notes by the place where you originally created your note. For example, if you traveled to another state, province, or country, Evernote would track that you took notes in that particular region.

The image here shows one note taken in California and seven notes taken in Florida.

To view these notes, just tap the markers (push pins).

Evernote Synchronization and Settings

Tap the **Sync** soft key to view your synchronization settings.

The free account type limits the amount of information you can store on Evernote servers. If you use the application lightly, or mainly for text notes, the free version should be fine. If you use a lot of images or voice notes, then you will want to check out the premium version.

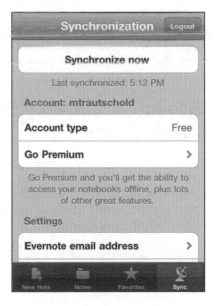

If you scroll down the **Synchronization** screen, you can check out your total usage of your free (or paid) account.

The free account gives you 40MB of data, which is more than 50,000 text notes but many fewer voice and picture notes. Tap the **Approximate notes remaining** option to get a feel for how many picture or voice notes this might include.

If you are running out of space, you can upgrade by touching the **Go Premium** option in the top of the **Synchronization** window.

Viewing or Updating Evernotes on Your Computer or Other Mobile Device

As mentioned, all your notes get synced to the Evernote web site wirelessly and automatically. You can then log in to your account from your PC, Mac, iPod touch, iPhone, or BlackBerry to check out or update your notes (see Figure 23–8). This is a great feature if you have multiple devices and you would like to stay up-to-date or add notes from any of them.

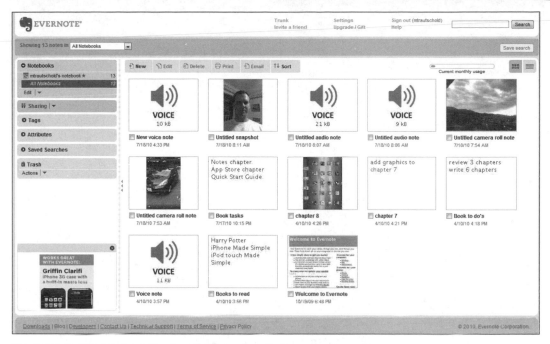

Figure 23–8. *Viewing your notes from the Evernote web site on your computer*

Chapter 24

Bluetooth on the iPod touch

In this chapter, we will show you how to pair your iPod touch with any Bluetooth device, regardless of whether it is another computer, stereo speakers, or a wireless headset.

Thanks to the technology known as A2DP, you can also stream your music to a capable Bluetooth stereo.

> **NOTE:** You must have a capable third-party Bluetooth adapter or Bluetooth stereo to stream your music via Bluetooth technology. Also, there is soon to be AVRCP profile support, so many music controls on a Bluetooth device (like Play, Pause, or Skip) will work quite well.

Think of Bluetooth as a short-range, wireless technology that allows your iPod touch to connect to various peripheral devices without wires. Popular devices are headsets, computers, and vehicle sound systems.

Bluetooth is believed to be named after a Danish Viking and king, Harald Blåtand, whose name has been translated as *Bluetooth*. King Blåtand lived in the tenth century and is famous for uniting Denmark and Norway. Similarly, Bluetooth technology unites computers and telecom. His name, according to legend, is from his very dark hair, which was unusual for Vikings. Blåtand means dark complexion. There does exist a more popular story that the king loved to eat blueberries, so much so that his teeth became stained with the color blue.

Sources:

- http://cp.literature.agilent.com/litweb/pdf/5980-3032EN.pdf
- www.cs.utk.edu/~dasgupta/bluetooth/history.htm
- www.britannica.com/eb/topic-254809/Harald-I

Understanding Bluetooth

Bluetooth allows your iPod touch to communicate with things wirelessly. Bluetooth is a small radio that transmits from each device. Before you can use a peripheral with the iPod touch, you have to "pair" it with that device to connect it to the peripheral. Many Bluetooth devices can be used up to 30 feet away from the iPod touch.

Bluetooth Devices That Work with the iPod touch

Among other things, the iPod touch works with Bluetooth headphones, Bluetooth stereo systems and adapters, Bluetooth keyboards, Bluetooth car stereo systems, Bluetooth headsets, and hands-free devices. The iPod touch supports A2DP, which is known as Stereo Bluetooth.

Pairing with a Bluetooth Device

Your primary uses for Bluetooth might be with Bluetooth headphones, Bluetooth stereo adapters, or a Bluetooth headset. Any Bluetooth headphones should work well with your iPod touch. To start using any Bluetooth device, you need to first pair (connect) it with your iPod touch.

Turning On Bluetooth

The first step to using Bluetooth is to turn the Bluetooth radio **On**.

1. Tap your **Settings** icon.

2. Then touch **General**.

3. You will see the **Bluetooth** tab in the right-hand column.

4. By default, Bluetooth is initially **Off** on the iPod touch. Tap the switch to move it to the **On** position.

TIP: Bluetooth is an added drain on your battery. If you don't plan on using Bluetooth for a period of time, think about turning the switch back to **OFF**.

General	**Bluetooth**
Bluetooth	OFF

Pairing with a Headset or Any Bluetooth Device

As soon as you turn Bluetooth **ON**, the iPod touch will begin to search for any nearby Bluetooth device—like a Bluetooth headset or stereo adapter (see Figure 24–1). For the iPod touch to find your Bluetooth device, you need to put that device into "pairing mode." Read the instructions that came with your headset carefully—usually there is a combination of buttons to push to achieve this.

TIP: Some headsets require you to press and hold a button for five seconds until you see a series of flashing blue or red/blue lights. Some accessories, such as the Apple wireless Bluetooth keyboard, automatically start up in pairing mode.

Once the iPod touch detects the Bluetooth device, it will attempt to automatically pair with it. If pairing takes place automatically, there is nothing more for you to do.

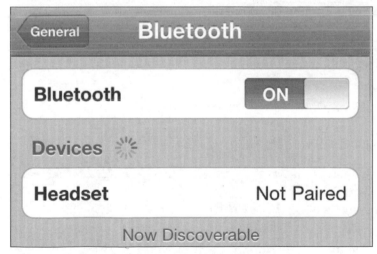

Figure 24–1. *Bluetooth device discovered but not yet paired.*

NOTE: In the case of a Bluetooth device, such as a headset, you may be asked to enter a series of numbers (passkey) on the keyboard itself. See Figure 24–2.

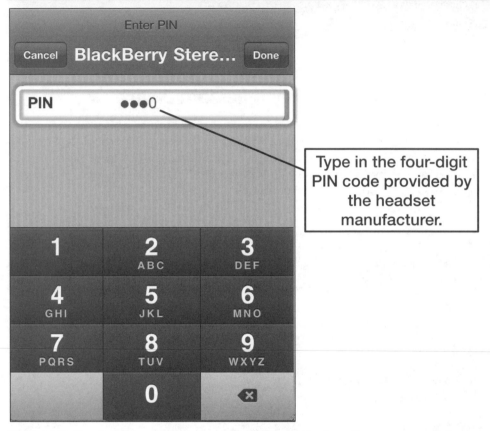

Type in the four-digit PIN code provided by the headset manufacturer.

Figure 24–2. *Type in the four-digit passkey when prompted during the pairing process.*

Newer headsets like the Aliph Jawbone ICON, used here, will automatically pair with your iPod touch. Simply put the headset into pairing mode and turn on Bluetooth on the iPod touch—that's all you have to do!

Pairing will be automatic, and you should never have to re-pair the headset again.

Bluetooth Stereo (A2DP)

One of the great features of today's advanced Bluetooth technology is the ability to stream your music without wires via Bluetooth. The fancy name for this technology is A2DP, but it is simply known as Stereo Bluetooth.

Connecting to a Stereo Bluetooth Device

The first step to using Stereo Bluetooth is to connect to a capable Stereo Bluetooth device. This can be a car stereo with this technology built in, a pair of Bluetooth headphones or speakers, or even newer headsets like the Jawbone ICON.

Put the Bluetooth device into pairing mode as per the manufacturer's instructions, and then go to the Bluetooth setting page from the **Settings** icon, as we showed you earlier in the chapter.

Once connected, you will see the new Stereo Bluetooth device listed under your Bluetooth devices. Sometimes it will simply be listed as "Headset." Just touch the device and you will see the name of the actual device next to the **Bluetooth** tab in the next screen, as shown here.

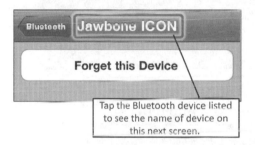

Tap the Bluetooth device listed to see the name of device on this next screen.

Next, tap your **Music** icon and start up any song, playlist, podcast, or video music library. You will now notice a small **Bluetooth** icon in the lower right-hand corner of the screen. Tap the **Bluetooth** icon to see the available Bluetooth devices for streaming your music (see Figure 24–3).

Figure 24–3. *Selecting a Bluetooth device.*

In the previous screens, we selected the **BlackBerry Stereo Gateway** by tapping it. Now, your music will start to play from the selected Bluetooth device. You can verify this again by touching the **Bluetooth** icon on the screen once more. You should see the **Speaker** icon next to the new Stereo Bluetooth device, and you should hear your music coming from that sound source as well.

Disconnecting or Forgetting a Bluetooth Device

Sometimes, you might want to disconnect a Bluetooth device from your iPod touch.

It is easy to get this done. Get into the Bluetooth settings as you did earlier in this chapter. Touch the device you want to disconnect in order to bring up the next screen, then tap the **Forget this Device** button, and confirm your choice.

> **NOTE:** Bluetooth has a range of only about 30 feet, so if you are not nearby or not using a Bluetooth device, turn off **Bluetooth**. You can always turn it back on when you are actually going to be using it.

This will delete the Bluetooth profile from the iPod touch. (See Figure 24–4.)

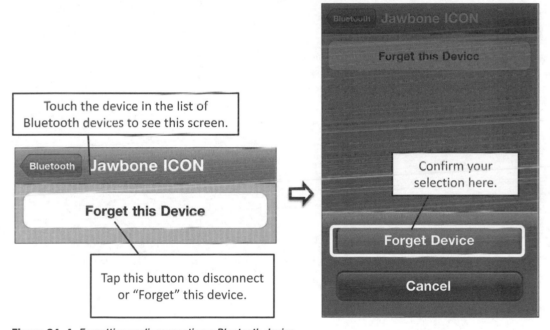

Figure 24–4. *Forgetting or disconnecting a Bluetooth device.*

Chapter 25

Utilities: Clock, Calculator, and Weather

The iPod touch is very useful for a great number of things. Some of the most simple things and apps are those you might find yourself using quite frequently. Your iPod touch comes pre-loaded with a few utilities that should prove quite useful.

In this chapter, we will show you how to use your clock, set alarms, and use the timer. We will also show you the features of the built-in calculator and compass.

Lastly, we will show you not only how to configure the built-in **Weather** app, but also a couple of other free weather apps you might want to add to your iPod touch.

You might want to see what time it is in London, Tokyo, or any other city around the world. You might want a wake-up alarm clock. How about a count-down timer to tell you when the pasta is finished boiling or a stopwatch to time how long it takes to get something done? All these can be done in the **Clock** app.

How about calculating the tip on your meal, or other simple, everyday calculations—what would 120 licenses of our Made Simple videos cost a company at $15.95 each? Use the calculator.

How about the weather for the next few days in your city, or any city in the world? Use the **Weather** app.

The World Clock App

Touch the **Clock** icon to launch the Clock.

Immediately, you see the World Clock feature. Usually, the standard clock is for Cupertino, CA—but you can easily add to that or delete it.

Adding a New World Clock Entry

It is very easy to add new entries to the **Clock** app.

1. Touch the "+" sign 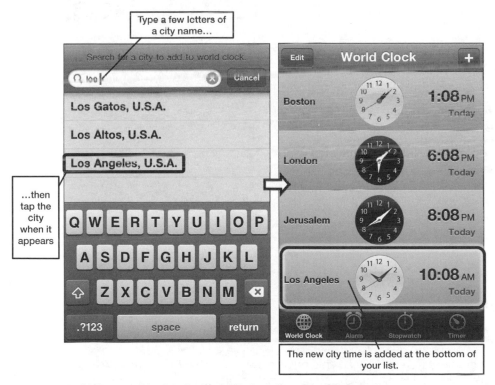 in the upper right-hand corner and the keyboard will pop up.

2. Type in the name of a city.

3. As you type, the iPod touch will show you entries that match your letters.

4. When you see the city you want, tap it to select it.

5. Once you do this, the new city is automatically added to the World Clock list. See Figure 25–1.

Figure 25–1. *Adding new cities into the World Clock section of the **Clock** app.*

Re-sorting or Deleting World Time Entries

1. Just touch the **Edit** button in the top left of the screen.

2. You will notice that each entry now has a red "-" sign.

3. When you touch the minus sign, it will rotate 90 degrees and a red **Delete** button will appear to the right.

4. Touch **Delete** and that particular World Clock entry will no longer be in the list.

To move a World Clock entry, do the following:

1. Touch and drag the three bars you see to the right of each entry.

2. Drop or let go of the entry when you have it in the correct location.

The Alarm Clock

The alarm clock feature is very flexible and powerful on the iPod touch. You can easily set multiple alarms. For example, you might set an alarm to wake you up on weekdays, and a separate one on weekends. You can even set a separate alarm to wake you up from your Tuesday and Sunday afternoon nap at 3:00pm.

To get started, tap the **Alarm** icon in the lower row of soft keys.

If you have alarms set, they will be displayed. If there are no alarms, tap the "+" sign in the upper right-hand corner to add a new one.

Adjust the time of the alarm by rotating the dials at the bottom of the screen.

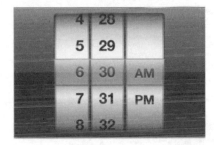

If this is a one-time alarm, then leave the Repeat set at **Never**. This setting will cause the alarm to automatically be set to **Off** after it rings.

Repeat	Never >

If the alarm does repeat, then adjust the repeating function of the Alarm by touching the **Repeat** tab. Touch the days of the week you would like the Alarm to be active.

> **TIP**: You may touch as many or as few days as you want.

Every Monday

Every Tuesday   ✓

Every Wednesday

Every Thursday

Every Friday

Every Saturday

Every Sunday

| Sound | Marimba > |

Adjust the sound the alarm makes by touching the **Sound** tab and then choosing an alarm sound from the list.

For silent alarms, set the sound to **None** at the top of the list to have an onscreen silent alarm—no sound will be made.

Tap **Back** when you are done.

To enable the **Snooze** feature, make sure the **Snooze** switch is in the default **ON** position.

NOTE: The pre-set snooze time is 10 minutes and could not be changed as of the writing of this book.

| Snooze | ON |

Standard

Marimba	
Alarm	
Ascending	
Bark	
Bell Tower	✓
Blues	
Boing	
Crickets	

A ringing alarm will wake up your sleeping iPhone.

1:12
Thursday, July 15

Alarm

Snooze

Snooze for 10 min...

...Or slide to stop.

slide to stop alarm

You can re-name your alarm by touching the **Label** tab. The keyboard will launch and you can type in a new name for that particular alarm.

Give your alarm a name that is easy to recognize.

Give your alarm a name that is easy to recognize.

NOTE: If you want to use this feature to wake up in the morning at different times on different days, you will need to set an alarm for each day of the week following the procedure.

Will an alarm turn on my iPod touch? **No**. If your iPod touch is completely powered off, the alarm will not turn it back on. However, if your iPod touch is just in sleep mode (see Chapter 1: "Getting Started"), then your alarms will ring just fine.

Using the Stopwatch

The iPod touch comes with a built-in stopwatch, which can be a very handy feature. Just touch the **Stopwatch** icon along the bottom row of the **Clock** app.

This is a very simple app. To start the stopwatch, tap the **Start** button and the clock will start to run.

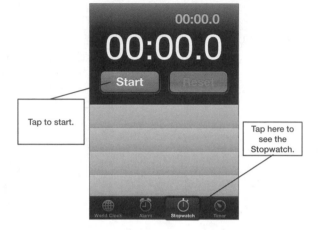

Tap to start.

Tap here to see the Stopwatch.

Showing "Lap" Times

You can either stop or lap the stopwatch after you start it.

Just touch the **Lap** button as if you were timing a sporting event like a track race.

1. Each lap time is shown in the list.

2. Drag them up/down to see all the lap times. When you are done, tap **Stop**.

Stopping and Resetting

Touch the red **Stop** button to stop the clock at any time.

You can then continue the timing by touching **Start** **Start** again.

Or touch **Reset** **Reset** to reset the clock back to zero.

Using the Countdown Timer Feature

Need to take something out of the oven in 30 minutes?

Need to take the pasta out in 8 minutes, but don't have a kitchen timer available?

Need to remember to turn off the sprinkler in 1 hour?

All these are perfect reasons to use the Timer, which gives you a great count-down timer.

Setting the Timer

Tap the **Timer** soft key inside the **Clock** icon to see the timer screen.

1. Slide the dials at the top with your finger, setting the hours and/or minutes.

2. In the screenshot here, we have the timer set for 30 minutes.

To change the sound you hear when the countdown timer reaches 0:00, touch the **When Timer Ends** tab.

Choose any other sound from the list of sounds, and touch the **Set** button when you are done.

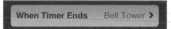

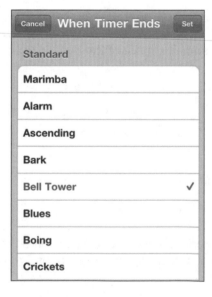

Turning Off (Sleeping) Your iPod After a Set Time

A great thing to be able to do is to set your iPod to turn off (go into sleep mode) at a set time.

Say you want to have your music play for 30 minutes and then turn off automatically. This is a good thing to set when you are going to sleep and want to listen to music but don't want to be bothered turning off your **Music** app.

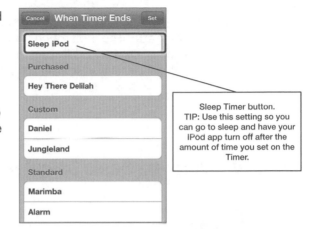

Sleep Timer button.
TIP: Use this setting so you can go to sleep and have your iPod app turn off after the amount of time you set on the Timer.

Starting the Timer

Once you have the time and sound set, just touch the green **Start** button to start the timer.

The screen will display a digital clock counting down to zero. You can cancel the timer at any time by simply touching the red **Cancel** button.

The Calculator App

One more very handy app included on your iPod touch is the **Calculator** app. The iPod touch Calculator can handle almost anything a typical family can throw its way, performing both basic and scientific calculations.

Calculator

Viewing the Basic Calculator (Portrait Mode)

 Click the **Calculator** icon to start the **Calculator** app.

In portrait mode (vertical) view, the **Calculator** application is a "basic" calculator. All functions are activated by simply touching the corresponding key to perform the desired action.

Need to store something in memory? Use the following keys to do so:

- M+ to add it into memory

- M- to subtract the number from memory

- MC to clear memory

- MR to recall the number in memory to the screen

Viewing the Scientific Calculator (Landscape Mode)

Just turn the iPod touch sideways into landscape mode (horizontal) view and the accelerometer in the iPod touch transforms the calculator into a scientific calculator. The keys become smaller, and the new scientific keys are added along the left-hand side of the calculator.

Turn the calculator back to its vertical position, and it will return to its basic functions.

The Weather App

The iPod touch comes with a very useful and easy-to-use **Weather** app built in.

After you set it up, a quick touch of the **Weather** icon  will show you the next six days of weather forecasts for your area.

It is easy to set up your location and other locations to check their weather on the **Weather** icon.

Getting Started with "Weather"

Tap the **Weather** icon. Unless you live in Cupertino, California, the default weather settings are not for your area. You will need to add your location.

1. Touch the small "*i*" in the lower right-hand corner to go to the Weather settings screen.

2. If the town selected is not one you wish to keep track of, just touch the red "minus" sign and you will be prompted to delete the location. See Figure 25–2.

Touch here to add a new location.

Touch here to add or edit your weather locations.

Switch between Fahrenheit and Celsius here.

Figure 25–2. *Adding or editing your weather location.*

Adding a New Location

1. Just touch the "plus" sign in the upper left corner to add a new location.

2. Type in the name of the city or town or the zip code (the iPod touch will start to display towns it thinks you are trying to type).

3. If it does not display suggestions as you type, touch **Search** after you type in your town.

4. When you see the town you want, just touch it.

You will be taken back to the Weather settings screen.

If it looks OK to you, just touch **Done** in the upper right-hand corner.

Deleting a Weather Location

To delete a weather location, do the following:

1. First get into the Weather settings screen by tapping the "i" in the lower right corner of the weekly weather screen.

2. Then tap the red minus sign to the left of the location name so you see the **Delete** button appear.

3. Finally, tap **Delete** and confirm to remove the location.

4. Tap **Done** in the upper right corner to complete your changes.

To delete a location, first tap here...

...then tap Delete.

Re-ordering the Locations in Weather

You can re-order the locations so your most important location is first on the list.

To re-order entries, touch and drag the three bars  you see to the right of each entry.

Drop or let go of the entry when you have it in the correct location.

Tap **Done** in the upper right corner to complete your changes.

Touch and Drag up/down to re-order

Moving Between Weather Locations

Once you have Weather set up for your various locations, you can then swipe from screen to screen, seeing the weather in all the cities you chose.

Touch and drag your finger across the screen to advance to the various Weather locations.

Other Weather Apps

The **Weather** app bundled with the iPod touch is certainly functional, but there are other alternatives. Most of the weather apps are free in the App Store, and some offer premium versions for a modest fee.

> **NOTE**: Most of the free weather apps are supported by ads in the app. For the most part, these are not intrusive.

The easiest way to find alternative weather apps is to go to the App Store and touch the **Categories** icon at the bottom. There is a separate category of the store simply called Weather. In the Weather category, touch **Top Free** at the top and then search for apps. See more about downloading apps in Chapter 20: "The Amazing App Store."

The Weather Channel

The Weather Channel is certainly one of the weather authorities today. **The Weather Channel** app takes a similar approach to the **Weather** app on the iPod touch.

When you first start the app, you will input your zip code or address so a custom home page with your weather can be created. The home page shows the current weather, with soft keys for **Hourly, 36 Hour**, and **10 Day** forecasts.

Along the very bottom are four icons: **Weather**, **Map**, **Severe**, **Video**, and **Info** (which gives indices). Each is fairly explanatory of the features contained.

AccuWeather

Another of the weather authorities, AccuWeather, has put together a very comprehensive weather app for the iPod touch.

Download the app from the App Store as we explained earlier.

You will be prompted to use your location for determining local weather—we recommend allowing AccuWeather to do this.

The home page of the app shows you the current temperature and conditions with a graphic of what the sky should look like. Like **The Weather Channel** app, there are soft keys to show different views.

The upper level of soft keys at the bottom of the screen shows buttons for **Current**, **Hourly**, and **15 Day** forecasts. There is also a soft key for **Indices**.

Below that are the main function keys of the app, **Weather**, **Radar**, **Video**, **Risk**, **Alarms**, and **Alert**.

Chapter 26

New Media: Reading Newspapers, Magazines, and More

In last chapter, we spoke about how the iPod touch has revolutionized the world of reading. Not only is the iPod touch unparalleled for reading e-books, it's also unequaled in viewing new media such as online newspapers and magazines, PDF files, and more. The iPod touch is even set to revitalize the comic book industry with comic books that look beautiful and are amazingly interactive.

In this chapter, we'll explore how to enjoy new media using the iPod touch's vivid screen and terrific touch interface.

Newspapers on the iPod touch

Remember the days when newspapers were delivered to the house? Invariably, if there was one puddle in the sidewalk, that was where the newspaper landed! You took it out of that plastic bag, shook it off, and tried to make out what was in section two – the section that got soaked.

Well, those days may be gone forever. You now have the opportunity to interact with the news and even get your paper delivered every day – but to your iPod touch instead of your driveway.

Many newspapers and news sites are developing apps for the iPod touch, with new apps seeming to appear every day. Let's take a quick look at three apps from the largest newspapers in the country (see Figure 26–1), paying special attention to how the iPod touch revolutionizes the act of reading the news.

Figure 26–1. *The front pages of various newspaper apps.*

Popular Choices: The New York Times, The Wall Street Journal, and USA Today

The New York Times, *The Wall Street Journal*, and *USA Today* all have circulations of millions of readers, but each paper has taken a different approach to bringing you the news on the iPod touch.

NOTE: You can always go and visit the dedicated web site for any news source. Some are optimized for the iPod touch, while others offer you a full web experience. Some require registration or a paid subscription to view the paper's full content.

The common denominator with all three apps for these papers is that you must first find, download, and install a news app on the iPod touch. Here are the steps:

1. Locate your desired news app in the App Store. You may find one or more news apps in the **Featured** section, and there's also a direct link to **News** under **Quick Links** at the bottom of the App Store home page.

2. Next, touch the **Categories** button at the bottom of the page and then touch the **News** icon. This will take you to all the news apps in the App Store. Browse or search for your desired news app, just as you would for any other app.

3. Once you locate the desired news app, download it as you would any other app.

> **NOTE:** Many news apps are free. Some are free to try, but require you to buy them to continue receiving them. Others offer limited free content, but you need to subscribe to gain access to their full content.

4. Once the app is downloaded, touch its icon to start it.

The New York Times App

The New York Times offers a slimmed-down version of the paper in its free iPod touch/iPhone app.

There are five soft keys at the bottom of the page for **Latest**, **Popular**, **Saved**, **Search**, and **More**. Each section carries a sampling of stories from those sections in the current day's paper.

Touching **More** shows you tabs for all sections of *The New York Times*.

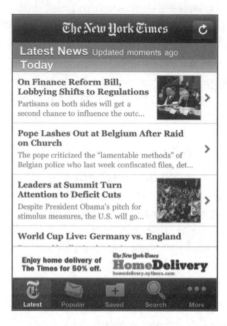

Navigating **The New York Times** app is as simple as touching an article and scrolling through. While reading a story, just touch the center of the screen and the soft keys on top and bottom appear.

To go back to the **Home** page, touch the **Latest News** button in the upper-left corner.

NOTE: If you are in another section – say *Technology* – the button in the upper-left corner will

say **Technology**.

To email an article, just touch the **Email** icon in the lower-left corner. This button is only available when you are inside an article, not on the **Home** page.

Touch the icon, and you can send the article through email, text message, or Twitter.

The Wall Street Journal App

The Wall Street Journal app takes a different approach to delivering the news. When the app launches, you'll be prompted to create an online account.

Once you've created the account, you have access to a subset of content from *The Wall Street Journal*.

Material that is unavailable to free-account users is marked with a small **Key** icon that indicates the material is locked.

If you fully subscribe to **The Wall Street Journal** app, all articles and tools become available.

Tap a video to watch it or tap a picture to view it and any related pictures.

Key shows this is "locked" and only viewable by paying subscribers.

Tap an article to read more.

To order the full subscription to **The Wall Street Journal** app for the iPod touch, touch a "locked" article and then the **Subscribe Now** button that appears on the next page. At the time of writing, a subscription for weekly access was about US $4 a week or about US $17 a month.

The articles without the **Key** icon are available to read. Touch an article and it loads onto the iPod touch.

Similar to **The New York Times** app, **The Wall Street Journal** app lets you simply scroll through to continue reading.

You'll notice that the **The Wall Street Journal** app's home page has a **Video** button next to the **Articles** button. Touch the **Video** button to look at the **Video** menu. Touch a video and it will start playing in the iPod touch's video player.

To access other sections of the paper, touch the **More** button in the lower-right corner.

USA Today App

While not as full-featured as its iPad equivalent, the **USA Today** app for the iPod touch is still a great source to get your iPod touch news. The app is available in the **News** category of the App Store.

Download the app as you did the other news apps.

When you first start the app, you will be asked to input your location so your local weather and news can be configured.

The sections of the paper are at the top of the home screen. Just slide from right to left and then touch the section of the paper you want to read.

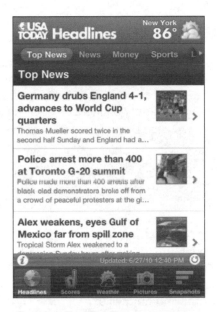

Moving Through and Enjoying Content

After you play for a while with all these news sites, you'll begin to realize that there is no real standard for moving around. This means you'll need to become familiar with each app's own way of navigating articles, as well as how to return to the main screen. Here's a short guide for generally navigating these types of apps; these features are common to **The New York Times**, **The Wall Street Journal**, and **USA Today** apps:

- **Showing or Hiding Control buttons or Captions:** Tapping the screen once usually shows hidden controls or picture captions. You can tap them again to hide them again.

- **Getting to the Details of an Article:** Usually, you just scroll through the articles, just as you would on a web page.

- **Viewing a Video:** Tap a video to start playing it. Usually, this plays the video in the same manner as any other video. See Chapter 10: "Viewing Videos, TV Shows, and More" to learn how to navigate videos on the iPod touch.

- **Expanding a Video or Image Size:** You can try pinching open in the video or image and then double-tapping it. Look for an **Expand** button, and you can also try rotating to landscape mode.

- **Reducing a Video or Image Size:** You can try pinching closed inside the video or image. Look for a **Close** or **Minimize** button, and you can also try rotating back to portrait mode.

Adjusting Font Sizes and Sharing, Emailing, or Saving an Article

The various apps for reading newspapers and other content usually include a button or icon for changing the font size. That same button or another one near it may also allow you to share, save, or email an article to a friend. Some apps allow you to share the article with a social networking site, such as Facebook or Twitter.

> **TIP:** Almost all newspaper or magazine apps let you change font sizes and email or otherwise share an article. Look for a button or icon that says **Tools**, **Options**, **Settings**, or something similar. In some apps, the font-size adjustment option shows as small **A** and large **A** icons.

In **The Wall Street Journal** app, touch the **More** button in the lower-right corner and then touch the **Options** tab on the next page to adjust options such font sizes, saving, or emailing an article:

If you choose **Save Article,** the article ends up in the **Saved Articles** section on the **Start** screen.

If you choose **Email Article,** the article is sent to the address you specify in an email.

If you want to change the font size, in the Options menu choose font size and just tap the larger or smaller letter to make the font bigger or smaller.

Options	Set Font Size

Instructions

Current Font Size: Large

You can decrease and increase the font size by tapping the buttons in the toolbar below.

Once you're satisfied with the size, tap the back button in the navigation bar above. Your setting is automatically saved.

The font sizes of the text you see here correspond exactly to the font sizes used in the articles.

A   A

In the **USA Today** app, the font size and share options are separate.

Touch the **Share Article** icon to email an article or share it with a social networking site.

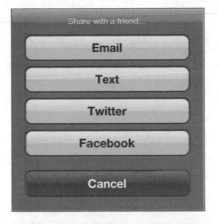

You can also touch the **info** button

to launch the **Settings & Info** menu.

Doing so brings up a page that lets you choose the font size, link the app to your **Facebook** and **Twitter** accounts, and set your default weather location.

Tap **Done** to return to the **Home** page.

The **New York Times** app has one button in the lower-left corner of the article screen for sharing the article.

You adjust the font size by using the **T-** and **T+** buttons at the bottom.

Magazines on the iPod touch

It is no secret that both newspapers and magazines have suffered declines in readership over the last few years. The iPod touch offers a totally new way of reading magazines that might just give the media industry the boost it needs.

Pictures are incredibly clear and brilliant in magazines on the iPod touch. Navigation is usually easy, and stories seem to come to life, much more so than in their print counterparts. Add video and sound integration right into the magazine, and you can see how the iPod touch truly enhances the magazine reading experience.

Some magazines, such as *TIME Magazine*, include links to live or frequently updated content. These might be called **Newsfeeds**, **Live Edition**, or **Updates**. Check for them in any magazine you purchase – they will give you the most up-to-date information.

> **TIP:** Make sure to check the user ratings for a magazine or other app before you purchase it. Doing so may save you some money and some grief!

The App Store is filled with both individual magazines you can purchase (these magazines sometimes include limited content from for free) and magazine readers that provide samples of many magazines that allow you to subscribe to weekly or monthly delivery of a given magazine.

Unlike newspapers, only a few magazines are available for free.

One magazine app with strong reviews is *GQ* **Magazine** for the iPod touch, which retails for US $4.99 per issue at the time of writing.

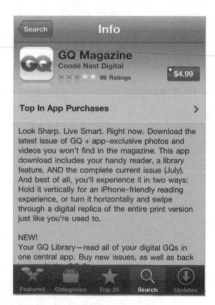

The Zinio Magazine App – a Sampler

The **Zinio** app takes a unique approach. This app is free in the App Store, and it gives you the ability to subscribe to hundreds of magazine titles. Reading an article in **Zinio** requires a few simple steps:

1. Login into the **Zinio** app. This takes you automatically to the **My Library** section, which has some free magazines you can download.

2. Download any free samples or choose the **Shop** button to purchase magazines.

3. Some magazines may be giving away full, free issues. Just look in the **My Library** section to see what is available.

To subscribe to any of the magazines featured in **Zinio**, touch the **Shop** button at the bottom of the screen.

You can navigate magazines by category along the left-hand side, or you can slide the icons at the bottom to see available magazines.

There are many popular magazines you can choose. The categories cover everything from art to sports and more. Prices vary, but often you can buy either a single issue or a yearly subscription.

For example, at the time of writing the latest issue of *Popular Mechanics* was $1.99 on **Zinio**, and a yearly subscription was $7.99.

Some of the subscriptions make great sense. A single issue of *Bike Magazine* (one of my favorites) was $4.99 at the time of this writing, while a yearly subscription was only $9.00.

A closer look showed me that there were more than 16 cycling magazines I could subscribe to.

Comic Books on the iPod touch

One genre of "new media" poised for a comeback with the advent of the iPod touch is the comic book. The iPod touch, with its high-definition screen and powerful processor, makes the pages of comic books come alive.

There are already a few comic book apps available, including one from the famous Marvel Comics. DC Comics has launched its own app, as well. This app was created by the same people who make the Marvel app, **Comixology** (they also make the more generic **Comics** app).

To locate the **Marvel Comic** app in the App Store, go to **Categories** and then **Books**. The app is free, and you can purchase comic books from inside the app.

At the bottom of the **Home** screen, you'll see five buttons: **My Comics**, **Featured**, **Free**, **Top 25,** and **Browse**. Purchases you make will be listed under the **My Comics** heading.

The App Store gives you the opportunity to download both free comics and individual issues for sale. Most sell for $1.99 per issue.

Each tab takes you to a new list of comics to browse, much like the iTunes store.

Touch the **Browse** button to browse by **Genre**, **Creator**, **Storylines**, or **Series**. Or you can try to find a particular comic by typing its name (or a portion thereof) into a search field.

You can read a comic book in one of two ways. First, you can swipe through the pages and read one after the other. Second, you can double-tap a frame to **Zoom** in, then tap the screen to advance to the next frame in the comic strip. From there, you can just swipe from right to left to advance a frame; or, if you want to go back, swipe from left to right.

To return to the **Home** screen or to see the onscreen options, just tap the center of the screen. You'll see a **Settings** button in the top-left corner. Touch this and you can **Jump to the First Page**, **Browse to a Page,** or go to the **Settings** menu.

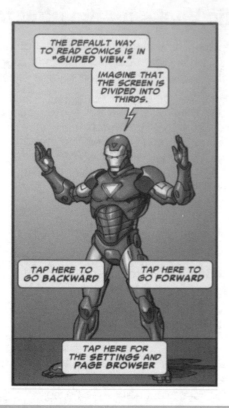

NOTE: The makers of this app, **COMIXOLOGY**, also make the **COMICS** app that contains the Marvel comics, as well as a bunch of others, including *Archie*, *Image*, and *Top Cow*. DC Comics is now also available.

The iPod touch as a PDF Reader

We've already showed you how to open up attachments, including PDF files, earlier in the book. You can now read PDF files in the **iBooks** app, but another great PDF reader is called **GoodReader**. The added benefit of **GoodReader** is that you can use Wi-Fi to transfer large PDF files.

You can find the **GoodReader** app in the **Productivity** section of the App Store. At the time of writing, this app costs only US $0.99.

> **NOTE:** The **iBooks** app can also read PDF files that are emailed as attachments. If **iBooks** is installed, just choose **Open in iBooks** when opening a PDF.

Transferring Files to Your iPod touch

One of the great things about the **GoodReader** app is that you can use it to wirelessly transfer large files from your Mac or PC to the iPod touch for viewing in the **GoodReader** app. You can also use **GoodReader** for document sharing in iTunes, as discussed in Chapter 3: "Sync Your iPod touch With iTunes." Follow these steps to transfer a file with **GoodReader**:

1. Touch the small **Wi-Fi** icon at the bottom left of the screen, and the **Wi-Fi Transfer Utility** pops up. You are prompted to type in either an IP address into your browser or a Bonjour address if you use the **Bonjour** service (see Figure 26–2).

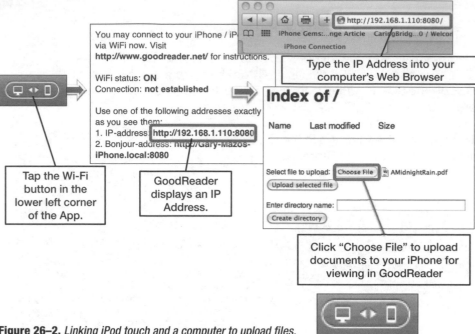

Figure 26–2. *Linking iPod touch and a computer to upload files.*

2. Type the address shown in the pop-up window from the **GoodReader** into a web browser on your computer. Now you can make your computer act as a server. You'll see that your computer and iPod touch 4 are now connected.

3. Click the **Choose File** button in the web browser on your computer to locate a file to upload to your iPod touch.

4. Once you've selected the file, click **Upload Selected File** and the file will be automatically transferred to your iPod touch inside **GoodReader** (see Figure 26–3).

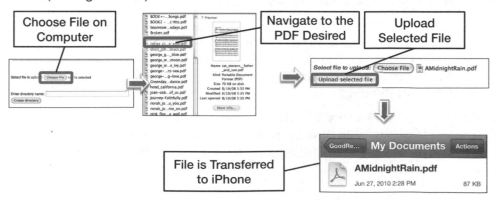

Figure 26–3. Uploading a file to iPod touch.

How is this useful? Well, for one of the authors (Gary), the iPod touch has become a repository for more than 100 pieces of piano sheet music. This means no more downloading PDF files, printing them out, putting them into binders, and then trying to remember which song is in which binder. Now, all his music is catalogued on his iPod touch. All he has to do is put the iPod touch on the piano, and he has access to all his music in one place.

> **NOTE:** You can also transfer **Word**, **Excel**, and **PowerPoint** files in the same manner. However, the document transfer utility in iTunes (see Chapter 3: "Sync Your iPod touch With iTunes" for more information on this utility) probably provides an easier way to do this.

Navigating the **GoodReader** PDF viewer is quite easy. This app is more sensitive than others, so tap the center of the screen quickly to bring up the onscreen controls. You can then go to your library or touch the **Turn Page** icon to turn the page.

The easiest way to move through pages is to touch the lower right-hand side of the screen to advance a page, or touch the upper-left side of the screen to go back a page. This becomes quite natural after a while.

You can also flick up or down to turn pages.

To go to another PDF file or another piece of sheet music, just touch the center of the iPod touch quickly and touch the **My Documents** button in the upper-left corner.

Connecting to Google Docs and other Servers with GoodReader

You can also use your iPod touch to connect to **Google Docs** and other servers with **GoodReader**. Follow these steps to do so:

1. In the **Web Downloads** tab, choose **Connect to Servers**.

2. Select **Google Docs.** (You can select a number of different servers, including mail servers such as MobileMe iDisk, Public iDisk, Dropbox, box.net, FilesAnywhere.com, MyDisk.se, and WebDAV Server. You can also select FTP servers.)

3. Enter your **Google Docs** username and password to log in.

4. Once you've established a connection, a new **Google Docs Server** icon will appear under the **Connect to Server** tab on the right-hand side of the page.

5. Tap the new **Google** tab to connect to the server (an Internet connection is required).

6. Now you'll see a list of all the documents you have stored on **Google Docs**. Tap any document and select the file type to download it. Usually PDF works well for this. (Google docs will show a **Save As...** dialog where you can choose PDF as the file type. The nice thing about PDF files is that they are easier to work with.)

7. Once the file is downloaded, it will appear on the left-hand side of **GoodReader** and you can simply touch it to open it.

Chapter 27

Find Your Way with Maps

Mapping on your iPod touch is very convenient and pretty amazing. As we explore the power of the **Maps** app in this chapter, you'll see how to find your location on the map and get directions to just about anywhere. You'll learn how to change views between classic **Map**, **Satellite**, and **Hybrid**. You'll also see how, if you need to find the best route, you can check the **Traffic and Construction** view using **Maps**. If you want to find the closest pizza restaurant, golf course, or hotel to your destination, that's easy, too. And you can use Google's **Street View** right from your iPod touch to help you get to your destination. It is easy to add an address you have mapped to your contacts. There's also a digital compass feature that is fun to play with.

Getting Started with Maps

The beauty of the iPod touch is that the programs are designed to work with one another. You've already seen how your contacts are linked to the **Maps** app; just look back at Chapter 15: "Working with Contacts" for more information on this topic.

The **Maps** app is powered by **Google Maps** – the leader in mobile mapping technology. With **Maps** you can locate your position, get directions, search for things nearby, see traffic, and much more.

Simply touch the **Maps** icon to get started.

Determining Your Location (the Blue Dot)

When you start the **Maps** program, you can have it begin at your current location. Follow these steps to determine your location:

1. Tap the small **Blue Arrow** icon at the lower-left corner.

Find my
Current
Location

2. **Maps** will ask to use your current location—touch **OK** or **Don't Allow**.

    We suggest choosing **OK**, which makes it much easier to find directions from or to your current location.

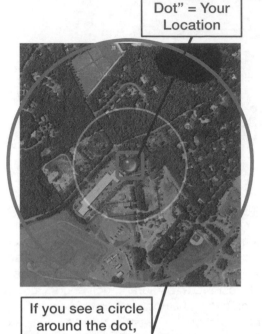

The "Blue Dot" = Your Location

If you see a circle around the dot, then your location is approximate.

NOTE: You might wonder how **Maps** knows where you are since your iPod is not connected to a cell network. The iPod uses Wi-Fi location (every Wi-Fi connection broadcasts a location) to show your spot on the map. If you are not connected to Wi-Fi (see Chapter 5: "Wi-Fi Connectivity," for more information on using the iPod touch's built-in Wi-Fi), then you won't see a location.

Changing Your Map Views

The default view for **Maps** is **Map** view, a basic map that shows a generic background overlaid with streets and their names. **Maps** can also show you a **Satellite** view or a combination of **Satellite** and **Map** views called **Hybrid** view. Finally, it includes another view called **List** view; this view appears only when you perform a search that generates a list of turn-by-turn directions. You can switch among all the views using the following steps:

1. Touch the turned-up edge of the map in the lower-right corner.

2. The corner of the map turns up to reveal buttons for views, traffic, pins, and more (see Figure 27–1).

3. Tap the view you'd like to switch to:

- **Map** is a regular map with street names (see Figure 27–2).

- **Satellite** is a satellite picture with no street names (see Figure 27–1).

- **Hybrid** is a combination of the **Satellite** view and the classic **Map** view; that is, it is a **Satellite** view with street names (see Figure 27–2).

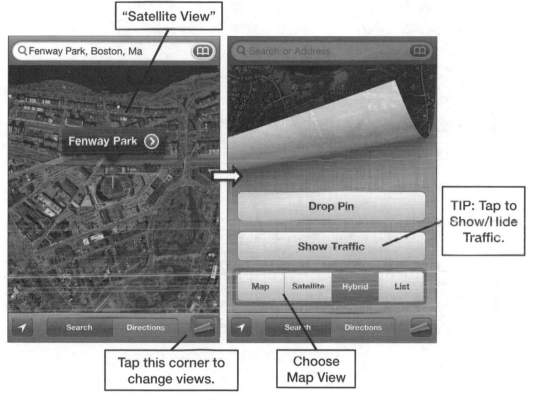

Figure 27–1. *The Satellite view and changing to another map view.*

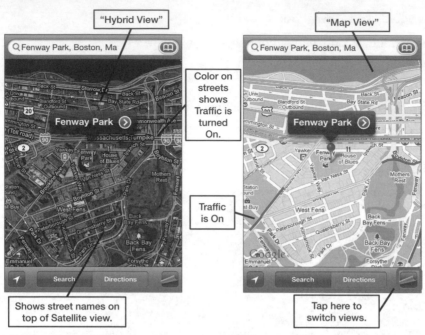

Figure 27–2. *Hybrid and Map views with traffic enabled.*

As noted, **List** view is available only when your search produces multiple results (like "pizza 32174") or you've asked for directions, as shown in Figure 27–3.

Figure 27–3. *List views for directions and search results.*

Checking Traffic

Not only does your **Maps** program tell you how to get somewhere, but it can also check traffic along the way. This feature is supported only in the United States for now. Follow these steps to check the traffic along your route:

1. Tap the lower-right corner of the map to see the options.

2. Touch **Show Traffic**.

On a highway, if there is a traffic situation, you will usually see yellow lights instead of green ones. Sometimes, the yellow light will flash, alerting you to traffic delays.

You may even see **Construction Worker** icons to indicate construction zones.

Maps uses color on major streets and highways to indicate the speed that traffic is moving:

- Green indicates traffic is moving at 50 MPH or more.

- Yellow indicates traffic is moving at 25–50 MPH.

- Red indicates traffic is moving at less than 25 MPH.

- Gray (or no color) indicates that no traffic data is currently available.

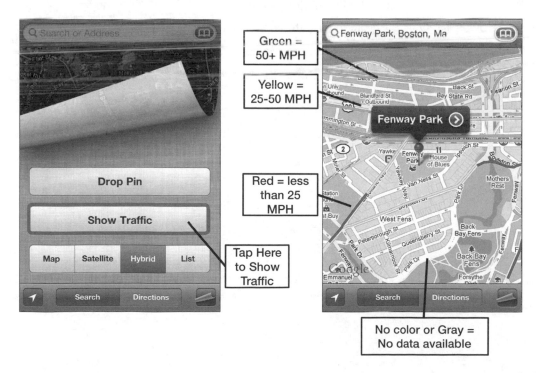

Searching for Anything

Because **Maps** is tied to **Google Maps**, you can search for and find just about anything: a specific address, type of business, city, or other point of interest, as shown in Figure 27–4. Follow these steps to search for a specific location:

1. Touch the **Search** bar in the top-right corner of the screen.

2. Type in your address, a point of interest, or the town and state you would like to map on your iPod touch.

Google Maps Search Tips

You can enter just about anything in the search, including the following:

- First name, last name, or company name (to match your **Contacts** list)

- 123 Main Street, City (some or all of a street address)

- Orlando Airport (to find an airport)

- Plumber, painter, roofer (any part of a business name or trade)

- Golf courses + city (to find local golf courses)

- Movies + city or ZIP/postal code (to find local movie theaters)

- Pizza 32174 (to search for local pizza restaurants in ZIP Code 32174)

- 95014 (the ZIP code for Apple Computer headquarters in California, United States)

- Apress

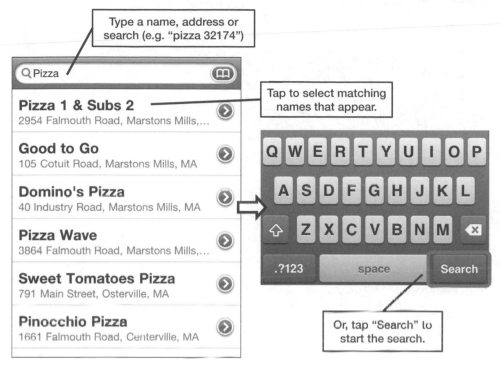

Figure 27–4. *Searching in the Maps app.*

To use numbers, tap the **123** key on the keyboard. For letters, tap the **ABC** key to switch back to a letter keyboard.

Mapping Options

Now that your address is on the **Maps** screen, a number of options become available to you. Follow these steps to view and access these options:

1. Touch the **Blue Arrow** icon next to the address to see some of these options.

2. If you have mapped one of your contacts, you'll see the contact details, as shown in Figure 27–5. **Maps** will also pull up contact information for specific searches. You can also get directions, share a location, or add a location as a bookmark.

NOTE: You can also tap and hold the address to bring up the **Copy** pop-up menu.

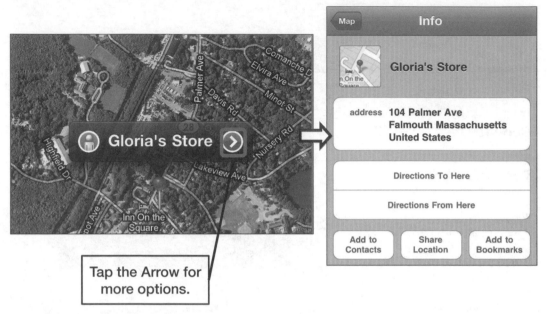

Tap the Arrow for
more options.

Figure 27–5. *Touching the information button to see the mapped contact details.*

Working with Bookmarks

Bookmarks work in **Maps** very much as they do in the web version of the app. A bookmark simply creates a record of places you've visited or mapped and want to remember in the future. It is always easier to look at a bookmark than to perform a new search.

Adding a New Bookmark

Bookmarking a location is a great way to make it easy to find that place again. Follow these steps to create a bookmark for a location.

1. Map a location, as shown in Figure 27–6.

2. Touch the blue **Information** icon next to the address.

3. Touch **Add to Bookmarks**.

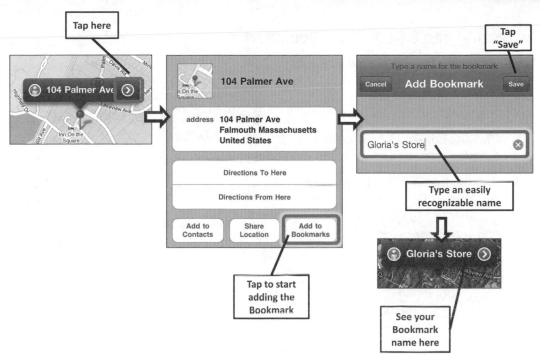

Figure 27–6. *Adding a bookmark.*

4. Edit the bookmark name to make it short and recognizable – in this case, you edit the address to simply say **Gloria's Store**.

5. When you are done, just touch **Save** in the top-right corner.

TIP: You can search for bookmark names just as you search for names in the **Contacts** app.

Accessing and Editing Your Bookmarks

To view your bookmarks, follow these steps:

1. Tap the **Bookmarks** icon next to the search window in the top row.

2. Tap any bookmark to immediately jump to it.

3. Tap the **Edit** button at the top of the bookmarks to edit or delete bookmarks. Tapping this button lets you accomplish the following tasks:

   - To reorder the bookmarks, touch and drag the right edge of each bookmark up or down.

   - To edit the name of a bookmark, touch it and retype the name. After editing the name, touch the **Bookmarks** button in the top left to get back to your list of bookmarks.

   - To delete a bookmark, swipe to the left or right on the bookmark, and tap the **Delete** button.

   - Tap the **Done** button when you are finished editing your bookmarks.

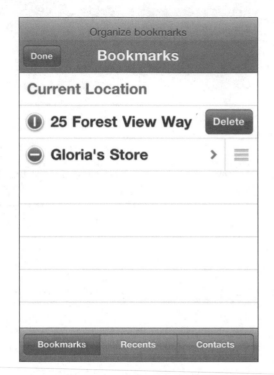

Adding a Mapped Location to Contacts

It is easy to add a location you have mapped to your contact list; follow these steps to do so:

1. Map an address.

2. Tap the **Arrow/Information** icon.

3. Tap **Add to Contacts** Add to Contacts .

4. Tap either **Create a New Contact** or **Add to Existing Contact**.

5. If you choose **Add to Existing Contact**, you then scroll through or search your contacts and select a name. The address will automatically be added to that contact.

Searching for Establishments Around Your Location

One of the great features of **Maps** is that you can use it to find businesses near your current location. Follow these steps to do so:

1. Map a location on the map, or use the blue dot for your current location.

2. Tap the search window. Assume you want to search for the closest pizza restaurants, so you type **pizza**. All local pizza restaurants will be mapped.

3. Notice that each mapped location may have a **Street View** icon on the left and the **Information** icon on the right.

4. If you want to zoom in or out, you can pinch the screen open or closed, or you can double-tap the screen.

5. Just as with any mapped location, when you touch the blue **Information** icon, you can see all the details, including the pizza restaurant's phone number, address, and web site.

6. If you want directions to a given restaurant, just touch **Directions to Here**, and a route is instantly calculated.

> **NOTE:** If you touch the **Home Page** link, you will exit **Maps**, and **Safari** will start up. You will then need to restart **Maps** again when you're done.

Zooming In and Out

You can zoom in and out in the familiar way by double-tapping and pinching. To zoom in by double-tapping, just double-tap the screen as you would on a web page or picture.

Dropping a Pin

Let's say you're looking at the map, and you find something you'd like to set either as a bookmark or as a destination.

In the following example, you are zooming in and looking around greater Boston. You stumble upon Fenway Park and decide it would be great to add it to your bookmarks. Follow these steps to do so:

1. Map a location or move the map to a location where you'd like to drop the pin.

2. Tap the lower-right corner of the map.

3. Tap **Drop Pin** (see Figure 27–7).

4. Now drag the pin around the map by touching and holding it. Move it right onto Fenway Park.

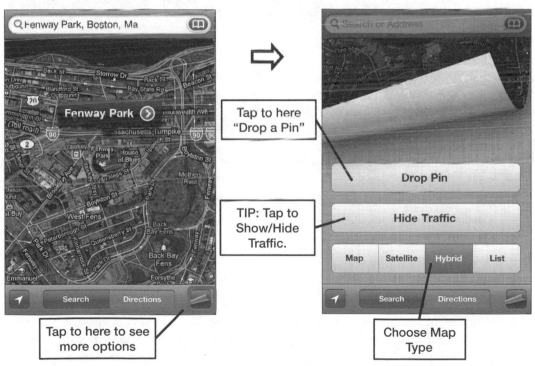

Figure 27–7. *How to drop a pin.*

TIP: You might wonder how can you determine the street address of any location on the map. When you drop a pin, Google Maps will show you the street address. This is very handy if you find a location by looking at **Satellite** or **Hybrid** view but need to get the street address.

Dropping a pin is also a great way to keep track of where you parked, which is especially helpful in an unfamiliar location.

Using the Street View

Google's **Street View** (Figure 27–8) is really fun in **Maps** on the iPod touch. Google has been hard at work photographing just about every address across the United States and elsewhere. The pictures are then fed into the company's database, and that's what shows up when you want to see a picture of your destination or waypoint.

NOTE: Google's **Street View** is currently in a small number of countries at the moment. The list of places supported includes much of North America, Western Europe, Australia, and now South Africa.

If there is a **Street View** available, you will see a small icon to the left of the address or bookmark on the map – a small orange **Person** icon.

In this example, Gary wants to check the **Street View** of his wife Gloria's store on Cape Cod, so he follows these steps:

1. In this case, he maps the address by tapping on the work address under Gloria's name on his **Contacts** list. He could have mapped it by typing an address in the search window, by searching for a type of business, or by touching the address in the **Contacts** app.

2. To the left of Gloria's name is the **Street View** icon. He taps the icon to immediately shift to a **Street View** of the address.

3. What is very cool is that he can navigate around the screen in a 360-degree rotation by swiping left, right, or even up or down, looking at the places next to and across the street from the destination he's reviewing.

4. To return to the map, he touches the lower-right corner of the screen.

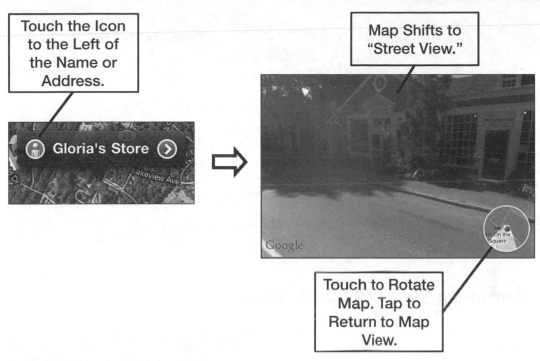

Figure 27–8. *Using Google's Street View app.*

Getting Directions

One of the most useful functions of the **Maps** program is that it lets you easily find directions to or from any location. Let's say you want to use the current location and get directions from Gloria's store to Fenway Park in Boston.

Tap the Current Location Button First

To find directions to or from your current location, you don't have to waste time typing your current address – the iPod touch will assume you want directions from where you are unless you specify otherwise. You may need to tap the **Current Location** button a few times until you see the blue dot on the screen.

Now you can do one of two things:

- Tap the **Directions** button at the bottom.
- Touch the **Blue Arrow** icon as you did previously and then select **Directions from Here** (see Figure 27–9).

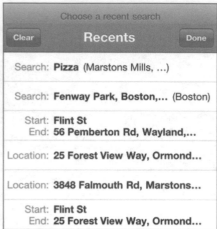

Figure 27–9. *Choosing Directions From Here and then Recents.*

Choosing a Start or End Location

Choosing a start or end location is also easy. Simply follow these steps to do so:

1. Touch the **Blue Arrow** icon above the pin.

2. Tap **Directions From Here**.

3. Now you can tap **Bookmarks**, **Recents**, or **Contacts** to find your destination. In this case, you tap **Bookmarks**.

4. Tap **Fenway Park**.

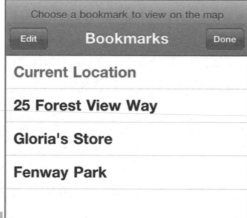

> **NOTE:** As soon as you touch the **Directions From Here** button, your recent searches will be automatically displayed, as in Figure 27–9. You can also touch the **Destination** box and type in a destination.

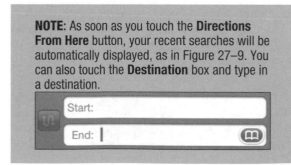

5. After you select Fenway Park from **Bookmarks**, the routing screen takes you to an overview screen.

6. A green pushpin is dropped at the start location, and a red one is dropped at the end location—in this case, Fenway Park.

Looking at the Route

Before you start the trip, you will see a **Start** button in the lower-right corner of the screen. Tap the **Start** button, and the routing directions begin. The **Start** button changes to **Arrow** icons that allow you to move between the steps in the trip.

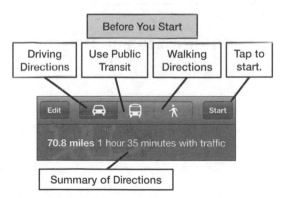

As Figure 27–10 shows, you can look at the route either as a path on the map or as a list.

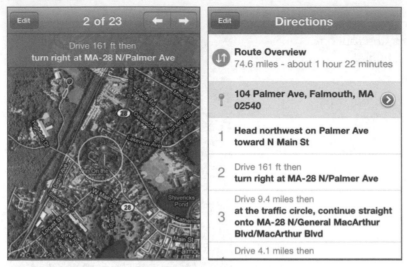

Figure 27–10. *Two ways of viewing directions.*

You can move the screen with your finger to look at the route, or just touch the arrows at the bottom to show the route in step-by-step snapshots.

You can also touch the **List** button, which will show detailed step-by-step directions.

Switching Between Driving, Transit, and Walking Directions

Before you start your directions, you can choose whether you are driving, using public transportation, or walking by tapping the icons on the left side of the blue bar at the top of the directions screen, as shown in Figure 27–11.

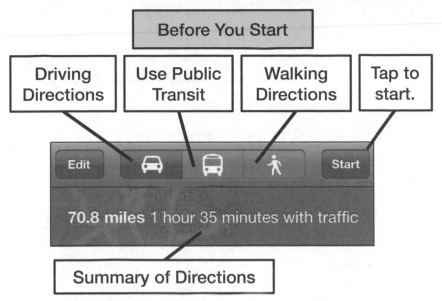

Figure 27–11. *Choosing your mode of transportation.*

Reversing the Route

To reverse the route, touch the **Reverse** button, which is at the top of the screen, between the **Start** and **End** fields. This can be useful if you're not great about reversing directions on your own or if your route relies on many one-way streets.

Maps Options

Currently, the only setting that affects your **Maps** app is **Location Services**, which is critical for determining your current location. Follow these steps to use the **Location Services** option:

1. Touch the **Settings** icon.

2. Tap the **General** tab in the left column.

3. Now find the **Location Services** switch about halfway down. Move this switch to the **ON** position; doing so enables **Maps** to approximate your location.

NOTE: Keeping the **Location Services** switch **ON** will reduce battery life by a small amount. If you never use Maps or don't care about your location, then set it to **OFF** to save your battery life. Remember: If you are not connected to Wi-Fi, your iPod can't locate you.

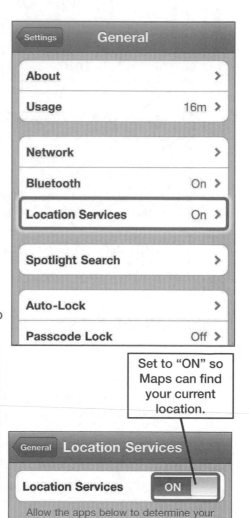

Set to "ON" so Maps can find your current location.

Chapter 28

Troubleshooting

The iPod touch is usually highly reliable. Occasionally, like with your computer or any complicated electronic device, you might have to reset the device or troubleshoot a problem. In this chapter, we give you some useful tips to help get your iPod touch back up and running as quickly as possible. We'll start with some basic quick troubleshooting and move into more in-depth problems and resolutions in the "Advanced Troubleshooting" section.

We also cover some other odds-and-ends related to your iPod touch and give you a list of resources where you can find more help with your iPod touch.

Basic Troubleshooting

First, we will cover a few basic tips and tricks to get your iPod touch back up and running.

What to Do If the iPod touch Stops Responding

Sometimes, your iPod touch won't respond to your touch—it freezes in the middle of a program. If this happens, try these steps to see whether the iPod touch will start responding (see Figure 28–1):

1. Click the **Home** button once to see whether that exits the app to the **Home** screen.

2. If one particular app is causing trouble, try double-clicking the **Home** button to open the **App Switcher** bar. Then press and hold *any* icon in the **App Switcher** bar until they all shake and a red circle with a minus sign appears in the upper-left corner of the

icon. Tap the red **circle** icon to close the app.

3. If the iPod touch continues to be unresponsive, try pressing the **Sleep/Power** key until you see **Slide to Power Off**. Then press and hold the **Home** button until you return to the **Home** screen—this should quit the program.

4. Make sure your iPod touch isn't running out of power. Try plugging it in or attaching it to your computer (if it's plugged in) to see whether it will start to respond.

5. If holding the **Home** button doesn't work, you will need to try to turn off your iPod touch by pressing and holding the **Power/Sleep** button for three to four seconds, and then slide the **Slide to Power Off** slider at the top of the screen. If you cannot power off the iPod touch, then see the following instructions about how to reset the iPod touch.

6. After you power off the iPod touch, wait a minute or so, and then turn on the iPod touch by holding the same **Power** button for a few seconds.

7. You should see the Apple logo appear on the screen. Wait until the iPod touch starts up, and you should be able to access your programs and data.

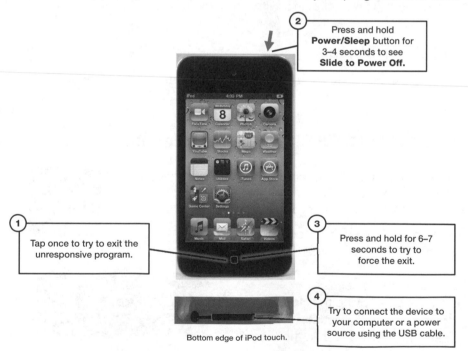

2 Press and hold **Power/Sleep** button for 3–4 seconds to see **Slide to Power Off.**

1 Tap once to try to exit the unresponsive program.

3 Press and hold for 6–7 seconds to try to force the exit.

4 Try to connect the device to your computer or a power source using the USB cable.

Bottom edge of iPod touch.

Figure 28–1. *Basic troubleshooting steps.*

If these steps don't work, you will need to reset your iPod touch.

How to Hard-Reset Your iPod touch

Resetting your device is your last response to an unresponsive iPod touch. It is perfectly safe, and it usually fixes many problems (see Figure 28–2).

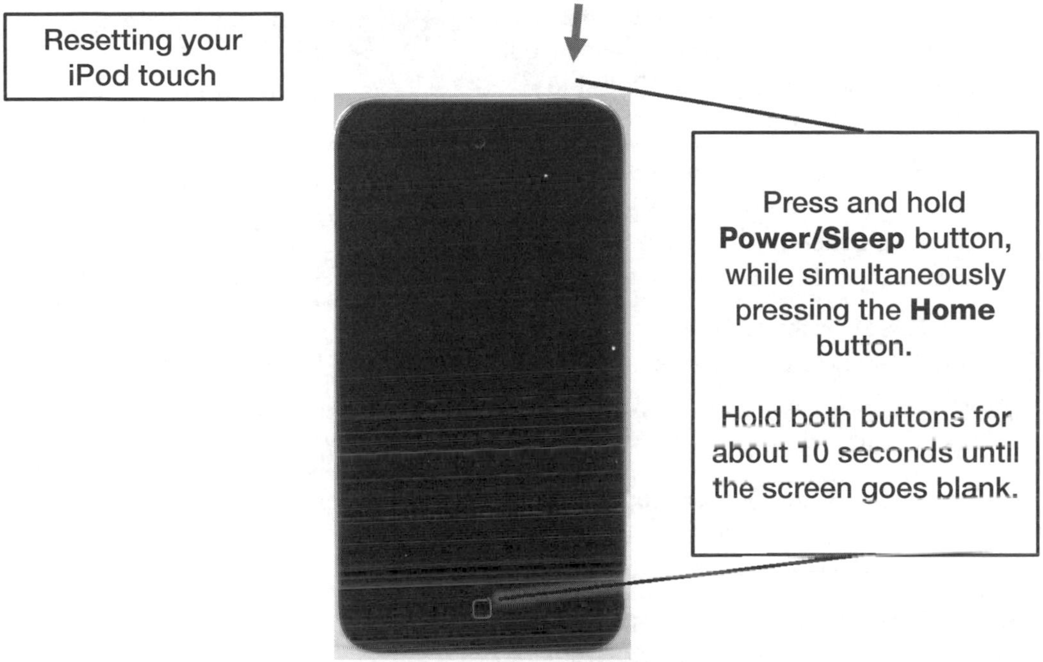

Resetting your iPod touch

Press and hold **Power/Sleep** button, while simultaneously pressing the **Home** button.

Hold both buttons for about 10 seconds until the screen goes blank.

Figure 28–2. Resetting your iPod touch.

Follow these steps to hard-reset your iPod touch:

1. Using two hands, press and hold the **Home** button and the **Power/Sleep** button at the same time.

2. Keep both buttons held down for about eight to 10 seconds. You will see the **Slide to Power Off** slider. Ignore that, and keep holding both buttons until the screen goes blank.

3. After a few more seconds, you should see the Apple logo appear. When you see the logo, just release the buttons, and your iPod touch will be reset.

How to Soft-Reset Your iPod touch

There are various things you can reset in the **Settings** app, from the **Home** screen layout, to the network settings, to all the data on your device.

1. Tap the **Settings** icon.

2. Tap **General**.

3. Swipe up to see the bottom of the page.

4. Tap **Reset**.

5. Tap **Reset All Settings** to reset the network, keyboard, **Home** screen layout, and location warnings. Tap **Reset** to confirm in the pop-up window.

6. Tap **Erase All Content and Settings** to erase everything from your iPod touch. Then tap **Erase** to confirm in the pop-up window.

7. Tap **Reset Network Settings** to clear all your Wi-Fi network settings.

8. Tap **Reset Keyboard Dictionary** to reset the spelling dictionary.

9. Tap **Reset Home Screen Layout** to return to the factory layout, from when you first received your iPod touch.

10. Tap **Reset Location Warnings** to reset the warning messages you receive about allowing apps to use your current location.

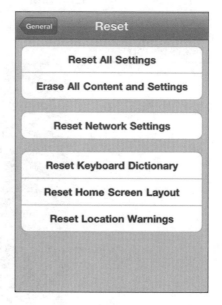

No Sound in Music or Video

Few things are more frustrating than hoping to listen to music or watch a video, only to find that no sound comes out of the iPod touch. Usually, there is an easy fix for this problem. Follow these steps to try to fix issues with playing music or video on your iPod touch:

1. Check the volume by using the **Volume Up** key in the upper-left edge of your iPod touch. You might have accidentally lowered the volume all the way or muted it.

2. If you are using wired headphones from the headphone jack, unplug your headphones, and then put them back in. Sometimes, the headset jack isn't connected well.

3. If you are using wireless Bluetooth headphones or a Bluetooth stereo setup, then try these steps:

a. Check the volume setting (if available on the headphones or stereo).

b. Check to make sure the Bluetooth device is connected. Tap the **Settings** icon. Tap **General**, and then tap **Bluetooth**. Make sure you see your device listed and that its status is **Connected**. If it is not connected, then tap it and follow the directions to pair it with the iPod touch.

> **NOTE:** Sometimes you may actually be connected to a Bluetooth device and not know it. If you are connected to a Bluetooth Stereo device, no sound will come out of the actual iPod touch.

4. Make sure the song or video is not in **Pause** mode.

5. Open the iPod touch music or video controls. Double-clicking the **Home** button should open the **App Switcher**. Swipe from left to right to see your iPod controls. Verify the song is not paused or the volume is not turned down all the way, as shown here.

Your volume is turned down. Slide to right to turn up.

This play button shows your music is paused. Tap to play.

6. Follow these steps to see whether you or someone else has set the **Volume Limit** on the iPod touch:

a. Tap the **Settings** icon.

b. Swipe down the page, and tap **Music**.

c. See whether **Volume Limit** is **On**.

d. Tap **Volume Limit** to check the setting level. If the limit is unlocked, simply slide the volume to a higher level.

e. If it is locked, you need to unlock it first by tapping the **Unlock Volume Limit** button and entering the four-digit code (see Figure 28–3).

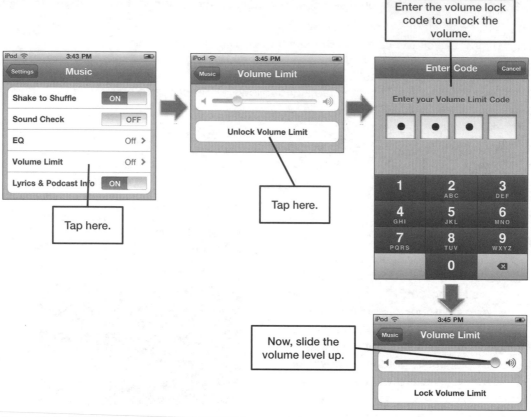

Figure 28–3. *Checking the volume limit in settings.*

If none of these steps helps, check out the "Additional Troubleshooting and Help Resources" section later in this chapter. If that doesn't help, then try to restore your iPod touch from a backup file using the steps in the "Restore Your iPod touch from a Backup" section in this chapter. Finally, if that does not help, then contact the store or business that sold you your iPod touch for assistance.

If You Can't Make Purchases from iTunes or the App Store

You have this new, cool device, and let's say you go to the iTunes store or the App Store. What if you receive an error message or you are not allowed to make a purchase? Follow these steps to try to resolve this issue:

1. Both stores require an active Internet connection. Make sure you have an active Wi-Fi connection. For assistance, check out Chapter 5: "Wi-Fi Connectivity."

2. Verify that you have an active iTunes account. We show you how to set up a new iTunes account in the "Create an iTunes Account" section of Chapter 29: "Your iTunes User Guide."

Advanced Troubleshooting

Now we will delve into some more advanced troubleshooting steps.

Remember to Reregister with Your iTunes Account

Every iPod touch is associated with an iTunes account. That association allows you to purchase iTunes music, videos, and apps from your iPod touch. It is also this association that allows you to play music from your iTunes account on your computer on your iPod touch.

Sometimes, your iPod touch might "lose" its registration and connection with the **iTunes** account. Usually, this is a very simple fix. Just connect your iPod touch to the computer via the USB cable, and the **iTunes app** will walk you through the process of reassociating your iPod touch with your iTunes account. We show the detailed steps for how to do this in Chapter 1: "Getting Started."

If you have trouble registering your iPod touch through iTunes, then Apple provides an online resource that you can get to from your computer or iPod touch web browser. Type this into your web browser:

https://register.apple.com/cgi-bin/WebObjects/GlobaliReg.woa

You should see a screen similar to the one shown in Figure 28–4. Follow these steps to reregister your iTunes account:

Figure 28–4. *The online registration site from Apple's login page.*

1. Complete the information, enter your Apple ID and password, and click **Continue**.

2. Depending on what you are registering, select either **One product** or **More than one product**. In this case, we chose **One product** (see Figure 28–5).

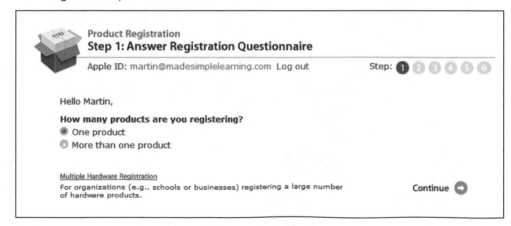

Figure 28–5. *Step 1 on Apple's online registration site.*

3. Now, choose the category, product line, and product. In this case, we chose **iPod touch** category, **iPod** product line, and **iPod touch**. This moved us through Steps 2–4 at once (see Figure 28–6).

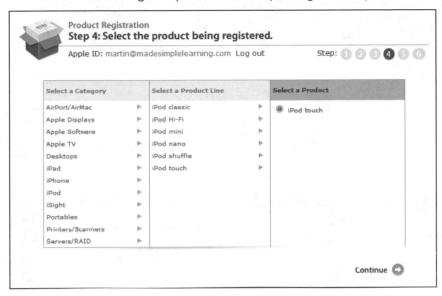

Figure 28–6. *Steps 2–4 on Apple's online registration site.*

4. Now you need to enter your iPod touch serial number and other information that describes how you will use the iPod touch.

TIP: To locate the serial number, connect your iPod touch to your computer and load the **iTunes** app. Click your iPod touch in the left nav bar, and click **Summary** in the top nav bar. The serial number is at the top of the **Summary** screen, as shown in Figure 28–7.

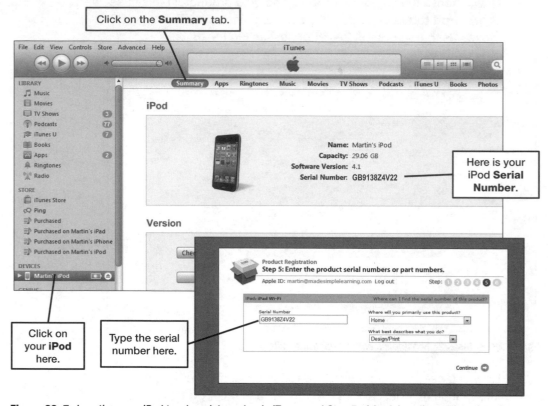

Figure 28–7. *Locating your iPod touch serial number in iTunes and Step 5 of Apple's online registration site.*

5.   Now click **Continue**, and you should see the confirmation screen shown in Figure 28–8.

6.   Click **Continue** to complete the registration of your iPod touch.

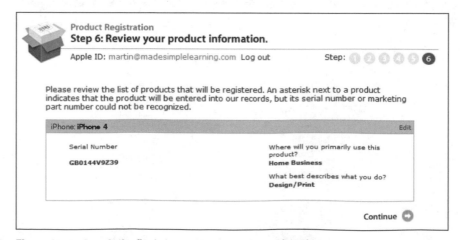

Figure 28–8. *Step 6, the final step, on Apple's online registration site.*

When Your iPod touch Does Not Show Up in iTunes

Occasionally, when you connect your iPod touch to your PC or Mac, your iPod touch may not be recognized by the **iTunes** app, and it will not appear in the left nav bar.

In Figure 28–9, after you connect your iPod touch to your computer, you should see it listed in the left nav bar under **DEVICES**, as shown in the image on the right side. In the image on the left side, you will notice that there is no device shown, even though your iPod touch is connected to the computer.

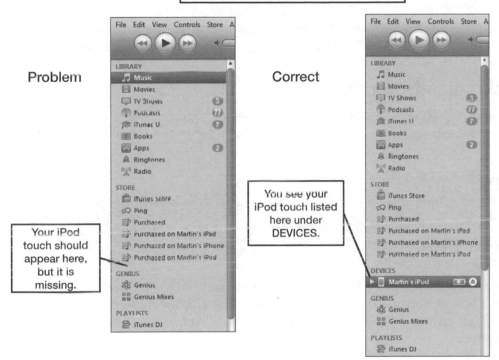

Figure 28–9. *Verifying your iPod touch is listed in the left nav bar in iTunes when connected to your computer.*

There are a few steps you can take to try and get your iPod touch recognized so it appears in iTunes

1. Check the battery charge of the iPod touch by looking at the battery level in the top right of the **Home** screen. If you have let the battery run too far down, the **iTunes** app won't see your iPod touch until the level of the battery rises a bit.

2. If the battery is charged, try connecting the iPod touch to a different USB port on the computer. Sometimes, if you have always used one USB port for the iPod touch and switch it to another port, the computer won't see it.

3. If this still does not fix the problem, try disconnecting the iPod touch and restarting the computer. Next, reconnect the iPod touch to the USB port.

4. If this still does not work, download the latest update to the **iTunes** app, or completely uninstall and reinstall iTunes on the computer again. If you do try this option, make sure you back up all the information in the **iTunes** app.

We have included detailed steps showing you how to upgrade to the latest version of **iTunes** in the "Upgrade iTunes" section of Chapter 29: "Your iTunes User Guide."

Synchronization Problems

Sometimes, you might be having errors when synchronizing your iPod touch with your computer (PC or Mac). How you work on the problem depends on your sync method.

Using iTunes to Sync

If you are using the **iTunes** app to sync your personal information, then follow these steps:

1. First, follow all the steps we outlined in the "iPod touch Does Not Show Up in iTunes" section in this chapter.

2. If the iPod touch still will not sync but you can see it in the left nav bar of the **iTunes** app, then go back to Chapter 3: "Sync Your iPod touch with iTunes," which explains how you can check your sync settings very carefully.

Using Apple's MobileMe or Microsoft Exchange to Sync

If you are using the **MobileMe** service or **Microsoft Exchange** method to sync your email and personal information, follow these troubleshooting steps:

1. Both **MobileMe** and **Exchange** sync require a wireless Internet data connection in order to sync your email and personal information. Verify that you have a live data connection by checking Table 1 in the Quick Start guide's "Reading the Connectivity Status Icons" section.

2. If you do not have a wireless data signal, then verify your Wi-Fi connection is set up correctly (see Chapter 5: "Wi-Fi Connectivity").

3. After you have verified your connection, you need to check that your sync settings are correct on your computer and on your iPod touch, as shown in Chapter 4: "Other Sync Methods."

> **TIP:** Sometimes the problem can be as simple as the fact your password has changed. If this is the case, then make sure to correct your password on your iPod touch for your sync settings. These are found by tapping your **Settings** icon, then tapping **Mail, Contacts and Calendars**. Finally, tap the account name and adjust the password.

Reinstalling the iPod touch Operating System (with or Without a Restore)

Sometimes, you might have to do a clean install of your iPod touch operating system to get your iPod touch back up and running smoothly. If an update is currently available, such as the 4.1 update that was available during the writing of this book, then this process will also result in upgrading your iPod touch software.

> **TIP**: This process is virtually identical to the process of updating your iPod touch with a new version of the operating system.

During this process, you will have three choices:

- If you want to return the iPod touch to its normal state with all your data, then you will have to use the **Restore** function in the **iTunes** app.

- If you plan on getting a clean start and tying the iPod touch to an iTunes account, then you would use the **Setup a new iPod touch** function at the end of this process.

- If you plan on giving away or selling your iPod touch, then you would simply eject the iPod touch from the **iTunes** app at the end of this process (before doing a restore or new setup).

> **CAUTION**: This restore process will wipe your iPod touch totally clean. You will need to resynchronize and reinstall all of your apps and enter your account information, such as email accounts. This process could take 30 minutes or longer, depending on how much information you have synced to your iPod touch.

To reinstall the iPod touch operating system software with the option of restoring data to your iPod touch from a previous backup, follow these steps:

1. Connect your iPod touch to your computer, and load the **iTunes** app.

2. Click your **iPod touch** in the **DEVICES** category in the left nav bar.

3. Click **Summary** in the top nav bar.

4. You will see the iPod touch information screen. Click the **Restore**
    button in the middle screen, as shown in Figure 28–10.

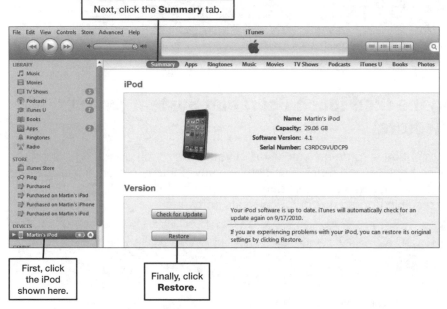

Figure 28–10. *Connecting your iPod touch and clicking the Restore button in iTunes in the Summary screen.*

5. Now you will be asked whether you want to back up. Click **Backup** just
    to be safe.

6. On the next screen, you are warned that all data will be erased. Click
    Restore or **Restore and Update** to continue (see Figure 28–11).

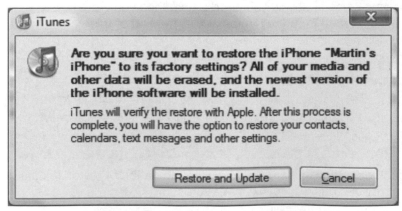

Figure 28–11. *Backing up before you restore in iTunes*

7. You will see an **iPod touch Software Update** screen. Click **Next >** to continue.

8. You will see the **Software License Agreement** screen. Click **Agree** to continue and start the process.

9. The **iTunes** app will download the latest iPod touch software, back up and sync your iPod touch, and then reinstall the iPod touch software completely. In the process of doing so, it will erase all data and restore your iPod touch to its original state. You will see status messages at the top of the **iTunes** app.

10. After the backup and sync, your iPod touch screen will go black. Next, the Apple logo will appear, and you will see a status bar under the logo. Finally, a small pop-up window will appear in the **iTunes** app to tell you the update process is complete. Click **OK** to be brought to the **Set Up your iPod touch** screen and then follow these steps:

    a. If you want to keep your iPod touch clean (i.e., without any of your personal data), then select the top option, **Setup as a new iPod touch**. You might want to use this option if you are setting up this iPod touch for someone else (you will need that person's Apple ID and password).

    b. If you are giving away or selling your iPod touch, simply click the **Eject** icon next to the iPod touch, and you're done (see Figure 28–12).

Figure 28–12. *Ejecting the iPod touch if you are giving it away or selling it.*

    c. Select **Restore from the backup of:** and verify that the pull-down is set to the correct device.

11. Finally, click **Continue**.

12. If you chose to restore, then after a little while you will see a **Restore in Progress** screen on your iPod touch and a status window in the **iTunes** app that says "Restoring iPod touch from backup…" with a time estimate.

13. Next, you will see a little pop-up window saying, "The settings for your iPod touch have been restored." In a few seconds, you will see your iPod touch appear in the left nav bar under **DEVICES** in the **iTunes** app:

a.   If you sync your information with the **iTunes** app, then all data will be synced now.

b.   If you use **MobileMe**, **Exchange**, or another sync process, then you will probably have to reenter passwords on your iPod touch to get those sync processes back up and running.

Additional Troubleshooting and Help Resources

Sometimes you may encounter a particular issue or question that you cannot find an answer to in this book. In the following sections, we provide some good resources that you can access from the iPod touch and from your computer's web browser. The iPod touch on-device user guide is easy to navigate and may provide you some quick information that you seek. The Apple knowledge base is helpful if you are facing a troubleshooting problem that is proving especially difficult to resolve. The iPod touch/iPod touch-related web blogs and forums are good places to locate answers and even ask unique questions you might be facing.

On-Device iPod touch User Guide

Follow these steps to use the on-device iPod touch user guide:

1.   Open your **Safari** web browser to view the online user guide for your iPod touch.

2.   Tap the **Bookmarks** button in the bottom row of icons.

3.   Swipe to the bottom of the list and tap **iPod touch User Guide**.

If you don't see that bookmark, then type this address into the **Safari** address bar on your iPod touch: `help.apple.com/iPod touch`.

> **TIP:** To view the manual in PDF format from your computer, go to `http://support.apple.com/manuals/iPod/`.

Once you get to the user guide on your iPod touch, you should see a screen similar to the one shown in Figure 28–13.

The nice thing is that you already know how to navigate the guide. Tap any topic to see more information about that topic – either another list of subtopics or detailed information.

Read the topic or tap another link to learn more.

Tap the button to the right of the screen to back out one level.

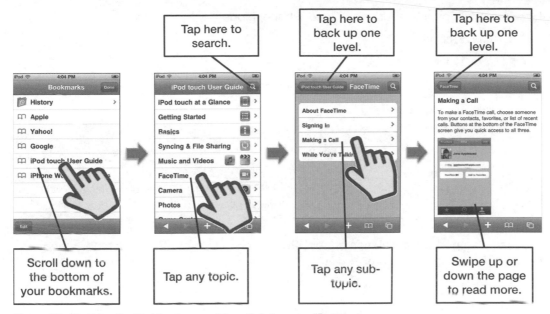

Figure 28–13. *Using the iPod touch manual from Safari on your iPod touch.*

The Apple Knowledge Base

The Apple Knowledge Base provides a lot of helpful information about your iPod touch. On your iPod touch or computer's web browser, go to this web page:

www.apple.com/support/iPod/

Next, click a topic in the left nav bar to get started.

iPod touch-Related Blogs

One of the great things about owning an iPod touch is that you immediately become part of the world-wide camaraderie of iPod touch owners.

Many iPod touch owners would be classified as *enthusiasts* and are part of any number of iPod touch user groups. These user groups, along with various forums and web sites, serve as a great resource for iPod touch users.

Many of these resources are available right from your iPod touch, and others are web sites that you might want to visit on your computer.

Sometimes you might want to connect with other iPod touch enthusiasts, ask a technical question, or keep up with the latest and greatest rumors. The blogs are a great place to do that.

Here are a few popular iPod touch (and iPhone) blogs:

- www.tipb.com
- www.iPhonefreak.com
- www.gizmodo.com (see the iPod touch section)
- www.ilounge.com

TIP: Before you post a new question on any of these blogs, please do a search on the blog to make sure your question has not already been asked and answered. Also, make sure you are posting your question on the right section (e.g., iPod touch) of the blog. Otherwise, you may incur the wrath of the community for not doing your homework first!

You can also perform a web search for "iPod touch blogs" or "iPod touch news and reviews" to locate more blogs.

iPod touch's Soulmate: iTunes

Your iPod touch is inextricably tied to **iTunes**—the e-commerce center of Apple. **iTunes** is not only where you buy music, videos and apps, it's also where you organize all of the great content you can use on your iPod touch. Use the new **Ping** social networking in iTunes to keep up to date with your favorite artists and friend's taste in music. You can even use **Ping** to meet up with frends and buy tickets for upcoming concerts. Learn how to purchase exciting new content—and even how to find it for free. Learn something new with iTunes U or find give your music library a fresh new feel using the Genius mix. We even help you learn how to save money with iTunes Home Sharing.

Chapter 29

Your iTunes User Guide

In this chapter, we will show you how to do virtually everything you might want to do with **iTunes**. We cover the new **iTunes** version 10 with the cool new social networking feature called **Ping** (see Figure 29-1). We will help you get **iTunes** installed and updated, and take you on a guided tour. We will also describe all the great ways to organize and view your music and videos to get ready to put them on your iPod touch.

Besides **Ping**, we will cover **iTunes DJ**, the **Genius** feature, and the money-saving **Home Sharing** feature. We will also show you how to import music CDs, DVDs, PDF, and e-book files, and get album artwork for all your music. We will even teach you about authorizing computers to share content using **iTunes**. Finally, we will provide some useful iTunes troubleshooting tips.

> **NOTE:** If you are looking to set up your iPod touch for the first time, please check out Chapter 1: "Getting Started." If you are trying to sync your computer to your iPod touch using **iTunes**, please check out Chapter 3: "Sync Your iPod touch with iTunes."

If you need to install the iTunes software on your computer, please jump to the "Downloading and Installing iTunes Software" section later in this chapter. If you already have the iTunes software installed, then go to the "Updating iTunes Software" section to make sure you have the latest version.

Figure 29–1. *The iTunes screen showing the Ping feature, new in version 10.0.*

Seeing If iTunes Is Already Installed

If you are a Windows PC user, then first look for the **iTunes** icon on your desktop, and double-click it. If you don't find it, then click the **Windows** logo or **Start** button in the lower-left corner and type **iTunes**. If you don't see **iTunes** appear in the search results, then you might not have **iTunes** installed. If that's the case, then follow the steps in the "Downloading and Installing iTunes Software" section, which follows. If **iTunes** is installed, you will see it appear—just click the icon to start it up and skip to the "iTunes Guided Tour" section.

If you are a Mac user, **iTunes** is installed by default with your computer. Check to see if the **iTunes** icon is on your desktop or desktop dock. If you see it, then double-click it and skip to the "iTunes Guided Tour" section. If you do not see the **iTunes** icon, then start **Finder**, and click **Applications**, and look for **iTunes** in the alphabetical list of apps.

Downloading and Installing iTunes Software

If you have never installed **iTunes** before on your computer, you can download the software directly from the Apple web site by following these steps:

1. Open a web browser on your computer, such as Apple **Safari**, Microsoft **Internet Explorer**, Google **Chrome**, or Mozilla **Firefox**.

2. Type in the web address www.itunes.com/download into the top of your browser, and then press **Enter**. This web address works for both Windows PC and Mac users.

3. Next, select the software that matches your computer's operating system, assuming that you're given a choice.

4. If you are given a choice to run or save the software, choose **Run** so that the installation will start automatically once the download is complete.

5. If the installation does not start right away, then locate the file you downloaded (Windows users should look for a file with a name like iTunes.exe and Mac users should look for something like iTunes_Install.dmg). Double-click the install file to start the installation.

6. Follow the onscreen instructions to install **iTunes**.

Updating iTunes Software

This process is easy because **iTunes** checks by default and will automatically let you know if a newer version is available for download. After you start **iTunes**, if a newer version of **iTunes** is available, you will see a pop-up window similar to Figure 29–2.

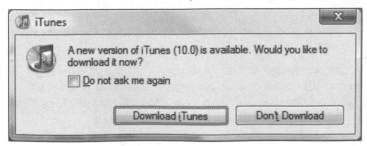

Figure 29–2. *The Apple software update screen.*

After you click **Download iTunes**, you will be taken to the **iTunes** web site. Select the appropriate software for your computer and click the **Download Now** button.

Follow the onscreen instructions to install the updated **iTunes** on your computer.

> **TIP:** To determine your computer operating system on Windows, click the **Start** button or **Windows** logo in the lower-left corner. Then right-click **Computer** and select **Properties**. On the Mac, click the **Apple** logo in the upper-left corner and select **About This Mac** from the menu.

What iTunes Can Do For You

The **iTunes** software on your computer can allow you to do many things, including the following:

- *Buying apps, music, videos, TV shows, and more (or downloading them for free)*: You can purchase or download free apps, music, movies, TV shows, podcasts, iBooks, PDF files, audiobooks, and educational content (from **iTunes U** – This is the area in iTunes devoted to educational content from universities and other institutions of learning, much of it free!).

- *Organizing your media*: You can use the various views and automatic playlists, and set up your own custom playlists.

- *Social Networking:* Using the new **Ping** feature in **iTunes**, you can follow your favorite artists and learn what music they are talking about. You can also share your favorite music with your friends, and you can even see who is going to the concert next weekend.

- *Syncing your music, videos, contacts, and more to your iPod touch:* You want to be able to take all your great music and videos with you on your iPod—use **iTunes** to sync it and go. (See Chapter 3: "Sync Your iPod touch with iTunes" for help syncing.)

- *Playing your music, videos, and audio content:* It serves as a great media player for your computer to play all your media, including music, videos, TV shows, and podcasts.

- *Backing up and restoring your iPod touch*: It lets you back up and restore your iPod touch data.

Common Questions About iTunes

What follows is a list of frequently asked questions about **iTunes** for the iPod touch, followed by short answers that address the core concern or issue raised by the question.

*Is the **iTunes** software on my computer the same as the **iTunes** app on my iPod touch?*

The **iTunes** software on your computer does the same job as a number of apps on your iPod touch. You need the following apps on your iPod touch to do all that **iTunes** can do on your computer: **Music**, **Videos**, **iTunes**, **iBooks**, and the **App Store**.

I have an iPhone, iPad, or another iPod; can I share music and videos with my new iPod touch?

Yes! You can definitely keep listening to all your music and sharing all your videos on all of your Apple devices, including your new iPod touch.

*Can I use my existing **iTunes** software and account?*

Yes! This is fine; you can use the same **iTunes** software already installed on your computer, as well as your existing iTunes account to set up your iPod touch.

Can I use my purchased apps from my iPhone, iPod touch, or iPad?

Yes and no. Older iPod touch and iPod touch apps will work; however, iPad-specific apps will not work on your iPod touch.

iTunes Guided Tour

After you have the latest version of **iTunes** installed (which was 10 at the time of writing this book), you're ready to take a quick guided tour of the **iTunes** interface on your computer. The nice thing is that the interface looks very much the same on PCs and Macs.

When you first start **iTunes**, you will see the main window with the top controls to play your music or videos (see Figure 29–3). You will also see the left navigation (nav) bar, which lets you select from your library, the **iTunes Store**, your iPod touch (when connected), shared media, **Genius** playlists, and your own playlists. The top nav bar adjusts depending on what you have selected in the left nav bar. Also, the center main window adjusts depending on selections from the left and top nav bars, and what is inside the main window itself.

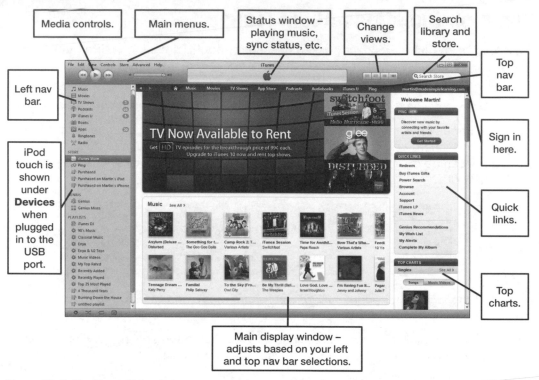

Figure 29–3. *The iTunes Main window.*

Starting from the top left of the main window, you can see the following menus, controls, windows, and other visual elements:

- *Main menus*: These are located just above the media controls, and they provide access to all the actions **iTunes** can perform through a logical and convenient set of menus. While a lot of the functionality in these menus is available in buttons and toolbars, these menus are where you'll find what you're looking for in a logical list.

- *Media controls*: These buttons let you play, pause, or skip to the next song or video, as well as adjust the volume.

- *Status window*: Located in the top-middle section of **iTunes**, this window shows you the status of what is currently going on (sync status, whether you're playing a song/video, or any other related messages).

- *View adjustment buttons*: These buttons allow you to adjust views between **List**, **Grid**, or **Cover Flow** views. (These are only active when you are in your own media libraries.)

■ *Search box*: This box allows you to search your library or the **iTunes Store** for a particular song, video, TV show, or anything else based on the text you enter.

■ *Sign-in link*: Located just below the search box in the upper-right corner, this button allows you to sign into the **iTunes Store** or create a new Apple ID. Notice that the figure to the right shows **martin@madesimplelearning.com** instead of **Sign in**, because Martin has already signed in with his Apple ID.

■ *Top nav bar*: This set of buttons under the status window will vary depending what you have selected in the left nav bar. Sometimes there are very few buttons; other times they will stretch across the screen. Click any of these buttons to change the content shown in the main window.

■ *Left nav bar*: This nav bar allows you to view your library (e.g., music, videos, TV shows, and podcasts), the **iTunes Store** and **Ping**, your purchased content, any currently connected devices (your iPod touch, iPod, iPhone, etc.), shared libraries, **Genius** mixes, and your own playlists.

■ *Main window*: This is where you can see all the content based on your selections in the left and top nav bars. For example, if you selected your iPod touch in the left nav bar and **Apps** in the top nav bar, you would see a screen similar to the one shown in Figure 29–3.

Apple Video Tutorials for iTunes

In addition to all the information provided in this book, you can find some good video tutorials from Apple to help you start using the **iTunes** app. You can check these tutorials out from within the **iTunes** app by clicking the **Help** menu and selecting **iTunes Tutorials**.

Using Ping in iTunes

As we mentioned, **Ping** is the new social networking feature focused on music, available for the first time in **iTunes** version 10. It allows you to follow your favorite artists as well as your friends, share your likes and dislikes with people, find out about local concerts, and more.

Getting Started and Creating Your Profile

To get started, click **Ping** in the **Store** section in the left nav bar of **iTunes**. Then click the [Turn On Ping] **Turn On Ping** button in the main window. You will need to sign into **iTunes** again to get started with **Ping**. Then you will need to create your profile for **Ping**. Enter your first and last name, enter your gender, add an optional picture, tell where you live, give a brief bio, and finally select up to three music genres you like.

Click **Continue** to select how music is displayed on your profile. The default is **Automatically display all music I like, rate, review, or purchase**. However, you can adjust this to meet your preferences. Click **Continue**.

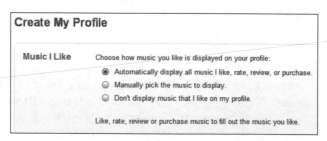

Finally, you can choose to allow people to follow you with or without approval (the default) or not allow them to follow you at all. Select your choice, and then click **Done** to finish setting up your **Ping** profile.

After you complete your setup, you will see a page similar to this one, with recommendations based on music you have purchased in the **iTunes Store**. To start following artists, click the **Follow** buttons at the bottom or type a search to follow a friend or artist.

You can also click the **Invite** button to invite your friends to join **Ping**.

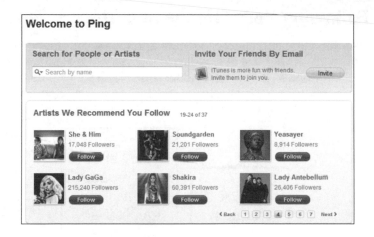

If you want, you can invite your friends by email by clicking the **Invite** button and entering their email addresses.

Following Your Favorite Artists

To find artists to follow, type their name in the search window of the **Ping** screen. When you see them appear, click the **Follow** button. We searched for and found the Rolling Stones, but note that this is not the group the Rolling Stones— this is a person who has taken the name.

CAUTION: Make sure this says **Artist**, not **People**, if you want to follow an artist.

CAUTION: Some people have (or have used) the same name as artists, so make sure to click the **Show Artists** link to the right of the search window. Otherwise, you might end up following Peter Gabriel the beer-drinking German who enjoys alternative, electronic, and rock, instead of the artist Peter Gabriel.

Following Your Friends and Other People

Use the same find feature to locate and follow your friends and others. In the example in Figure 29–4, we have decided to follow Gary Mazo, so we search for his name. After clicking **Follow**, a pop-up window is displayed, telling us that **Ping** will have to send my name, photo, and email address to Gary so he can approve our request. Figure 29–4 shows what Gary will see on his iPod touch when Martin requests to follow him.

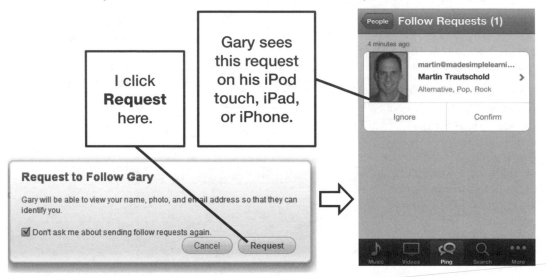

Figure 29–4. *Follow request from iTunes Ping as it appears on your mobile device.*

Recent Activity Feed

The heart of **Ping** is all the updates you receive from the artists and people you are following. In order to see this information, you need to scroll down under the people and artist follow recommendations to see your recent activity page (see Figure 29–5). This will show all the recent activity of you and your followed friends and artists. It's very similar to your Wall in Facebook. It allows you to provide comments, "like" what you see posted, and read comments from other followers. Have fun, let your opinion be heard, and get in on the conversation!

If the friends that you follow allow you to see their purchases, you can comment on those as well. Of course, **iTunes** makes it easy for you to purchase albums or songs that your friends purchase with the handy **Buy** button next to the listed item.

Figure 29–5. *The iTunes Ping recent activity page gives you the ability to add a comment or say that you like something.*

Concerts: Find Out and Share with Friends

When you click an artist's page in **Ping**, you can see if they have any upcoming concerts scheduled by looking for the **Concerts** box in the lower-right corner of the page. The accompanying image shows upcoming concerts for U2. Click the **See All** link in the title bar of the box to see all details and tell people if you're going to any of these concerts.

After clicking the **See All** link, you will see details of all concerts. You can click the **I'm Going** button to show others that you're attending and the **Tickets** button to try purchasing tickets. If you click **I'm Going**, you can add a comment about your post for your friends to see—maybe tell them what seat you have so they can find you.

Seeing What Artists Like in Ping

If you go to some artists' pages in **Ping**, you can see what music they like in the upper-right corner. In this image, we can see that U2 likes Elbow, TV on the Radio,The National, and more. Click any of the album covers to listen to and even purchase songs from the album.

Using Ping Drop-Down Menu for a Song

Next to all your songs in most of the **iTunes** views, you will see a little **Ping** drop down menu. Click the **Ping** menu to **Like**, **Post** or **Show Artist Profile**. You can also view the iTunes store to see more songs by that artist, album or even more songs in the same genre as shown to the right.

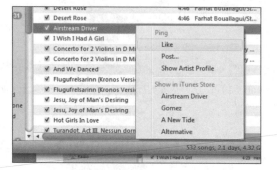

Viewing Ping in the Right Column

As you move between items in your music library, you will soon notice that **Ping** will show up at the top of the right column. You can say if you **Like** the song or **Post** a comment on the song from this right column.

Ping Mobile

You can access **Ping** right from the **iTunes** app on your iPod touch. To see **Ping**, start up your **iTunes** app on your iPod touch, and then tap the **Ping** soft key in the bottom row. Notice that you can switch between **Activity**, **People**, and **My Profile** by tapping those tabs along the top. The image to the right shows the **People** tab. This is where you can approve follow requests and follow more people or artists.

Changing Views in iTunes

There are many ways to view your music, videos, and other media in **iTunes** on your computer. Getting familiar with these views on your computer will help you understand your iPod touch as well, because your iPod touch also has many of the same views. There are four customizable views in **iTunes**: **Song List**, **Album List**, **Grid**, and **Cover Flow**.

> **NOTE:** **Album List** view is new in **iTunes** version 10.0. It is a nice view because it groups your songs by album and shows you the album art in the **Album** column.

Song List View

Click the leftmost of the view icons to see **List** view (see Figure 29–6). You can re-sort the list by any column by clicking that column's heading. For example, to sort by name, you would click the **Name** column heading. To reverse the sort order, just click the same column heading again. **List** view can be especially helpful for finding all the songs by a particular artist or on a particular album.

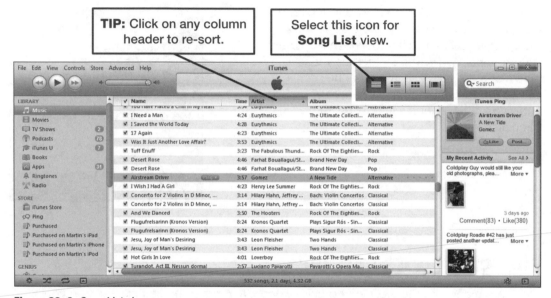

TIP: Click on any column header to re-sort.

Select this icon for **Song List** view.

Figure 29–6. *Song List view.*

Album List View

As we mentioned, this is a new view in **iTunes** version 10.0. Click the second view icon to see **Album List** view (see Figure 29–7). You can re-sort the list by any column by clicking that column's heading. For example, to sort by name, you would click the **Name** column heading. To reverse the sort order, just click the same column heading again. This **List** view can be especially helpful for finding all the songs by a particular artist or on a particular album.

Figure 29–7. *Album List view.*

Grid View

Click the third icon to show **Grid** view (see Figure 29–8). This is a very graphical view, and it is helpful if you want to quickly find album or poster art.

Figure 29–8. *Grid view.*

Cover Flow View

Click the rightmost icon to see **Cover Flow** view (see Figure 29–9). This is a fun view because it is visual, and you can quickly flip through the images using the slider bar to browse through the album covers. Like **Grid** and **Album List** views, this view provides an easy way to find an album when you know what the cover looks like.

Figure 29–9. *Cover Flow view.*

Playing Songs, Videos, and More

If you are new to **iTunes**, these basic pointers can help you get around the app (see Figure 29–10):

- *Playing a song, video, or podcast*: Double-click an item to start playing it.

- *Controlling the song or video*: Use the **Rewind**, **Pause**, and **Fast Forward** buttons, in addition to the **Volume** slider in the upper-left corner, to control the playback.

- *Moving to a different part of the song or video*: Just click the diamond in the slider bar under the song name at the top of the window and drag it left or right as desired.

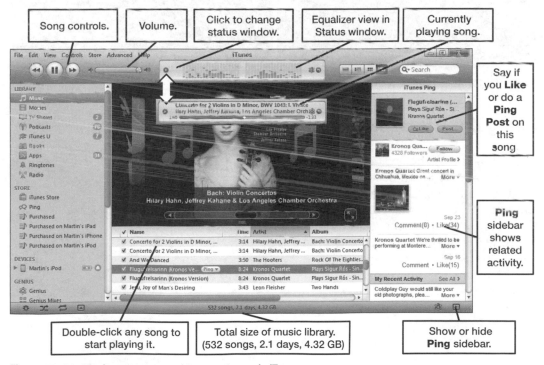

Figure 29–10. *Playing your songs, videos, and more in iTunes.*

iTunes Visualizer

There is a very interesting visual feature of **iTunes** that is quite entertaining. It looks like a screen saver that reacts to the music you are playing. There are two versions: the iTunes Classic Visualizer and the new iTunes Visualizer. To see the Visualizer, from the menu, select **View ➤ Show Visualizer** (alternatively, on Windows you can press **Ctrl+T**, and on the Mac you can press **Command+T**). To change between the Classic and New Visualizer, from the menu, select **View ➤ iTunes Visualizer** or **iTunes Classic Visualizer**. See Figure 29–11 for examples of the two visualizers.

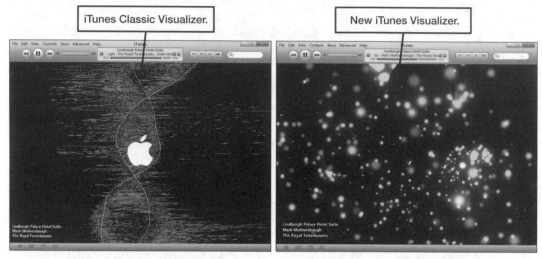

Figure 29–11. *iTunes Classic and New Visualizers.*

Using the iTunes Equalizer

You can enhance the sound of your music by matching the built-in equalizer to the type of music you are listening to. To view the **iTunes Equalizer**, from the menu, select **View ➤ Show Equalizer** (or, on Windows press **Ctrl+Shift+2**, and on the Mac press **Command+J** and check **Equalizer**). You can choose from over 20 preset settings, including **Classical**, **Rock**, **Pop**, and **R&B**, and you can modify the settings to fit your individual tastes.

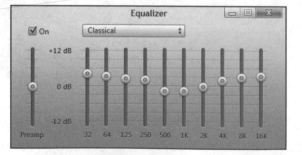

iTunes Mini Player

Sometimes you want to keep **iTunes** playing on your computer, but you don't want it taking so much screen real estate. Luckily, **iTunes** has a built-in miniature version called the Mini Player.

To show the Mini Player, from the menu, select **View ➤ Switch to Mini Player** (or, on Windows press **Ctrl+M**, and on the Mac, press **Shift+Command+M**). To switch back to regular view, press the same shortcut key.

Drag the lower-right corner to see the status window.

iTunes DJ

If you want to listen to your music in a new order without running out of songs, you should try out **iTunes DJ**. To start it, click **iTunes DJ** at the top of your **Playlists** section in the left nav bar.

iTunes DJ will play a continuous mix of music based on your entire music library or a single playlist. To adjust the source, click the drop-down menu next to **Source** at the bottom of the screen.

You can see the list of songs that the DJ is about to play in the **iTunes DJ** main window. To change the order in which the songs will be played, you can simply drag and drop the song higher or lower in the list, as shown in Figure 29–12.

Figure 29–12. *iTunes DJ, and moving the order of songs to be played.*

You can also add songs to the **iTunes DJ** list or play them next by right-clicking the song in your library and selecting **Add to iTunes DJ** or **Play Next in iTunes DJ**.

Apple Remote App

One fun thing to do is use the **Remote** app on your iPod touch or other Apple device. To get started, start up the **App Store** on your iPod touch and do a search for **Remote**. The **Remote** app from Apple, Inc. is free, so be careful not to purchase one of the paid apps that appear. Make sure you are downloading the **Remote** app made by Apple.

After you get the app installed on your iPod touch, tap it to start it up. Then you need to connect the app to iTunes on your computer by entering a four-digit passcode.

1. On your iPod touch, tap the **Remote** app to start it (see Figure 29–13).

2. Tap **Settings** in the upper-left corner of the **Remote** app.

3. Tap **Add Library**, and you should see a four-digit passcode.

4. On your computer, start up **iTunes**. In the **Devices** section, your iPod touch should now be displayed with the **Remote** icon next to it. Click it to get started.

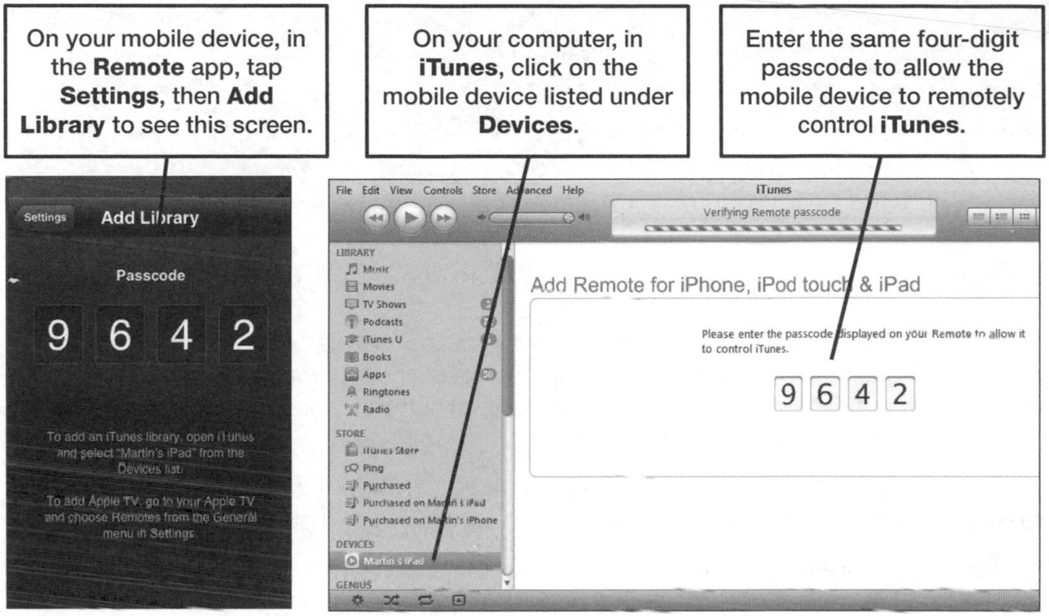

Figure 29-13. *Connecting your mobile device (IPod touch, iPhone or iPad) to iTunes using the Apple Remote app.*

Now, with your iPod touch (or other Apple device) connected, you can remotely control iTunes—play, pause, skip a song, even change playlists—virtually anything you can do related to playing music when sitting at your computer!

AirPlay: Wirelessly Stream Your iTunes Music Around Your House

Apple has had the AirTunes feature for a while, which allows you to stream your ITunes music to specifically designed wireless speakers throughout your house. Recently, Apple changed the name to AirPlay, and has expanded the number of manufacturers that build this new standard into their speaker, dock, and stereo systems. AirPlay even transmits information from **iTunes** about the currently playing song, including song name, artist name, time played, and time remaining. AirPlay will work audio-only with Airport Express and also stream video with Apple TV.

To make sure the next speakers, dock, or stereo you purchase is compatible, look for language such as "Apple AirPlay Compatible" in the product description or packaging. Many manufacturers have products with this new standard already, including iHome, Sony, Denon, Marantz, B&W, and JBL.

> **TIP:** Use the **Apple Remote** app (described in the "Apple Remote App" section of this chapter) to control **iTunes** when you have music streaming through your wireless speakers—even when you are nowhere near your computer! This is a great feature to help you enjoy and control your music throughout your house with your iPod touch.

Using iTunes Search

If your library does not already contain hundreds or thousands of songs and other media, it will soon! How do you quickly find that special song you are in the mood for right now? The quickest way to locate an individual song or video is to use the search field in the upper-right corner of the **iTunes** app.

First, in the left nav bar, click the type of content you wish to find. For example, click **Music** to find songs, **Podcasts** to find podcasts, **Apps** to find apps, and so on.

After selecting the category of media in the left nav bar, then in the search field, start typing any part of a name of a song, artist, composer, album, podcast, TV show, app, or audiobook.

You will notice that, as soon as you type the first letter, **iTunes** will narrow your search results (shown in the main window) by that letter. In this case, **iTunes** is finding all matching songs/videos that have the letter (or series of letters) that match any part of the artist, album, composer, or song/video name.

In Figure 29–14, we clicked **Podcasts** and typed **Marketplace** into the search window to find the podcasts of the NPR radio show *Marketplace*.

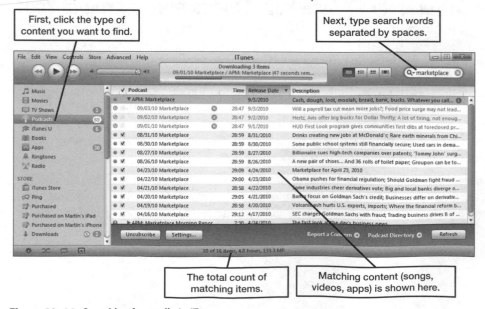

Figure 29–14. *Searching for media in iTunes.*

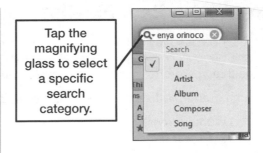

TIP: If you want to narrow your search by a specific category such as artist, composer, song name, or title, then click the little magnifying glass in the search field to see a drop-down list. Click any item in the drop-down list to narrow the search using that item.

Tap the magnifying glass to select a specific search category.

Ways to Search iTunes

You can type any combination of words to match the item you are trying to find. For example, assume you know that the song you want has the word "love" in the title, and the song is by U2. You could just type in those two words, separated by a space – "Love U2" –which will immodiately show all matching items (see Figure 29-15). In this case, only two songs match, so you can quickly double-click the song you want to listen to. Search is also contextual. This means that if you are in your music library, the search function will search for music, whereas if you are in your apps library, the search will look only for apps. In every search, both your own library and the App Store web site will be searched.

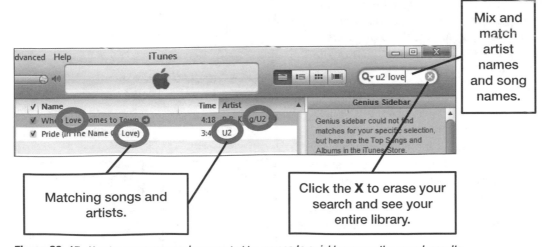

Mix and match artist names and song names.

Matching songs and artists.

Click the **X** to erase your search and see your entire library.

Figure 29–15. *Use two or more words separated by spaces to quickly narrow the search results.*

When you are done searching, click the little **X** in the circle next to the search words to clear out the search and see all your songs and videos again.

Creating a New Playlist

You may be used to listening to all the music on a particular album, but you will soon find the benefits of creating your own custom playlists. These are lists of particular songs that you group together. You can create a normal playlist or a smart playlist.

You can group playlists however you like, as in this example:

- Workout music
- Favorite U2 songs
- Traveling music

> **TIP:** You can create playlists in your iTunes library or directly on your iPod touch. To create a playlist for your computer, click any existing playlist under the **Playlists** heading in the left nav bar. To create a new playlist directly on your iPod touch, click your iPod touch, listed under **Devices** in the left nav bar. Depending on what you have highlighted in the left nav bar, your new playlist will be created either on the computer or on the iPod touch.

Creating a Normal Playlist

A normal playlist is one in which you can drag and drop songs manually onto your new playlist.

Once you have decided whether to create your playlist on your iPod touch or on your computer, you are ready to get started. Follow these steps to create a new normal playlist:

1. Press **Ctrl+N** (or **Command+N** on the Mac) to select a new playlist from the **File** menu. Or, you can simply click the **New Playlist** button in the lower-left corner of **iTunes**, as shown to the right.

2. Type the name of your playlist in the entry that appears in the left nav bar.

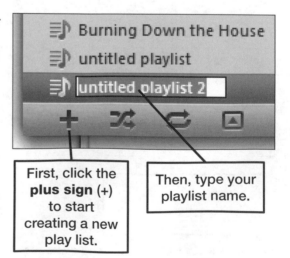

First, click the **plus sign** (+) to start creating a new play list.

Then, type your playlist name.

> **TIP:** If you want to create a new playlist with songs very similar to another playlist, then right-click the playlist and select **Duplicate**.

After creating and naming your playlist, you are ready to add songs to your new playlist (see Figure 29–16). To select from your entire library, click **Music** on the **Library** tab.

To select songs from an existing playlist, click that playlist.

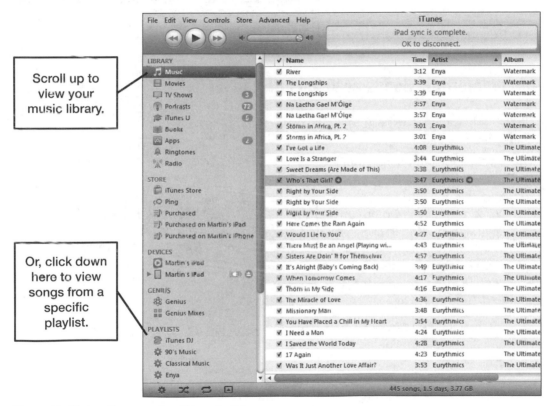

Figure 29–16. *Locating songs to add to a playlist.*

Adding Individual Songs

You can easily add individual songs to your new playlist:

1. Click any individual song to select it, and then keep holding down the mouse button as you drag the song over to your new playlist.

2. To put the song into the playlist, drop it by letting go of the mouse button when the song name you are dragging is over the name of the playlist.

Click and drag any song over to your playlist.

Drop the song on your playlist.

Adding Multiple Songs or Videos (Not in a List)

You can add multiple items in two simple steps:

1. To add selected songs that are not listed sequentially, press and hold the **Ctrl** key (Windows) or the **Command** key (Mac), and then click the individual songs/videos. Once you are done selecting songs/videos, release the **Ctrl/Command** key.

2. After all the songs/videos are selected (highlighted), click one of the selected songs, and drag and drop the entire selected group onto your playlist.

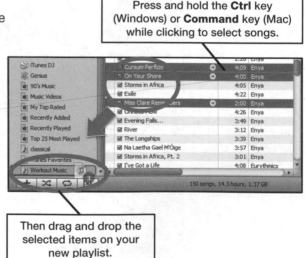

Press and hold the **Ctrl** key (Windows) or **Command** key (Mac) while clicking to select songs.

Then drag and drop the selected items on your new playlist.

Adding a List of Songs or Videos

You can also add a list of songs/videos using a pair of steps:

1. To add a list of songs/videos to a playlist all at once, press and hold the **Shift** key. While pressing the **Shift** key, click

the top item in the list and then click the bottom item. Both items clicked, as well as all the items between them, will be selected.

2.   After all the songs/videos are selected (highlighted), click one of the selected songs, and drag and drop the entire selected group onto your simple playlist.

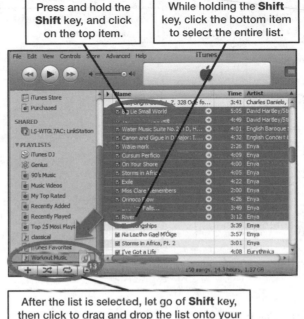

Press and hold the **Shift** key, and click on the top item.

While holding the **Shift** key, click the bottom item to select the entire list.

After the list is selected, let go of **Shift** key, then click to drag and drop the list onto your Playlist.

Creating a New Smart Playlist

A smart playlist is one that **ITunes** creates for you based on your selections. You can create a smart playlist, for example, for your ten most played songs, specific artists, or a specific genre, and you can even limit the playlist to a certain size based on the number of songs or their size (in MB or GB).

To start creating a smart playlist, select **File ▶▶ New Smart Playlist**. Or, on Windows, you can press **Ctrl+Alt+N** and then select **New Smart Playlist** from the **File** menu, and on the Mac you can press **Command+Option+N** and just input the search parameters.

Figure 29–17 illustrates that you have many options for creating a smart playlist. All of the default playlists you see in **iTunes** are smart playlists. Default categories include **90's Music**, **Classical Music**, **Music Videos**, **My Top Rated**, **Recently Added**, **Recently Played**, and **Top 25 Most Played**.

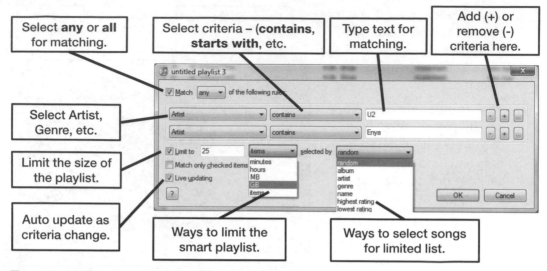

Figure 29–17. *The smart playlist settings screen.*

Editing a Smart Playlist

The best way to get a feel for how the smart playlist function works is probably to check out some of the preset smart playlists. To edit a smart playlist, select **Edit Smart Playlist** from the **File** menu. In Figure 29–18, you can see the smart playlist for **90's Music**; you can also see that it will pull all music and music videos from 1990 to 1999. Check out a few other default smart playlists to start to learn how the myriad options interact to create a very powerful playlist function.

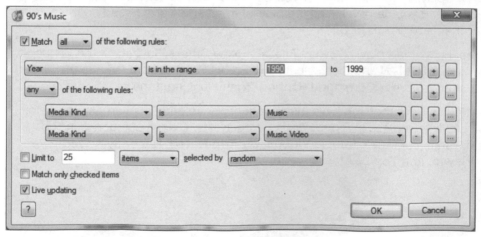

Figure 29–18. *The smart playlist settings screen for 90's Music.*

NOTE: The **Live Updating** feature of smart playlists allows them to scan whenever you play a song or add any new media (e.g., songs, videos, etc.) to your library; it then includes any new songs that it deems may fit the criteria of the smart playlist. This makes the playlists really dynamic.

The iTunes Genius Feature

The **iTunes Genius** feature can do all sorts of fun things to help enhance your music and video library in **iTunes**. You can take advantage of it by following these steps:

1. Click **Genius** in the left nav bar, and then click the **Turn On Genius** button. If you don't see the **Genius** item, then click **Store** and then **Turn On Genius** from the **iTunes** menu.

2. If you are not already logged into the **iTunes Store**, you will be asked to log in. If you do not yet have an Apple ID, then please jump to the "Creating an iTunes Account" section later in this chapter to learn how to create one.

3. Read and agree to the **Genius** license agreement to continue.

4. Next, you will see a window on your screen for some time (longer if your library is large) that says the **Genius** feature is starting up.

5. In order for the **Genius** feature to work correctly, **iTunes** needs to understand the types of music and videos you have in your library. It will use this information to help make suggestions on similar music or videos that you don't yet own, but might want to purchase. When this step is done, you will see a final success screen telling you **Genius** is now set up. Now you are ready to start using the **Genius** feature!

TIP: You can use the **Genius** feature on your iPod touch, but only after you have enabled it on your computer (as just described).

You can think of the **Genius** feature as your personal shopper, who knows your tastes and makes good recommendations (**Genius** suggestions). You can also think of the **Genius** feature as your personal DJ, who knows the music that goes well together and will create a great playlist for you (**Genius** playlists).

Creating Genius Mixes and Playlists

Follow these steps to create a **Genius** mix and playlist:

1. Right-click a song in your library that you would like for your **Genius** playlist and select **Start Genius**.

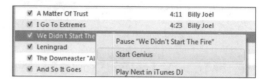

2. After you click the **Start Genius** drop-down item, the screen will immediately change to show you the **Genius** mix of all songs that **iTunes** thinks match the type of song you selected (see Figure 29–19); these suggestions are based on computer algorithms and feedback from other **iTunes** users. You may be surprised at the list of music or even artists that you would not normally put together into a playlist.

> **TIP: Genius** mixes and playlists provide a great way to keep your music library fresh, helping you to put together songs that go well together—often in combinations that you might not have thought about yourself.

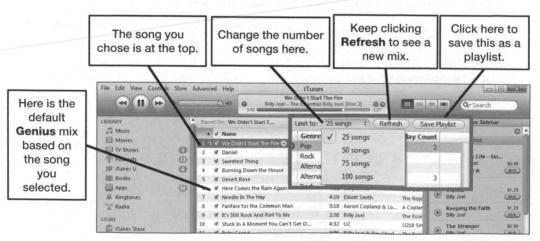

Figure 29–19. *The options for the Genius Mix screen.*

3. On the **Genius Mix** screen, you have options to change to 25, 50, 75, or 100 songs. Click the **Refresh** button to see a new (usually slightly different) mix/playlist.

4. If you like the mix and want to save it as a playlist, click the **Save Playlist** button in the upper-right corner. Notice that the playlist is saved under the **Genius** section in the left column. The default name of the playlist is the name of the song you first clicked. You can change this name by double-clicking the playlist name. You will see it turn into editable text; from here, you can type a new name.

NOTE: In iTunes version 10.0, the **Genius** sidebar was replaced by the **Ping** sidebar. It is unclear as to whether Apple plans to bring the **Genius** sidebar back in future releases of **iTunes**.

Turning Off Genius

To turn off the **Genius** feature and remove all your **Genius** mixes and playlists, select **Store** from the **iTunes** menu, and then choose **Turn Off Genius**.

Updating Genius

If you have added a lot of music, videos, or other content to your **iTunes** library, periodically you will want to send an update to the **Genius** function in **iTunes**. To send this update, select **Store** from the **iTunes** menu, and then choose **Update Genius**.

How to Back Up and Restore Your iTunes Library

In order to protect the sizable investment in your iTunes music, videos, and more, you should periodically back up your library. You can use the built-in CD or DVD burner in your computer to backup your library, but this process becomes cumbersome if you have a large media library. When you have a larger iTunes library, you should backup your library to an external hard disk.

Backup with CDs or DVDs (for Smaller Libraries)

For smaller iTunes libraries, you can use CDs or DVDs to backup your media. To do this, select **File ➤ Library ➤ Backup to Disc** from the **iTunes** menu. Then you will see a window with several options, as shown in Figure 29–20. We recommend selecting the default and backing up everything; however, you could also choose to back up just iTunes purchases. After you insert all the disks required for the backup, you will see a backup complete message. If you have recently backed up to disc, then you can save time and space by checking the **Only back up items added or changed since last backup** box.

> **TIP:** If you need to backup to DVD or CDs, we highly recommend opting for the DVD method to do the backup, since it can hold four to eight times the content of a CD.

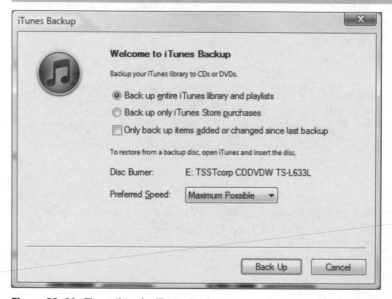

Figure 29–20. *The options for iTunes backup.*

To Restore from CDs or DVDs

All you need to do to start restoring your library is to insert the first backup CD or DVD and iTunes will ask you if you would like to restore from the backup disc.

Some items are not restored when you restore your library using the drag and :

- Play count

> **TIP:** You can also restore individual files by clicking on the backup disk under the Devices listed in the left nav bar. Then drag-and-drop files from the backup to your library. However, a few items are lost from restored files such as bookmarks of last played

Backup to External Hard Disk (for Larger Libraries)

As your iTunes library grows larger, it could take you dozens or even a hundred or more DVDs or CDs to complete the backup, so you should use an external hard disk instead. This method works best only when your iTunes library is located in a single folder.

Step 1: Make Sure All Media is In a Single Folder

You can use iTunes to move all your media to a folder by a command.

1. From the iTunes menu, select **Edit ➤ Preferences** (Windows) or **iTunes ➤ Preferences** (Mac).

2. Then click on the **Advanced** tab and check the box next to **Copy files to iTunes Media folder when adding to library** in the middle of the page.

3. Click **OK**.

4. From the iTunes menu, select **File ➤Library ➤ Organize Library** to see the window to the right.

5. Check both checkboxes as shown and click **OK.**

6. This will result in all your media to be copied to a single iTunes media folder.

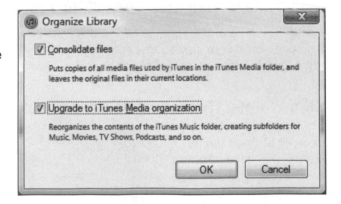

Step 2: Drag and Drop Your Library to the External Hard Disk

This assumes you have purchased and connected an external hard disk. If you don't have one, you can find one by visiting your local computer store or doing a web search for external hard disk for your computer operating system type: Windows or Mac.

1. Open up a window on your computer and locate your iTunes library. The default media location for your iTunes library is:

   Windows XP: \Documents and Settings\username\My Documents\My Music\

   Windows Vista or Windows 7:\Users\username\music\iTunes\iTunes music\

   Mac OX X: /Users/username/Music/

2. Open another window on your computer for your external hard disk.

3. Drag and drop the iTunes library onto the external hard disk window to copy all the files. This will take quite a while if your library is very large, but at least you won't be swapping disks every few minutes!

Restoring from an External Hard Disk Backup

First, close **iTunes**, then follow the steps below.

Step 1: Copy Your Library Back to Your Computer

Use the reverse of the steps above to drag and drop your library from the external hard disk back onto your computer. You may want to put the library in the same location as the original iTunes library for simplicity sake. See above for the default locations.

Step 2: Open iTunes and Select the Library

In order to open the newly copied library, you have to open iTunes a special way.

1. On Windows, hold down the **Shift** key while you open **iTunes**. On a Mac, hold down the **Option** key. Make sure to keep the key pressed until you see the small window shown to the right. If you let go too soon,

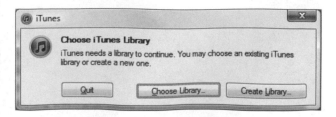

then iTunes will open
normally.

2. Select **Choose Library** and locate the library you just copied from your external
hard disk.

3. Click **Open** (Windows) or **Choose** (Mac) to open the iTunes library file.

This should allow you to restore your iTunes library by opening the file you just copied
from your external hard disk.

The Home Sharing Feature

If you have several people in your home that use **iTunes**, and they are all connected
together on a home network, then the **Home Sharing** feature will help you share your
content (music, videos, and more) across your computers with **iTunes** enabled. Follow
these steps to take advantage of the **Home Sharing** feature:

1. Pick the account to use for the **Home Sharing** feature. All computers connected
with the **Home Sharing** feature have to use the same iTunes account and
password to log in and be connected. You will usually want to pick the account
that has the most purchased content or the content you would like to share across
all the computers.

> **NOTE:** Even though you can see other people's content and play it on **iTunes** on your computer,
> you need to import shared content into your own library if you want to enjoy it on your iPod touch
> (or iPhone or iPad).

2. Set up the **Home Sharing** feature and authorize each of the other
computers. You can get started with **Home Sharing** much as you can
with the **Genius** feature. Click **Home Sharing** under the **Shared** heading
in the **iTunes** app's left nav bar, as shown in Figure 29–21. If you do not
see **Home Sharing** in the left nav bar, then from the menu, go to
Advanced ➤ Turn Off Home Sharing, and then **Advanced ➤ Turn On
Home Sharing**. That should fix the issue.

> **NOTE:** All versions of videos and movies purchased or rented from the **iTunes Store** are
> protected by digital rights management (DRM) using FairPlay. However, such DRM-protected
> content can be played on up to five authorized computers (PC or Mac). Rented DRM content,
> such as a rented movie, must be physically transferred to one machine or device at a time.
> Protected music can be authorized on up to five computers, and music can be synced to a large
> number of mobile devices, as long as those mobile devices sync to only a single computer.

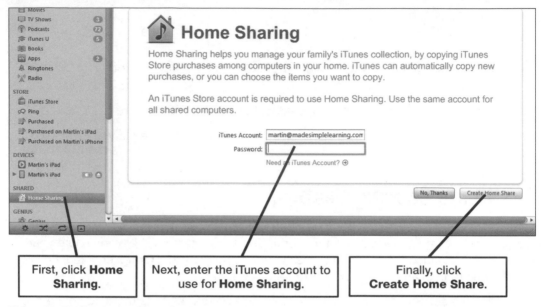

First, click **Home Sharing**.

Next, enter the iTunes account to use for **Home Sharing**.

Finally, click **Create Home Share**.

Figure 29–21. *Starting the Home Sharing feature.*

3. Repeat step 2 on every computer you want to give access to your home-shared content. Make sure that you use the same iTunes account on every computer; this could be a little confusing at first, but it's important to use the same account. On the other computers, you will probably have to authorize the computer to play iTunes content. The **iTunes** app will notify you if you need to authorize the computer by popping up a window.

NOTE: Up to five computers can be authorized as home-sharing computers.

4. Click **Yes** to continue. Once authorization is complete, you will see a screen showing how many of your five total authorizations have been used up. To learn more about authorizing or deauthorizing computers, see the "Authorizing and Deauthorizing Computers" section later in this chapter.

5. Start enjoying the shared content. Once the **Home Sharing** feature is enabled on at least two computers, the second computer will then see the shared content underneath the **Shared** heading in the left nav bar in **iTunes**. To start viewing, playing, and importing this shared content, click the shared library, as shown in Figure 29–22.

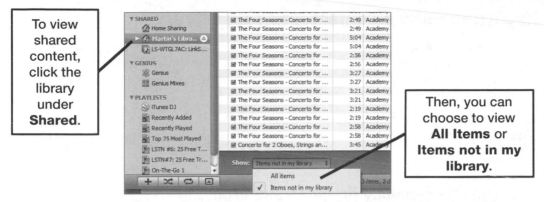

To view shared content, click the library under **Shared**.

Then, you can choose to view **All Items** or **Items not in my library**.

Figure 29–22. *Viewing a home-shared library and filtering to view all items, or those not in your own library.*

Filtering a Home-Shared Library to Only Show Items Not in Your Library

Once you get up and running with a home-shared library, you will notice that there is a switch at the bottom of the screen that allows you to show only those items that are not in your library (see Figure 29–22). This is a great way to quickly assess what you might need to add (i.e., import) to your library from the shared library.

Two Types of Shared Libraries

You will see two logos in the **Shared** category on the left nav bar of **iTunes**. Each type of logo shows you whether the library is a fully shared library (the **House** icon) or a listen-only type of library (the **Stack of Papers** icon). Table 29–1 describes the differences.

Table 29–1. *Fully Shared vs. Listen-Only Libraries*

Types of Shared Libraries	What This Means
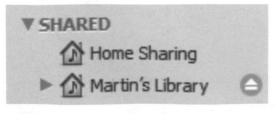 Fully Shared Library (the **House** icon)	Martin's library is fully enabled for home sharing—you can view, listen, and import (add) items from this library.
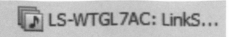 Listen-Only Library (the **Stack of Papers** icon)	LS-WTGL7AC is a listen-only and view-only library. You cannot import any songs from this library to your own library.

Importing Shared Content into Your Library

When you are viewing a home-shared library, you can listen to anything in that library, as long as your computer has been authorized to do so. If you hit any authorization issues, please refer back to Chapter 3: "Sync Your iPod touch with iTunes." In that chapter, we show you how to authorize your computers for **iTunes**.

You can manually drag and drop content into your library, or you can set up the **Home Sharing** feature to automatically import all new purchases from the home-shared iTunes account.

Importing by Manually Dragging and Dropping

The drag-and-drop method for importing works well if you want to grab a few songs or videos from the shared library. Simply click the songs or videos to highlight them, and then drag them over to your library.

You can also click the songs/videos to highlight them, and then click the **Import** button in the lower-right corner to do the same thing.

Automatically Importing New Purchases

Follow these steps if you want to share all new purchases from the home-shared iTunes account to the library on another device or computer automatically:

1. Click the home-sharing library you would like to import from in the left nav bar.

2. Click the **Settings** button in the lower-right corner of the **iTunes** screen.

3. Now you will see a small window pop up that is similar to the one shown to the right. Check off those items to be automatically transferred from the home-shared library into your library.

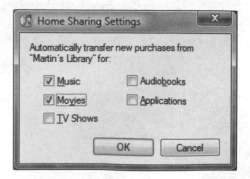

4. Click **OK** to save your home-sharing settings.

Toggling Home Sharing Off and On

Once you have enabled the **Home Sharing** feature, you may want to turn it off at some point. You do this by going to the **iTunes Advanced** menu and selecting **Turn Off Home Sharing**. To turn it back on, repeat this by going to the same **Advanced** menu and selecting **Turn On Home Sharing**.

Troubleshooting Home Sharing

Sometime you will see a "Computer Not Authorized" error, even though your computer has already been authorized on the **Home Sharing** account. Usually this happens because the content (e.g., song or video) that you are trying to view or listen to from the home-sharing account was purchased by an account other than the home-shared iTunes account. To correct this problem, follow these steps:

1. Locate the person in your home who originally purchased the song.

2. Ask him to authorize your computer. (If you hit any authorization issues, then you'll find Chapter 3: "Sync Your iPod touch with iTunes," useful; this chapter explains how to authorize your computers for **iTunes**.)

3. Once your computer is authorized, you should be able to enjoy the music or video.

Creating an iTunes Account

If you have already registered for an iTunes account using an Apple ID or AOL screen name, then you need to sign in (see the "Signing into the iTunes Store" section later in this chapter for information on how to do this).

If you want to buy or download free songs, books, apps, videos, TV shows, and more, you will need to acquire them from the **iTunes Store**. You can do so by following these steps:

1. Click the **Sign In** button in the upper-right corner, as shown in Figure 29–23. If you do not yet have an iTunes account, then click the **Create New Account** button and follow the instructions to create your new account. If you already have an account, enter your Apple ID or AOL screen name and password, click the **Sign In** button, and skip ahead to the "Signing into the iTunes Store" section. This is where you'll enter you're Apple ID or AOL account details, if you have them.

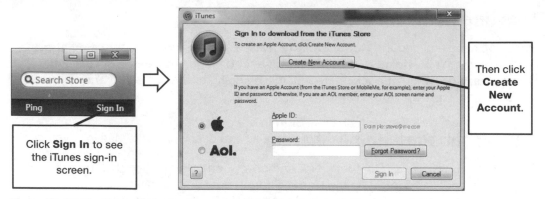

Figure 29–23. *The iTunes Store sign-in screen, where you can start creating a new account.*

2. When you click the **Create New Account** button, you will see a new account welcome screen; click **Continue** to move on.

3. Read and accept the terms and conditions by clicking the check box at the bottom of the screen, and click **Continue** to move on.

4. On the next screen, you set up your Apple ID (your login name for the **iTunes Store**), your password, and your secret question and email preferences. If you do not want email notification, be sure to uncheck the boxes at the bottom of the page. Click **Continue** to move on.

5. On the next screen, you are asked to enter your billing information. Note that you can create a US-based account without billing information. Also, you can enter an iTunes gift card to receive credit, so you do not need to enter a credit card or PayPal account. This screen contains your preferred billing information, which will be used when you buy music, videos, and iPod touch apps (from the **App Store** app on your iPod touch). Click **Continue** to move on. Please note that the contents of this screen may vary slightly depending on the country in which you are located.

6. Depending on your locale, you may need to verify your county, province, or other local taxing authority. Next, click **Done**.

7. Now you should see a screen that asserts you have correctly set up your iTunes account. Click **Done** to finish.

Signing into the iTunes Store

If you've successfully created an iTunes account, or you already own one, then the wonders of the **iTunes Store** are now yours to explore! The following sections show you most of the things you can do once you're signed in. But first you need to sign in.

To do this, begin by clicking the iTunes **Sign In** button to take you to the sign-in screen, where you'll then be asked to enter your Apple ID and password. Alternatively, you can enter your AOL screen name and password.

Getting to the iTunes Store

You can always get back to the **iTunes Store** by clicking the **iTunes Store** link under **Store** in the left nav bar.

Buying or Getting Free Media from the iTunes Store

After signing in or creating a new account, you will be able to search the store for any artist, album, composer, or title.

To find all the songs by a particular artist, type that artist's name into the search box in the upper-right corner. You could also search by part or all of a particular song's name. Once you press the **Enter** key, you will be presented with all the matching items from the **iTunes Store** (see Figure 29–24).

> **TIP:** Use the **Power Search** feature shown in the upper-left corner of the main **iTunes** window to further narrow your search. Also note that you can refine your search by using the **Filter by Media Type** box just below **Power Search**. Filter the search by music, movies, TV shows, apps, audiobooks, podcasts, iTunes U, or Ping.

You can then navigate around and purchase individual songs with the **Buy** buttons at the bottom.

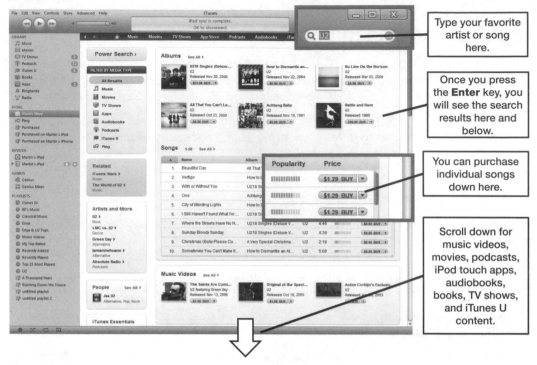

Type your favorite artist or song here.

Once you press the **Enter** key, you will see the search results here and below.

You can purchase individual songs down here.

Scroll down for music videos, movies, podcasts, iPod touch apps, audiobooks, books, TV shows, and iTunes U content.

Figure 29–24. *Searching for and buying songs in the iTunes Store.*

After you click the **Buy** button, you will need to log in, unless you have previously instructed **iTunes** to keep you logged in for your purchases.

CAUTION: If you are at a public computer or are worried that someone might access your computer and buy stuff without you knowing, then don't check the **Remember password for purchasing** box!

After you log in, you will see a pop-up window if you have just clicked the **Buy** button.

If you don't want to see this dialog box every time you buy something, then check the box at the bottom pop-up window that says **Don't ask me about buying songs again**, and then click the **Buy** button.

Now the song, video, or other item you purchased will be queued up to be downloaded to your local library in the **iTunes** app on your computer.

Making Sure All Items Are Downloaded

After you purchase a song, video, app, or other item from the **App Store**—or if you have just authorized this computer on your account—you should click the **Downloads** link that appears under the **Store** category heading in the left nav bar.

Any items currently being downloaded will show a status bar in the main **Downloads** window. You will see a **Done** status message when the items are completely downloaded to your computer.

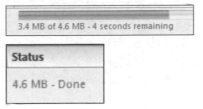

You will need to see a status of **Done** before you can put the purchased item onto your iPod touch. If you see a pop-up window asking whether you want **iTunes** to download all your purchased items, then click **Yes**.

Redeeming an iTunes Gift Card

At some point, you may receive an iTunes gift card. Follow these steps to learn how to redeem the value of the card to your iTunes account.

> **NOTE:** iTunes gift cards are country specific. In other words, a US gift card will only work for a US iTunes account.

1. If you are not already signed in, then sign into your iTunes account by clicking the **Sign In** link in the upper-right corner of **iTunes**.

2. Click the little drop-down arrow to the right of your iTunes Apple ID, where you saw the **Sign In** link, and select **Redeem** from the drop-down list.

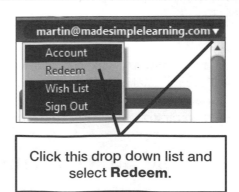

Click this drop down list and select **Redeem**.

3. On the **Redeem** screen, you will need to enter the code from the back of the gift card (see Figure 29–25). You may need to scratch off the silver/gray covering to see the card's code.

4. Click the **Redeem** button.

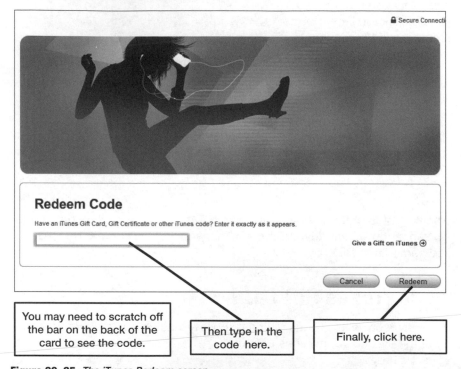

Figure 29–25. *The iTunes Redeem screen.*

5. To verify that the gift card is being applied to the correct iTunes account, you will need to sign in or re-enter your password.

6. Click the **Sign In** button, or the **View Account** button (if you're already signed in).

7. When the gift card has been successfully applied to your account, you will see the total amount of the card in the upper-right corner of the **iTunes** screen, right next to your sign-in name. Now you can use this gift card credit to buy stuff from the **iTunes Store**.

Getting Your Stuff into iTunes

If you have music CDs, DVDs, e-Books, and PDF files you want to enjoy on your iPod touch, you will first have to import them into your iTunes library on your computer. We show you how in this section.

Importing Music CDs

If you are of legal drinking age, then it's likely that you have a few music CDs in your home library. If you are over 40, that likelihood goes up to 100 percent. So, how do you get all your best CDs loaded onto your iPod touch? Accomplishing this is a two-step process:

1. First, you must load the CDs into iTunes.

2. Then you must sync or manually transfer those CD songs to your iPhone. (We show you how to sync or manually transfer with **iTunes** in Chapter 3: "Sync Your iPhone with iTunes.")

In order to import your music from a CD, insert the CD into your computer's CD drive. You may see a pop-up inside **iTunes** that asks whether you would like to import the CD as shown. Click **Yes** to import the CD.

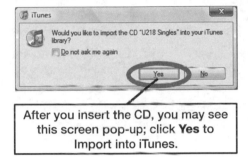

After you insert the CD, you may see this screen pop-up; click **Yes** to Import into iTunes.

If you did not receive this pop-up window, then you can manually start the CD import into **iTunes** by clicking the **Import CD** button in the lower-right corner. Also notice that the CD appears under the **Devices** list in the left column (see Figure 29–26).

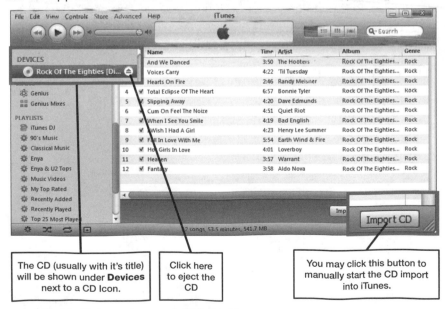

The CD (usually with it's title) will be shown under **Devices** next to a CD Icon.

Click here to eject the CD

You may click this button to manually start the CD import into iTunes.

Figure 29–26. *Working with a music CD inside iTunes.*

Importing Movies from DVDs

Some of the more recent DVDs and Blu-rays that you can purchase may have two versions of the movie: one for your DVD or Blu-ray player, and an extra digital copy that can be loaded automatically into **iTunes**.

Usually, there will be text on the DVD box that states that there is an extra digital copy for your computer. You can check whether this copy exists by inserting the DVD into your computer's DVD drive and opening **iTunes**. If the digital copy exists, then **iTunes** will automatically detect it and ask whether you would like to import the movie.

CAUTION: Most DVDs or Blu-rays do not provide this extra digital version, which is meant to be loaded and watched on your computer and mobile devices. These standard DVDs or Blu-rays are copy-protected and cannot normally be loaded into **iTunes**. However, if you do a web search for "load DVD into iTunes," you may find some software products (such as **Handbrake**; at see http://handbrake.fr) that allow you to *rip* or *burn* your DVDs into **iTunes**. We strongly urge you to obey copyright laws; if you use software like this, you should only use the DVD on your own computer or iPod touch, and never share the movie or otherwise violate the copyright agreement.

Importing e-Book (PDF and iBook Format) Files

If you want to read a PDF file or e-book (in the industry standard ePub format set by the International Digital Publishing Forum) on your iPod touch, you will first need to get the file into **iTunes** to sync it to your iPod touch. There are a couple of ways to get e-books into **iTunes**. You can use the drag-and-drop method or the menu commands to add files or folders to the library.

The Drag-and-Drop Method

This is a great way to add a single file or just a few files.

1. Locate the file on your computer.

2. Click and drag that file into your library in **iTunes**. Let go of the mouse to drop this file into your library. A box will be drawn around your library, as shown in the image to the right. When you see the box, you can let go of the mouse button.

3. Since the file is readable by the **iBooks** app, you should then see the file appear in the **Books** section of your library.

Using Menu Commands

Using menus works well if you have an entire folder or multiple folders of files you want to move into **iTunes**.

> **TIP:** This method works for e-books and also other content such as music.

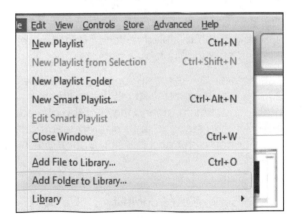

1. From the **iTunes** menu, choose **File**, and then select **Add Folder to Library** to add an entire folder of content, or **Add File to Library** if you have only one file to add.

2. Now navigate to the folder or file you wish to add and click **Select Folder** (or **Open**, for a single file).

3. All iBooks-readable files will be added to **iTunes**.

Getting Album Artwork

iTunes can automatically get the album art for most songs and videos; however, if you need to manually retrieve this artwork, follow these steps:

1. Start **iTunes**.

2. Go to the **Advanced** menu.

3. Select **Get Album Artwork**.

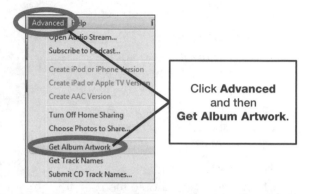

Click **Advanced** and then **Get Album Artwork**.

NOTE: You will need to have an iTunes account already and be logged in for this to work correctly.

Authorizing and Deauthorizing Computers

As mentioned previously, you can authorize up to five different computers to play your iTunes media (e.g., music and movies).

Here's a question that you may hear quite often: *Someone else has authorized my computer to play her songs; can I now load and listen to these "authorized songs" on my iPod touch?*

The short answer is maybe. The answer is no for all songs purchased on **iTunes** prior to January 2009. It is also no for all songs purchased with DRM protection. These songs are tied specifically to one person's mobile device (iPad, iPhone, or iPod touch).

The answer is yes for all songs purchased without DRM protection enabled. Early in 2009, iTunes announced that it would start selling some songs and videos without DRM protection, which means they can be played on multiple iPhones and iPod touches. Follow these steps to authorize or deauthorize your computer to be able to play songs on your computer and possibly your iPod touch from someone else's iTunes library:

1. Start up **iTunes**.

2. To authorize a computer, go to the **Store** menu and select **Authorize This Computer....** To

deauthorize a computer, go to the **Store** menu and select **Deauthorize This Computer...**.

NOTE: You will need to know your iTunes or AOL username and password for this to work.

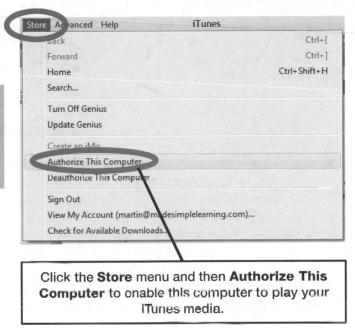

Click the **Store** menu and then **Authorize This Computer** to enable this computer to play your iTunes media.

3. Enter your Apple ID, or if you prefer, click the radio button next to AOL and enter your AOL screen name and password.

4. Next, click the **Authorize** or **Deauthorize** button.

iTunes Troubleshooting

In this section, we will provide a few tips and tricks to help you deal with some common issues you might encounter when using **iTunes**. We also have an entire chapter devoted to troubleshooting (see Chapter 28: "Troubleshooting") if you cannot find answers to the problems you encounter in this section.

What to Do If the iTunes Automatic Update Fails

The automatic update may fail If you have the About iTunes.rtf text file open, or you have another related file open that cannot be closed by the installer automatically. If you locate and close the problem file, you should be able to retry the automatic update.

If you see a message similar to the one shown to the right, then you will have to manually install the update. Follow these steps to do so:

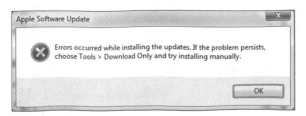

1. From the **Apple Software Update** screen, select the **Tools** menu and then **Download Only**.

2. You will see the download status screen (shown in the image to the right of step 1). Once the download is finished, a new window should pop up, showing the downloaded files ready for you to install manually (see Figure 29–27).

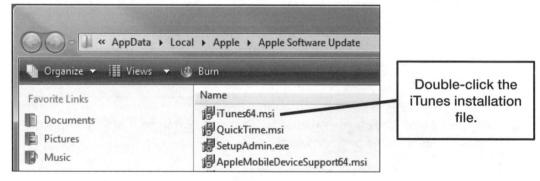

Figure 29–27. *Apple Software Update manual install folder (Windows PC).*

3. To manually start the install, double-click the **iTunes** installer file, as shown in Figure 29–27. The file may be slightly different from the one shown in the figure (e.g., iTunes.msi or iTunes64.msi), depending on the operating system on your computer.

4. From here, you need to follow the **iTunes** installation screens.

Fixing the Apple ID Security Error

If you try to log in with your Apple ID, you might receive an error message at the top of the screen that looks similar to this one:

> To use this Apple ID you must first login to the My Info Web page then provide additional security information.

If this happens, then you will have to log in to the Apple Store web site, enter a security question/answer, and then add the month and day of your birth.

To correct this error, follow these steps:

1. Open a web browser on your computer and go to www.apple.com.

2. Click the **Store** link in the left portion of the top nav bar, and then hover your mouse over the **Account** link in the upper-right corner to see a drop-down list. Select **Account Information** from this list (see Figure 29–28).

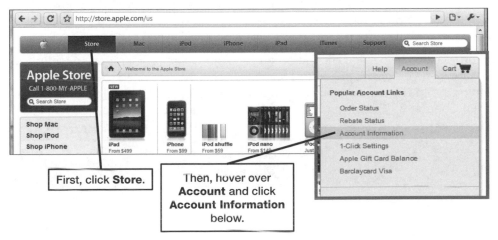

Figure 29–28. *Getting to your account information to correct your security information.*

3. If you clicked **Account**, then you will need to select the **Change account information** link from the next screen.

4. Log In with your Apple ID and password (the one that caused the error).

5. Most likely, your security question and answer or your birth month and date are blank. You need to add this information, type your password twice, scroll to the bottom of the screen, and then click the **Continue** button.

You should now be able to use your Apple ID and password to register your iPod touch.

> **CAUTION:** Apple will never send you an email asking you for your password or asking you to log in and enter your password. If you receive such an email, it might be a scam. Don't click any links in such an email. If you are concerned about your iTunes account, log in through the **iTunes** app to manage it.

How Do I Get My Music Back If My Computer Crashes?

The good news is that you'll probably have a lot, or perhaps all, of your music on your iPod touch. We can't help you get your computer back up and running in this book if the initial reboot isn't successful. However, we can tell you about how you can get your music back from your iPod touch to your **iTunes** app once your computer is running again.

So, if your only copy of your music, videos, and other content resides on your iPod touch, iPod, or iPad, then you need to use a third-party tool to copy your music from that mobile device back into **iTunes** app on your computer, once you've got your computer up and running again.

Do a web search for "copy iPod touch or iPod to iTunes" and you will find a number of both free and paid software tools to accomplish this task. We recommend using a free trial of any software before purchasing it to make sure it will meet your needs.

This solution will also help if you encounter the problem where all your iPod touch music is grayed out when you view it from **iTunes**. In that case, you will need to copy all your iPod touch music to **iTunes**, and then start fresh with the sync or manual transfer steps described in Chapter 3: "Sync Your iPod touch with iTunes."

CAUTION: Please do not use this third-party software to create unauthorized copies of music, videos, or other content that you have not legitimately purchased.

Index

■Special Characters and Numbers

■A

D

■S

U

■ V

W

Making Technology Simple

What individuals say about
our video tutorials:

*"Turns on the light for features that
are not intuitive!"*
- Lou

"Easy to follow. I learned a lot!"
- Nicky

"Short & sweet! Definitely recommend!"
- Sandy

"Just what I needed – concise and relevant!"
- Dan S.

*"Our BlackBerry users have gained an
hour a day in productivity and we've
reduced help desk calls by 50% with the
Made Simple Learning videos."*
- 3,000 Users, Fortune 500 Company

*"I would definitely recommend these videos to
anyone in a BES administrator or BlackBerry
technical support role for any size company!"*
- 250 Users, Mid-size Company

*"Having the videos right on the Blackberry
makes all the difference in the world. I get far
fewer questions, and I've heard a lot of the Bold
users getting excited that they've "found" new
features that are helpful to them."*
- 60 Users, Small Company

For You

Get Started Today!

1. Go to **www.madesimplelearning.com**.
2. Purchase any of our video tutorials or
   guide books right from our site.
3. Start learning in minutes.

For Your Organization

Get Started Today!

1. Request a quote by e-mail from:
   info@madesimplelearning.com
2. We set you up with a free trial.
3. Try before you buy.

*3-minute Video Tutorials
About Your iPod touch
Viewed on your PC or Mac*

*Mobile Video Training
About Your iPod touch
On Your iPod touch*